Mastering
Windows® 7 Deployment

Mastering

Windows® 7 Deployment

Aidan Finn

Darril Gibson

Kenneth van Surksum

Wiley Publishing, Inc.

Acquisitions Editor: Agatha Kim

Development Editor: Candace English

Technical Editors: Johan Arwidmark and Mikael Nyström

Production Editor: Christine O'Connor

Copy Editor: Elizabeth Welch

Editorial Manager: Pete Gaughan

Production Manager: Tim Tate

Vice President and Executive Group Publisher: Richard Swadley

Vice President and Publisher: Neil Edde

Book Designers: Judy Fung and Maureen Forys, Happenstance Type-O-Rama

Compositor: Jeff Lytle, Happenstance Type-O-Rama

Proofreader: Jen Larsen, Word One New York

Indexer: Nancy Guenther

Project Coordinator, Cover: Katherine Crocker

Cover Designer: Ryan Sneed

Cover Image: © Pete Gardner/DigitalVision/Getty Images

Dear Reader,

Thank you for choosing *Mastering Windows 7 Deployment*. This book is part of a family of premium-quality Sybex books, all of which are written by outstanding authors who combine practical experience with a gift for teaching.

Sybex was founded in 1976. More than 30 years later, we're still committed to producing consistently exceptional books. With each of our titles, we're working hard to set a new standard for the industry. From the paper we print on, to the authors we work with, our goal is to bring you the best books available.

I hope you see all that reflected in these pages. I'd be very interested to hear your comments and get your feedback on how we're doing. Feel free to let me know what you think about this or any other Sybex book by sending me an email at nedde@wiley.com. If you think you've found a technical error in this book, please visit http://sybex.custhelp.com. Customer feedback is critical to our efforts at Sybex.

Best regards,

Neil Edde
Vice President and Publisher
Sybex, an Imprint of Wiley

To my friends and family who have supported me over the years.

—Aidan Finn

To my wife Nimfa. Thanks for sharing your life with me and continuing to enrich my life in so many ways.

—Darril Gibson

Acknowledgments

Thanks to Agatha Kim for inviting me on this project. I truly enjoy working on the Mastering series books with Agatha and her team. The editors are top-notch and provide consistently helpful advice. I also appreciated all of the excellent suggestions provided by the technical editor, Johan Arwidmark, even if we didn't have room for all of them.

—*Darril Gibson*

I would like to thank my wife, Miranda, and kids, Colin and Caitlin, for their support while I was working on the chapters for this book. I would also like to thank Rhonda Layfield for providing me with this opportunity, and a special thanks to Johan Arwidmark and Mikael Nyström for doing the technical review. I would also like to thank Candace English, Agatha Kim, Christine O'Connor, and other people involved for helping me make some great chapters about deployment.

—*Kenneth van Surksum*

About the Authors

Aidan Finn (B.Sc., MCSE, MVP) has been working in IT since 1996. He has worked as a consultant, contractor, and system administrator for various companies in Ireland and with clients around Europe. In recent years, Aidan has worked with VMware ESX, Hyper-V, and Microsoft System Center. Currently, Aidan is a senior infrastructure consultant in Dublin, Ireland.

Aidan is the leader of the Windows User Group in Ireland. He regularly speaks at user group events and conferences about Windows Server, desktop management, virtualization, and System Center. Aidan was also a Microsoft Most Valuable Professional (MVP) on System Center Configuration Manager in 2008. He was awarded MVP status with virtual machine expertise in 2009. He is a member of the Microsoft Springboard STEP program and is one of the Microsoft System Center Influencers. Aidan has worked closely with Microsoft, including online interviews, launch events, and road shows, and has worked as a technical reviewer for the Microsoft Official Curriculum course on Windows Server 2008 R2 virtualization.

Darril Gibson is the CEO of Security Consulting and Training, LLC. He has written, co-authored, and contributed to more than a dozen books, and regularly consults and teaches on a wide variety of IT topics. Most of the books he's been involved with are available on Amazon by searching for "Darril Gibson." He has been a Microsoft Certified Trainer (MCT) since 1999 and holds a multitude of certifications, including MCSE (NT 4.0, Windows 2000, and Windows 2003), MCITP (Windows 7, Windows Server 2008, and SQL Server), Security+, CISSP, and ITIL Foundations. Darril lives in Virginia Beach with his wife of over 18 years and two dogs. Whenever possible, they escape to a cabin in the country with over 20 acres of land where his dogs wear themselves out chasing rabbits and deer, and he enjoys long, peaceful walks.

Kenneth van Surksum is a consultant from the Netherlands, focused on Microsoft System Center products. He currently designs and implements several System Center products at companies in the Netherlands, working for INOVATIV. Kenneth has more than 10 years of experience in IT and in particular with deployment, starting with building unattended installation infrastructures for deploying Windows NT for a large bank in the Netherlands, evolving over time to newer operating systems and new methods of deployment. Kenneth is also a Microsoft Certified Trainer (MCT) and teaches classes in the Netherlands. He is also a Microsoft Most Valuable Professional (MVP) with the Expertise Setup & Deployment.

About the Contributing Author

Mikael Nyström is a Microsoft MVP and Senior Executive Consultant at TrueSec, with an extremely broad field of competence. He has worked with all kind of infrastructure tasks in all kind of environments, enterprise to small business. He is working deep within products such as SCOM, ConfigMgr, SCVMM, SCDPM, Hyper-V, MDT, SharePoint, Exchange, SharePoint, and Active Directory. Mikael is a very popular instructor and is often used by Microsoft for partner trainings as well as to speak at major conferences such as TechEd, MMS, etc. Lately Mikael has been deeply engaged in the development of Windows 7 and Windows Server 2008 R2 as a member of the TAP team.

Contents at a Glance

Contents

Introduction

Deploying Microsoft operating systems can be quite complicated, but it doesn't have to be. The setup program is completely different from what you have known in the past with OSs like Windows XP and Windows Server 2003. There are now configuration passes to perform during the installation and new tools to help you get the job done. In this book we start at the beginning of a deployment project and work our way through deploying OSs, applications, drivers, and packages. And more importantly, we don't stop there. Re-imaging machines today is a valid and useful troubleshooting step. We'll show you how to maintain your images to keep them current even months down the road.

While most of the tools covered in this book are free—the time spent learning them could be costly. After all, time is money, right? In this book, we strive to make learning these tools as easy as possible by giving you our crib notes. We'll share all the tips and tricks we have learned as well as the pitfalls and most commonly made mistakes so you won't waste valuable time making the same mistakes.

Who Should Read This Book

This book is for people who want to learn how to use Microsoft's deployment tools—all the tools! From installation through advanced configuration and troubleshooting, you'll find it here. For those of you reading this book, you'll probably fall into one of three basic groups of readers:

◆ IT pros who have been in the industry for a short time who understand basic networking infrastructure concepts like Active Directory Domains, Domain Naming Services (DNS), and the Dynamic Host Configuration Protocol (DHCP) and who want to further their knowledge in the deployment of Microsoft operating systems

◆ More experienced IT pros who have been involved in deploying Microsoft operating systems using tools like Ghost and Altiris who want the flexibility and cost-effectiveness of Microsoft's tools

◆ IT pros who have been around a while and used some of the Microsoft deployment tools but want to learn how to integrate the tools together to get the most robust deployment solution

How to Use This Book

There is more than one way to use this book. You could start with Chapter 1 and read the entire book to become a true Microsoft deployment expert. The chapters are organized as a real-world deployment project and take you through determining which of your existing machines are ready for Windows 7 to deploying an image complete with an OS, all your applications, drivers, and packages. There are many ways to deploy an image; each tool has its positive and negative aspects and you need to be aware of them before you choose the tool that is right for your environment. Or you can read only the chapters that interest you—but a word of caution here: If you decide to only read the MDT 2010 U1, WDS, or SCCM, chapters please be sure to read Chapters 3 and 4. These chapters explain in great detail the tools that all the other tools are built on. To troubleshoot MDT, WDS, or SCCM, you need to know the underlying tools. Another way to use this book is searching for resolutions to issues you have encountered. There is nothing wrong with using the book in this manner, but you'll get a more-well rounded understanding of the tools if you know all the pieces and how they fit together.

What You Need

You don't need to create a test environment (be it virtual or physical) to follow along with each chapter's step-by-step instructions, but it would certainly help you gain a much more in-depth understanding of the tools.

What Is Covered in This Book

Chapter 1: Does Your Hardware Measure Up? walks you through the process of implementing the Microsoft Assessment and Planning Toolkit, and using it to assess the infrastructure for a Windows 7 deployment project. This chapter also shows you how you can produce reports from the MAP database.

Chapter 2: Evaluating Applications for Windows 7 Compatibility looks at each step in the process of ensuring that your line-of-business (LOB) applications execute in a reliable manner when we you deploy Windows 7 to your desktop environment.

Chapter 3: Installing Windows 7: Meet the Panther peeks into the three different phases of the installation process: the preinstallation phase, the online configuration phase, and the Windows Welcome phase. The chapter also includes steps you can use to perform a clean installation and an upgrade and explores basics on licensing and activation, including the use of retail keys and original equipment manufacturer (OEM) keys.

Chapter 4: Cloning the Panther: Automating Windows 7 Installation shows you how to use the WinPE to create bootable media, add additional tools such as ImageX, and then capture an image.

Chapter 5: Migrating the Existing User Data helps you maintain your users' data, settings like Internet Explorer favorites and desktop settings, and application settings to make your users' environment look and feel as close as possible to their old environment (Vista or XP).

Chapter 6: Windows Deployment Services: The Basics will show you how to install and configure Windows Deployment Services (WDS) with images that are complete with drivers and applications.

Chapter 7: WDS from the Client's View walks you through the WDS client experience where you will start working with client machines to access the services that WDS provides.

Chapter 8: Tweaking Your WDS Server focuses on the advanced WDS features.

Chapter 9: Microsoft Deployment Toolkit 2010 shows you how to install MDT along with the required software and hardware. You'll learn how to put an image together and deploy it.

Chapter 10: MDT's Client Wizard teaches you how to customize the MDT's client wizard, showing you how to silence pages in the wizard and add rules and logic to the deployment.

Chapter 11: Fine-Tuning MDT Deployments dives into the advanced features of MDT, including selection profiles and linked deployment shares.

Chapter 12: Zero Touch Installations shows you how to create template images and deploy them from a central console to targeted PCs on an ad hoc and on a scheduled basis.

Chapter 13: Taking Advantage of Volume Licensing helps you choose which volume license key type to use and shows you how to track your licenses with the Key Management Service.

How to Contact the Authors

The authors welcome feedback from you about this book or about books you'd like to see from them in the future.

You can reach Aidan by writing to aidanfinn@hotmail.com. For more information about his work, please visit his website at www.aidanfinn.com and follow him on Twitter @joe_elway.

Darril loves hearing from readers, and you can reach him at darril@mcitpsuccess.com.

To contact Kenneth, write to kenneth@vansurksum.com or visit his LinkedIn profile at www.linkedin.com/in/kennethvansurksum. For more information about his work, please visit his website at http://www.techlog.org.

Sybex strives to keep you supplied with the latest tools and information you need for your work. Please check their website at www.sybex.com, where we'll post additional content and updates that supplement this book if the need arises. Enter **Windows 7** in the Search box (or type the book's ISBN—**9780470600313**), and click Go to get to the book's update page.

Chapter 1

Does Your Hardware Measure Up?

Your boss or customer will start the conversation with one question when you propose to upgrade the desktop infrastructure to Windows 7: How much will it cost? Licensing might come into the equation and it may not. That's usually a pretty simple calculation. What is more difficult is calculating the number of hardware upgrades or replacements that will have to be performed to bring the computers up to the required specifications for Windows 7 and the relevant desktop applications.

This chapter introduces you to Windows 7, its editions, and the hardware requirements of the operating system. Armed with this information, you'll be ready to perform an assessment of the network to identify the machines that are suitable for Windows 7, those that might require an upgrade, and those that should be replaced.

The Microsoft Assessment and Planning (MAP) Toolkit is a free suite that you can use to assess the existing IT infrastructure for a number of Microsoft product deployments, including Windows 7 and Office 2010. This chapter walks you through the process of planning the implementing MAP and using it to assess the infrastructure for a Windows 7 deployment project.

We finish the chapter by showing how you can produce reports from the MAP database. These reports can be presented to your boss or customer or they can be used by you to plan any hardware changes that must be implemented before you proceed with a Windows 7 deployment.

In this chapter, you will learn to:

- Identify the Windows 7 requirements

- Plan for and use the Microsoft Assessment and Planning Toolkit

- Produce reports and proposals from the Microsoft Assessment and Planning Toolkit

Meet Windows 7

Windows 7 is the newest Microsoft desktop operating system and is the successor to Windows Vista. As with Windows Vista, and Windows XP before that, there are a number of editions of Windows 7:

- Windows 7 Starter

- Windows 7 Home Basic

- Windows 7 Home Premium

- Windows 7 Professional

- Windows 7 Ultimate

- Windows 7 Enterprise

We won't go into detail on the first three; the Starter edition is available via original equipment manufacturers (OEMs) only and is used mainly for netbook systems, and Home Basic and Home Premium editions are focused on the end consumer market. This leaves us with the Professional, Ultimate, and Enterprise editions.

The Professional edition is the normal business edition of Windows 7 that will be sold with OEM computers. It has the usual features you would expect from a business edition, including the ability to join a domain and be managed using Group Policy.

The Ultimate and Enterprise editions inherit features from the same editions of Windows Vista and also introduce the new Better Together features, which are designed to work with Windows Server 2008 R2. The Better Together features are as follows:

BitLocker and BitLocker To Go BitLocker is a disk-encryption solution that is intended to protect against accidental loss or theft of computers. The entire contents of the hard disk are encrypted and are unusable for unauthorized users. BitLocker can be centrally managed using Active Directory.

Many organizations have protected their laptops against loss or theft using disk encryption but have still managed to make the wrong sort of headlines when removable media (such as flash drives) disappeared with private, sensitive, or customer data on them. The liabilities of transporting such data on removable media are huge. BitLocker To Go provides a way to encrypt removable media on Windows 7 Enterprise or Ultimate editions. The contained data can be accessed using a preshared password. The encrypted data can be accessed on other versions of Windows such as Windows XP with that password. Administrators can manage BitLocker To Go using Group Policy and can even force its usage for all removable media.

DirectAccess One of the most difficult things an administrator has to do is train end users how to use a virtual private networking (VPN) client and then field help desk questions related to its usage. These calls are typically very repetitive. For example, an administrator might call to complain that he cannot connect to an internal SharePoint site. The cause might be that they are not connecting their VPN client first. A user might call to complain that they find the VPN client cumbersome to log into or use. Many organizations use third-party VPN clients and identity-verification devices that complicate the login process.

DirectAccess gives you VPN-like access to internal network resources without a visible VPN client. The DirectAccess client identifies requests to internal resources and creates a secure tunnel to the network for the connection and associated network traffic. This is often a highly desirable feature—one that the mobile workforce (including the executives) will desire greatly. The mobile worker can simply access that private SharePoint site while working on the Internet. There are no clients to start or additional passwords to remember.

BranchCache It has been the ambition of many large organizations to simplify the infrastructure and reduce the costs (financial and administrative effort) of managing the branch office network. The key to this is to remove servers from the branch offices. The difficulty is that end users will still want to be able to access SharePoint sites and file servers, which will now be located in a remote central site at the other end of a high-latency WAN connection.

Transferring a small file over that connection will take much longer than it would have with a local file server.

BranchCache provides a way to cache centrally located web or file server content in the branch office, either using desktops (in a peer-to-peer network) or a Windows Server 2008 R2 server. Client machines will retrieve files from the cache rather than from the remote share if they are unchanged. The process will respect file locks and access permissions on the central share. This will drastically improve the download (not the upload) experience for branch office users.

BranchCache is a valuable solution and even improves how management solutions such as System Center Configuration Manager will operate in a branch office network.

Federated Search   IT systems exist so that information workers in the business can have access to and share information. This allows workers to make informed decisions. Where is this information stored? Ideally the local PC hard drive has no information stored on it. But information will be scattered throughout file shares and SharePoint sites across many servers, and possibly in many geographic locations. Federated Search makes it possible to find this information from a single search mechanism on a Windows 7 computer.

AppLocker   Businesses need solutions to control what software is running on the network. AppLocker provides a white list solution that is controlled by administrators using Active Directory Group Policy. This prevents software such as unlicensed products, malware, and resource-wasteful products from being allowed to start up.

Unlike software restriction policies, AppLocker is based on the application's publisher-generated digital signature. This allows more flexible rules that do not require as much administrative effort. For example, you can allow all versions or higher of a specific product. This would allow for product upgrades by Windows Update, System Center Configuration Manager, or third-party solutions, without disabling the product.

AppLocker allows a business to tightly control what products can be used on the network and brings control back to the IT department and the business.

Virtual Desktop Infrastructure Optimizations   Windows 7 has been optimized to provide a better end-user experience when used in a virtual desktop infrastructure (VDI). This is a solution where the desktop operating system is installed in virtual machines that are running on virtualization solutions such as Windows Server 2008 R2 Hyper-V, VMware ESX, or Citrix XenServer.

Multilingual User Interface   The Multilingual User Interface (MUI) is a language shell that can sit on top of an installation of Windows 7. Users can choose to change the language of the interface to suit their needs. This is a solution that is typically used in multinational organizations. A single standard image can be created for all sites and users, and the MUI packages can be bundled into it.

Windows 7 Hardware Requirements

Most organizations that are deploying Windows 7 will probably be using Windows XP as their current desktop operating system. They also likely will have desktop and laptop computer hardware. Windows 7 has much higher hardware requirements than Windows XP. You will have to know the requirements of Windows 7 so that you can identify the desktops and laptops that must be either upgraded or replaced.

Those organizations that bought PCs recently would have been purchasing machines that were designed for Windows Vista but were downgraded to Windows XP. We have some very good news for you; these machines will be probably fine for Windows 7. The hardware requirements are pretty much identical.

Knowing the minimum requirements for Windows 7 is useful for a couple of reasons. First, exams tend to feature questions about minimum requirements. Being able to recall these facts will score you a few easy points on your next certification exam. Second, the usual experience for a consultant, engineer, or administrator in this situation is that they are offered antique computers that are collecting dust in a storage room. You can use the minimum requirements to identify which machines will be useful and which should be sent to a recycle facility. However, remember that these are the *minimum* requirements. That means that these are the most basic specifications that you will need to get Windows 7 running. These specifications will not suffice for a typical office machine. They also won't meet the requirements of higher-end applications.

WINDOWS 7 REQUIREMENTS REFERENCE

The official Windows 7 requirements statement can be found here:

    www.microsoft.com/windows/windows-7/get/system-requirements.aspx

The core minimum requirements for Windows 7 are as follows:

Processor The processor should be 1 GHz or faster. You can use either a 32-bit (x86) or a 64-bit (x64) processor thanks to Windows 7 having 32-bit and 64-bit builds. Many organizations are choosing to deploy the 64-bit builds of Windows 7 to future-proof their desktop network and to maximize the security.

Windows 7 will support up to 32 logical processors or cores in a single processor with a 32-bit build. It can support a massive 256 cores with a 64-bit edition.

A few power users may require multiple processors (sockets rather than logical processors). The Windows 7 Professional, Ultimate, and Enterprise editions will support up to two physical processors (with multiple cores each). The other editions will support only one processor (with multiple cores).

Memory The minimum requirements for memory are 1 GB of RAM for a 32-bit installation and 2 GB of RAM for a 64-bit installation.

However, this amount of memory would not be sufficient in practice. The typical Windows XP office computer could run with 512 MB of RAM but was usually configured with 2 GB of RAM. Realistically, you will want to add more than the minimum to suit the applications that are installed on the computer. For example, a kiosk machine will probably be fine with the minimum amount of RAM so that it can run a web browser. However, a Windows 7 computer that is being used by a graphics artist will require much more RAM.

Table 1.1 shows the maximum amount of memory that is supported by each Windows 7 edition.

TABLE 1.1:   Maximum memory supported by Windows 7

EDITION	32-BIT LIMIT	64-BIT LIMIT
Enterprise	4 GB	192 GB
Ultimate	4 GB	192 GB
Professional	4 GB	192 GB
Home Premium	4 GB	16 GB
Home Basic	4 GB	8 GB
Starter	2 GB	2 GB

The information in Table 1.1 makes it pretty clear that power users will want to use 64-bit installations of Windows 7 because of the support for much larger amounts of memory.

Hard Disk Space   A 32-bit installation requires 16 GB of disk space and a 64-bit installation requires 20 GB of disk space. This does not account for the applications that will be installed on the computer and the various service packs and patches that will be deployed to it. You should also allow for additional space if your organization uses Offline Files or allows users to store files on their computer.

Graphics Card   A DirectX 9 graphics processor with Windows Display Driver Model (WDDM) 1.0 or higher is required.

Some features of Windows 7 have additional hardware requirements:

Internet Access   Internet access is required to access online features such as the Web and direct online activation with Microsoft, and to download Windows Updates directly from Microsoft.

Games   Games typically have publisher-specified graphics card and memory requirements that are higher than that of Windows 7.

Video Playback   You will require a better graphics device and more memory to display high-quality video.

DVD Drive   You need a DVD drive to install Windows 7 using the Microsoft-supplied media. This book shows you several methods for installing Windows 7 without using a DVD drive.

BitLocker   A Trusted Platform Module (TPM) 1.2 chip is required to use BitLocker.

Windows XP Mode   Microsoft supplies a virtual machine with a free copy of Windows XP Professional to users of the Enterprise, Ultimate, and Professional editions of Windows 7. This requires an additional 1 GB of RAM on the Windows 7 computer.

You now know the requirements of Windows 7. The challenge is to use this information to identify what you need to do with your existing computers so that you can deploy the new desktop operating system. This is where you may start to use the Microsoft Assessment and Planning Toolkit.

Using the Microsoft Assessment and Planning Toolkit

The Microsoft Assessment and Planning (MAP) Toolkit is a free tool that you can use to assess an existing IT infrastructure to deploy one of several Microsoft products, including Windows 7 and Microsoft Office 2010. The tool will remotely connect to machines that it discovers on the network using Windows Management Instrumentation (WMI), retrieve information from them, and store the information in a SQL Server database. You can view information in the MAP console and you can produce reports. These reports can be presented to management for business planning or can be used by you to plan hardware upgrades or replacements. We will be focusing on how MAP can be used in a Windows 7 deployment.

MAP is updated pretty regularly by Microsoft to include assessment features for new products. The newest version of MAP as of this writing was 5.0. You can find the latest version here:

```
http://technet.microsoft.com/solutionaccelerators/dd537566.aspx
```

Planning and Installing MAP

Let's look at the machine requirements for MAP and how to prepare the network for it before we show you how to install MAP to perform an assessment for a Windows 7 deployment project.

MAP SYSTEM REQUIREMENTS

The hardware requirements for MAP are as follows:

- 1.6 GHz processor
- 1.5 GB of RAM
- 1 GB of available disk space
- Network adapter card
- Graphics adapter that supports 1024 768 or higher resolution

A dual-core 1.5 GHz or faster processor is recommended for Windows Vista, Windows 7, Windows Server 2008, or Windows Server 2008 R2. For Windows Vista, Windows 7, or Windows Server 2008 R2, 2.0 GB of memory is recommended.

The performance of MAP queries and report generation is a direct result of the storage, memory, and processor resources that are available to it. MAP will perform better if you provide it with more resources and faster disks.

MAP can be installed on either the 32-bit or 64-bit edition of the following operating systems:

- Windows Server 2008 R2
- Windows 7

- Windows Server 2008

- Windows Vista Ultimate, Enterprise, or Business Edition

- Windows Server 2003 R2

- Windows Server 2003 with Service Pack 1 or later

- Windows XP Professional with Service Pack 2 or later

The following additional software components must be installed before you install MAP:

- .NET Framework 3.5 SP1 (3.5.30729.01)

- Windows Installer 4.5

- Microsoft Office Word 2007 SP2 or Word 2010

- Microsoft Office Excel 2007 SP2 or Excel 2010

- Microsoft Office Primary Interop Assemblies for Microsoft Office 2007

- All updates for Windows and Office that are available via Windows Update

You can install the Microsoft Office Primary Interop Assemblies for Microsoft Office 2007 from the Microsoft Office 2007 setup media.

SQL Server 2008 R2 Express Edition will be installed and used to store any MAP databases by default. You may choose to prevent this and use a database called MAPS on any of the following:

- Microsoft SQL Server 2005

- SQL Server 2008

- SQL Server 2008 R2

NETWORK CONFIGURATION

MAP uses agentless communications to talk to computers on your network. This requires administrative access on the machines, access rights, and firewall exceptions to be created.

You will need a user account with local administrative rights for every computer that is to be assessed. The easy solution is to use a domain administrative user account. You should *not* do this. You may already have a domain-based user account that you can use for this remote connectivity.

Many organizations will choose to outsource the Windows 7 deployment project to consultants or contractors. These organizations will be hesitant to share the credentials of important user accounts. It may also be possible that large organizations will have delegated administration or budget units in the network. This means that more than one user account will be required to assess the computers.

You can quickly grant local administrative rights to a domain-based user account using the Restricted Groups feature of Group Policy. The policy will (within a few hours, depending on Group Policy refresh settings) grant local administrative rights to all computers that inherit the policy. This will allow you to quickly use one or more user accounts to perform an assessment without using a domain admin user—and without running around to every computer to set up a user with administrative rights.

The process will start with some basic Group Policy engineering. You should identify a location to link a new Group Policy Object (or edit an existing one). This organizational unit (OU) will contain all the computers that will inherit and apply the new setting (for a new local administrative user). You might need to identify a number of locations to link a single policy depending on your OU architecture and placement of computer objects. You might also need to create or edit more than one Group Policy Object (GPO) if you need to configure more than one local administrative user for different parts of the organization within the Active Directory domain. This process will need to be repeated if there are computers to be assessed in more than one domain or forest. That is because a GPO can only apply within a single domain.

A small lab network is used in this book to demonstrate the discussed technologies. All of the computers are members of a domain called `deploy.com`. A server called `DeploySrv` is used to install the deployment technologies.

A number of desktop computers will be used to demonstrate bare-metal installations, upgrades, and possibly remote administration. You will need some machines with no operating system and some that are installed with Windows XP.

Suppose a domain-based user account called `deploy\map` has been created to provide administrative access to all computers to be assessed by MAP. The user account `deploy\map` has been made a member of a domain-based security group called `MAPGroup`. This process will make `MAPGroup` a member of the local Administrators group on each PC that inherits the new policy, thus making `deploy\map` a local administrator on every targeted computer. You can use the Group Policy Management tool to create and manage Group Policy. This tool is installed on domain controllers (Full Installation rather than Server Core) or on computers that have had the Remote Server Administration Tools installed. You can use Group Policy Management to navigate to the OU where you want to link your new policy. Right-click on the OU in question and from the context menu select Create A GPO In This Domain, And Link It Here. Name the new GPO object in the New GPO dialog box. You can see the new GPO in Figure 1.1.

FIGURE 1.1
The New GPO

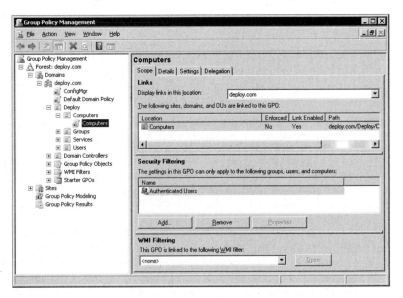

CAREFUL APPROACH TO NEW GROUP POLICY OBJECTS

You should always limit the scope of a new policy to a set of test machines. This will allow you to check your new policy without doing any harm to production systems.

Ideally you will limit the number of GPOs in a domain. However, some administrators will choose to create a new GPO for new policy settings that are created. This allows administrators to quickly apply it and, more importantly, quickly remove it in case there is a problem. The new policy settings can be merged into an existing GPO.

You can edit the new GPO by right-clicking it and selecting Edit. This opens the Group Policy Management Editor, which is shown in Figure 1.2. The policy we want to discuss is Restricted Groups. You can find this setting in Computer Configuration ➤ Policies ➤ Windows Settings ➤ Security Settings.

FIGURE 1.2
Group Policy Management Editor

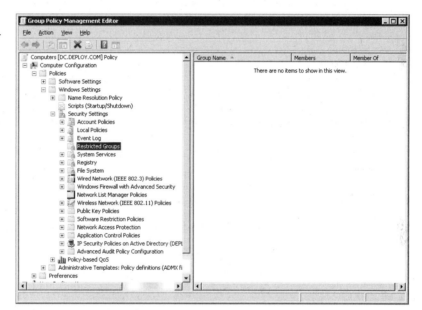

EXISTING RESTRICTED GROUPS POLICY

You should not go through this process if there is already a policy for controlling the local Administrators group membership. You should edit the existing policy to add the user account that will be used by MAP to connect to the computers.

The Restricted Groups policy setting works by editing the contents of a local user group on a computer. Say we want to grant local administrative access to MAPGroup on the computers that we want to assess. We are going to manage the MAPGroup security group rather than the local Administrators group. You can add a group to manage by right-clicking on Restricted Groups and selecting Add Group. This opens the Add Group dialog box, shown in Figure 1.3.

FIGURE 1.3
The Add Group
dialog box

A new dialog box opens, allowing you to control the membership of the `MAPGroup` security group. This policy setting, when applied or refreshed, will add the group to the group that we'll specify in a moment.

You can specify which groups `MAPGroup` will be made a member of by clicking the Add button beside This Group Is A Member Of. This opens the Group Membership dialog box, where you specify the group or groups that you want `MAPGroup` to be added to. You would specify Administrators in this example, as shown in Figure 1.4.

FIGURE 1.4
The Group
Membership
dialog box

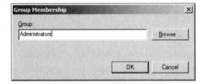

You can close Group Membership to return to DEPLOY\MAPGroup Properties. The contents of the This Group Is A Member Of section are updated to include the Administrators group (Figure 1.5).

You can wait for this policy to apply to the computers that inherit the policy (all computers in deploy.com ➤ Deploy ➤ Computers in this example), or you can force the policy to apply on each of your test machines by running this command on them:

```
gpupdate /force
```

`Deploy\MAP` is a member of `Deploy\MAPGroup`. `Deploy\MAPGroup` is now a member of the Administrators group on the computers that you want to assess. That means you can use `Deploy\MAP` to perform the assessment with administrative rights. Now you have the required administrative rights to assess the required computers. You must follow this up by ensuring that you can communicate with them across the network.

MAP does not use an agent to discover and assess computers. Instead, it uses Windows Management Instrumentation (WMI) to connect to the computers and collect data over the network. There are a few requirements for this:

Remote Registry Access An exception must be made for this service in the Windows Firewall for computers to be assessed. This will open TCP port 135. Any network devices or firewalls between your MAP machine and your computers must also allow this traffic.

Enable File and Printer Sharing You must enable this setting on computers if they have the Windows Firewall enabled. TCP 139 and 445 as well as UDP 137 and 138 are the affected ports. Network appliances and firewalls must allow this traffic.

Remote Registry Service   This service is used by MAP to identify which roles are installed and to gather performance information.

Windows Management Instrumentation Service   The WMI service must be enabled and running.

Local Administrator Credentials   MAP uses WMI to remotely access each computer. This will use the previously configured administrator credentials to get administrative access to each machine.

FIGURE 1.5
Administrators
Restricted Group
members

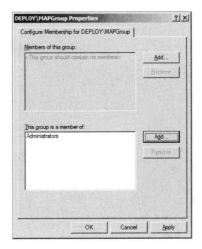

You can configure each of these manually, by script, or by using GPOs in an Active Directory domain. We will be working with GPOs.

Legacy operating systems such as Windows XP x64 will require a few additional changes:

Windows XP x64   The nondefault Windows Installer Provider must be installed on 64-bit installations. This can be done by installing WMI Windows Installer Provider under Management and Monitoring Tools in Add/Remove Programs in the Control panel.

Windows NT 4.0   Admittedly, it's very unlikely that you'll be assessing any Windows NT 4 machines to install Windows 7 on. However, you might have some machines that you may want to replace. You will need to install the WMI Core on machines with this operating system. This is available at:

```
http://www.microsoft.com/downloads/details.aspx?familyid=AFE41F46-E213-4CBF-9C5B-
FBF236E0E875
```

We are using Group Policy once again to configure a number of settings to make the network access configurations. You will start by configuring the sharing security model for local user accounts. Select Computer Configuration ➢ Policies ➢ Windows Settings ➢ Security Settings ➢ Local Policies ➢ Security Options. You should configure Network Access: Sharing And Security

Model For Local Accounts to use the Classic: Local Users Authenticate As Themselves setting, as shown in Figure 1.6.

FIGURE 1.6
Network Access
Model for Local
User Accounts

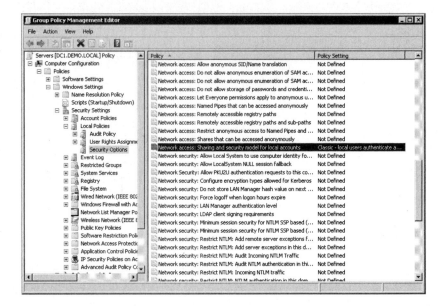

You will need to start working on the firewall next. Navigate to Computer Configuration ➢ Policies ➢ Administrative Templates ➢ Network ➢ Network Connections ➢ Windows Firewall ➢ Domain Profile. You will enable Windows Firewall: Allow Inbound Remote Administration Exception. You can see in Figure 1.7 that there is a bit more to this setting. You will also need to configure the IP address of the MAP machine. In this example it is 192.168.1.22.

The Windows Firewall: Allow Inbound File And Printer Sharing Exception policy must also be configured. You will enable it and enter the IP address of the MAP machine in the same way you just did to enable remote administration.

You have not completed the firewall rule requirements for MAP. The Remote Registry and the Windows Management Instrumentation services need to be running. It is possible that the services are stopped. Some organizations will disable Remote Registry as a part of a security hardening process. It won't be dangerous to enable Remote Registry if you are managing the Windows Firewall. The Allow Inbound Remote Administration Exception policy that we just configured will restrict access to the service to one IP address: the MAP machine. Now you will learn how to set these services to run automatically using Group Policy.

Navigate to Configuration ➢ Policies ➢ Windows Settings ➢ Security Settings ➢ System Services. In the right-hand pane you will see all of the services can be managed using Group Policy. Let's start with the Remote Registry service. Double-click on it to manage the settings. In Figure 1.8 you can see that you must select the Define This Policy Setting check box and then set the service to Automatic. You can optionally restrict who will have the rights to locally manage the service by clicking Edit Security and using the usual Windows permissions dialog box to choose the permitted users and groups. You should then repeat this process for the Windows Management Instrumentation service.

FIGURE 1.7
Allow Inbound
Remote Adminis-
tration Exception

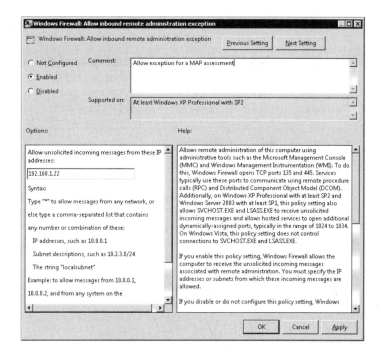

FIGURE 1.8
Configuring the
Remote Registry
Service Policy

It is possible that you will have computers to assess that are members of workgroups. The firewall exemptions and access configurations will have to be set up using manual configuration or by using a script. You will also need to change the Network Access: Sharing And Security Model For Local Accounts local policy setting from Guest to Classic. More information on that process can be found here:

http://technet.microsoft.com/library/cc786449.aspx

Your network and the computers are ready for assessment. It is time to turn your attention to the MAP machine.

INSTALLING MAP ON THE SERVER

Install the operating system and prerequisites for MAP on the machine that you will install MAP on. You can use the free SQL Server Express Edition on that machine. By default, the Express Edition is downloaded and installed by the MAP installer. Alternatively, you can use a purchased version of SQL Server. You can do so by installing a SQL instance called MAPS on the server before starting the MAP installer.

Real World Scenario

MAP AND CONSULTING

It is possible to perform many discrete MAP projects with a single MAP installation. This would allow a consultant, for instance, to install MAP once, perform many assessments, and produce reports for many customers without having to rebuild the infrastructure from scratch every time. However, there might be some security concerns about a consultant bringing a laptop into several customer sites and plugging it into their networks. It is possible to prepare a virtual machine (which is just a couple of files) with an operating system, the software requirements, and MAP. You can deploy a copy of the exported virtual machine in each customer site for which you must do an assessment. This arrangement would allow MAP to be up and running in a few minutes.

You can download the latest version of MAP from the Microsoft site and start the installation when you are ready. The opening screen in the installation wizard is shown in Figure 1.9. A check box, which is selected by default, allows you to automatically download device compatibility and application updates. The ability to download the very latest compatibility information is useful because one of our concerns in a Windows 7 assessment is device and driver compatibility with the new operating system. This option will require that the MAP machine have access to the Internet.

The Microsoft Assessment And Planning Toolkit Setup wizard will proceed to check the MAP prerequisites on the machine. If you receive a prerequisite check failure message, a link will lead you to more information about the failure(s). You will have to install any missing prerequisites and restart the installation if you do get a warning like this. You can continue the wizard if all the prerequisites are installed.

The Installation Folder screen will appear. The default folder location is `C:\Program Files\ Microsoft Assessment and Planning Toolkit`.

FIGURE 1.9
MAP installation
welcome screen

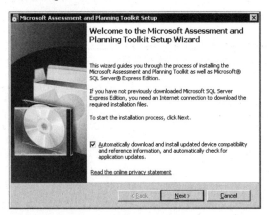

The SQL Server Express screen (Figure 1.10) lets you configure how SQL Server Express will be installed. The default option is to allow the wizard to download and install the files. The second option, Install From Previously Downloaded Installation Files, enables you to use a copy of the setup files for SQL Server Express that you might have previously downloaded for other projects. You might use this option if your MAP machine does not have Internet access and you can copy the SQL Express files using some form of removable media.

FIGURE 1.10
The SQL Server
Express screen

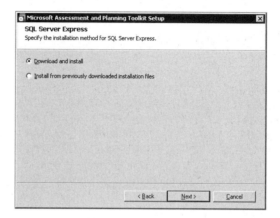

You will be informed that the setup wizard will install and configure MAP and SQL Server Express (if necessary). Give the installation some time, and unless something goes wrong, you'll see an Installation Successful screen, which will allow you to terminate the setup wizard and start the Microsoft Assessment and Planning Toolkit.

Everything is in place now. You have a user account with administrative rights on the machines to be assessed for Windows 7 readiness. You have configured the Windows Firewall on the machines and established the required access rights. You have installed MAP on a machine, and you now can start discovering computers on your network and assessing them.

Performing a Windows 7 Readiness Assessment

You have reached the point where you can launch the Microsoft Assessment and Planning Toolkit console from the Start menu. You will be asked to select an existing MAP database (to continue working on a project) or create a new one (to start a new assessment project), as you can see in Figure 1.11. You must enter a database name if you want to create a new one.

We'll start by taking a quick tour of the MAP console. You can access a collection of reference material related to the possible projects that MAP can be used in by clicking on the Reference Material bar in the bottom left (Figure 1.12).

FIGURE 1.11
Select or create a
MAP database.

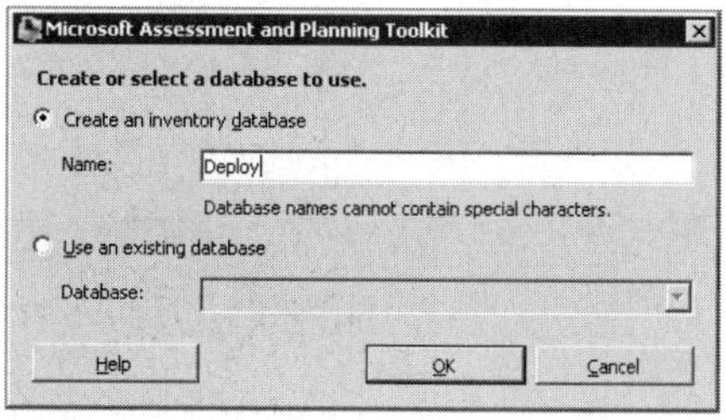

FIGURE 1.12
MAP reference
material

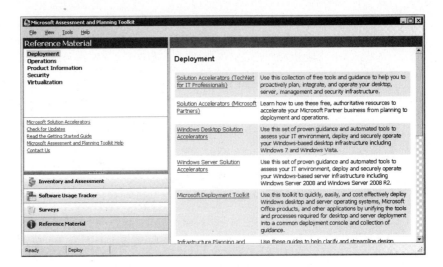

The Surveys wunderbar is strangely named. It provides you with links to more reference material. There is a link in MAP to take you to a website called IPD Assessment Guide And Scenario Selection Tool. The content included will help you choose the correct desktop solution or solutions for your organization.

The Software Usage Tracker wunderbar takes you to a feature that was introduced in MAP. Many organizations struggle to keep track of their licensing. Some licensing schemes, such as Microsoft's Enterprise Agreement, require an annual report on which the organization's license fees are based. Microsoft added software usage tracking to the MAP accelerator to help with this need. You can learn more about this functionality by reading the Software Usage Tracker Guide, which you will find in the Microsoft Assessment And Planning Toolkit program group in the Start menu.

Now we get to where you will spend most of your time in a deployment project: the Inventory And Assessment wunderbar, shown in Figure 1.13.

FIGURE 1.13
The Inventory
And Assessment
wunderbar

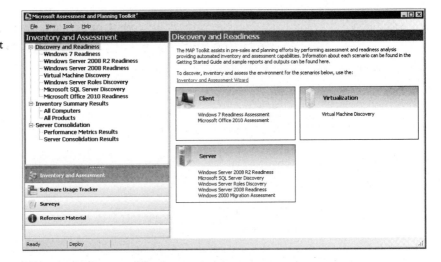

You can expand each of the items in the navigation pane on the left to see the many ways you can use MAP. MAP can be used for the following:

◆ Windows 7 readiness

◆ Windows Server 2008 R2 readiness

◆ Windows Server 2008 readiness

◆ Virtual machine discovery

◆ Windows Server roles discovery

◆ Microsoft SQL Server discovery

◆ Microsoft Office 2010 readiness

The final item might be of interest to you if you are doing a Windows 7 deployment. You can use MAP to assess a network for an Office 2010 deployment. You may choose to deploy Office 2010 as a part of your Windows 7 project.

We're going to return to performing an assessment of your machines for a Windows 7 deployment. Click on Windows 7 Readiness and you will see a screen indicating that you have not performed a discovery of computers that you could install Windows 7 on (Figure 1.14). You can start this process by clicking on the Inventory And Assessment Wizard link.

Clicking that link launches the Inventory And Assessment Wizard, which starts with the Inventory Scenarios screen (Figure 1.15). Here you can see the possible scenarios where you can use MAP to perform a discovery of computers:

◆ Windows-Based Computers

◆ Linux-Based Computers

◆ VMware-Based Computers

◆ Exchange Server

◆ SQL Server

FIGURE 1.14
Not enough inventory data

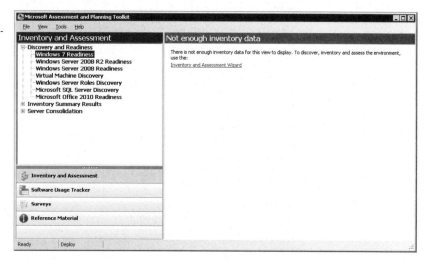

FIGURE 1.15
The Inventory Scenarios screen

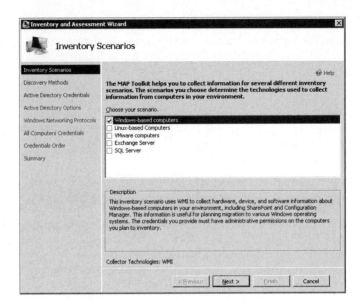

Windows-Based Computers is selected by default. This is the option that you will use for a Windows 7 readiness assessment. Click the Next button to continue to the next screen.

GETTING SOME HELP

Microsoft got a lot of criticism about its documentation for the Windows Vista deployment technologies. Redmond listened and a lot of very positive changes were made. You'll find usable and understandable built-in documentation in the deployment products that you use to deploy Windows 7. For example, you can press the F1 key to get help while using the Inventory And Assessment Wizard.

Figure 1.16 shows the Discovery Methods screen. Here you can select the ways that MAP will discover computers that will be assessed. The possible methods are as follows:

Use Active Directory Domain Services (AD DS)   This method is selected by default. The computer accounts from your domain are used in the discovery process. The scope can be limited to a domain, an OU, or a container. It is limited to 120,000 computer objects per domain. The AD DS method will not discover any additional computer objects beyond 120,000. Microsoft recommends that this method not be used with the Windows networking protocols method because it will take more time to complete the process.

Use Windows Networking Protocols   This discovery method uses the WIN32 LAN Manager APIs to query the Computer Browser service. This method is used to discover computers in workgroups and Windows NT 4–based domains. Microsoft recommends that this method not be used with the AD DS method because it will take more time to complete the process.

Use System Center Configuration Manager (SCCM) System Center Configuration Manager (also known as SCCM or ConfigMgr) is Microsoft's enterprise deployment and management solution. We will look at it more in Chapter 12, "Zero Touch Installations," where you will learn to push out a Windows 7 image to SCCM-managed computers without touching them. The SCCM discovery method will use the database of SCCM-managed computers to assess potential machines for installing Windows 7.

FIGURE 1.16

The MAP discovery methods

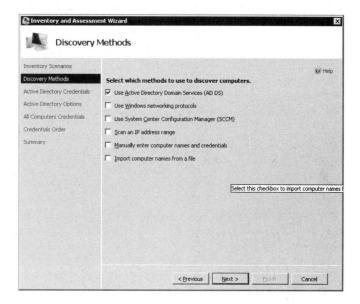

Scan An IP Address Range There may be little in common between the physical infrastructure (network) and the logical network (Active Directory domains or OUs). This method allows you to target a set of IP addresses for your discovery. That way, you can be very specific in how you assess your infrastructure. For example, you can bring a laptop with MAP installed around to each branch office in a multinational company and target each local LAN without impacting the WAN.

Manually Enter Computer Names And Credentials You use this method if there are a few known machines that you want to target and the previously discussed methods are either unsuitable or too much work. For example, you might have performed an AD DS discovery and then want to target just a handful of known workgroup member machines.

Import Computer Names From A File There may be a scenario where Computer Browser is not enabled or you cannot query Active Directory. If so, you can specify computer names, NetBIOS names, or fully qualified domain names (FQDNs) in a simple text file, with one computer name per line.

We're using the AD DS discovery method in this example because we can target a particular OU that contains all of the machines we want to assess and they are contained within a single site. Choose the Use Active Directory Domain Services (AD DS) check box and click Next.

The Active Directory Credentials screen (Figure 1.17) asks you to enter the credentials that will be used by MAP to connect to Active Directory and to identify the computer account objects that will be assessed. This account must be a domain member with read permissions for the required OUs. Fill in the appropriate information, then click Next.

FIGURE 1.17
Active Directory discovery credentials

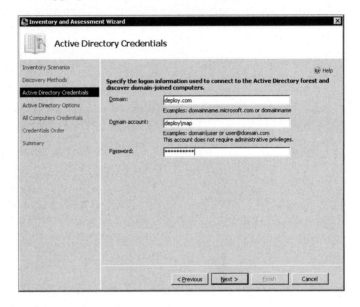

The Active Directory Options screen (Figure 1.18) allows you to do either of the following:

◆ Assess all computers in all OUs and/or containers in all domains in the forest

◆ Assess computers in specified OUs and/or containers and in specified domains

FIGURE 1.18
Active Directory Options

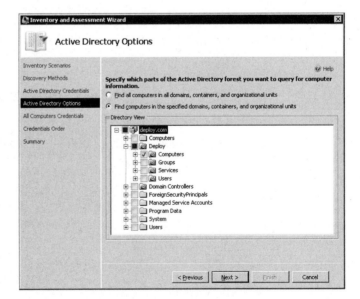

In this example, we are going to assess all computers in deploy.com ➤ Deploy ➤ Computers. Choose the Find Computers In The Specified Domains, Containers, And Organization Units radio button, and click Next.

You may be wondering when you'll get to use that domain-based user account that you spent so much time on to grant it local administrative rights on your computers. The All Computers Credentials screen is that user account's time to shine! The screen is empty by default, as shown in Figure 1.19.

FIGURE 1.19
All Computers
Credentials

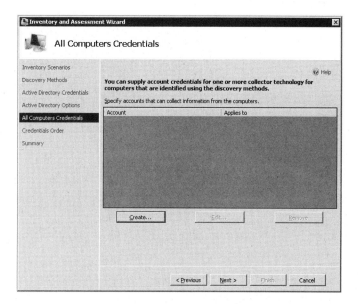

Click the Create button to add a set of credentials to remotely connect to the computers that are being assessed. Figure 1.20 shows how `deploy\map` will be used. You can use more than one account. Some organizations have several IT units within a single domain or forest and want to limit the administrative scope of accounts such as the MAP discovery account. You can quickly add an account by clicking the Save And New button. Otherwise, just click the Save button to save your entered credentials and continue.

FIGURE 1.20
Account Entry

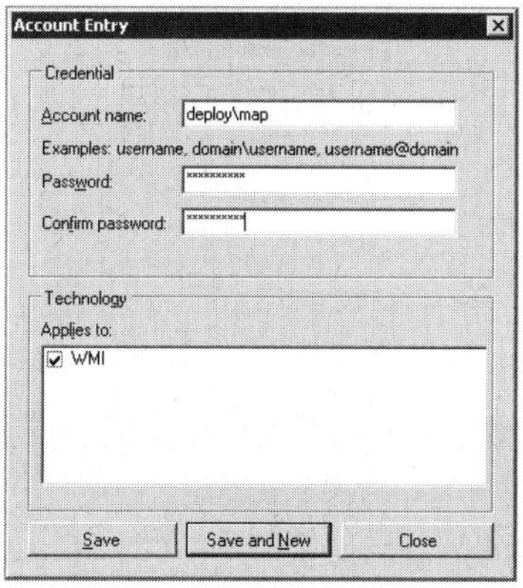

The All Computers Credentials screen is updated to show the entered credentials, as shown in Figure 1.21.

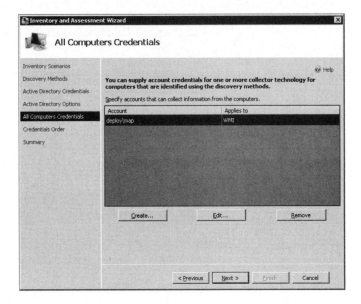

If you do enter more than one set of credentials in the All Computers Credentials screen, you will want to define the order in which they will be tried when MAP connects to computers using WMI. To control this ordering, in the Credentials Order screen (Figure 1.22) select a set of credentials and click the Move Up or Move Down button. When you're finished, click Next.

FIGURE 1.22
Credentials Order

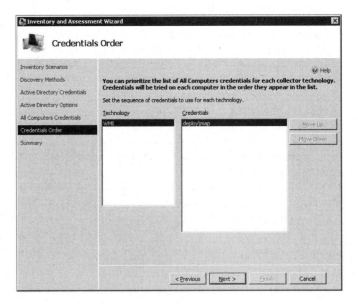

The Summary screen lists the configuration of the discovery. You can proceed with the discovery if you are happy. Figure 1.23 shows the status of the running discovery. You can close this window and monitor the discovery progress in the bottom of the MAP console.

FIGURE 1.23
Discovery status

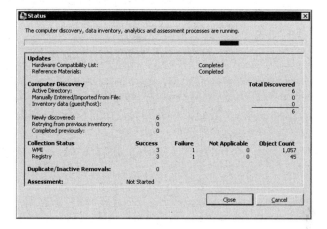

The Windows 7 Readiness view is updated with some initial Windows 7 Readiness Summary Results (see Figure 1.24 a bit later) when the discovery is completed. The initial discovery is now complete. You can perform more discoveries of different types if you have to add more computers to the current MAP database.

 **Real World Scenario**

HOW COMPLETE IS MAP, REALLY?

You may have a few questions if you have tried to use MAP. You may have noticed, for example, that the number of discovered machines is less than what you really have. The problem is that MAP depends on the machines being available on the network to assess. MAP does not have an offline assessment method. That means that any computers that are used by mobile users (laptops, tablets, etc.) will not be assessed.

You can try to run your assessment a few times to get a more complete picture of your end-user infrastructure. Unfortunately, there will always be a few machines that won't be hit. You could do a manual assessment if it is just a few machines. This won't be realistic in a larger organization. In that circumstance, you could use the MAP results to identify trends to predict costs and required upgrades/replacements.

There is a catch to running a discovery that is based on a database such as Active Directory. The domain might contain computer accounts that are no longer valid. It is a good idea to clean up computer accounts that are no longer valid before using MAP. You can use OldCmp (www.joeware .net/freetools/tools/oldcmp/index.htm) to quickly identify such computer account objects and either move them to a special OU that is outside the discovery scope or delete them.

Produce MAP Reports and Proposals

The MAP database should now contain information about discovered computers and their specifications. You can start to use this data to identify machines that are suitable for Windows 7, those that need to be upgraded, and those that need to be replaced.

The Windows 7 Readiness Summary Results (Figure 1.24) presents you with an initial assessment of your infrastructure based on the gathered data and some assumptions that are defined by default within MAP. There are four possible categories that each audited machine can fall into:

Ready For Windows 7   Any machine in this category can be successfully installed with Windows 7 based on the default specified requirements.

Not Windows 7 Ready   Machines in this category are not currently able to meet the requirements for Windows 7 but they can be upgraded.

Cannot Run Windows 7   Machines in this category cannot be upgraded to run Windows 7 and will have to be replaced.

Insufficient Data   You will likely see a number of machines in this category after your first discovery pass. These are machines that MAP discovered but could not communicate with. For example, a computer account might be discovered in Active Directory or SCCM but the machine might be offline or not have the required firewall/access configurations, or MAP might not have administrative access to the machine.

The readiness summary in the example shows that, before any hardware upgrades, our existing computers are not ready for Windows 7. With some hardware upgrades, five of the discovered seven machines will definitely be Windows 7–capable. Two machines have insufficient data for an assessment.

FIGURE 1.24
Initial Windows 7
Readiness Summary Results

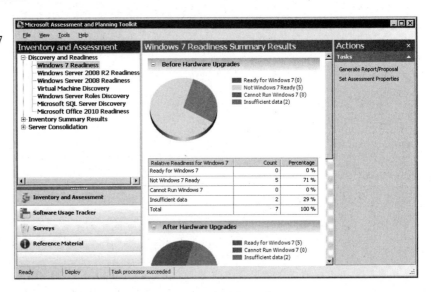

We should investigate why none of our machines have fallen into the Ready For Windows 7 category. We can do this by running a report based on the collected data and the assessment. Take the following steps:

1. Click on the Generate Report/Proposal link in the Actions pane to create a report.

2. A job status window appears, as shown in Figure 1.25. You can close this window and reopen it by clicking the job status button, which appears at the bottom of the MAP console.

FIGURE 1.25

Generating job status reports

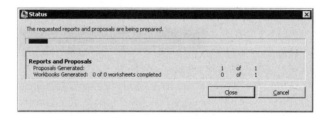

3. The reports are saved into the My Documents folder of the currently logged-in user in a subfolder called MAP\<MAP database name>. Open a Windows Explorer window in that folder from the MAP console using the Saved Reports And Proposals option on the View menu. Figure 1.26 shows this folder. A Word document (a proposal) has been generated. We'll come back to that later.

FIGURE 1.26

MAP reports and proposals

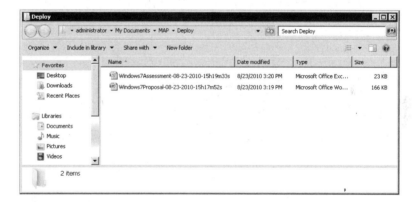

An Excel spreadsheet (a report) has also been generated. This is what we are interested in right now.

4. Open the spreadsheet and navigate to the ClientAssessment worksheet to view the reasons for any machines not being in the Ready For Windows 7 category. You can see in Figure 1.27 that the five computers do not have a DVD-ROM drive.

Many organizations choose to purchase computers that do not include a CD or DVD drive. This can save a small amount of money per machine and it can reduce the possibility of misuse of business property. As you will learn in Chapter 6, "Windows Deployment Services: The Basics," you do not need an optical drive to install Windows. Many organizations choose to use quicker and more flexible network-based installations.

FIGURE 1.27

Reason for not being Windows 7 ready

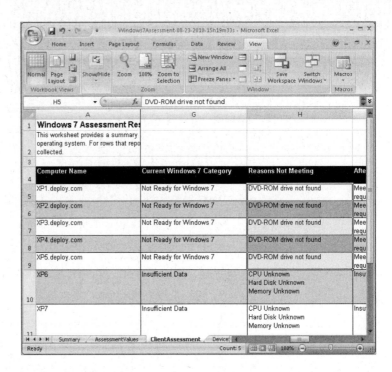

5. Take some time to look around this spreadsheet report. It will be the basis of your future work in the Windows 7 deployment project. There are a number of worksheets, which are detailed in Table 1.2.

TABLE 1.2: The Excel report

WORKSHEET NAME	DESCRIPTION
Summary	This is a summary of the categorization of the discovered machines.
AssessmentValues	The assessment values that are used to categorize machines are listed here.
ClientAssessment	This worksheet lists every assessed machine and the reason for its categorization.
DeviceSummary	Devices that are attached to or inside of assessed machines are summarized in this worksheet. This includes information on where a driver can be sourced from. For example, a driver might be included with the Windows 7 media, it might be available from Windows Update, it might be available from the hardware vendor, or you might need to replace the device.

TABLE 1.2: The Excel report *(CONTINUED)*

WORKSHEET NAME	DESCRIPTION
DeviceDetails	Details on every discovered device are listed here, including actions that need to be taken if the attached machine is upgraded to Windows 7.
MinimumAfterUpgrades	This worksheet lists the actions that must be taken to bring discovered computers up to a point where they meet the minimum requirements for Windows 7.
RecommendedAfterUpgrades	This worksheet lists the actions that must be taken to bring discovered computers up to a point where they meet the recommended requirements for Windows 7.
DiscoveredApplications	Every application and version of that application is listed, including the number of machines that it was discovered on. You will use this information to test compatibility with the new operating system and obtain support information when it is installed on Windows 7.

6. Return to the MAP console and click the Set Assessment Properties link to open the dialog box shown in Figure 1.28. Here you can see the Microsoft-listed Windows 7 requirements. This is what is being used by MAP to assess each computer that MAP has discovered. You will probably find that these requirements are inappropriate for your organization.

FIGURE 1.28
The default assessment properties

Some devices, such as the DVD-ROM, may offer a more complete experience but may not have a business reason to be installed in your Windows 7 computers.

Additionally, as mentioned previously, the Microsoft minimum hardware requirements are probably too low for a business desktop computer. Would you really want to use machines with 1 GHz processors, 16 GB of disk space, and 1 GB of RAM? An information worker would find that machine incapable of doing the work that is required. You will likely want to raise these hardware requirements to something significantly higher based on your application requirements.

7. Select the Use Custom Settings option and modify the selections and entered hardware sizes to meet your requirements (Figure 1.29). Notice that the If DVD-ROM Is Not Found, Flag Machine As Not Ready option has been deselected. This should change the assessment categorization of our five machines.

FIGURE 1.29
The customized assessment properties

Note that the assessment properties will change the minimum hardware specifications rather than the Microsoft recommended hardware requirements for a standard installation of Windows 7.

8. Click the Run Assessment button to save the changes and to instruct MAP to rerun the assessment using the previously gathered data.

You can see in Figure 1.30 that the five computers are now appearing as Ready For Windows 7 in the Windows 7 Readiness Summary Results. Unfortunately, there are still two machines with an Insufficient Data status. You should try to identify which machines are no longer valid and rerun the assessment in the hope of gathering data from those that might have been offline before.

FIGURE 1.30
Updated Windows 7 Readiness Summary Results

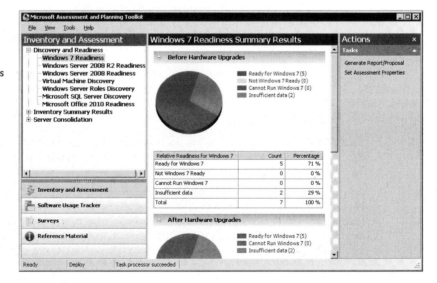

9. When you have discovered and assessed as many machines as you can in the organization and you have configured the assessment properties appropriately, rerun the
   Generate Report/Proposal job to create the documents based on the latest information in
   the MAP database.

10. Return to the folder containing your MAP reports and proposals. Check out the Word
    document that was mentioned in step 3 (Figure 1.31). It is a proposal aimed at decision
    makers such as your manager or a customer.

FIGURE 1.31

The MAP-generated
proposal document

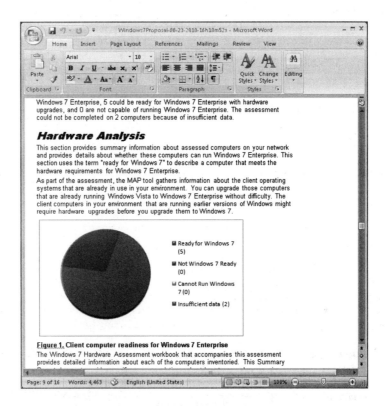

You could perform a single discovery of all machines to create a single MAP database. You would then set the assessment properties and generate reports for each of the user categories in the organization. You would have to edit each report to filter out each of the unwanted machines. The result will be that you have three reports, with each one containing an assessment for each of the machine groups (managers, IT consultants, and developers).

Alternatively, you could create a single MAP database for each of the user groups. That means you would need to have some way to separate the machines using your discovery process. For example, an AD DS discovery would require that there be a management OU, an IT infrastructure consultant OU, and a developers OU. Each database discovery would target the appropriate OU. You could set the assessment properties for each database to suit the needs of the machines in that database and then produce three reports and proposals.

You can rerun a discovery by navigating to Discovery And Readiness in the navigation pane and clicking on the Inventory And Assessment Wizard link.

The document shows the summary data that we mentioned earlier. The document starts by introducing Windows 7. It then goes through the assessment to discuss the work that must be completed to deploy the new operating system. It contains high-level information such as the following:

- Hardware upgrade recommendations
- Device driver analysis
- Application summary

You can take this Word document and customize it to meet your requirements.

You now know how to install MAP, discover computers with it, perform an assessment of the hardware based on built-in and customized system requirements, generate reports that include hardware and application information, and generate a proposal document that can be presented to a manager or a customer.

The Bottom Line

Identify the Windows 7 requirements. You should know the minimum Windows 7 requirements and understand the difference between minimum and recommended requirements.

Master It You are working as a consultant in a client site. The client is a publishing company. You are performing an assessment of the desktop and laptop computers with the intent of doing a Windows 7 deployment. You have been invited to a meeting to discuss the reports. A junior IT manager wants to reduce the amount of hardware upgrades to save money. She has stated that the minimum Windows 7 requirements should have been used in the assessment. What will your response be?

Plan for and use the Microsoft Assessment and Planning Toolkit. MAP can be installed and used in a number of ways, depending on the organization and the project.

Master It You are working as a senior engineer in a multinational organization. You have been tasked with performing an assessment of all desktop and laptop computers in the organization for a deployment of Windows 7. The project manager has told you that you must not impact the WAN connections in any way. How will you perform the assessment?

Produce reports and proposals from the Microsoft Assessment and Planning Toolkit. MAP can produce a report and a proposal from a MAP discovery and assessment database.

Master It You work for a software development company that is planning to deploy Windows 7. You have been asked to generate an assessment based on two hardware requirements: one for the support desk with low requirements and one for the developers with high requirements. Each group is contained within an Active Directory organizational unit. How will you perform the assessment and generate the necessary reports and proposals?

Chapter 2

Evaluating Applications for Windows 7 Compatibility

One of the greatest challenges to deploying a new desktop operating system in an organization is application compatibility. Even a small organization can have dozens of applications, some of which run only on legacy versions of Windows, such as Windows XP. Typically you'll find that it's some critical application that causes issues. Imagine what it must be like for large organizations like corporations or schools where there are thousands of applications. Even discovering compatibility issues must seem like a daunting process, let alone resolving those issues.

Many of the difficulties users and organizations had with Windows Vista were compatibility issues. Drivers couldn't be found, and essential applications wouldn't install or run correctly. Things improved over time with a solution in the form of the Application Compatibility Toolkit (ACT) from Microsoft.

Microsoft made a real commitment to resolve compatibility issues for those who were migrating from legacy operating systems to Windows 7 with the 5.6 version of ACT. Solutions are now available to identify applications and drivers in your organization, test those applications, resolve basic issues with drivers and applications, reuse existing compatibility solutions, and develop your own in-house solutions for more complex issues using fixes from a collection of over 300 possibilities. In this chapter, we will look at each of these steps in the process to ensure that your line-of-business (LOB) applications execute in a reliable manner when you deploy Windows 7 to your desktop environment.

In this chapter, you will learn to:

◆ Plan for and install the Application Compatibility Toolkit

◆ Use ACT to identify incompatible applications

◆ Use ACT and XP Mode to solve compatibility issues

Application Compatibility

Most organizations around the world were heavily invested in Windows XP for many years by the time Windows Vista was released. Application developers were producing products just for Windows XP. Driver developers often only considered Windows XP. When organizations tried to deploy Windows Vista, they started having issues. Many of the driver issues were resolved over time. But one major issue prevented many organizations from deploying Windows Vista: LOB and other critical applications just would not work on Vista. Vista did change how Windows worked quite a bit. Those compatibility issues did not go away with Windows 7. In fact, it's likely that Windows 7 will behave almost identically as Windows Vista with legacy applications. It seems that many of the causes for application failure weren't due to these changes. Here are some examples:

Despite a huge public testing program prior to the release, many application developers chose not to get involved. These developers either believed that Vista would not be successful enough or they bought into the myth that the subsequent release of Windows would be a return to the XP-style operating system.

Many developers or application publishers either moved on or went out of business. This prevented willing customers from being able to upgrade or repair incompatible applications.

Many customers who used applications chose not to upgrade their applications to Vista-supported versions. Customers cited reasons such as compatibility issues with other systems or lack of available funding.

Many legacy applications require you to have administrative rights. Users tried unsuccessfully to update things like the Windows folder or secure locations in the Registry or the file system. Windows Vista introduced User Account Control (UAC). When you log in as an administrative user, you are given two tokens. The first gives you administrative rights. The second is a standard user token. UAC tries to protect your computer by logging you in with that standard user token. This can cause issues with those applications requiring administrative rights if users do not know how to interact with UAC.

Some developers didn't heed the best practice advice from Microsoft when developing their software. A very basic example of this is when an application checks the operating system version. The check might be something like `if OperatingSystemVersion not = 5.1 then fail`. That meant the application would only work on XP, even though every other feature of the application would be fine on Vista. Sometimes developers tried to "fix" bugs they found in XP through their application. Microsoft fixed those bugs in Vista, and this caused the application to behave in an unexpected manner.

Microsoft released ACT with Windows Vista to aid in detecting known incompatible applications, testing others, tracking your process, and developing workarounds for issues. ACT aided in resolving many of the issues but not all of them. There were two problems with this solution:

◆ Despite Microsoft's efforts, not many people know about ACT. You cannot use what you do not know about.

◆ Sometimes an application just cannot be made to work on anything but Windows XP.

Over time Microsoft stepped up its efforts. As the release of Windows 7 approached, those efforts increased. Version 5.6 of ACT was released in conjunction with Windows 7. It increased your ability to resolve issues using workarounds referred to as *mitigations,* or *shims.* But you still had those few occasions when ACT wasn't able to help or perhaps wasn't appropriate when you needed a quick fix. Microsoft took its desktop virtualization product, Virtual PC, and redeveloped it as an application compatibility solution. Windows Virtual PC for Windows 7 allows you to run a free (on the business editions) copy of Windows XP Service Pack (SP) 3 Professional as a virtual machine (VM). You can install your XP applications in XP Mode and access them through seamless windows on your Windows 7 installation using shortcuts on the Windows 7 Start menu.

SHIM OR MITIGATION?

The two words are interchangeable. When you talk to an application compatibility person, they use the word "shim." The ACT applications use the more formal "mitigation."

It appears now that for almost every application out there, you should have a way to get it working on a Windows 7 PC. We're going to spend the rest of this chapter discussing the solutions provided by Microsoft, and we'll explain how you can best employ them to prevent application compatibility from becoming a barrier to your upgrade to Windows 7.

When you set out working on the application compatibility issue, you will need to have a process. Every organization will have a different process. Figure 2.1 shows you a sample process that you can use.

FIGURE 2.1
An application compatibility workflow

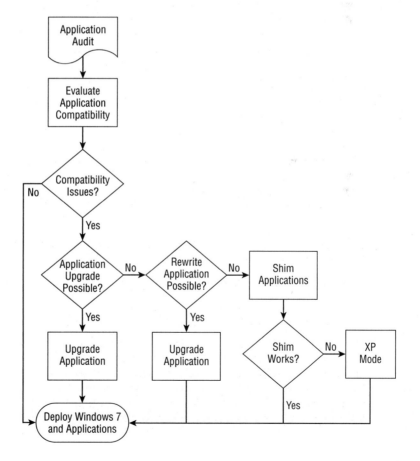

The process starts with identifying the applications found in the organization. From there you need to work out whether each application found is compatible with Windows 7. If the application is compatible, then no further work is required. If it isn't, then you try to fix it by either upgrading or rewriting the application so that it does support Windows 7. If neither approach works, you will have to create a mitigation or shim to "trick" the application into thinking that it is working on Windows 7.

If that doesn't work, you then move on to using virtualization. You attempt to install the application in a VM that's running a legacy operating system such as Windows XP. Microsoft's XP Mode is a free (to those who have a Business, Ultimate, or Enterprise edition of Windows 7) and pretty clever solution. It provides a Windows XP VM that runs on the Windows 7 computer. The end user might not even notice that it's running on their PC because their Start menu icons for the XP Mode applications appear on the Windows 7 Start menu and the applications run in seamless windows, hiding the XP VM in the background. This strategy can increase administrative workloads because there is another operating system to install, manage, and secure.

A similar solution is Microsoft Enterprise Desktop Virtualization (MED-V), which is a part of the Microsoft Desktop Optimization Pack (MDOP), a suite that is available to customers (for a fee) if they have acquired Software Assurance as a part of their licensing. MED-V provides a centrally managed VM that is distributed to user computers. The VM can run a legacy operating system, such as Windows XP, and can be installed with legacy applications that will not work on Windows 7.

Another solution is to use Remote Desktop Services (previously called Terminal Services). You can run centralized machines with a legacy operating system such as Windows Server 2003, install the applications there, and provide Remote Desktop access for your users.

These virtualization solutions come at some cost, be it licensing or additional management, but they allow you to provide access to functional legacy applications until you find a version or alternative that will work correctly on Windows 7.

The Application Compatibility Toolkit

Microsoft provides the free-to-download Application Compatibility Toolkit (ACT) to help you get legacy applications working on Windows 7. Using it, you can go through the process of identifying your legacy applications, test them, track your progress, and even create shims to fool those applications into believing that they are running on Windows 7. You will now learn how to plan for ACT, install it, and use it to resolve application compatibility problems.

Choosing an ACT Architecture

To plan for ACT, you will need to understand how it works. There are two basic ways to use ACT. It contains a number of tools for creating shims to mitigate application compatibility issues. A simple, quick installation of ACT allows you to do that. However, to make the most of ACT, you will probably use the Application Compatibility Manager (ACM) tool.

ACM allows you to deploy an agent called a data collection package (DCP) to selected PCs, or even all of them, to gather information about the applications and application versions that are out "in the wild." The DCPs will create periodic data files and send them to a file share of your choosing. A central ACT installation, the Log Processing Service, will process the files from this file share and store the information in a SQL database. Administrators and engineers can use ACT to connect to the SQL database. This allows them to generate reports, connect with

Microsoft to download up-to-date information on compatibility issues, and track the progress of the project. Finally, ACT contains tools that can be used on test and development machines to create shims to enable otherwise incompatible applications to work on Windows 7.

ACT is pretty flexible, and you can architect your configuration to suit the project and the organization you are working in. The configuration can vary from the all-in-one-machine installation to a multisite setup that allows dozens of people across continents to collaborate on a corporate solution.

Figure 2.2 shows the most basic architecture that you might use while learning the product or while working in a small organization.

FIGURE 2.2
Basic ACT architecture

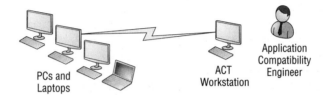

PCs and Laptops

ACT Workstation

Application Compatibility Engineer

All of the ACT components are installed onto a single machine with this basic installation, labeled as ACT Workstation. This can be a single server, PC, laptop, or even a VM. Using the latter option offers some advantages. Virtualization obviously reduces costs for the organization. Consultants can even build a VM with no data and reuse it in different customer sites, minimizing the time required to start working on the solution for their customers.

The SQL installation that you use for the single-machine and single-user architecture can be the free SQL 2008 Express. Only local users and applications can use this database, and the database is limited to 4 GB. You will need to use one of the paid-for editions of SQL Server 2008 if you need to use the database remotely or if the database will be larger than 4 GB.

With the installation illustrated in Figure 2.2, the administrator is doing all the testing and development work on a single machine. That's not an ideal solution because you never know if one application will contaminate the computer and affect the work you do with other applications. It's for this reason that you should consider using a number of test machines, as shown in Figure 2.3.

FIGURE 2.3
ACT with multiple test machines

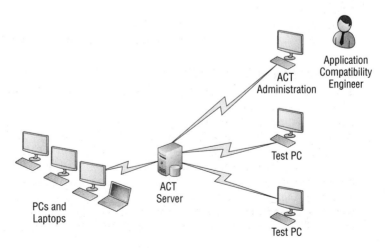

ACT Administration

Application Compatibility Engineer

Test PC

PCs and Laptops

ACT Server

Test PC

There are a few ways you can approach having test machines. A cost-effective solution is to use virtualization. Microsoft's Virtual PC for Windows 7 and Hyper-V Server 2008 R2 are free products that you can use for this purpose. Virtualization allows you to create a sample or template machine that you can redeploy for every application solution that you work on. This is a speedy solution too. Alternatively, you can use machines that are typical of the organization. It's important to do this if you are working with applications that integrate with the hardware.

Larger organizations may seek a different solution. It may be necessary to have a large database and to allow many administrators to work on it at once. Figure 2.4 shows how you can achieve this goal in a single network.

FIGURE 2.4
ACT with multiple engineers

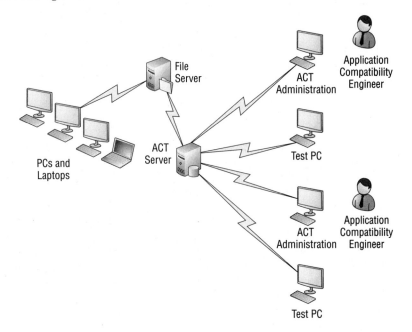

A paid-for edition of SQL is used to host the ACT database in this scenario. It is possible to place the file share on the SQL server or on a different machine. There's a good chance that you will use an existing SQL server for the ACT database. The owners of that machine probably won't like the idea of a file share being created on it, so you can use another file server for this role.

The DCP that you deploy to the desktops and laptops on your network will upload a file to the file share on a configurable periodic basis. This file contains information about the applications on the network. This process could cause an issue for your wide area network (WAN). The files may be small, but few network administrators will be thrilled about additional frequent traffic using up the WAN bandwidth. You can create agents for each collection of machines that you wish to target for data collection. This approach allows you to specify a local file share in each branch office. You can see this in Figure 2.5.

All that remains now is to get the data back to the central file share from the local file shares for processing by ACT. You could use some file replication mechanism such as Distributed File System Replication (DFS-R), schedule copy tasks during off hours using a tool like Robocopy, or even burn a few weeks' worth of data on a DVD and send it by courier.

Consider how the organization and the application compatibility project will be run. Then choose the most suitable ACT architecture. The great thing about ACT is that it is very modular and will allow you to adapt to changes in the project. We're now going to show you how to install ACT using the architecture shown previously in Figure 2.3.

FIGURE 2.5
ACT on the wide area network

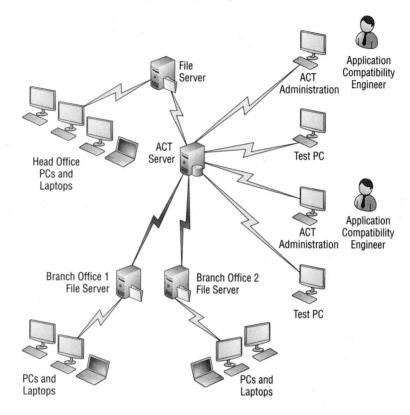

Installing ACT

A simple installation of ACT is not far from a next-next-next operation. The first thing to do is download ACT. ACT 5.6 is the current version as of this writing. You can find it at http:// technet.microsoft.com/en-us/library/cc722067(WS.10).aspx. Microsoft is always in the process of developing and improving the ACT product, so it's a good idea to do a search for the latest version at the start of any project to ensure that you are up-to-date.

The requirements for ACT are as follows:

Operating Systems   Windows 2000 Service Pack 4, Windows 7, Windows Server 2003 Service Pack 1, Windows Vista, or Windows XP Service Pack 3

Database Components   Microsoft SQL Server 2008, Microsoft SQL Server 2005, Microsoft SQL Server 2005 Express Edition

Other Software Requirements   Microsoft .NET Framework, version 3.5.0

As we mentioned in the planning section, you'll need to figure out which SQL license to use. A single-machine deployment of ACT that uses the ACT tools only locally can use the free SQL Express 2008. Any project requiring databases more than 4 GB in size or use of the ACT tools on many machines will need a purchased edition of SQL.

SQL CONFIGURATION AND RECOMMENDATIONS

If you plan on using an existing SQL server for the ACT database, then you will probably not have rights to do any administration on that server. That means you will need to get the server owner or a database administrator to manually create the database. They can do that by running the `CreateDB.sql` script, which you will find in `\ProgramData\Microsoft\Application Compatibility Toolkit`. You run the script by using the Query Tool in SQL Server Management Studio. Alternatively, you open the command prompt and run `osql -E -S <serverName> -I CreateDB.sql`.

When you split SQL Server from the computer where the Log Processing Service will run, then you need to do some further configuration work. Any user and/or local service account(s) that will be used to run the ACT Log Processing Service must have the db_datareader, db_datawriter, and db_owner roles on the ACT database. If you cannot grant the db_owner role due to security or policy reasons, you must grant each of the following rights to every stored procedure to the user(s) or local service account(s):

◆ SELECT

◆ INSERT

◆ UPDATE

◆ DELETE

◆ EXECUTE

Any user account that will run ACM must have the db_datareader and db_datawriter database roles on the ACT database.

Let's begin by installing our ACT onto our deployment server called `deploysrv.deploy.com`. We have previously installed SQL Server 2008 Standard and applied the latest SP and updates. That will support our example project, on which many engineers are concurrently working.

Download the ACT installer and run it. You'll have to go through the usual splash and End User License Agreement screens. Pick the default location for the installation. The product set will install after a few minutes. If you're new to ACT, you get the option to view an introductory video at the end of the installation. As you can see in Figure 2.6, a number of tools are installed.

You can now work with the compatibility tools to fix your applications. We're not going to do that yet, however. Instead, we'll explore how to use ACM to detect your desktop applications and track your progress through the application compatibility project.

ACM will allow you to create a DCP, which will be installed on your targeted PCs and will gather information about the applications on those PCs. The data is uploaded to a file share, referred to as the ACT log share, that you will specify. The ACT Log Processing Service will then process the data and enter it into the ACT database.

THE APPLICATION COMPATIBILITY TOOLKIT | **41**

By default, ACM has no configuration. Before you do anything with it, you should create a file share for the ACT logs that are created by the DCP. Ensure that all the computers you target can create files in this file share. In this example, you will create the C:\ACTLogs folder and share it as \\DeploySrv\ACTLogs.

You will see the screen in Figure 2.7 when you start up the ACM application for the first time.

FIGURE 2.6
ACT is installed.

FIGURE 2.7
Welcome to the
ACT Configuration
Wizard.

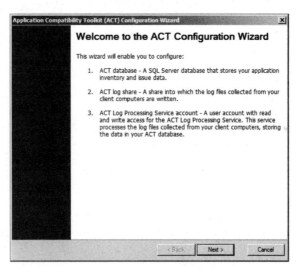

Figure 2.8 shows the next screen. Here you configure ACM for this machine. You need to choose between two options:

Enterprise Configuration   You will choose this option if this is the computer that will process the log files. It can also be used to view the reports.

View And Manage Reports Only   You will choose this option if ACM will only be used for administration on this computer. This allows you to then select a preexisting and prepopulated ACT database.

We are setting up the initial ACM server, so choose to create an enterprise configuration.

The next screen allows you to configure the SQL database for this ACM installation. You can either create a new database on an existing SQL Server or connect to an existing ACT database. You should read the sidebar "SQL Configuration and Recommendations" if you are using a remote SQL server in case any of the included scenarios and configurations apply to your environment.

In Figure 2.9 you can see that DeploySrv, the server you are working on, has been selected and the name of the new database has been entered. Clicking Create will create the database and allow you to progress through the wizard.

FIGURE 2.8
Select the ACM configuration.

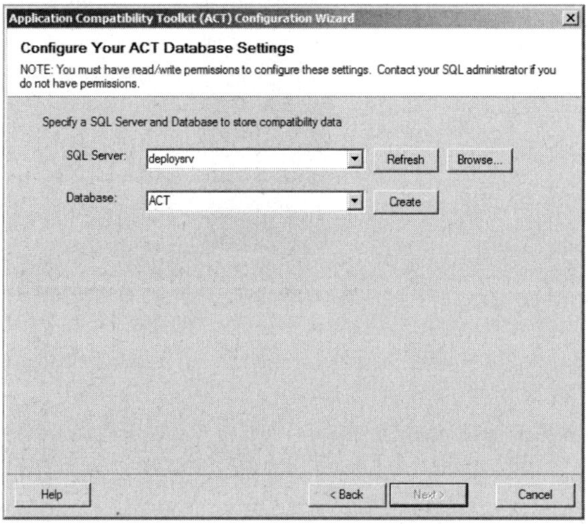

FIGURE 2.9
Create an ACT database.

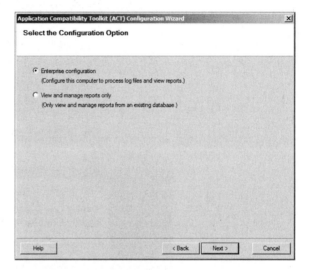

Figure 2.10 shows the next screen. Here you specify the location on the server where you created the ACT log share. We previously created and shared C:\ACTLogs.

If you are running the ACM Log Processing Service on the same server as the log share and SQL server, then you can run the service as Local System. However, you may need to configure the service to log on as a user account if the log share and SQL database are on different machines.

Figure 2.11 shows the screen where you can configure the service. Note that you must ensure that the user account has rights to access both the log share and the SQL database.

FIGURE 2.10
Select the ACT
logs share.

FIGURE 2.11
Specify the Log
Processing Service
credentials.

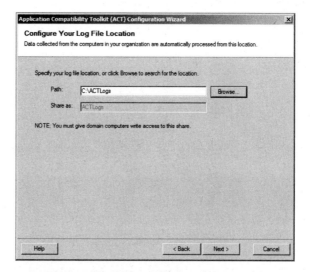

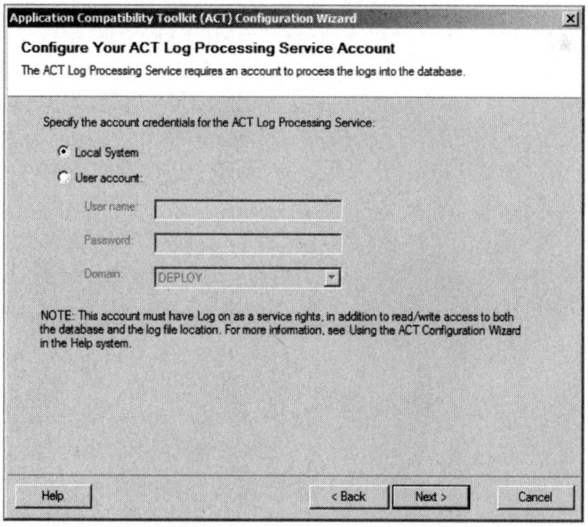

The final screen in the wizard allows you to join the Community Experience Program (disabled by default) and to automatically check for and download updates (enabled by default). At this point, ACM will launch.

In this example scenario, we used a Windows 7 PC called Admin1 to manage our ACT project. You'll be able to do all the ACM administration from the comfort of your Admin1 PC—just make sure your user account has been assigned with the db_datareader and db_datawriter database roles on the ACT database.

Your installation experience is going to be quite similar to what you have just done on DeploySrv. You will configure ACM to use the View And Configure Reports configuration and to use the recently created ACT database on the DeploySrv server.

You are now ready to start gathering information from the PCs on your network.

Using the Application Compatibility Manager

At this point you have already learned how the Microsoft Assessment and Planning (MAP) toolkit can be used to identify what applications and drivers are out there in your desktop and laptop network. It gives you a lot of information that you can use to identify drivers and applications that can cause blocking issues with a Windows 7 deployment. What you are going to learn about now is how to use ACM, a component of ACT, to discover the applications on your network.

WHAT ELSE DOES THE ACM DO?

In addition to discovering applications, ACM can do the following:

◆ Download information on vendor support statements and an analysis by the greater community for each application.

◆ Track the progress of your project.

GATHERING APPLICATION COMPATIBILITY DATA

At this point you should have ACM open and be viewing the screen shown in Figure 2.12.

The detail pane illustrates what you need to do to use ACM. You need to create a DCP to collect data for ACM to use. From this, you can analyze the data and generate reports. Then you can use the other ACT tools to test any applications with issues and create shims to make them work on Windows 7.

You will now create a DCP. This is an MSI (Windows Installer) file that you will deploy to PCs. It will run as a service on those PCs and gather information. A file will be periodically sent to the ACT log share for the Log Processing Service to use.

You can create a DCP by clicking on the link in this introductory screen or by double-clicking in the detail pane of the Collect window. That opens the screen shown in Figure 2.13.

FIGURE 2.12
Application Compatibility Manager

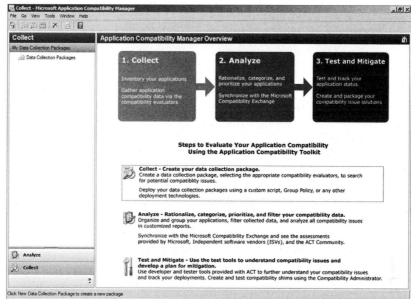

FIGURE 2.13
Creating a data collection package

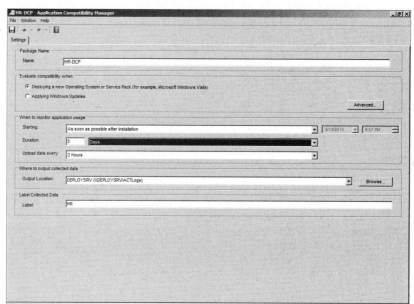

The first thing you need to do is name the DCP. Note that ACM will also assign this name to the MSI installer file it creates. You should use a descriptive name that suits the PCs you are targeting with this collection.

You now need to specify why you are performing this analysis. In a Windows 7 deployment project, choose Deploying A New Operating System Or Service Pack (for example, Microsoft Windows Vista). You can also deploy a DCP to perform application compatibility analysis when deploying Windows updates.

Click the Advanced button to open the dialog box shown in Figure 2.14. The Advanced Settings dialog box allows you to select which evaluators you want to enable in the DCP—that is, what sort of data the DCP will collect. Notice that you can do the following:

◆ Collect an inventory

◆ Evaluate UAC compatibility

◆ Evaluate Windows compatibility

USING TWO DATA COLLECTION PACKAGES

Normally you will have performed a discovery of applications using the Microsoft Assessment and Planning Toolkit, as discussed in Chapter 1, "Does Your Hardware Measure Up?" If you have not done this assessment, you can create two DCPs instead of one.

Configure the first DCP to collect an inventory only. This allows you to identify your future workload and triage applications. You can then create and deploy a second DCP that evaluates UAC compatibility and Windows compatibility.

At the bottom of the Advanced Settings dialog box is a check box named "Prompt users to restart if required by the installation (Microsoft Windows 2000 only)." Other operating systems are not affected by this check box.

FIGURE 2.14
Advanced DCP
Settings

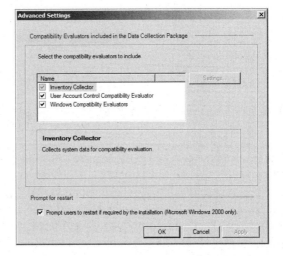

Back on the DCP creation screen in Figure 2.13, you can configure the monitoring of application usage. Normally you will want to start monitoring as soon as the DCP is able to. However, you can alter that. For example, maybe you want to pre-deploy the DCP and specify that it start working at a later date and time. The DCP will have a limited shelf life. It will stop functioning after a specified number of minutes, hours, or days, as defined by you in the Duration field.

Be careful with the Upload Data Every setting. This setting defines how often the DCP will upload collected data to the ACT log share. The file may only be a few hundred kilobytes, but imagine hundreds or thousands of computers all uploading that data at once. It could become a distributed denial-of-service (DDoS) attack on your network or file server! Plan this carefully, taking into account placement and selection of log shares, numbers of PCs, and the choice of upload frequency.

You can specify the location of the log share in the Where To Output Collected Data area. You can use this ability to specify a log share location in a branch office scenario. For example, your ACT server might be in Chicago. You might be creating a DCP for an office in Dublin, Ireland. Using the Output Location pull-down, you can configure PCs in Dublin to use a local share. You can then configure some controlled way to get the log share data back to the log share on the ACT server for the Log Processing Service to use.

The final setting is Label. You can use this setting to tag the collected data. You can later use this tag to filter data for reporting and analysis reasons.

In this example, the DCP will be deployed to the Human Resources (HR) department. The DCP is named HR and the label is configured as HR so the data for this department can be easily retrieved.

When you are finished, you can choose one of two actions from the File menu. You can save the DCP to the database, allowing you to revisit it later. The DCP will not be created and it will not gather any data. You could think of it being in a draft state. You can double-click on it to edit it again.

You can also save and create the DCP. This will create the MSI file to a location of your choice. This approach allows you to install the DCP.

How you install the DCP depends on your organization and what you are doing with it. The DCP is an MSI file and that gives you lots of options, including but not limited to the following:

Use "sneaker net."   Someone will run from PC to PC to install the DCP by hand. This might be OK in small organizations, small departments, or in a lab, but it will be an ordeal for larger networks.

Use Active Directory startup scripts.   You can run the installer using a startup script that is defined in an Active Directory Group Policy Object that applies to the computers of your choosing.

Use Active Directory Group Policy.   You can create a Group Policy Object to assign the MSI file to the computers of your choice.

Use System Center Configuration Manager.   This will likely be the choice for many larger organizations. A package can be quickly created from the DCP MSI file and advertised to a collection that contains the targeted computers.

A new service is created when you install the DCP on a computer. You can see this in Figure 2.15, where we have deployed the HR DCP to a Windows XP computer.

FIGURE 2.15
The ACT Data
Collector Service

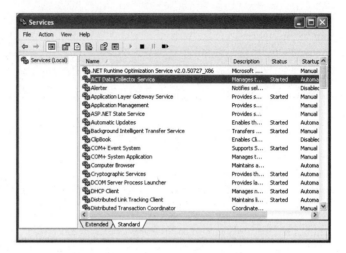

FORCING THE DCP TO CREATE A LOG

When you are testing and trying out the process of creating a data collection provider, you might want to force the DCP to generate logs on an as-needed basis rather than according to the configured schedule. You can do this by manually restarting the ACT Data Collector Service on the PC.

After a while you will start to see files added to the log share, as shown in Figure 2.16. The DCP will upload two XML cabinet files to the log share. These files are compressed and may be even less than 100 KB. The first is quite small and gives a status update. The second contains the inventory from the DCP. The Log Processing Service will expand these files and move the contents into the \Processed folder as the files are processed.

FIGURE 2.16
The ACT log share

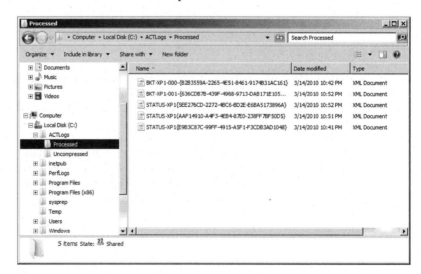

BRANCH OFFICE AND LOG SHARE FILES

You probably won't have a Log Processing Service that directly processes the DCP data in the branch office ACT log shares. You can transport or replicate those files to the central ACT log share for the Log Processing Service to use.

You can safely delete these files as long as the ACT SQL database is reliably backed up. You can use these files to re-create the ACT database if you lose it.

The Log Processing Service can be managed in the Services snap-in (Figure 2.17). Check that this service is running if you notice that the DCP data is no longer being processed. A failed service will be noticeable if XML cabinet files are not being moved from the root of the ACT log share into the "processed" subfolder.

FIGURE 2.17
The ACT Log Processing Service

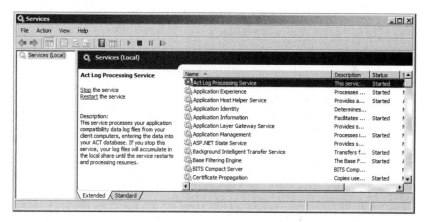

Once you reach this point, you should have data in the ACT database that you can start to use. We'll now look at viewing this data and making use of it.

USING THE APPLICATION COMPATIBILITY DATA

Once your data collection packages start returning data, you can begin viewing, analyzing, and using that data in the ACM. To do this, you will go into the Analyze view (Figure 2.18).

The navigation pane called Quick Reports on the left side of the screen allows you to do compatibility analysis and tracking for Windows 7 and for older operating systems such as Windows Vista and Windows Vista with SP1 or SP2. Under each operating system, you can see the applications, application installation packages, computers, and devices that were found. Drilling into each one gives you more information. We will focus on the Applications report data for Windows 7. Click on that in the Quick Reports navigation pane and the Application Report, and you'll see the screen shown in Figure 2.19.

FIGURE 2.18
The ACM
Analyze view

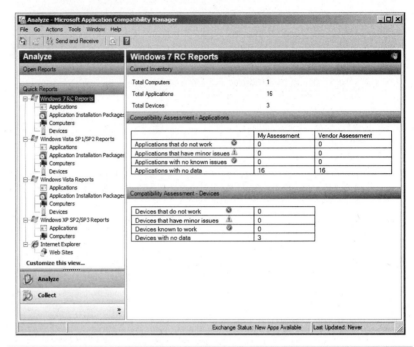

FIGURE 2.19
ACM Application
Report

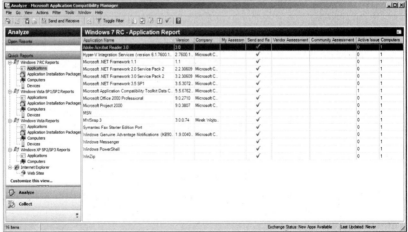

The view presents a number of columns by default. You can right-click on the column names to add or remove columns to show your preferred data.

Each row shows an individual application version that was found in your scans. The network that was used in this example is small but is obviously dated; you can see applications such as Office 2000 Professional and Project 2000 are running on the XP computer in the lab network. You can see the application name, the version, and the publisher. The rest of the columns are where things get interesting!

There's possibly going to be a lot of data here. Using the Toggle Filter button on the toolbar, you can restrict what is shown in the Application Report. This reveals a way of creating a Boolean algebra statement based on the columns of data and values that were gathered by the DCP. You could restrict the view to applications that have a specific vendor or community assessment. Or you could filter the view to data with one of your DCP labels. You can see an example of that in action in Figure 2.20.

FIGURE 2.20
Filtering the application assessment data

At this point you might be thinking, "I have hundreds [or thousands] of applications. Do I have to test every single one?" That's a pretty daunting project. Here's the great news: the work may have already been done by Microsoft, the application vendor, and others like you who have already gone through this process and shared their data. What you will do now is see how to get those assessments into your database, thus vastly reducing the amount of work you need to do.

On the toolbar you can see a Send And Receive button. If you click this button, you can exchange data with Microsoft, where those preexisting assessments are stored. You might have some applications that you do not want to share data about. That's fine; if you right-click on the application you can set the Send And Receive Status to either Do Not Send To Microsoft or Send To Microsoft. Click Send And Receive when you are ready to share your assessment data (if you have any) and to download other assessments. A pop-up window appears to let you know that data, including applications, your assessments, your IP address, and your device list, will be uploaded. You can review this data before sending it. You can even save it to a text file.

When you click Send in the Send And Receive Data wizard, you'll see the progress of the upload and download. The Application Report will be updated with the various assessments' data when that completes.

You can see in Figure 2.21 that only two of the applications have an assessment by their vendors. But check out the Community Assessment column. That's the work that has been done by other people like you. They've already tested these applications on Windows 7 and submitted the overall result:

Green Check Mark   The test was successful.

Amber Exclamation Point   The application works but has some sort of problem. Or maybe there is a workaround of some kind. Double-clicking on Microsoft Office 2000 Professional reveals that Microsoft recommends an upgrade.

Red X   The application could not be made to work.

READ THE BUILT-IN DOCUMENTATION

Microsoft made a big effort to improve the documentation associated with all the deployment technologies in the buildup to the release of Windows 7. We strongly recommend that you read this documentation. In the case of ACT, you can find it in the help file.

You can view more detailed information by double-clicking on the application to open the window shown in Figure 2.22.

FIGURE 2.21

Application assessment

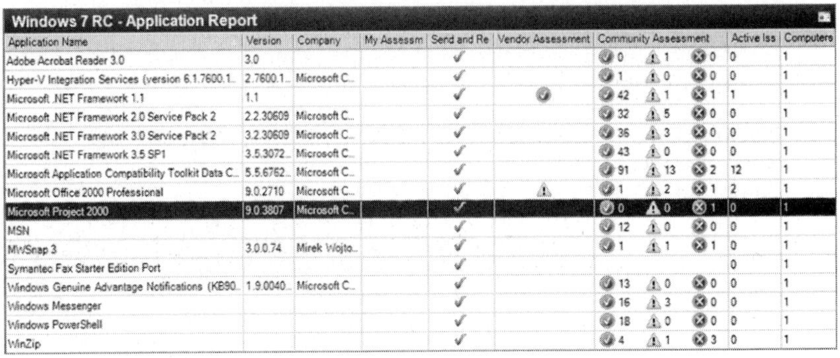

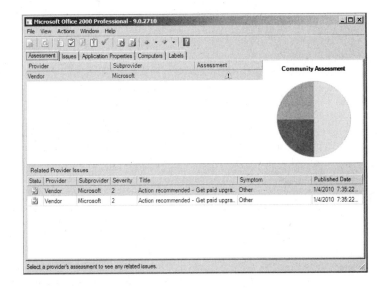

FIGURE 2.22

Viewing application assessment details

The window is split into a number of tabs. The Assessment tab reveals the summary data. The vendor (the original publisher) assessment is visible in the top pane if the data is made available by the vendor. The pie chart shows what results the community got with their testing. The Related Provider Issues pane at the bottom shows what actions might be necessary to get the application working.

The Issues tab also shows the issue summary information, and you can double-click on it to get a more detailed view (Figure 2.23).

Back in the application assessment window, you will also find these tabs:

Application Properties This tab reveals details about what the application looks like when it is installed. This includes file information, the associated MSI (installer) file(s), any entries in Add/Remove Programs (or Programs and Features in newer operating systems), shell extensions, Registry values, and any associated services.

Computers   This tab shows the computers on which the DCP detected this application.

Labels   This tab lists the labels that you created in your DCP to track your DCP usage and data. For example, we used "HR" as a label earlier in the chapter. This label would be present in all data produced by that DCP. This allows you to track the locations of incompatible applications based on your labeling and targeted installations of the DCP.

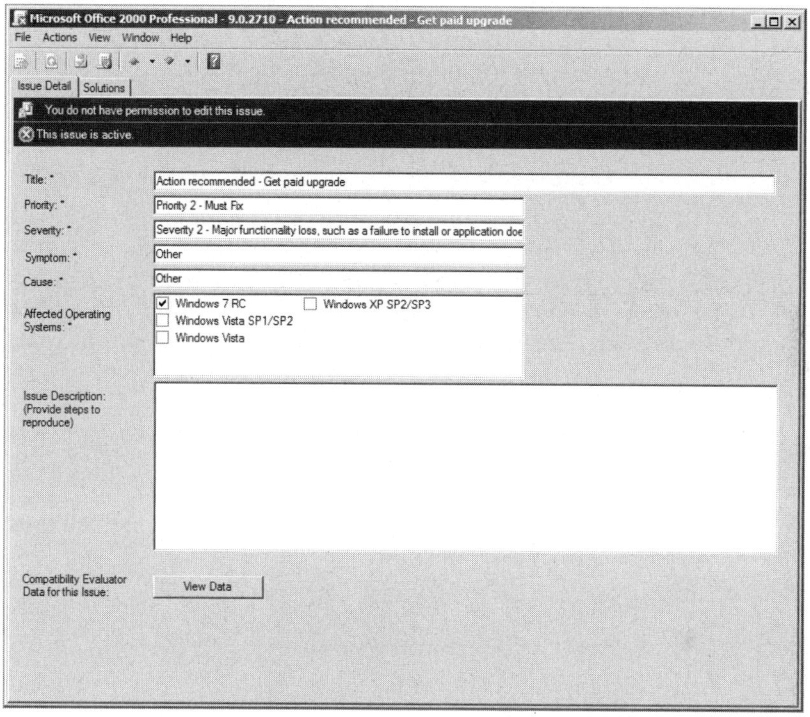

FIGURE 2.23
Viewing application issue details

At this point you are ready to start creating required mitigations and testing your applications. You can use the downloaded assessment data to plan your testing. How you do this depends on your organization, but here's one suggestion:

Applications with a 100% OK (check-mark) Status   You will either perform no testing or just the most basic of tests.

Applications with a Warning (Exclamation Point) Status   You will do any recommended actions or create required shims before performing in-depth tests on the application.

Applications with a Mostly or 100% Status   You either need to find an alternative application or look at using XP Mode to run the application on Windows 7 PCs.

When you create your test and mitigation plan, you can assign a priority to each application. Do so by right-clicking on the application and selecting Set Priority. The values here vary from Unspecified, Priority 4 – Unimportant, all the way up to Priority 1 – Business Critical.

TESTING APPLICATION COMPATIBILITY

You can deploy Windows 7 PCs or virtual machines to your application testing team. Consider the following:

♦ It's a good idea to use template machine images that are redeployed every time you run a test or create a shim. That way, one application will not contaminate another. This strategy allows you to identify any basic application/Windows 7 compatibility issues.

♦ There's a good chance that you'll want to test the applications on Windows 7 machines with no software and Windows 7 machines with typical software configurations for different departments. That approach will reveal complex issues if they exist.

♦ Please don't forget to test the applications using a user account that truly represents the end user. For example, most of your tests will probably be done as a nonadministrative user.

As the project moves along, your team can use ACT on their computers and connect to the ACT database. That means no one needs to log directly into the ACT server. Just ensure that each person has the required database permissions as we discussed earlier. Each team member will be able to set the assessment by right-clicking on the application and choosing Set Assessment. Here are the possible assessment values for an application:

♦ Green check mark: The application works.

♦ Amber exclamation point: There are problems or there are solutions.

♦ Red X: The application will not work.

Also, as progress is made you will right-click on the application and select Set Deployment Status. You can choose from:

♦ Not Reviewed

♦ Testing

♦ Mitigating

♦ Ready To Deploy

♦ Will Not Deploy

At the end of this phase of the project, you will have an assessment that you can use for your "go/no go" decision making. In large organizations, you will sit down or communicate with each application owner to decide a course of action for that application. Do you deploy it as is, deploy it with a fix, or not deploy it? The latter will probably require an alternative application to be sourced and tested. Note that the deployment status of each application should either be Ready To Deploy or Will Not Deploy.

REPORTING

We all know that project managers love reports. You can quickly produce an Excel spreadsheet using File ➤ Export Report in the Application Compatibility Manager. You can then manipulate or format the data for your reports.

You've gone from knowing what applications you have to being ready to deploy applications. Next we'll look at the process of creating workarounds to the problems that were found.

USING ACT CONNECTOR FOR CONFIGURATION MANAGER 2007

System Center Configuration Manager (ConfigMgr) is Microsoft's medium and large organization solution for managing hundreds or thousands of computers. It normally contains a repository of information about the computers, operating systems, and software that it has detected and is able to manage. Microsoft has a free download, Application Compatibility Toolkit Connector (ACT Connector), that allows you to integrate ConfigMgr with ACT 5.6. You can download it from www. microsoft.com/downloads/en/details.aspx?FamilyID=567be755-1d64-471d-8376-6b463491654b&displaylang=en.

When you install ACT Connector, you will need to grant the ConfigMgr service account access to the ACT database. You can then configure ConfigMgr to integrate into the ACT database. This allows you to run a number of reports from the ConfigMgr reporting site that will contain information from ConfigMgr and from ACT.

You can also use ConfigMgr to distribute your DCP. Unfortunately, it does not provide an alternative way to gather DCP data. That data will still be uploaded to the DCP file share that you configured when you created the DCP. However, this is a cool way to provide delegated people with access to your application compatibility reports.

Resolving Application Compatibility Issues with Shims

Most application incompatibilities occur when the application makes a request to the operating system. A very basic one is when an application asks, "Hey! What operating system are you?" Windows XP would respond, "I am 5.1." Windows Vista would respond, "I am 6.0," and Windows 7 would respond "I am 6.1." Applications that are coded to only accept 5.1 would fail to launch.

WINDOWS 7 VERSION

Did you notice that Windows 7 is actually version 6.1? There's a good reason for that. Microsoft was the recipient of a lot of negative thoughts when people couldn't get their applications to work on Windows Vista. They wanted to avoid the same issues with Windows 7. They aimed to ensure that as many applications as possible worked on Windows 7 if they worked on Windows Vista. And you know what? They were successful at doing that. One trick they used was to only increase the minor version number instead of the major version number of the operating system.

So Windows 7 jumped to 6.1 from version 6 of Windows Vista. Why would they do that? Many applications only check the major version when they install or run. They simply might not care about the minor version. This little solution prevents many compatibility issues.

ACT allows you to create mitigations or workarounds in the form of a shim. This shim...well, there's no other way to put this...it's a liar. You instruct Windows to lie to the application via the shim. Alternatively, you can think of it as an interpreter that sits between specified applications and the operating system. So in the case of "What operating system are you?" you can create a shim that instructs Windows to lie to that particular application and respond with "5.1" instead of "6.1." The application might have no other compatibility issue and you end up with a fully working LOB program. Your project team will attempt to create these shims whenever an application has compatibility issues and a newer version or developer fix isn't available. We're going to focus on this process for while.

USING THE STANDARD USER ANALYZER AND STANDARD USER ANALYZER WIZARD

Many legacy applications require administrative access to run. This is a problem with most business networks. That's because we like to restrict users to standard users so that we can control security, configuration, and compliance systems. Typical of IT security, we need to find a middle ground between security and the business operations. Windows 7 has some virtualization features that can fool some operations. For example, attempts to write to restricted parts of the Registry or file system will be redirected to more suitable locations in the user's profile. But we still have issues where an application checks to see if the user is an administrator. The application may fail to start because of this hard check, even though no functionality may be affected.

Both the Standard User Analyzer (SUA) and the Standard User Analyzer Wizard allow you to do this testing and develop a fix to make the application work in this scenario. You will need to download and install the Microsoft Application Verifier from www.microsoft.com/downloads/en/details.aspx?familyid=c4a25ab9-649d-4a1b-b4a7-c9d8b095df18&displaylang=en to use the SUA tools.

STOCK VIEWER—A VERY BROKEN APPLICATION

Microsoft thought of us when it came to trying out, learning, and demonstrating the ACT. They wrote an application called Stock Viewer and released it to the public. It proved so popular that it was included in the setup for ACT 5.6. It is also available for download at http://blogs.msdn.com/b/cjacks/archive/2008/01/03/stock-viewer-shim-demo-application.aspx.

This application will simulate a number of the problems found with legacy applications when you run it on Windows 7. For example, it requires administrative rights but it is not aware of UAC. This gives you a perfect playground to try out many of the possible solutions that you can create with ACT. We will be using Stock Viewer to demonstrate methods for testing and fixing applications.

Your shim creation and application testing process will probably start with the SUA tools. This administrative issue is just the tip of the compatibility iceberg. The rapid process of using SUA to fix application administrator access problems may end up providing a quick win for many compatibility problems. That makes it a good place to start.

Let's delve into working with Microsoft's sample Stock Viewer application and you can see the problem and the tools in action.

The best way to see the problem is to log in as a user that does not have administrative rights on the test PC. Launch Stock Viewer in this scenario and you'll be greeted by a Permission Denied dialog box (Figure 2.24). You are correctly informed that you are not logged in as administrator. IT has decided that no users should have administrative rights on their PC. IT also believes that Stock Viewer will be able to run with no issues on Windows 7—once we sort out that administrator rights check.

The application does start up but it does have problems. We will have to fix this issue using the SUA tools. We're going to start with the SUA Wizard. The wizard is a simple next-next-next tool for creating a fix for the application's issue. You can find the tool on the Start menu under All Programs ➤ Microsoft Application Compatibility Toolkit ➤ Developer And Tester Tools. Launch it and you'll see the screen shown in Figure 2.25.

You will tell the tool to shadow a particular executable, that is, the application that you will run. You can supply any parameters that would normally be used with the executable to configure the program execution. You can then click the Launch button to run the program you are shadowing or fixing.

FIGURE 2.24
The application requires administrative rights.

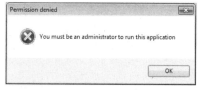

FIGURE 2.25
Launch the Standard User Analyzer Wizard.

At this point, the program will run and experience all the problems you should now be already familiar with. That allows the SUA Wizard to see the issues. Run the program, test it thoroughly, and then exit it. You'll now be asked by the wizard if the program ran without having any problems. If you click Yes, then the wizard will exit without making changes. If your program complained about administrative rights, then click No to create a fix. That brings up a screen (Figure 2.26) showing a potential fix for your application. This screen contains one or more shims that will be associated with your program's executable.

Three interesting shims have been configured. LocalMappedObject resolves a problem where an application tries to create a file mapping object in the Global namespace. The Global namespace hides the complexities of physical storage. This is not possible without administrative rights. With this shim enabled, the application will create the file mapping object in the Local namespace. Take a look at CorrectFilePaths. That will use virtualization to prevent Stock Viewer from trying to write into a location that the user has no access to. ForceAdminAccess is also an interesting one. That's the one that will fix the core issue at hand. It won't run the program as an administrator. Instead, it will trick the application into believing that the user is an administrator.

FIGURE 2.26
Potential shims in
the SUA Wizard

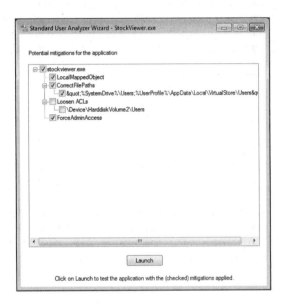

You now must launch the program again. This time it will temporarily use the shims to run. This is a chance to test the potential fix before saving it. This is a good idea because there's a good chance the SUA fix won't be enough to get all functionality in your program running. Click the Launch button again and thoroughly test your application. The SUA Wizard will again sit back and wait for the program to exit.

When you do exit the tested program, you are again asked if the application ran without any issues. If your answer is No, you will be returned to the previous Potential Mitigations screen. You can enable or disable mitigations. If you skip this, then you are asked if you want to try something else:

Run The Standard User Analyzer   That is, run the full tool, not the wizard.

Mark The Application As 'RunAsAdmin'   This option tells Windows the program should always be run as an administrator.

Export The Mitigations So Far   We'll come back to this option in a moment.

Exit   Abandon all hope of the SUA tools helping this application!

If you responded Yes to the mitigations fixing your problem, then you will get the option to export your mitigation. That will create an MSI file, which you can install on every PC that will have this application. MSI files can be easily deployed using MSIEXEC via startup scripts or Group Policy, or by using advance software deployment solutions.

DEPLOYING A MITIGATION WITH CONFIGURATION MANAGER

Medium and large organizations may use products such as System Center Configuration Manager or System Center Essentials for deploying applications. To eliminate mistakes, you can automate the deployment of your Standard User Analyzer–generated mitigations with your applications. This is possible by creating a package and program from the mitigation MSI. You can then specify the mitigation's package installer program as a dependency for your fixed application. Any advertisement of that application will preinstall the mitigation if it is not already present on the client computer.

The SUA will produce the same sort of fix as the SUA Wizard, but it gives you a look under the covers to see what is going on. With more experience of application compatibility engineering, you'll be able to interpret this data to figure out complex problems.

Just like with the wizard, SUA requires that you specify the executable for the application and any required parameters. The Launch Options area on the right contains two configurable options. The Elevate check box is enabled by default. According to Microsoft, this option enables the application to run either as a standard user or an administrator. Clearing the check box will cause the application to run as administrator. That will give SUA the opportunity to identify issues that might occur when a normal user runs the program. The Disable Virtualization check box is grayed out when Elevate is enabled. Microsoft recommends disabling it if a lot of data will be created in virtualized locations on the PC by the application. In Figure 2.27 we have configured SUA to shadow Stock Viewer with the Elevate option turned off. Clicking Launch starts the program that you want to test and fix.

FIGURE 2.27
Standard User
Analyzer

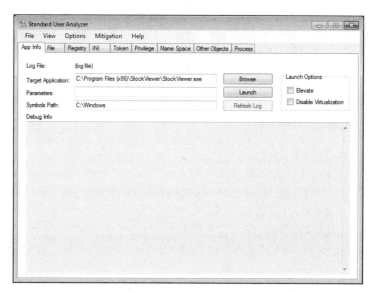

As before with the wizard, you test the program and see all the faults, allowing SUA the opportunity to create fixes. You can see in Figure 2.28 that a lot more information about the analysis is there for you to check out. Debug Info shows you actions performed. Each of the tabs, such as File, Token, Name Space, and Other Objects, reveals more information.

FIGURE 2.28
Testing the application with the Standard User Analyzer

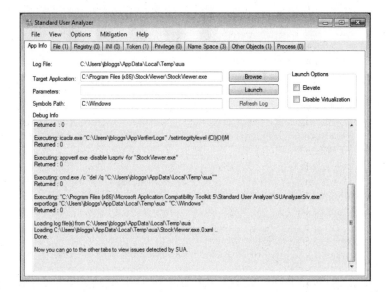

Click to open the Mitigation menu, where you have three options. As it stands right now, SUA has generated a possible fix but has done nothing with it. You can test that mitigation by choosing Apply Mitigations. Then rerun and retest the application. You can then choose Undo Mitigations to uninstall the possible fix. If you're happy with the fix, you can choose Export Mitigations As MSI.

So there you go; that's the Standard User Analyzer tools. It's quite possible that you can quickly fix issues for applications associated with administrator rights very quickly with either one of these tools. If you took the time to try out more of the Stock Viewer functions, then you'll already know that it is a very "broken" application. SUA isn't a panacea, either, as it doesn't fix enough of the problems. Make sure you have undone any mitigations created in SUA. It's now time to move on to the big gun.

CREATING SHIMS

You saw a few shims being created when we looked at the Standard User Analyzer. There are over 300 shims that you can use in ACT 5.6. An automated tool like SUA can only do so much for you. Sometimes you need to get under the hood yourself and get some grease on your hands.

A lot of things can prevent an application from working correctly:

◆ The operating system version is different and the application check is very specific.

◆ A verification of the version of Internet Explorer finds a newer, unsupported version.

◆ File or Registry paths have changed or there is a lack of access rights.

◆ The Windows GUI, Aero, is quite advanced and can cause trouble for some legacy applications.

◆ An application may need to spawn off another program that requires an elevated UAC token to execute but it doesn't know how to.

◆ Some applications can develop minor issues that could be safely ignored (after testing) but cause the program to crash.

◆ Annoying error boxes can repeatedly appear because of minor issues that can be ignored.

Now you are probably wondering, "I can test an application but how do I really know what's wrong with it?" Tools are available that you can use to help identify the root causes of any failures. If you use the SUA, then you've already installed the Application Verifier (Figure 2.29). You can configure this tool to shadow an application, and it will generate logs of faults that were detected. Another tool that will prove to be very helpful is Process Monitor (ProcMon), a free download from the Microsoft Sysinternals site at `http://technet.microsoft.com/sysinternals/bb545027.aspx`. This tool allows you to watch how an application interacts with the file system and the Registry while it runs. When you see an application failure, you can look back through recent activity and see exactly what it tried to do. And there is always the good old-fashioned eyeball test. Sometimes the application will tell you exactly what is wrong; for example, it will work only with Internet Explorer 6 (IE6).

FIGURE 2.29
Application
Verifier

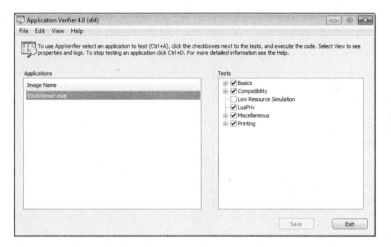

Very often an application, such as a `setup.exe`, will do a basic check of the operating system. This is typical of driver installers that were written specifically for Vista. The OS check will fail but the driver or program will work fine on Windows 7 if they can only get installed. As you can see in Figure 2.30, you can right-click on an executable file and create shims for it using the Compatibility tab. You can pick an operating system that the shim should pretend to be, such as Windows XP SP2, for administrative access, and control the screen resolution or colors. This quick solution may provide a handy fix.

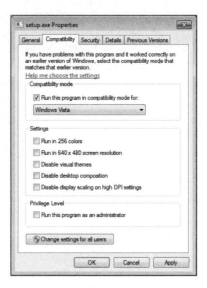

FIGURE 2.30
Application
compatibility
properties

We're going to continue to work with Stock Viewer because it contains a number of problems that are quite common. Start up Stock Viewer on a PC with no shims or mitigations installed. You'll get the usual administrator access warning. On the Tools menu there is a Show Me A Star option. That will also fail because the PC has Windows 7, not Windows XP. Clicking the Browse button reveals that Stock Viewer will only work with IE6. If you click Options ➤ Save Preferences, then you'll get a failure because a standard user cannot write to the default location. If you click Tools ➤ Show Me A Star, the tool will fail to launch because the operating system is Windows 7, not Windows XP. Finally, if you click File ➤ Update Kernel, you will see that this fails because you are trying to update a protected system file. Even with administrator access, you won't be able to do this on Windows 7. We're going to do our best to fix all of these issues by creating shims in the ACT Compatibility Administrator.

COMPATIBILITY ADMINISTRATOR REQUIRES ADMIN RIGHTS

Strangely enough, you are going to want to do some compatibility fixing on the Compatibility Administrator application. It requires that you run the program with your elevated UAC token or administrator access instead of with a standard user token/rights. It's all too easy to click the Start menu entry for the program without right-clicking and picking Run As Administrator. The program will start but it won't work correctly. A handy fix is to right-click on the menu entry, select the Compatibility tab, and check the Run As Administrator check box. Now the program will always seek administrator access when you run it.

Launch the Compatibility Administrator and you'll get the window shown in Figure 2.31. The navigation pane on the left shows a number of things. The System Database has three entries:

Applications   This is an extremely useful place to start with any application you find a problem with. Microsoft maintains a database of shims for existing applications. This one contains over 6,500 fixed applications. There is a possibility that the fix you need is already here if you're using a well-known off-the-shelf application with compatibility issues. We'll come back to that in few moments.

Compatibility Fixes   These are the potential shims that can be used to change how things work. An example might be a Registry redirect.

Compatibility Modes   There is a subtle difference between compatibility modes and fixes. A mode is something like a setting, such as Windows XP SP2 or a 640×400 screen resolution.

FIGURE 2.31
The Compatibility
Administrator

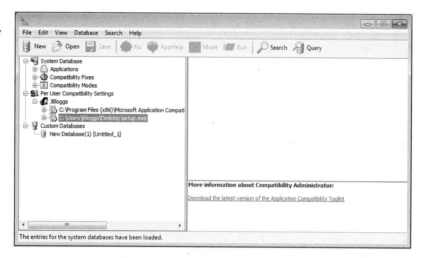

Per User Compatibility Settings shows the currently installed shims for the currently logged-in user. You can see the fixes for the `setup.exe` driver installer and for the Compatibility Administrator.

Custom Databases is where all the magic happens. This is where you can create a database of shims for each of your applications that will require a compatibility fix. Compatibility Administrator takes a different approach to deployment than you found in SUA. Instead of creating one MSI for each application, it is possible to create a single database file with an SDB extension for your entire organization. You can then deploy that SDB to every PC on your network and fix all possible compatibility issues. Of course, you could go with an alternative solution and have smaller SDB files for departments or offices, or even per-application SDB files.

DEPLOYING AN SDB FILE

Every Windows 7 PC has a program in C:\Windows\System32 called sdbinst.exe. You can use this program to install the fixes contained in an SDB file. You can install an SDB file with:

    sdbinst.exe <name of SDB file>

You can uninstall an SDB file with:

    sdbinst.exe -u <name of SDB file>

This means you can use solutions like startup scripts and advanced software deployment solutions such as Configuration Manager to run the program using the SDB file as a parameter. Have a look at any package program in ConfigMgr; all it does is run an executable with a parameter. There's nothing to stop you from doing that with the sdbinst.exe that's found on the client computer using an SDB file that's located on the network as the parameter.

You can include your SDB files in a Windows 7 deployment image. Doing so reduces the work required to deploy legacy applications. However, you might want to limit what you include in the image for troubleshooting reasons. You might also want to maintain a centralized library with complete control in case you need to change the SDB file at a later point.

A default custom SDB file is present in the Compatibility Administrator. You can either rename it to suit your needs or open a preexisting one by clicking the Open button.

Two tools will help you navigate the database and fixes on your ACT PC:

Search Using this tool, you can point at a folder on the PC to search for programs with a compatibility fix. You can then double-click on the found programs to view the details of the fix.

Query This tool allows you to search your database based on application name, filename, and various other properties.

Let's look at creating a fix for an application that already exists. Start by renaming the custom database. Right-click on Custom Database in the console and choose Rename. It's good to follow naming standards. For our example, rename this database to **deploy.com** (to match our domain). We have identified that Photoshop CS2 is on the network and is having issues with Windows 7. There isn't a budget to upgrade to a newer version, so we will have to deploy a fix. Click Query and enter the name of the program. You can use % as a wildcard. So you can enter either **Photoshop CS2** to get a precise result or **Photoshop%** to view everything starting with the word Photoshop. Note that the search tool is not case sensitive. Our search brought up the results in Figure 2.32.

FIGURE 2.32
Querying for an application fix

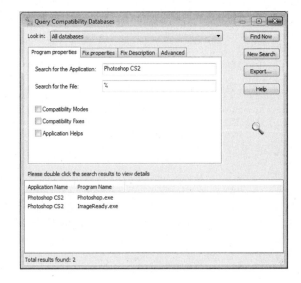

Two programs were tagged as Photoshop CS2. It turns out that there is another program in the package that also needs to be fixed. Double-click one of them and you are brought to the application in the database, as shown in Figure 2.33.

Each application is boldface in the detail pane. You can now right-click an application (or even the fix in the detail pane) and select Copy. Browse back to your custom database and paste the application. Repeat this for each required application. You can see in Figure 2.34 that you can add many applications into the database. There are even noncommercial applications like old games that you thought might never see the light of day again after your upgrade to Windows 7.

FIGURE 2.33
The application in the database

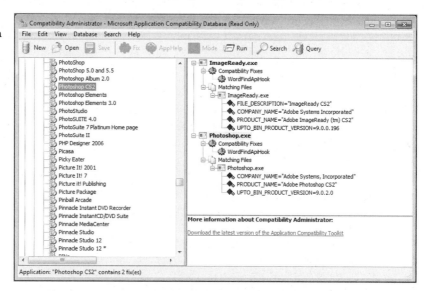

FIGURE 2.34
A completed SDB

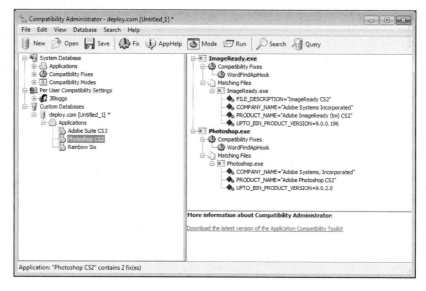

Before you go any further with testing this database, you need to save it. This will create the SDB file in the location of your choosing. If you use multiapplication SDB files, you need a strict testing and change control process to avoid nasty calls at 3:00 a.m., angry "conversations" with the boss, and searches of employment websites.

Now you can right-click on the custom database and install it onto your PC for testing. A new node will appear in the navigation pane on the left called Installed Databases. Expand it to reveal your fixes. Now you can test those applications on this PC. Note that an application only loads the associated shims when it starts up. A running application will not dynamically load any associated shims until you restart it. Remember to uninstall the database from the PC when you have finished by right-clicking on it under Installed Databases and selecting Uninstall.

That's all well and good if your application is one of those in the Applications database. But what if you have a lesser-known or a custom application that cannot be fixed or upgraded? Stock Viewer comes to mind. You will have to create shims for it by hand based on the faults you identified.

First, create a new application in the custom database. Do so by right-clicking on the database and selecting Create New ➤ Application Fix. The Create New Application Fix wizard appears (Figure 2.35). You should populate the fields with the name of the application, the vendor, and the location of the application executable.

FIGURE 2.35
Create New Application Fix wizard

The next screen allows you to choose operating system modes (for example, Windows XP SP2 or Windows 2000) or compatibility modes for screen resolution and colors. Normally you will not choose any of these options and move ahead to the next screen.

The first problem we will deal with is the check for administrator access. You saw earlier with SUA that the ForceAdminAccess compatibility fix (shim) fooled the application into thinking that it was running with an administrator's rights. Scroll down through the available shims in the Compatibility Fixes list box (Figure 2.36) and check that shim. If you click Next you will see all the detail involved in creating the application fix. Click Finish and you get a new application fix in your database. If you save and install that database, you should now be able to run Stock Viewer without the annoying warning about administrator rights.

FIGURE 2.36
Selecting an application compatibility fix

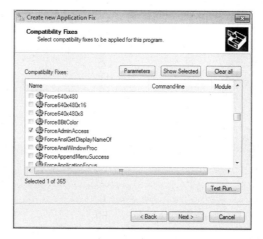

That's the first fix done. You can go back and edit the application fix by right-clicking on it in the detail pane and selecting Edit Application Fix. You'll return to the wizard's compatibility fix screen.

There are four fixes in Stock Viewer that we can use to solve problems that we encountered when we first discussed Stock Viewer:

VirtualRegistry   This fix allows you to redirect requests by the application from one Registry location to another.

CorrectFilePaths   This fix allows you to redirect file operations from an unavailable location (it's simply not there or a standard user has no permissions) to a valid location where the user has permissions to read and/or write.

WRPMitigation   Windows Resource Protection (WRP) only allows "trusted installers" to modify system files and Registry items. This fix lies to an application every time it tries to modify a protected resource that it has no rights to modify.

OS Version Lie   There is a compatibility fix for each lie you wish to present to an application—for example, Win2000SP3VersionLie and WinXPSP2VersionLie.

Let's configure each of the compatibility fixes now to get the aforementioned features of Stock Viewer working. When you select a compatibility fix, you can configure the command line for it by clicking parameters. This step is required for some fixes, such as when you specify a location to protect and an alternative location for the application to use. Table 2.1 shows the syntax of the fixes we will employ.

TABLE 2.1:   Stock Viewer compatibility fixes syntax

COMPATIBILITY FIX	PARAMETERS IN THE COMMAND LINE
VirtualRegistry	IE60 or ADDREDIRECT(*OldPath^NewPath*)
CorrectFilePaths	"*OldPath:NewPath*"
WRPMitigation	None required
WinXPSP2VersionLie	None required

MAKE CHANGES ONE BY ONE

When you are dealing with complex technology, making many changes at once can make it difficult to understand what caused the results. As with any other complex IT operations, you should try to make one application fix at a time and test it. You can then undo that fix, tweak it, or add another fix, all in a predictable manner.

Let's go through these parameters and see how to use them to fix our problem. The first one is VirtualRegistry, which we'll use to fix our IE6 issue. Windows 7 comes with IE8 and you cannot downgrade it. You can see two solutions in Table 2.1. The first one, IE60, is a prepackaged cheat from Microsoft to quickly tell any associated application that Internet Explorer 6 is installed. You can also use IE401 for Internet Explorer 4.01, or IE55 for Internet Explorer 5.5. There are lots more of these, which you can find on Microsoft TechNet at `http://technet` `.microsoft.com/library/cc749368(WS.10).aspx`.

That's fine for Internet Explorer. But what if there's some other Registry cheat you need to create? The solution is to use `ADDREDIRECT(`*OldPath^NewPath*`)` to create a new value with a setting in an alternative location. For example, create a REG_SZ called **Version** with a value of **6.0.2404.0** in `HKEY_LOCAL_MACHINE\Software\Microsoft\Internet Explorer 6`. You need to create a new one for this example because the `Version` value already exists in the `Internet Explorer` key. The value of the new version key will be `6.0.2404.0`.

Now you can set the parameter of VirtualRegistry to tell the application to go to the new `Internet Explorer 6` key instead of the original `Internet Explorer` key:

```
ADDREDIRECT(HKLM\Software\Microsoft\Internet%20Explorer^ HKLM\Software\Microsoft\
Internet%20Explorer%206)
```

There are two things to note with this `ADDREDIRECT(`*OldPath^NewPath*`)` solution. The command will use `HKLM` and not `HKEY_LOCAL_MACHINE`. You will also need to use `%20` to replace space characters.

Next you have to deal with the pesky Save Preferences menu option. That will use the CorrectFilePaths fix with this command:

```
"C:\Windows\Downloaded Program Files\StockViewer.ini;%appdata%\StockViewer.ini"
```

What you have done there is fool the application into thinking it will use the old file location in `C:\Windows` that the user has no access to. Instead, you are using an alternative location. `%appdata%` is an environment variable that points to the user's own profile where they can save their personal settings.

WRPMitigation is pretty simple. You just check the box and there are no parameters to set. Any attempt by the application to modify protected files will, of course, not succeed. But the application will be told that the actions did succeed, thus preventing unwanted failures. Be careful with this fix in case there are other dependencies on those updated files within the application.

The last one you will use for Stock Viewer applies to another executable that Stock Viewer starts on your behalf: the Show Me A Star tool. This is just a demo tool that uses features of Windows XP to display a star on the screen. This won't work on Windows 7 without a fix. You can find that program, `DWM Composting Rendering Demo.exe`, alongside `StockViewer.exe` in `C:\Program Files\StockViewer`. (It may be `Program Files (x86)` if you are using a 64-bit Windows 7 installation.) You will need to add another application to fix your customer database in the Compatibility Administrator for that executable. Then you can add the OSVersionLie (WinXPSP2VersionLie, in this case) compatibility fix.

At this point you should have all the aforementioned features of Stock Viewer working. Of course, there are more broken features in there, and there are hundreds of compatibility fixes. You can find a lot more information in the help file and on Microsoft TechNet at `http://technet.microsoft.com/library/cc722305(WS.10).aspx`. Here's a few fixes that you might find useful:

DisableDWM   This fix will prevent the application from using the Aero interface of Windows Vista and Windows 7.

FakeLunaTheme   Color may be important in some applications. A few legacy applications may not have the vivid colors they should have on Windows Vista or Windows 7.

IgnoreAltTab   This fix tells the application to ignore the following key sequences or keys: Alt+Tab, Alt+Esc, Ctrl+Esc, the Windows logo key, and the Application Key (Microsoft Natural Keyboard only).

IgnoreException   Microsoft warns that you should use this fix only if you have to. That's because IgnoreException doesn't have a filter for valid or invalid exceptions.

IgnoreMessageBox   Using the caption and text from an identified message box, you can prevent the message box from being displayed to a user.

RunAsAdmin   With this fix, the program requires administrative access and must ask for it if it doesn't already have it.

RunAsInvoker   The program should run as the current standard user but it currently asks for administrative rights. This fix will prevent that.

VirtualizeDeleteFile   Pretend that a file was successfully deleted by an application in scenarios where it cannot be deleted.

By now, you should have the tools and know-how to fix most applications that have compatibility issues. But there are always a few exceptions to the rule. For example, what if you need to use Internet Explorer 6 for a LOB website application that you can't fix? You can't install IE6 onto Windows 7. We're going to look at the last solution in our application compatibility catalog now.

Deploying XP Mode

Sometimes you just can't get an application to work on Windows 7 no matter what you do. You've found no upgrades, there is no vendor or third-party fix, you can't rewrite it, and all your efforts with ACT have failed. You have come to the conclusion that the only thing you can do is run the application on Windows XP. That used to mean installing two PCs at the user's desk. That increases hardware, licensing, power, and maintenance costs. It also frustrates the user.

What if you could give the user an XP VM that would run on their Windows 7 computer? What if you could make the applications installed on it look like they are running in Windows 7? The Start menu icons from the VM would appear on the Windows 7 Start menu. Any XP program would run in a seamless window on the Windows 7 desktop, keeping the XP machine hidden behind the scenes. That sounds pretty good, doesn't it? That's exactly what Microsoft accomplished with Virtual PC for Windows 7.

Microsoft rewrote Virtual PC to coincide with the release of Windows 7. The focus was on producing an application compatibility solution. It has Start menu integration and allows VM programs to run in a seamless window. If you are running Windows 7 Enterprise, Ultimate, or the Professional editions, you are entitled to download and use XP Mode. XP Mode is a VM that is set up and uses a special Windows XP Professional with Service Pack 3 license. It is special because it is nontransferrable and you cannot build a custom XP virtual machine for free.

The basic concept is that you install Virtual PC for Windows 7 and XP Mode on every Windows 7 PC that requires XP to run legacy applications. The legacy applications are installed in the XP virtual machines. End users can then enjoy their new Windows 7 PCs with all the new enterprise functionality that they provide, while continuing to use those legacy applications that just won't work on anything but XP.

There are a few things that administrators and engineers need to know. The XP virtual machine is a computer all its own. It has its own security boundary, its own network and IP configuration (even though it shares the NIC of the Windows 7 PC), and its own storage in the form of a virtual hard disk (VHD) file. It will need to be a member of the Active Directory forest to allow the end user to use a single set of credentials. It will also need management and security. That means any automated software deployment needs to manage the VM as well as the host Windows 7 computer. You have to patch it and you have to maintain antivirus on it. It is a whole other computer, just without a physical presence.

That extra management is probably why you should try to think of XP Mode as a temporary solution. Your overall aim should be to get all applications running on Windows 7. Some may take longer than others. Some may require time-consuming replacements with alternative solutions. And that's where XP Mode comes in and does a nice job.

MDOP AND MED-V

If you license your desktop and laptop computers with Software Assurance, you are entitled to purchase the Microsoft Desktop Optimization Pack (MDOP). MDOP includes an enterprise desktop virtualization solution called MED-V. As we mentioned earlier, MED-V lets you create centrally managed VM images, allowing you to quickly and easily update VMs that are deployed onto your physical PCs.

Installing Virtual PC for Windows 7

To install XP Mode, you will need to download (www.microsoft.com/Windows/Virtual-PC/default.aspx) and install Virtual PC for Windows 7. The requirements for it are as follows:

◆ 1 GHz or faster 64-bit processor

◆ 2 GB of RAM or more for 32-bit systems, 3 GB or more for 64-bit systems

◆ 20 MB for the installation plus 15 GB disk or more per virtual machine

◆ Windows 7 Home Basic, Home Premium, Enterprise, Professional, or Ultimate edition

When XP Mode and Virtual PC for Windows 2007 were originally released, there was another requirement for your PC: the CPU had to have the virtualization assistance feature. You had to check the CPU model and check on the AMD or Intel web sites to see whether CPU virtualization assistance was a feature of the CPU. In addition, the OEM BIOS had to allow you to turn on the virtualization assistance feature.

The CPU assisted virtualization requirement stung many Windows 7 early adopters (and virtualization enthusiasts). They had computers with supported CPUs, but the computer manufacturer did not offer a way to turn it on in the BIOS and they refused to create updates to change this. Third-party hacks were available, but they would violate your warranty and you had to be willing to accept 100 percent of the associated risks.

The update to XP Mode resolves this issue. During the writing of this book, Microsoft released an update (available on the same web page as Virtual PC for Windows 7 and XP Mode) for XP Mode to do away with the requirement of CPU assisted virtualization. This update allows many more machines to run the application compatibility solution. If you plan to run Vista or Windows 7 VMs in Virtual PC for Windows 7, you still have to turn on this feature in the BIOS for performance reasons. To do so, follow these steps:

1. Enable the hardware features in your BIOS if you have them

2. Download the Virtual PC for Windows 7 installer and run it. It's a pretty basic installer that will require a reboot.

A new folder and item called Windows Virtual PC will be created on your Windows 7 Start menu. Clicking that opens an Explorer window with a location of C:\Users\<Your Username>\Virtual Machines (Figure 2.37). This is the default location for your VMs.

You can create your own custom VMs by clicking Create Virtual Machine. Define the name, location, memory, how it will network, and what storage it should use. Then provide a CD/DVD or ISO file to install an operating system.

That brings us to XP Mode, Microsoft's prepackaged Windows XP installation. There is also a Start menu item under Windows Virtual PC for XP Mode. It cannot do anything until you install it.

Installing XP Mode

You can download XP Mode from the same website where you got Virtual PC for Windows 7 (www.microsoft.com/Windows/Virtual-PC/default.aspx). First you have to run and install Genuine Advantage to check for piracy and activation—download and install the plug-in and then enable it. The nearly 500 MB download will then begin. Note that you are only licensed to run XP Mode on Windows 7 Enterprise, Ultimate, or Professional edition.

FIGURE 2.37
Virtual PC for
Windows 7

XP MODE MEMORY

By default, the virtual machine will be assigned 512 MB of RAM. You may need to add more memory. Understand that this will consume slightly more than that amount from the physical host. You can add more RAM to the VM by shutting it down, opening Windows Virtual PC, and editing the XP Mode VM's settings.

Make sure you consider XP Mode memory as early as possible when planning the desktop deployment project.

The setup consists of two parts. The installer extracts and prepares the XP Mode on your PC. That's a pretty simple routine. Every user who then uses the PC will get his or her own XP Mode installation. This will be based on the template VHD, Windows XP Mode `base.vhd`, which is located in `C:\Program Files\Windows XP Mode`.

The Windows XP Mode Setup then kicks off by asking you to accept the license agreement. The next screen asks you to enter a location for the VM and to enter credentials for it, as you can see in Figure 2.38. You go through the usual "protect my computer" screen and then the VM is created by copying the template. Three new files are added to the specified location:

VHD   This is the virtual hard disk, a file that simulates a hard disk and contains the operating system, program files, and data on the VM.

VMC   This is the VM's configuration file.

VSV   This is a save state file and used when the VM hibernates.

FIGURE 2.38
Windows XP Mode
setup

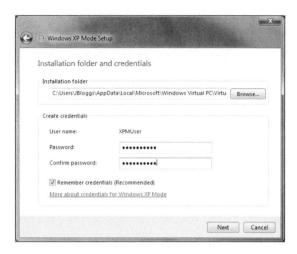

Note that any subsequent users will be able to start the Windows XP Mode Setup program to create their own VM by running Windows XP Mode Setup from the Start menu.

The setup routine launches a new window to let you further configure the VM. This process can take a little while. If your Windows 7 PC is configured for sound, you will eventually hear the XP Mode machine log in automatically. The full screen appears, revealing the XP desktop (Figure 2.39). You'll only use this program to set up software in the VM.

FIGURE 2.39
Windows XP Mode
full screen

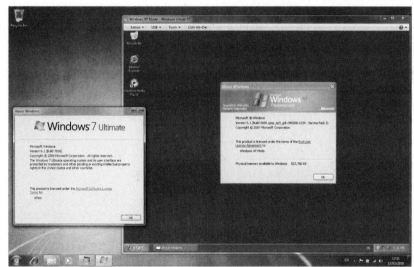

You'll notice a few handy tools on the menu at the top of the full screen. The USB menu allows you to capture any devices plugged into the Windows 7 host so that the VM can use them. The Tools menu lets you disable the Integration Features. These features enable advanced functionality for the VM, such as seamless windows. You can also use the Settings menu to reconfigure the VM. The Ctrl+Alt+Del option allows you to pass that key sequence to the VM via a mouse click. You can also use Ctrl+Alt+End to use that key sequence directly in the VM without affecting the Windows 7 host.

If you open Windows Explorer in the VM, you will see that the physical drives of the Windows 7 host are available as network drives. Your VM can also mount an ISO file or a physical CD/DVD. And, of course, it can access the network.

This means you have many ways to install your legacy applications (that ACT couldn't fix) and your management systems (such as antivirus and the Configuration Manager client). You saw in the Application Compatibility Manager that an XP machine was using Microsoft Office 2000 and that no fix, other than an upgrade, was available. There are companies that use legacy server applications that might not support a newer version of Office, so the old one must be maintained. And those same companies may need a newer version on Windows 7 to work with new LOB applications. XP Mode to the rescue!

You can install any remaining legacy applications with Windows 7 compatibility issues in your XP Mode VM, just as you would on any physical computer. When it's done, you can open the Start menu of the Windows 7 PC. The shortcuts for the newly installed XP Mode applications should be present, as shown in Figure 2.40. If they aren't, you can move them to the All Users Start Menu in the VM, found at `C:\Documents and Settings\All Users\Start Menu`. By the way, that's a handy way to get Internet Explorer 6 and Outlook Express from XP Mode working on Windows 7.

Now you need to test them. Shut down the VM. When it has shut down, click one of the XP Mode Start menu items. The VM should start up behind the scenes.

FIGURE 2.40
The XP Mode Start
menu shortcuts

CREATING A CUSTOMIZED XP VM

Suppose you want to create your own template from scratch. You need to ensure that you have the appropriate licensing; for example, Software Assurance on the desktop provides the rights to run up to four free VMs. Alternatively, you would have to purchase the license for each operating system installed into a VM.

Creating a custom XP VM also requires the following:

◆ Integration Features installed

◆ Windows XP Service Pack 3

◆ The Update for Windows XP SP3, to enable RemoteApp (www.microsoft.com/downloads/en/details.aspx?familyid=E5433D88-685F-4036-B435-570FF53598CD&displaylang=en)

You then need to prepare the VM for deployment. That process involves using Sysprep and a `sysprep.inf` file to create an unattended mini-setup. Once the machine is prepared with Sysprep, shut it down.

Next, deploy the VHD to the desired location on the client computers. Microsoft provides a script that lets you automatically create a VM from your customized VHD file. You must run this script from an elevated command prompt:

```
cscript CreateVirtualMachine.wsf -p:<path to VHD> -vn:<virtual machine name>
```

A progress bar appears to indicate that the VM is starting up. You'll also see it appear if the VM has entered hibernation. The VM will normally hibernate when all XP Mode applications have been closed. If there are any problems or if you need to install or remove any programs, you can click the Windows XP Mode Start menu item to relaunch the full XP desktop. You'll soon see how you can do very cool and useful things, like run two versions of Office or Internet Explorer on the one Windows 7 computer, as shown in Figure 2.41.

FIGURE 2.41
IE8 and IE6 running simultaneously

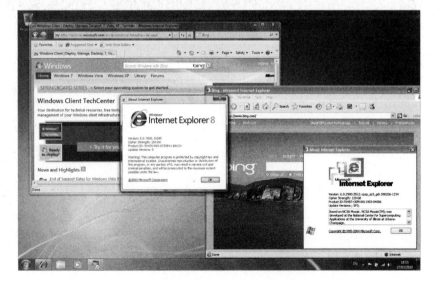

CONFIGURING GROUP POLICY SETTINGS FOR XP MODE

A number of Group Policy settings must be configured for XP Mode to work correctly. The following must be configured (default settings) on the Windows 7 host at Local Computer Policy\ User Configuration\Administrative Templates\Windows Components\Remote Desktop Services\RD Gateway:

◆ Set RD Gateway Authentication Method: Enabled or Not Configured

◆ Enable Connection Through RD Gateway: Enabled or Not Configured (Allow Users To Change This Setting: Enabled)

◆ Set RD Gateway Server Address: Enabled or Not Configured

The following must be configured (default settings) on the XP Mode virtual machine at Local Computer Policy\Computer Configuration\Administrative Templates\Windows Components\Terminal Services:

◆ Allow Users To Connect Remotely Using Terminal Services: Enabled

◆ Remove Disconnect Option From Shut Down Dialog: Enabled

◆ Client/Server Data Redirection: Not Configured

Make sure you work with your Active Directory administrators to ensure that these settings remain on any Windows 7 computers or XP Mode machines that are domain members. If either XP Mode or Virtual PC for Windows 7 starts to misbehave, you will probably want to start looking at the resulting Group Policy for your VM and your host Windows 7 PC using Group Policy Manager.

Advanced Deployment of XP Mode

There are a few advanced ways that you can use to deploy Windows XP Mode, and we'll discuss them in this section. For more information, check out the Microsoft-published whitepaper and scripts for performing advanced deployments of Windows XP Mode. You can find them at:

www.microsoft.com/downloads/en/details.aspx?FamilyID=9f142a1a-a7b7-4d0b-bd56-d9627f39c14f

SILENT INSTALLATION

You can perform silent installations of Virtual PC for Windows 7 and XP Mode. This is possible using two scripts. The first will silently install Virtual PC when run from an elevated command prompt:

```
cscript InstallWindowsVirtualPC.wsf -p:<path to the MSU for Virtual PC>
```

The next script will silently install XP Mode when run from an elevated command prompt:

```
Csript InstallAndCreateWindowsXPMode.wsf -p:<path to WindowsXPMode.exe>
```

Thanks to scripts like these, you can use startup scripts or advanced software deployment solutions like Configuration Manager to install XP Mode on your Windows 7 PC automatically.

GENERAL TIPS FOR ENSURING COMPATIBILITY

Here are a few suggestions to keep the process running as smoothly as possible:

◆ You can never have too much information. Make use of the Application Compatibility Administrator and start gathering information as soon as possible. That will help with realistic planning and scheduling.

◆ If you have Configuration Manager, you should configure the ACT Connector to produce reports with unified data.

◆ Work closely with the business and identify owners of business applications. Some applications may be redundant or obsolete; only those business owners will know this.

◆ Use virtualization to build a test and development network. You can build template VMs with ACT already installed and store them in a library. This will allow you to quickly test and fix applications on clean machines.

◆ Involve power users when and where you can to test applications. They understand the application more than anyone else can.

◆ Make use of the community. If you purchased an off-the-shelf solution, someone else may have already fixed any compatibility issues.

The Bottom Line

Plan for and install the Application Compatibility Toolkit.   The Application Compatibility Administrator allows for a flexible deployment based on the scale of the organization and the design of the network.

> **Master It**   You have been assigned the task of designing an ACT deployment for a large organization. There are many branch offices, some with lightly used high-speed links, some with moderately used high-speed links, and some with congested slow-speed links. You must design the solution so that enough data is gathered to plan any application compatibility operations while not affecting company operations.

Use ACT to identify incompatible applications.   The Application Compatibility Toolkit provides tools for identifying applications with compatibility issues.

> **Master It**   You have a large library of applications. Many of them are off-the-shelf purchases. You wish to avail yourself of as much community and vendor knowledge as possible to speed up the process of identifying compatibility issues. What is the best course of action?

Use ACT and XP Mode to solve compatibility issues.   When combined with Virtual PC for Windows 7, Windows XP Mode provides you with a way to run legacy applications that have no possible fixes on Windows 7 computers.

Master It   You are working as a consultant. A client site is replacing Windows XP with Windows 7. They have a small number of laptop users who need to run a critical application that does not work on Windows 7. All attempts to resolve this issue with ACT have failed. You have been asked to find a way to make the application work when the users are roaming and to make it as simple as possible to use. What can you do?

Chapter 3

Installing Windows 7: Meet the Panther

When installing Windows 7, you'll first have to identify the edition that will meet your needs. You can choose from three primary editions for your organization. After you pick the edition you want, you can decide on one of several methods to install Windows 7. The method you use primarily depends on whether you're upgrading or refreshing an existing computer or replacing the computer. These methods also affect how you can restore users' data using the User State Migration Tool (USMT), which is explained in greater depth in Chapter 5, "Migrating the Existing User Data."

This chapter peeks into the three phases of the installation process: the preinstallation phase, the online configuration phase, and the Windows Welcome phase. The chapter also includes steps you can use to perform a clean installation and an upgrade.

After the installation, Windows 7 needs to be activated. This chapter presents some basics on licensing and activation, including the use of retail keys, original equipment manufacturer (OEM) keys, multiple activation keys (MAKs), and the Key Management Service (KMS). Chapter 13, "Volume Licensing," expands on these topics.

In this chapter, you will learn to:

◆ Choose the correct edition of Windows 7

◆ Identify the correct method to install Windows 7

◆ Install Windows 7

◆ View the current activation status

Choosing the Right Edition of Windows 7

When you are planning to migrate to Windows 7, one of the first decisions you'll need to make is which edition to use. There are several editions and each has different capabilities. Some editions are for home use only; others are intended for use within businesses or organizations. Windows 7 Ultimate is used in both homes and organizations.

The following editions are available:

◆ Windows 7 Starter

◆ Windows 7 Home Basic

◆ Windows 7 Home Premium

- ◆ Windows 7 Professional
- ◆ Windows 7 Enterprise
- ◆ Windows 7 Ultimate

This chapter focuses only on the editions deployed within an organization: Windows 7 Professional, Windows 7 Enterprise, and Windows 7 Ultimate.

Windows 7 Professional

The Windows 7 Professional edition is intended for small businesses but can also be used by home users who want additional capabilities beyond those of the Windows 7 Home Premium edition. It is available in both 32-bit and 64-bit versions.

Some of the capabilities are as follows:

Aero Glass   This feature adds several graphical features to Windows. It includes live thumbnails on the Taskbar and Aero Peek, which allows open windows to appear transparent.

Domain Membership   If your organization has an existing domain, a Windows 7 Professional computer can join it. This allows you to manage the computer with Group Policy and significantly increases security capabilities.

Windows XP Mode   You can install Windows XP Mode to run legacy applications on the Windows 7 system. This is useful if you have applications that worked in Windows XP but do not work correctly in Windows 7.

File Encryption   The Encrypting File System (EFS) is available with the NTFS (New Technology File System, the standard filesystem of recent Windows releases). Users can encrypt files so that other users cannot view the contents.

The Ability to Back Up to a Network Location   All editions can back up data with the Backup and Restore Center. However, this edition adds the capability to back up data to a drive located on the network in addition to backing up to locally attached drives.

Dynamic Disks   You can convert drives to dynamic disks. Dynamic disks support Redundant Array of Independent Disks (RAID).

Touch-Screen Support   If the monitor supports it, you can use touch-screen capabilities with Windows 7 Professional.

Remote Desktop   You can enable Remote Desktop so that an administrator can remotely connect to the Windows 7 Professional system for remote administration. You can also use a Windows 7 system to remotely connect to other systems.

Software Restriction Policies   You can use software restriction policies to control what applications can or cannot run on the system. Although you can use software restriction policies on a Windows 7 Professional system, you won't be able to use the newer AppLocker features. You can configure AppLocker on a Windows 7 Professional system, but AppLocker policies are not enforced. AppLocker is enforced only on systems running Windows 7 Enterprise or Ultimate editions.

Games are disabled by default in the Professional edition. However, they are installed and can be enabled by adding them through the Turn Windows Features On Or Off applet in Control Panel.

Windows 7 Enterprise

Only organizations that have a Software Assurance contract with Microsoft are able to purchase Windows 7 Enterprise edition through a volume licensing program. In other words, individuals can't buy it via standard retail channels.

Windows 7 Enterprise comes in both 32-bit and 64-bit versions, and includes all the features of Windows 7 Professional, plus some additional features:

BitLocker Support   You can encrypt entire hard drives with BitLocker and encrypt portable USB flash drives with BitLocker To Go.

AppLocker Support   AppLocker is an improvement compared to software restriction policies and gives administrators more control over what software can run. A significant addition is the ability to control who can run specific software based on group membership.

Ability to Switch Between Languages   Multilanguage support allows you to use the same system to switch between as many as 35 different languages.

DirectAccess Support   This feature can be used instead of a virtual private network (VPN) and allows clients to connect directly to internal Windows Server 2008 or Windows Server 2008 R2 servers over the Internet.

BranchCache Support   BranchCache can be used in remote offices to cache data that is retrieved from the main office over a WAN link. After one Windows 7 user retrieves a document, BranchCache caches it on a computer in the remote office and other users can then retrieve it from there. Data can be cached on Windows 7 computers, or on a Windows Server 2008 server in the remote office.

Remote Desktop Services   You can record audio over a Remote Desktop Services connection and use multiple displays with Remote Desktop Services. Note that Remote Desktop Services was previously known as Terminal Services but was renamed when Windows Server 2008 R2 was released.

Ability to Boot from Virtual Hard Disks   You can install Windows 7 onto a virtual hard disk (VHD) and configure the boot configuration data (BCD) store to boot to the VHD in a dual-boot or multiboot system.

Games are disabled by default in the Enterprise edition. However, they are installed and can be enabled. It's also possible to disable them using Group Policy.

Windows 7 Ultimate

The Windows 7 Ultimate edition is similar to the Enterprise edition except that you can purchase it through retail and OEM channels. It allows home users, and small organizations that don't have a Software Assurance contract, to enjoy the same capabilities of the Enterprise edition.

The primary difference between Windows 7 Enterprise and Windows 7 Ultimate is that games are enabled by default in the Ultimate edition.

The N, E, K, and KN Editions

There are some editions of Windows 7 sold in the European Union (EU) and South Korea that are a little different from versions sold in other places in the world. These editions grew out of legal action against Microsoft. The primary differences are related to Windows Media Player and Internet Explorer.

Windows 7 N   In 2004, Microsoft released a version of Windows XP called Windows XP N that, to comply with the EU requirements, did not include Windows Media Player. Microsoft also released Windows 7 N versions that are only sold in the EU. The current N editions of Windows 7 are the same as the regular editions except that Windows Media Player is not included. Users can download Windows Media for free.

Windows 7 E   In 2009, Microsoft released a version of Windows 7 called Windows 7 E, which did not bundle Internet Explorer with Windows 7. Later, the EU agreed to allow Internet Explorer to be installed with Windows 7. However, the first time users launch Internet Explorer, they see a screen that gives them a choice among several browsers.

Windows 7 K   The K edition is available in South Korea. It includes the same functionality as Windows 7 but does not include Windows Media Player. Users have links to a Media Player Center website and a Messenger Center website they can use to download these products if desired.

Windows 7 KN   The Windows 7 KN version is the same as the N version except it is available only in South Korea.

If you have a Windows 7 N or Windows 7 KN product and you want to enable the Windows Media features, you can install the Media Feature Pack. Details are available from Microsoft's Knowledge Base (KB) article 968211 (`http://support.microsoft.com/kb/968211`).

Speaking the Language: Four Ways to Use Windows Setup

Unless you purchase a computer with Windows 7 preinstalled, you'll need to install it. The installation DVD includes the Windows Setup program that you can use to install Windows 7 on a system. Windows Setup gives you two choices when installing it from a DVD. They are as follows:

Upgrade   Choose this option to update to a newer version of Windows and you can keep your applications, settings, and files. You can perform an upgrade only when you launch the installation DVD from certain Windows Vista or Windows 7 installations. It is not possible to upgrade from Windows XP. Note that upgrades aren't intended for large deployments, but you can use them in limited situations for small deployments.

Custom (Advanced)   This option installs a new copy of Windows 7 and is often referred to as a clean install. It doesn't keep applications or settings. If you modify partitions or volumes during the installation, existing files will also be lost.

PARTITION VS. VOLUME

Note that the terms *partitions* and *volumes* are interchangeable. A physical disk can be divided into partitions or volumes, which are known as C:, D:, and so on. In earlier operating systems, the term *partition* was more popular. In Windows 7, you'll see the term *volume* used much more often.

When installing Windows 7, you can use one of four basic methods discussed in the following sections:

◆ Deploying new bare-metal computers

◆ Upgrading computers

◆ Refreshing computers

◆ Replacing computers

Deploying New Bare-Metal Computers

A bare-metal install will install Windows 7 on a system that doesn't have any operating system on it, or on an existing system that has new hard drives.

When performing a new installation on a new computer, you can use the Setup program's built-in tools to manipulate the disks and volumes. When you're prompted to install Windows, the Setup program will scan the system and determine what disk drives and volumes are available, as shown in Figure 3.1. In the figure, only one unallocated hard drive is available. However, your system could have multiple hard drives and multiple volumes on any of the drives.

FIGURE 3.1
Choosing a location to install Windows 7

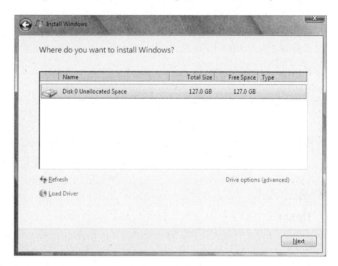

You can pick one of the available partitions, or click Drive Options (Advanced) to access additional menu options to manipulate the disks and volumes, as shown in Figure 3.2. For example, if you want to create two volumes, click New and divide the single hard drive into separate volumes.

Notice that you can also load drivers from this window. This can be useful if you're using a nonstandard hard drive that isn't recognized by the Windows 7 installation program.

Upgrading Computers

An upgrade will install the new operating system but keep existing applications and settings. You won't have to reinstall the applications from scratch. If you can upgrade using one of the supported upgrade paths, this will save you a lot of time and effort.

FIGURE 3.2
Drive options
to manipulate
partitions

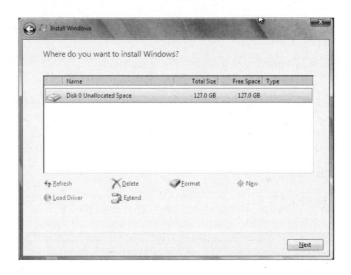

Unfortunately, there is a serious limitation with supported upgrade paths: you can't upgrade from Windows XP directly to Windows 7. Considering the majority of system PCs in organizations bypassed the upgrade from Windows XP to Vista, XP is what many organizations have in place.

Other *unsupported* upgrade paths start with the following:

♦   Any version of Windows before Windows Vista

♦   Windows Vista RTM (without a service pack)

♦   Windows 7 Beta, or Windows 7 release candidate (RC)

♦   Any Windows Server product

♦   Cross-architecture upgrades (x86 to x64 or 32-bit to 64-bit)

♦   Cross-language upgrades

♦   Cross store-keeping unit (SKU) upgrades such as Windows 7 N to Windows E

Table 3.1 shows the supported upgrade paths from Windows Vista to Windows 7.

TABLE 3.1:   Supported upgrade paths to Windows 7

FROM THIS WINDOWS VISTA EDITION (SP1 OR SP2)	TO THIS TO WINDOWS 7 EDITION
Business	Professional, Enterprise, Ultimate
Enterprise	Enterprise
Home Basic	Home Basic, Home Premium, Ultimate
Home Premium	Home Premium, Ultimate
Ultimate	Ultimate

You can also upgrade some Windows 7 installations using Microsoft's Anytime Upgrade. This product allows a user to purchase a computer with one version of Windows but then later upgrade to a different version. Table 3.2 shows the upgrade paths using Anytime Upgrade. The Anytime Upgrade path is built into the Windows 7 Professional edition. You can purchase an upgrade key either online or from an electronics store to upgrade the edition and unlock the advanced features.

TABLE 3.2:   Anytime Upgrade paths to Windows 7

FROM THIS WINDOWS 7 EDITION	TO THIS WINDOWS 7 EDITION
Home Basic	Home Basic, Home Premium, Professional, Ultimate
Home Premium	Professional, Ultimate
Professional	Ultimate
Starter	Home Premium, Professional, Ultimate

Refreshing Computers

The term *refreshing computers* means different things to different people. For many IT managers, a computer refresh means replacing the computers completely, including the hardware and operating system. However, in this context, the term refers to the process of installing a new operating system onto an existing computer. For example, the computer may currently be running Windows XP, but you will install Windows 7 on it to refresh it. The section "Replacing Computers" a bit later explains the process of replacing the computers.

When you refresh a computer, you often want users to have access to their settings and files from their existing systems. Thankfully, USMT gives you several options that you can use to migrate the user's data. USMT includes two primary tools known as ScanState and LoadState. You use ScanState to capture user state data and LoadState to restore it after the installation.

ScanState and LoadState are part of the Windows Automated Installation Kit (WAIK). Chapter 4, "Cloning the Panther: Automating Windows 7 Installation," explores the WAIK and Chapter 5 will dig into the syntax of the `ScanState` and `LoadState` commands, but this section provides an overview of the process.

Some of the scenarios include the following:

◆ PC refresh using a compressed migration store

◆ PC refresh using a hard-link migration store

◆ PC refresh using `Windows.old`

If you install Windows 7 on a system that has Windows installed and you don't modify the existing partitions, the setup program will recognize the previous installation and automatically move key data into a folder named `Windows.old`. You can then import the data back into the new installation.

Figure 3.3 represents the PC refresh using a compressed migration store. In this scenario, an administrator uses ScanState to collect the user state data before the refresh. It is stored over the network on a server. After the refresh, the administrator uses LoadState to load the user state data onto the same computer with the new operating system. This process is also called *wipe and load*.

You can perform a PC refresh using a hard-link migration store if you want to limit traffic over the network and you also have limited space on the existing computer. Figure 3.4 shows this method. ScanState collects the user state data before the refresh using the `/hardlink` option. ScanState stores the migrated data on the existing computer's hard drive. The administrator then removes the existing operating system and installs Windows 7 without deleting the migrated datastore. After the installation, LoadState loads the user state data onto the new operating system from the hard-link migration store.

Hard-link migration stores are explained in more depth in Chapter 5, "Migrating the Existing User Data." Instead of copying all the files needed for the migration, the `/hardlink` option creates a folder structure that points to the files on the hard drive. There are some restrictions as to when hard-link migrations can be used, but in general, if you're refreshing a computer you can perform a hard-link migration and this will improve the performance of the refresh. Even if you're not using hard links, you still want to store the migration data locally whenever possible.

FIGURE 3.3
PC refresh using a compressed migration store

ScanState captures data
LoadState restores data

Computer being refreshed

Migration store

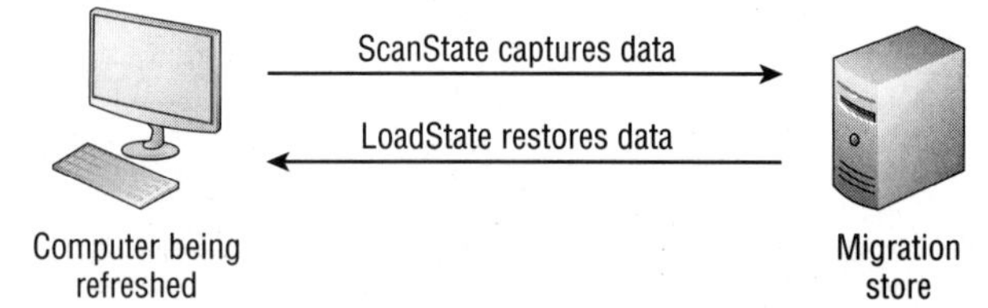

FIGURE 3.4
PC refresh using a hard-link migration store

Migration store

ScanState captures data
LoadState restores data

Computer being refreshed

Hard drive on computer being refreshed

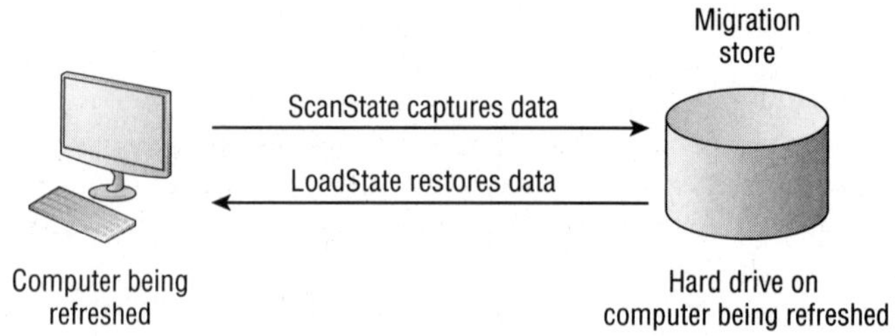

If you have enough hard drive space on the computer, you don't need to delete the existing installation. You can simply install Windows 7 as a clean install without modifying any of the hard drive partitions or volumes. Windows 7 will recognize that a previous installation of Windows exists on the system and will move key data to a folder named `Windows.old`. You can then use LoadState to restore the user state data to the new installation of Windows 7. Figure 3.5 shows this process.

FIGURE 3.5
PC refresh using
`Windows.old`

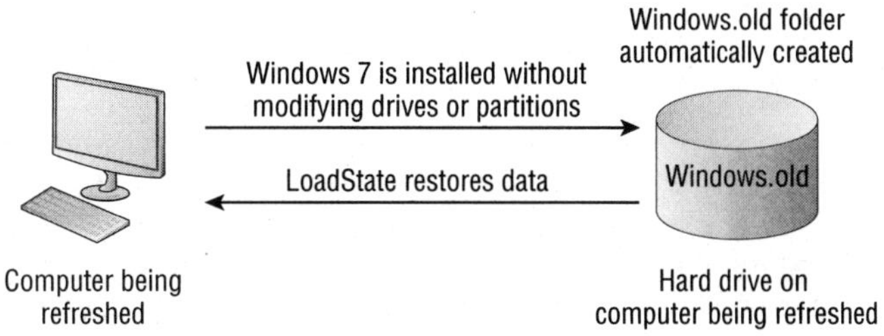

Windows 7 is installed without modifying drives or partitions

LoadState restores data

Windows.old folder automatically created

Windows.old

Computer being refreshed

Hard drive on computer being refreshed

Replacing Computers

Very often you'll replace computers in the organization and replace the operating system at the same time. In other words, users may be running Windows XP on their current systems, but they will receive a completely new computer with Windows 7 installed. However, users often want to preserve their user settings and data.

You can use USMT with ScanState and LoadState when replacing computers similar to how you can use it when refreshing computers. The primary difference is that you can't store the migration store on the existing computer. However, Figure 3.6 shows a common scenario you can use.

FIGURE 3.6
Migrating data
when replacing
computer

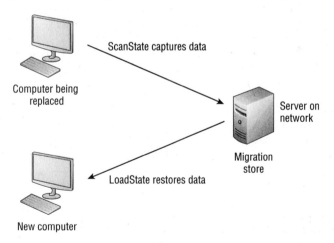

ScanState captures data

Computer being replaced

Server on network

Migration store

LoadState restores data

New computer

In this scenario, the administrator runs ScanState on the computer before replacing the computer. The migration store is stored on a server in the network. After the replacement, the administrator runs LoadState to restore the user's state data.

Windows Setup in Detail

Windows Setup uses several configuration passes to complete the installation. It may appear as though it's just one big installation, but the details have been segmented into these different passes. All of these passes are configurable using an answer file. The configuration passes are as follows:

windowsPE This configures the Windows preinstallation options and some basic Setup options. For example, you can partition a disk in this pass.

offlineServicing This pass can apply updates and packages such as software fixes and security updates.

generalize This pass is run only if an image has been prepared with the system preparation tool (Sysprep). Sysprep is run on a system prior to imaging it. It performs several cleanup actions, such as removing system-specific information like the computer name and security identifier (SID) to ensure the system can be imaged and deployed without any issues. Chapter 4 covers Sysprep in more detail.

specialize This pass creates and applies computer-specific information such as the computer name and the SID. You can configure the network settings, international settings, and domain information during this pass.

auditSystem This pass is used only if you boot into Audit mode after running Sysprep on a system. It processes the unattended setup settings that apply before a user logs on. It can be used for testing an image.

auditUser This pass is used only if you boot into Audit mode after running Sysprep on a system. It processes the unattended setup settings that apply after a user logs on. It is also used for testing an image.

oobeSystem This applies settings to Windows 7 before the Windows Welcome phase starts. It simulates the out-of-box experience (hence the oobe part of this pass's name) for the user.

Chapter 4 examines the Windows System Image Manager (WSIM), which is used to create an answer file. This answer file can include components for some of these passes. From a big-picture perspective, you'll see three phases of the installation:

◆ Preinstallation phase

◆ Online configuration phase

◆ Windows Welcome phase

Preinstallation Phase

In the preinstallation phase, the Windows Preinstallation Environment (Windows PE) is loaded. This basic Windows environment comes from the boot.wim Windows image file on the installation DVD. Several choices and options in this phase affect the installation.

The first choices are which language to install, the format of the time and currency, and the keyboard or input method, as shown in Figure 3.7.

You can press Shift+F10 at this point to access the command prompt. There are many advanced commands you can run from the command prompt that aren't available from the setup program. For example, you can use DiskPart to configure a VHD and install Windows 7 onto the VHD file.

The next screen is the Install Now screen. This screen also gives you access to the Repair Your Computer option in the lower-left corner, as shown in Figure 3.8. You can launch the Windows Recovery Environment (WinRE) by selecting Repair Your Computer.

FIGURE 3.7
Windows installation screen

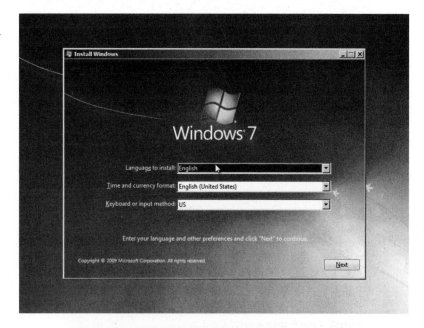

FIGURE 3.8
Windows 7 Install Now screen

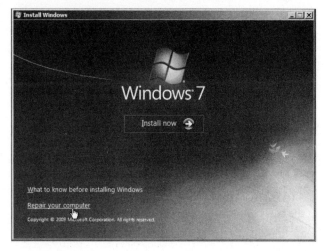

Next you'll see the Microsoft Software License Terms (formerly known as the end-user license agreement, or EULA). You must accept the license before you can continue. You'll then be given a choice between an upgrade or a custom installation. As mentioned previously, you can upgrade from only Windows Vista or Windows 7, and a custom installation is actually a clean installation.

Finally, you'll be given options to install additional drivers if necessary and configure the disks for the installation. You can partition disks as well as delete and format partitions using this screen. If you repartition any of the disks, you'll lose all the data on the partition. You should back up any data that you want before partitioning. Or you can wait to partition, expand, and shrink the disks after the installation if desired.

Ultimately, you'll need to pick a partition where Windows 7 will be installed. When you do so, Windows 7 will retrieve the image from the install.wim file located in the sources folder of the installation DVD.

Some installation DVDs include multiple images within the install.wim file, and some installation DVDs will include only one version. When there are multiple images, you are able to pick different editions of Windows 7 to install. However, the Windows product key is matched to a specific version. In other words, you can't purchase Windows 7 Home Premium and try to use that key to install Windows 7 Ultimate.

After the files are extracted from the install.wim file and copied onto the hard drive, the boot configuration data (BCD) store is created. The BCD store replaces the boot.ini file used in Windows XP and previous operating systems. It identifies which hard drive and which partition holds the Windows 7 operating system, and if multiple operating systems are installed on the same system, it includes details to provide users with choices. For example, you can configure a system to dual-boot between two versions of Windows 7, or between Windows 7 and another operating system. You can even configure a dual-boot system to boot between a regular installation of Windows 7 and an installation stored in a VHD file.

If you install Windows 7 with an answer file, you can include settings in the offlineServicing configuration pass that are applied during this phase.

Online Configuration Phase

The online configuration phase performs customization tasks for the system. This phase includes the Specialize pass.

You can configure installation programs to run during the configuration phase. In addition to typical applications, you can also configure scripts to run. You can use scripts to perform the configuration of the computer in any way desired. These scripts can be anything from basic batch files to more complex Visual Basic scripts.

Windows Welcome Phase

The last phase of the installation is the Windows Welcome phase. The user is prompted to enter a username, computer name, password, and product key. Additionally the user is prompted to choose how automatic updates will be completed and to identify the location of the computer. If you use an answer file, you can customize these Windows Welcome screens and messages.

Once the Welcome phase completes, the user sees the desktop. At this point, the installation is complete.

Performing the Windows 7 Installation

The best way to understand the installation steps is to install Windows 7. Even if you plan on automating the installation, you'll still need to create a reference computer with a clean installation if you want to modify the image.

For example, if you plan to create an image with several applications and preconfigured settings, you must first install Windows 7 on a computer, install the applications, and configure the settings. You can then capture this image and use it to deploy Windows 7 to the computers in your network. The only way you get around this step is if someone else is providing you with a preconfigured image.

 Real World Scenario

THE FEDERAL DESKTOP CORE CONFIGURATION

If you work in a U.S. federal agency, you may never have to install Windows 7. That's because the Office of Management and Budget (OMB) has mandated that all federal agencies running Windows must use a preconfigured Federal Desktop Core Configuration (FDCC) image.

This image was previously known as the Standard Desktop Configuration (SDC) used in the U.S. Air Force and then was fine-tuned and adopted for all federal agencies as the FDCC. It starts out in a known secure state and includes some core applications. By locking down a system and creating an image of the system in this secure state, the government is ensuring that new deployments start out secure.

Prior to adopting the FDCC, several agencies were repeating simple security errors by failing to take basic steps after installing Windows. The FDCC image has eliminated many of the basic security problems and helped the U.S. government raise its security posture. The FDCC does add a lot to security.

The FDCC was created by first installing Windows 7 just as you'll do in the steps in this chapter. Administrators then installed applications purchased for government use. Last, the administrators applied security settings. They ran Sysprep on this image to prepare it, and then the image was captured. Now, administrators in virtually any U.S. federal agency have this image available to deploy Windows.

Your organization may not use the FDCC, but you may want to create your own image. It starts with a clean installation. Future chapters show how you can create and deploy images developed from this installation.

Performing a Clean Installation

The following steps lead you through a clean installation of Windows 7 from the installation DVD:

1. Place the installation DVD into the system and restart it. The system will automatically load WinPE. You'll be presented with the first Windows 7 installation screen.

   At this point, you can access the command prompt by pressing Shift+F10. Using the command prompt can prove useful for advanced functions.

2. Select the appropriate language, time and currency format, and keyboard. Click Next.

3. The Install Now screen appears. Click Install Now. The Setup program starts.

4. After reviewing the license, select I Accept the License Terms and click Next.

5. You will be prompted to choose between an upgrade and a custom installation, as shown in Figure 3.9. Click Custom (Advanced).

6. The installation will take some time to complete and will automatically restart the computer. After the installation completes, you'll be prompted to provide a username and a computer name. Enter your first name in the Type A User Name text box. Note that when you do so, Windows will automatically create a computer name by appending -PC to your name. For example, if you enter `Darril` as the user name, it will create a computer name of `Darril-PC`. You can change the computer name if desired.

   You can use any letters, numbers, and the hyphen character for the computer name, but special characters are not allowed. It's best to keep it shorter than 16 characters so that it's compatible with NetBIOS names. After you enter a username and computer name, click Next.

7. You are prompted to enter a password, as shown in Figure 3.10. You can click Next without entering a password, but this isn't recommended. If you enter the password once, you also need to confirm it, as well as type in a password hint. Enter this information and click Next.

FIGURE 3.9
Choosing an
upgrade or new
installation

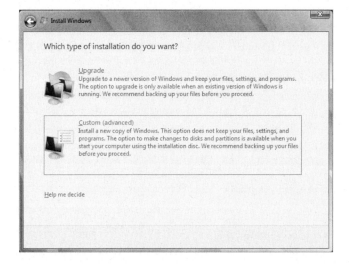

FIGURE 3.10
Prompt for
password and
password hint

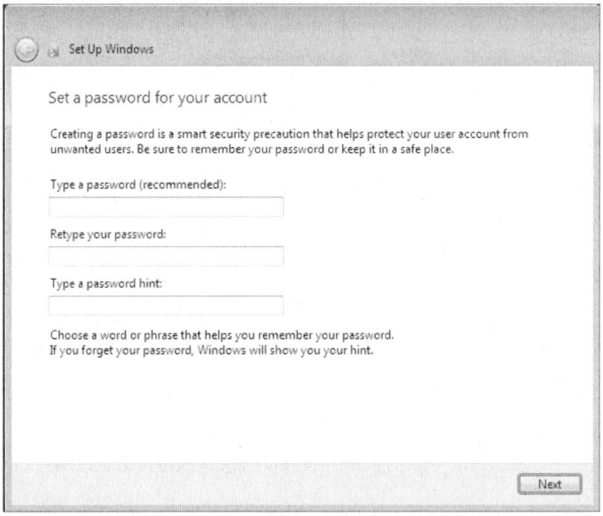

8. You are prompted to enter your Windows product key, as shown in Figure 3.11. The product key is provided with the installation DVD for retail versions. Organizations can use a multiple activation key (MAK) or Key Management System (KMS) server (see Chapter 13). Enter the appropriate key.

   Notice that Automatically Activate Windows When I'm Online is selected by default. Activation is explained in the next section. Click Next.

9. You are prompted to configure automatic updates, as shown in Figure 3.12. It's important to keep a system updated to ensure security vulnerabilities are patched, but you can choose something other than the recommend settings. Click your desired setting for Windows updates.

FIGURE 3.11
Entering the product key and enabling automatic activation

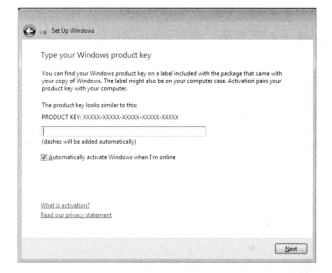

FIGURE 3.12
Configuring automatic updates

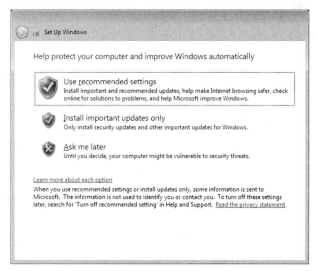

10. The Time Zone page will appear. Select your time zone from the drop-down box. You can also choose whether to automatically adjust the clock for daylight saving time. Finally, verify the date and time are correct and click Next.

11. If your computer has a network interface card (NIC) installed, you'll be prompted to enter the computer's current location. Select the location, and the Windows 7 desktop will appear. The installation will complete, prepare the desktop, and log you on with the username and password you provided.

That's it; Windows 7 is now installed.

Performing an In-Place Upgrade

There may be occasions when you want to perform an in-place upgrade to Windows 7. In other words, you have a compatible version of Windows Vista or Windows 7 and you want to perform an upgrade to Windows 7 on the same computer.

You should back up all important files on your system before the upgrade. While upgrades are usually seamless, if something does go drastically wrong, you'll still have your data if you've completed a backup first.

You can use the following steps to perform an upgrade:

1. Boot into your existing operating system and log on.

2. Place the installation DVD into the drive. If Autoplay doesn't start, use Windows Explorer to browse to the DVD drive. Double-click the `Setup.exe` program. If prompted by UAC, click Yes to continue.

3. When the Install Now screen appears, click Install Now. Setup will copy temporary files to your system.

4. You will be prompted to go online to get the last-minute updates for the installation. If you have access to the Internet, we recommend that you get these updates.

5. After you have retrieved and installed updates, you'll see the Microsoft Software License terms page. Review the license, select I Accept the License Terms, and click Next.

6. Click Upgrade. This will allow you to upgrade to a newer version of Windows and keep your files, settings, and programs.

7. You'll see the Upgrading Windows screen, shown in Figure 3.13. This process will take some time to complete and will automatically reboot your system several times. Even though the screen says the process may take several hours to complete, it won't take that long unless you're using a very, very old computer.

8. When the system completes, you'll be prompted to enter your product key. This screen also includes the Automatically Activate Windows When I'm Online check box. Enter your product key and click Next.

9. Next, you'll be prompted to configure automatic updates. Click on your selection to continue.

10. The Time Zone page will appear. Ensure the correct time zone, time, and date are selected and click Next.

11. You'll then see the logon screen for the same user account you used when you began the upgrade. Enter the user password and press Enter. After a moment, the desktop will appear, indicating the upgrade has completed. The `Windows.old` folder mentioned previously is not created when you upgrade the system. Since all of the user data and settings are migrated during the upgrade, you won't need this folder anyway.

FIGURE 3.13
Upgrading
Windows

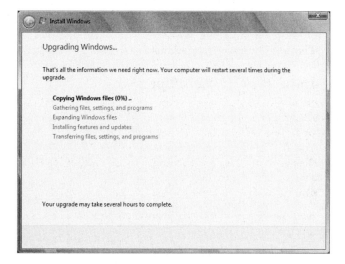

The Last Step: Licensing and Activation

It's estimated that over $40 billion is lost annually due to software piracy. Software development companies constantly try to identify ways to thwart the piracy of their software, whereas criminals try to identify ways to overcome the antipiracy techniques. It's a constant and ongoing battle.

Microsoft uses activation as an antipiracy measure. The goal is to reduce various forms of piracy, including casual copying. Casual copying occurs when one user copies the installation media and shares it with others in a way that violates the software license agreement.

Another form of piracy occurs when an illegitimate organization or individual copies the same licensed copy of Windows onto multiple computers that they sell. Some also package copies of Windows and sell them as retail versions. These copies are quite creative and come close to mimicking the actual product. Unsuspecting users may purchase a retail copy of Windows, or purchase a computer thinking they have purchased a fully functional computer with a valid operating system. Unfortunately, they find that the system won't activate since the product key has already been used.

If you use a valid copy of Windows, you can reuse the license on the same computer. For example, if the computer develops a problem and has to be rebuilt from scratch, you can still use the same license. However, if you install it on one PC and then you or someone else attempts to install it on another system, it will violate the license.

If the hardware on your computer changes substantially, the activation process may detect the change and force you to reactivate the computer. This prevents an image of an activated system from being deployed to multiple systems with the same key. The reactivation process is usually streamlined. However, there are occasions when the activation fails and you need to make a phone call to Microsoft to resolve it.

This section presents an overview on licensing and activation. Chapter 13 goes into much more depth on licensing, including the use of KMS and the Volume Activation Management Tool (VAMT).

Understanding Windows Activation

Activation is an antipiracy technology that verifies that Microsoft software products are genuine. It works by verifying the product key (the 25-key code) is authentic and hasn't been used by any more computers than permitted by the key. Some keys are multiple activation keys (MAKs) and are used by as many computers as specified by the license. Other keys are for only one computer. These single-use keys will not activate when used on any other computer after they have been used to activate a computer.

When you activate the system, the product key is combined with details on your system to create a unique installation ID. This installation ID is then submitted to Microsoft over the Internet or via phone. As long as the product key is valid, this activation process is seamless. The installation ID doesn't include any data that can be used to personally identify a user.

Windows 7 grants a 30-day grace period before activation is required. Four days after the installation, a daily pop-up reminds users to activate the system. These reminders will occur daily for 30 days. On day 31, the user will see a notification indicating that Windows must be activated to use all features. Additionally, several other changes occur reminding the user to activate. For example, the background changes to all black with text in the bottom right of the screen that says This Copy Of Windows Is Not Genuine.

Activating a New Computer

If the Automatically Activate Windows When I'm Online selection was selected during the installation, and the user has access to the Internet, activation will be automatic without any user intervention. If the user deselected this check box, a balloon reminder will periodically remind the user to activate Windows. Clicking on this balloon brings up the display shown in Figure 3.14.

You can also launch this screen from the command line by entering **slui** at the command prompt, or by clicking Activate Windows Now on the system properties page.

FIGURE 3.14
Activation screen

After activating a system or even when working on or troubleshooting a system, you may want to verify that the system has been activated. Figure 3.15 shows a system that has not been activated yet. You can view this screen by clicking Start, right-clicking Computer, and selecting Properties. You can compare this to Figure 3.16, which shows an activated computer.

If you installed Windows 7 without entering the product key, or the product key that you entered didn't successfully activate the client, you can enter or change the product key by clicking on the Change Product Key link in the computer properties screen. This screen allows you to enter or change the product key. However, you don't want to enter a different product key if your system has already been activated.

FIGURE 3.15
A Windows 7 system that hasn't been activated

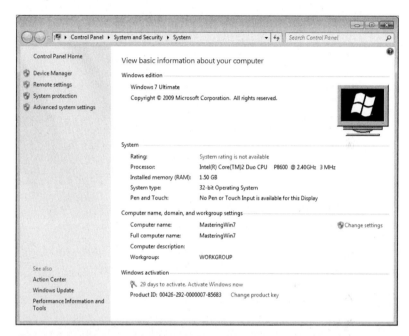

FIGURE 3.16
An activated Windows 7 system

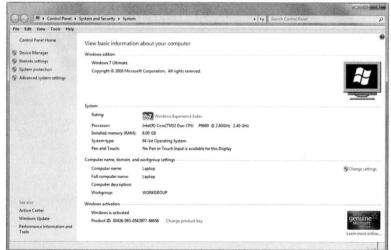

Notice that Figure 3.16 also has an icon for Genuine Microsoft software. This is part of the Microsoft Genuine Advantage program and is designed to help individuals determine if the copy of Windows they have is genuine and not a pirated copy. If the software you are running is not validated as genuine, you will not be able to access some downloads from Microsoft. For example, Microsoft Security Essentials, a free antimalware software program provided by Microsoft, cannot be downloaded, installed, or updated on a system if it hasn't been validated as genuine. If your system has passed the 30-day grace period without being activated, it will not be validated as genuine. However, once it's activated, it will pass the Genuine test.

If your system doesn't have access to the Internet, you can activate over the phone. This is an automated phone system. You'll be prompted to provide the 48 digits for the installation ID. The automated system will verify that the product key cryptographically embedded within the installation ID is valid, and you'll be provided with a confirmation ID. This confirmation ID will activate Windows 7.

Discovering the Four Types of Licenses

A Windows 7 product license includes the product key and is required to activate Windows 7. Microsoft currently has four different types of licenses for Windows 7, and each of them has different licensing terms. The four licenses are as follows:

◆ Retail

◆ Original Equipment Manufacturer (OEM)

◆ Multiple Access Key (MAK)

◆ Key Management Service (KMS)

The OEM and Retail licenses are each a single license purchased for a single computer. The MAK and KMS keys are used for multiple computers. Each of these is explained further in the following sections:

Retail   You can buy Windows 7 from retailers. It comes in a box and contains the installation DVD, a product key, a user's guide, access to product support, and the Microsoft Software License Terms. The retail version comes with a single product key and can be installed on only one system. Retail keys can be activated over the Internet or via the phone.

OEM   If you buy a computer with Windows 7 already installed, it comes with an original equipment manufacturer (OEM) license. For example, if you purchase a computer from HP or Dell, it will come with a Windows 7 version licensed to HP or Dell as the OEM.

The OEM license authorizes Windows 7 on that single computer but not any others. In other words, you can't transfer the Windows 7 license to another computer. OEM keys can be activated by the OEM or by the user over the Internet or via the phone.

MAK   Organizations that have enrolled in the Microsoft Software Assurance program can purchase a multiple activation key (MAK), which uses Microsoft Volume licensing. The MAK is simply a key used on multiple computers for one-time activation. Computers using a MAK can be activated over the Internet or via the phone. Additionally, Volume Licensing uses a new type of product activation called Volume Activation, which wasn't used in previous editions of Windows. You can track MAK keys using the Volume Activation Management Tool (VAMT); see the following section.

KMS   The Key Management Service (KMS) has become Microsoft's recommended method of activating a large number of clients within an internal organization. It enables local activation for an unlimited number of systems based on the KMS key. You can use it for clients that have Internet access, and also for clients in secure networks without Internet access where it isn't feasible to activate them via the phone.

Chapter 13 explores KMS in great detail, including the installation and configuration of a KMS server, and the management of activation using KMS.

THE VOLUME ACTIVATION MANAGEMENT TOOL

The Volume Activation Management Tool (VAMT) is used to manage MAKs, KMS keys, and retail product keys within a network. It can be used for activation tasks for Windows Vista, Windows 7, Windows Server 2008, and Windows Server 2008 R2. The following are some of the benefits of the VAMT:

◆ Protect product keys by retaining them only in the VAMT console instead of including a key in an image or distributing it in plain text.

◆ Perform activations internally without connecting to Microsoft activation services. These activations can be performed remotely.

◆ Inventory and monitor activation and licensing status of systems. You can use it to perform license compliance audits.

As of this writing, the current version of the VAMT is 2.0. You can download it for free by going to Microsoft's download site (`www.microsoft.com/downloads`) and entering **VAMT**. Chapter 13 presents more details on the VAMT.

SOFTWARE LICENSING MANAGEMENT TOOL

The Windows Software Licensing Management Tool is a command-line tool built into Windows 7 and other Windows operating systems. It is actually a Visual Basic script called `slmgr.vbs` located in the `%windir%\system32` folder. You can use it to check licensing details. For example, Figure 3.17 shows the result of the `slmgr /dlv` query executed at the command prompt. DLV is short for *display license verbose* and provides detailed information on the license. Chapter 13 offers more details on how to use `slmgr` for several tasks beyond just retrieving information on the license.

FIGURE 3.17
Licensing details for a Windows 7 installation

The Bottom Line

Choose the correct edition of Windows 7.   One of the primary tasks you'll have when considering Windows 7 is to determine what edition to purchase. Different editions have different capabilities, and if you purchase the wrong edition, you may not have the desired capabilities.

Master It   Your organization purchases licenses using Software Assurance contracts with Microsoft. Management wants to use the AppLocker capabilities of Windows 7. What edition should you select?

A. Windows 7 Business

B. Windows 7 Professional

C. Windows 7 Enterprise

D. Windows 7 Ultimate

Identify the correct method to install Windows 7.   There are some specific upgrade requirements that restrict your upgrade paths. However, tools are available that will assist with migrating data as long as you follow the procedures when installing Windows 7.

Master It   Your organization has Windows XP running on computers that will support Windows 7. You have purchased Windows 7 licenses and you want the computers to run Windows 7 when you're done. What should you do?

A. Perform a bare-metal install of the computers.

B. Perform an upgrade to Windows 7.

C. Replace the computers and use USMT.

D. Refresh the computers and use USMT.

Install Windows 7.   One of the basic deployment tasks of Windows 7 is performing an installation. While you may ultimately choose to create images and deploy the images, you still have to start with a basic reference computer.

Master It   Begin and complete an installation of Windows 7.

View the current activation status.   There may be times when you want to view the activation status of a system. You can use the slmgr command from the command prompt to view and manipulate the activation on any system.

Master It   Execute the command needed to view detailed activation information for a system.

Chapter 4

Cloning the Panther: Automating Windows 7 Installation

Images are an important topic to master when learning about Windows 7 deployment. All deployments of Windows 7 deploy images. The basic installation DVD includes images, and you can also use several tools to capture, manage, and deploy your own images in a production environment. Basic images include virtual hard drive (VHD) images, boot images, and install images. You can create a Windows 7 installation on a VHD image. Boot images boot into the Windows Preinstallation Environment (WinPE), and install images provide a fully functional installation of Windows 7.

This chapter shows you how to use the WinPE to create bootable media, add additional tools such as ImageX, and then capture an image. The Windows Automated Installation Kit (WAIK) provides you with several tools to capture, manage, and deploy images. You can use the Deployment Image Servicing and Management (DISM) tool to service these images offline by mounting the image and then adding drivers, packages, or features. The great strength of DISM is that you can service the image without deploying it to a computer. The WAIK also includes the Windows System Image Manager (WSIM), which you can use to create unattended answer files.

In this chapter, you will learn to:

◆ Create a dual-boot system using a VHD

◆ Prepare a system to be imaged

◆ Capture an image

◆ Modify an image offline

◆ Apply an image

◆ Create an unattended answer file

Getting Familiar with Microsoft Images

Installation of Windows changed quite a bit with Windows Vista, and Microsoft improved this imaging technology with Windows 7. Previously, you installed the operating system by copying individual files, often from the i386 folder of the installation disc. However, now the installation disc includes images in the form of a single file that you'll use for the installation of Windows 7.

Additionally, you can modify any installation of Windows 7 and create your own image. You can then use tools to deploy the images that you create. While this chapter focuses on using stand-alone tools such as the WAIK to install images, you'll see in later chapters that other tools use the same images. For example, Chapters 6, 7, and 8 cover Windows Deployment Services (WDS) that use the same types of images presented here. You can capture an image using the WAIK, and then copy it to the WDS server to deploy it to multiple systems using multicasting. You can also capture images with WDS.

Image Types: VHD and WIM

There are two overall types of images within Windows 7: virtual hard drive (VHD) images have a filename extension of `.vhd`, and Windows Imaging Format (WIM) images have an extension of `.wim`. You can boot to both VHD and WIM images.

A VHD image is a Windows 7 operating system with applications. You can create a VHD image when you begin an installation of Windows 7, install Windows 7 on the VHD, and then boot into VHD. Once the VHD is started, it works just like a normal installation. The section "Creating a Bootable VHD Image" later in this chapter shows you the process. Only the Windows 7 Enterprise and Ultimate editions support booting from VHDs. Although most features are available in a VHD image of Windows 7, there are some limitations. For example, a VHD image doesn't support BitLocker or dynamic disks.

The WIM images have two types: Windows preinstallation images (also called boot images) and operating system images (which include the full installation of Windows 7).

Preinstallation Images A preinstallation image boots into WinPE. This is a minimal Windows environment with limited services running. The installation DVD includes the `boot.wim` file that boots into WinPE. The section "Creating Bootable WinPE Media" later in this chapter shows you how to create your own customized WinPE. You can also create a Windows Recovery Environment (WinRE) bootable disc that extends the WinPE.

Operating System Images You can have either thin or thick operating system images. A thin image has only the operating system installed. The `install.wim` file on the installation DVD includes thin images of various editions of Windows 7. A thick image is a fully configured installation and has applications installed.

Creating a Bootable VHD Image

A VHD image is simply a VHD file that includes a fully functioning operating system. This is the same VHD image type used by Microsoft Virtual PC and Microsoft's Hyper-V virtual program (which is available on Server 2008 and Server 2008 R2). Windows 7 can also boot directly into a VHD file or use a VHD file as a dual-boot system. Because the VHD image is a single file, you can easily back up the entire operating system environment by copying the file. This approach has several benefits; you can:

Test application compatibility. You can install applications on the VHD image and test them for compatibility. If the application corrupts the operating system, you can simply shut it down, delete the corrupted VHD image, and copy your original VHD image back.

Create an isolated development environment. Application developers often need an isolated environment to develop, test, and debug applications. Bugs can sometimes affect the stability of the operating system. However, if an errant application corrupts the operating system, it can easily be restored by copying the original VHD image.

Test malware or other vulnerabilities.   Security professionals often need an isolated environment to test the effect of malware. It's not a good idea to do this in a live environment, but a system running on a virtual image can be isolated for testing.

VHD LIMITATIONS

While bootable VHDs have a lot of benefits, there are some limitations. First and foremost, you can create a bootable VHD with only Windows 7 Enterprise and Ultimate editions. Other Windows 7 editions don't support it. Other limitations include the following:

◆   BitLocker is not supported on Windows 7 VHD images.

◆   VHD images do not support hibernation.

◆   Bootable VHD images can't be compressed.

◆   The VHD can't be bigger than 2 TB.

◆   The VHD file must be located on an NTFS drive.

Follow these steps to create a bootable VHD image on an existing installation of Windows. (You can then install Windows 7 onto the VHD image using the steps in Chapter 3, "Installing Windows 7: Meet the Panther," for a clean installation. You'll end up with a dual-boot system that allows you to boot into Windows 7 normally or into the VHD file.)

1. Place the installation DVD into the system and restart it. The system will automatically load WinPE and you'll be presented with the first Windows 7 installation screen.

2. Press Shift+F10 to access the command prompt.

3. At the command prompt, enter **DiskPart** and press Enter. The DiskPart program will start and the prompt will change to DISKPART>.

4. Enter the following command to create a virtual disk file named `MasterWin7.vhd`:

    ```
    Create vdisk file = c:\MasterWin7.vhd maximum=40960 type=expandable
    ```

    The command creates a file about 2 MB in size, but it is dynamically expandable to 40 GB (40,960 MB). You can adjust the size based on your needs and available hard drive space. After the file is created you'll see a message indicating that DiskPart successfully created the virtual disk file. You can name the file something different but you must include the `.vhd` extension.

5. You can't manipulate the file until you select it, so select the virtual disk (vdisk) file with the following command:

    ```
    Select vdisk file=c:\MasterWin7.vhd
    ```

    If desired, you can view the selected disk by issuing the `List Vdisk` command. However, since the disk is not attached, it can't determine the type of the disk and it will be listed as Unknown.

6. Attach the vdisk file with the following command:

```
Attach vdisk
```

You can now view details on the vdisk with the `List Vdisk` command and it will show the file as Expandable.

7. Enter **List Disk** and press Enter. You'll see all your disks on the system. The 40 GB disk is listed with an asterisk (*) indicating it's selected; it has a status of Online, and it has 40 GB free.

8. Enter **Exit** to exit DiskPart.

9. Complete the Windows 7 installation. When prompted to select a disk, select the 40 GB disk you created with DiskPart to install Windows 7 on the VHD file. When you select the VHD disk file, the installation program presents a message telling you that "Windows cannot install to this disk." Don't believe it. It will.

Now you have a multiboot system. If desired, you can modify the boot configuration data (BCD) store to modify the boot options.

If you boot into Windows 7 normally, you'll see the file named `MasterWin7.vhd` at the root of C. If you want to use this image for any type of testing, first make a backup of this file. You can do so by simply copying the file. If future actions corrupt the file, you can copy the original back. Note that any data you store on this image will be lost if you haven't backed up the data somewhere else.

 Real World Scenario

CONVERTING A REGULAR INSTALLATION TO A VHD FILE

It's often valuable to convert a full operating installation into a VHD. Using the different VHD tools, you can easily create snapshots and roll back all changes to an installation, but this simply isn't possible with a regular installation.

For example, you may want to test the effect of an upgrade on a live system. You can create the VHD, apply the upgrade, and then perform testing. Once you've completed the testing, you can undo the changes to the VHD file to return it to the pre-upgrade status.

Mark Russinovich and Bryce Cogswell have written several utilities for Sysinternals, including one named Disk2vhd that you can use to create a VHD version of a physical disk. In other words, you can have a regular version of Windows 7 running and then use this tool to create a VHD file. You can then use the VHD file with Windows Virtual PC or Microsoft's Hyper-V virtual program.

You can read more about the free tool and download it from `http://technet.microsoft.com/ee656415.aspx`.

Of course, you can download many other valuable free Sysinternals tools. They are all available on Microsoft's site. For example, the Sysinternals utilities suite is available at `http://technet.microsoft.com/bb842062.aspx`.

Creating a Bootable WinPE Image

WinPE images are not intended to be a primary operating system. Instead, WinPE provides an interface for the user with enough access to the hardware to complete a full installation. You can boot to a WinPE image using a bootable CD, a USB flash drive, or a hard disk, or you can use a preboot execution environment (PXE) client to connect to a WDS server.

When you start the Windows 7 installation, Setup will load WinPE from the boot.wim file located in the \sources\ folder of the installation DVD. While the WinPE meets the needs of most users, you can customize it. For example, you can create your own bootable USB drive or CD and includes extra files like the ImageX utility to capture an image after booting to the WinRE.

Creating Operating System Images

Operating system images are also known as install images. They include a full operating system. A thin image (also called a basic image) is just the default operating system and nothing else. Thick images (also called custom images) include the operating system along with any customization and applications you may need.

A WIM file can hold multiple images. For example, install.wim on the installation DVD typically holds images for multiple editions of Windows 7. You can query the contents of an image file by issuing the following command at the WAIK Deployment Tools command prompt:

```
ImageX /info targetImageFile
```

The target is the location of the image file. For example, if your installation DVD is in the E: drive, the target location is e:\sources\install.wim and the command would look like this:

```
ImageX /info e:\sources\install.wim
```

Listing 4.1 shows a partial output from this query. We left all the details in for the first image (IMAGE INDEX="1") but included only the index number and name for the remaining four images.

LISTING 4.1   ImageX information included on the install.wim file

```
ImageX Tool for Windows
Copyright (C) Microsoft Corp. All rights reserved.
Version: 6.1.7600.16385

WIM Information:
----------------
Path:         e:\sources\install.wim
GUID:         {4db440bc-7222-4651-9192-1798c4b29bcb}
Image Count:  5
Compression:  LZX
Part Number:  1/1
Attributes:   0xc
              Integrity info
              Relative path junction

Available Image Choices:
```

```
------------------------
<WIM>
  <TOTALBYTES>2188572852</TOTALBYTES>
  <IMAGE INDEX="1">
    <DIRCOUNT>9044</DIRCOUNT>
    <FILECOUNT>45608</FILECOUNT>
    <TOTALBYTES>7936340784</TOTALBYTES>
    <CREATIONTIME>
      <HIGHPART>0x01CA0443</HIGHPART>
      <LOWPART>0x6568BDF8</LOWPART>
    </CREATIONTIME>
    <LASTMODIFICATIONTIME>
      <HIGHPART>0x01CA045F</HIGHPART>
      <LOWPART>0x905A47C2</LOWPART>
    </LASTMODIFICATIONTIME>
    <WINDOWS>
      <ARCH>0</ARCH>
      <PRODUCTNAME>Microsoftr Windowsr Operating System</PRODUCTNAME>
      <EDITIONID>Starter</EDITIONID>
      <INSTALLATIONTYPE>Client</INSTALLATIONTYPE>
      <HAL>acpiapic</HAL>
      <PRODUCTTYPE>WinNT</PRODUCTTYPE>
      <PRODUCTSUITE>Terminal Server</PRODUCTSUITE>
      <LANGUAGES>
        <LANGUAGE>en-US</LANGUAGE>
        <DEFAULT>en-US</DEFAULT>
      </LANGUAGES>
      <VERSION>
        <MAJOR>6</MAJOR>
        <MINOR>1</MINOR>
        <BUILD>7600</BUILD>
        <SPBUILD>16385</SPBUILD>
        <SPLEVEL>0</SPLEVEL>
      </VERSION>
      <SYSTEMROOT>WINDOWS</SYSTEMROOT>
    </WINDOWS>
    <NAME>Windows 7 STARTER</NAME>
    <DESCRIPTION>Windows 7 STARTER</DESCRIPTION>
    <FLAGS>Starter</FLAGS>
    <HARDLINKBYTES>3070770507</HARDLINKBYTES>
    <DISPLAYNAME>Windows 7 Starter</DISPLAYNAME>
    <DISPLAYDESCRIPTION>Windows 7 Starter</DISPLAYDESCRIPTION>
  </IMAGE>
  <IMAGE INDEX="2">
...
```

```
      <NAME>Windows 7 HOMEBASIC</NAME>
  ...
    </IMAGE>
    <IMAGE INDEX="3">
  ...
      <NAME>Windows 7 HOMEPREMIUM</NAME>
  ...
    </IMAGE>
    <IMAGE INDEX="4">
  ...
      <NAME>Windows 7 PROFESSIONAL</NAME>
  ...
    </IMAGE>
    <IMAGE INDEX="5">
  ...
      <NAME>Windows 7 ULTIMATE</NAME>
  ...
    </IMAGE>
  </WIM>
```

When working with images using either ImageX or DISM, you'll frequently need to know either the index number or the name. The index number is much easier to enter, but you may want to use the name to ensure you're working on the correct image.

While you probably won't have a need for an image file with multiple editions of Windows 7, you may want to create an image file with multiple versions of Windows 7 installations. For example, you can create one image that includes the software and configuration needed by sales people and name it **Windows 7 Sales**. You can create another image needed by personnel working in IT and name it **Windows 7 IT**.

A benefit of storing multiple images in a single WIM file is that the imaging format uses single file storage for efficiency. That way, if five images in a WIM file have an identical application named Notepad.exe, it is stored only once instead of five times.

Creating Your First Image

When imaging computers, you'll have different computers that you'll work with, as you can see in Figure 4.1.

You'll install tools such as the WAIK on the technician's computer, and you can then manipulate images and image files from that computer. The reference computer starts as a clean installation of Windows 7, and you make any configuration changes or add applications as desired. Once the reference computer is ready, you run Sysprep on the reference computer and capture the image. You can then deploy this image to the destination computers.

Because of a quirk, you need to consider the architecture of the target computers when choosing your technician's computer. Specifically, WSIM fails to create catalogs for an x86-based image if you run it from an x64-based computer. WSIM can create catalogs from both x86- and x64-based images on an x86-based computer, though.

FIGURE 4.1

Technician's, reference, and destination computers

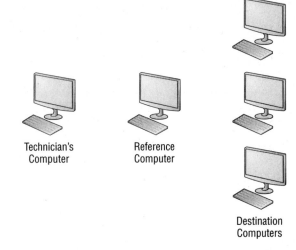

Technician's
Computer

Reference
Computer

Destination
Computers

Here are the high-level steps you'll take to manually capture an image:

1. Install the Windows Automated Installation Kit. You install it on a computer you're using for administrative purposes. In other words, don't install it on the computer you are imaging. The WAIK includes several tools you'll use during this process.

2. Create bootable media that includes ImageX. You can create either a bootable CD or bootable USB drive to boot into WinPE. You add the ImageX program before creating the bootable media so that it is available to you when you boot into WinPE.

3. Configure the reference computer. Install a clean installation of Windows 7 and configure it for your end users. You can configure any settings you want as well as install any applications you want your end users to have available to them when they receive the image.

4. Prepare the reference computer with Sysprep. The computer must be prepared with Sysprep. Sysprep will generalize any settings that must be generalized, such as the computer name, SID, and removal of the license key. Once Sysprep completes, the computer shuts down and should not be restarted normally until after the image is captured.

5. Boot to WinPE with your bootable media. Boot the reference computer to the WinPE. You can boot into the WinPE using multiple methods, including using bootable media you've created.

6. Capture the image with ImageX. After booting into WinPE, you can access the command prompt to capture the image using the ImageX command. You can then store the image on any media that will be accessible to the destination computers.

Using the Windows Automated Installation Kit

The Windows Automated Installation Kit (WAIK) is a group of tools you can use on the technician's computer to help with the deployment of Windows 7.

These tools include the following:

Deployment Tools Command Prompt   You can use this prompt to run commands such as dism, oscdimg, and imagex. When you launch it, the prompt temporarily modifies the path to include the path to these tools and starts in the C:\Program Files\Windows AIK\Tools\ PETools folder.

Windows System Image Manager   You can use this tool to create answer files. This tool is explored in the section "Using Windows System Image Manager" later in this chapter.

Documentation Folder   The Documentation folder includes access to several links. It includes a link to an HTML file that includes step-by-step instructions, links to three separate help files, and an additional folder named SDK (Software Deployment Kit) for software developers.

VAMT 1.2 Folder   This folder includes Volume Activation Management Tool (VAMT) version 1.2 help files and tools, which you can use for managing activation. You can also download VAMT version 2.0 as a separate download.

You can use these tools to capture or deploy an image, and perform offline maintenance of images. Offline maintenance means that you aren't booted into the operating system; instead, you are modifying the contents of the WIM file. You can use the WAIK tools to expand the contents of a WIM file into files and folders on the technician's computer. You can modify the files and folders as desired, and then restore them into the image.

The WAIK is available as a free download from Microsoft. You can get it by going to Microsoft's download site (www.microsoft.com/downloads/) and entering **WAIK** in the Search All Download Center text box. The Windows AIK for Windows 7 download (KB3AIK_EN.iso) file should be listed on the first page. It's about 1.7 GB in size so will take a little time to download even with a high-bandwidth connection.

After you download the ISO image, you can burn it to a DVD using Windows 7's built-in feature. Simply place a writable DVD into your DVD burner, right-click the ISO file, and select Burn Disc Image.

Once you have the DVD, you can use the following steps to install it:

1. Place the DVD into your DVD drive. If Autoplay doesn't start automatically, use Windows Explorer to browse to the drive and double-click StartCD.exe. If prompted by User Account Control (UAC), click Yes to continue. You'll see a screen similar to Figure 4.2.

2. Click Windows AIK Setup.

3. When the welcome page appears, click Next.

4. Review the license terms and select I Agree. Click Next.

5. Accept the default installation folder of C:\Program Files\Windows AIK\ and click Next.

6. On the Confirm Installation page, click Next to start the installation.

7. When installation completes, click Close.

8. Click Start ➢ All Programs ➢ Microsoft Windows AIK. You'll see all the WAIK tools within this Start menu folder.

FIGURE 4.2
Installing the
WAIK

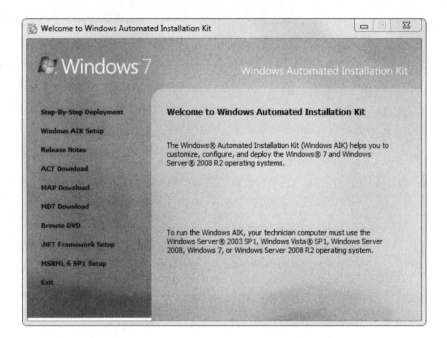

Creating Bootable WinPE Media

You can create your own bootable WinPE disc. You can then use this disc to boot to WinPE on any system to capture or deploy an image using ImageX. The following section includes steps you can use to create a bootable USB drive or bootable CD. These steps assume you have installed the WAIK on your system.

WinPE can be created for x86, AMD64, or IA64 systems. The commands are slightly different depending on which version you need. The x86 version is used for 32-bit systems, the AMD64 version is used for 64-bit versions (including Intel 64-bit systems), and the IA64 version is used for Itanium systems. You need to use the version based on the architecture of the target system. In other words, you could be creating the WinPE on a 32-bit technician's computer but plan on using the bootable media on a 64-bit target system, so you would use the commands to create the AMD64 version.

The two most common architectures are x86 and x64, so the following steps show the commands for each of these versions. The x86 procedure is provided first in each step.

1. Launch the Deployment Tools command prompt by clicking Start ➤ All Programs ➤ Microsoft Windows AIK ➤ Deployment Tools Command Prompt.

2. At the command prompt, enter the following command:

```
copype.cmd x86 c:\WinPE_x86
```

For a 64-bit version, use this command:

```
copype.cmd amd64 c:\WinPE_amd64
```

You can name the destination folder anything you want. It doesn't need to be named `WinPE_x86` or `WinPE_amd64`. This will copy several files and folders into the target folder.

3. Use the following command to copy the `winpe.wim` file into your WinPE folders as the `boot.wim` file:

```
copy c:\winpe_x86\winpe.wim c:\winpe_x86\ISO\sources\boot.wim
```

For a 64-bit target system, use the following command:

```
copy c:\winpe_amd64\winpe.wim c:\winpe_amd64\ISO\sources\boot.wim
```

4. Use the following command to copy the `ImageX.exe` file into your WinPE folders. Additional steps in the "Capturing an Image Using ImageX" section later in this chapter will show you how to use the ImageX tool to capture an image after booting into the WinPE.

```
copy "c:\program files\Windows AIK\Tools\x86\imagex.exe" c:\winpe_x86\iso\
```

For a 64-bit target system, use the following command:

```
copy "c:\program files\Windows AIK\Tools\amd64\imagex.exe"
```

```
c:\winpe_amd64\iso\
```

5. Create an `.iso` image with the `oscdimg` (operating system to CD image) command. The `-n` switch specifies that long filenames can be used. The `-b` switch specifies the location of the boot sector file (`etfsboot.com`), and there aren't any spaces between the `-b` switch and the location. The following command creates an `.iso` image in the `C:\winpe_x86\` folder from the contents of the `C:\winpe_x86\iso` folder:

```
oscdimg -n -bc:\winpe_x86\etfsboot.com c:\winpe_x86\ISO
c:\winpe_x86\winpe_x86.iso
```

For a 64-bit version, use the following command:

```
oscdimg -n -bc:\winpe_amd64\etfsboot.com c:\winpe_amd64\ISO
c:\winpe_amd64\winpe_amd64.iso
```

6. Place a blank CD into your CD-ROM burner. Launch Windows Explorer and browse to the folder holding the `.iso` image (`C:\WinPE_x86` or `C:\WinPE_amd64`). Right-click over the `.iso` file and select Burn Disc Image.

At this point, you have a bootable CD that you can use to boot a system to WinPE, and it includes the ImageX tool. Remember, if you plan to use this to deploy a 64-bit image, make sure that you use the 64-bit version.

With the size of USB flash drives constantly increasing while their prices decrease, you may want to create a bootable USB drive. You can do so by following these steps. Be careful, though: these steps will delete all the data on your USB flash drive, so make sure you copy all your data off the drive before starting. Additionally, these steps assume you've already created the WinPE image folders.

1. Insert a USB flash drive into your system.

2. Launch a command prompt with administrative permissions by clicking Start, typing **Command** in the Start Search text box, right-clicking over Command Prompt, and selecting Run As Administrator. If prompted by UAC, click Yes to continue.

3. At the command prompt, enter the following command to access the DiskPart tool:

   `DiskPart`

4. At the DiskPart prompt, enter the following command:

   `List Disk`

   You'll see an output similar to the following:

Disk ###	Status	Size	Free	Dyn	Gpt
Disk 0	Online	465 GB	1024 KB		
Disk 1	Online	298 GB	2048 KB		
Disk 2	Online	14 GB	0 B		

   Identify which disk is your flash drive. On our sample system, Disk 2 is our USB flash drive and it's listed as 14 GB, so we'll use Disk 2 in our examples in these steps.

5. Enter the following command at the DiskPart command prompt, ensuring you are using the number of your own USB drive:

   `Select Disk 2`

   The next step will delete all the data on your flash drive so ensure you have backed up any data you want to keep before continuing.

6. Use the following command to remove all the data on your disk.

   `Clean`

   You'll see a message that says DiskPart succeeded in cleaning the disk. At this point, the data on the flash drive is gone.

7. Enter the following command to create a primary partition on the drive:

   `Create Partition Primary`

   DiskPart will create it and display a message that DiskPart succeeded in creating the specified partition.

8. Enter the following command to select the partition you just created:

   `Select Partition 1`

   DiskPart will select it and display a message that Partition 1 is now the selected partition.

9. Mark the partition as Active with this command:

```
Active
```

DiskPart will display a message that DiskPart marked the current partition as active.

10. Format the partition with the following command:

```
Format quick FS=fat32
```

DiskPart will format the drive while displaying its progress. When it's done, it will display a message that DiskPart successfully formatted the volume. If desired, you can also format the partition with NTFS by using the command `Format quick FS=NTFS`.

11. Enter the following command to have your operating system assign a drive letter to the USB drive:

```
Assign
```

DiskPart will display a message that DiskPart successfully assigned the drive letter or mount point.

12. Exit DiskPart with the following command:

```
Exit
```

13. Use Windows Explorer to determine what drive letter was assigned to your USB flash drive. The following examples assume the drive letter is *x:* but you'll likely have a different drive letter assigned.

14. Copy the contents of the ISO folder created earlier onto the USB drive with the following command. Substitute the letter *x:* with the drive that was assigned to your flash drive and determined in the previous step. The /e switch copies all subdirectories, including empty ones:

```
xcopy c:\winpe_x86\iso\*.* /e x:\
```

That's it. At this point, you have a bootable USB drive. The great thing about a bootable USB drive is that if it is big enough, you can carry the image and the WinPE on the same flash drive. In other words, you use the flash drive to boot the system to WinPE and then deploy the image from the USB. You can also use this flash drive to capture an image you prepared with Sysprep, as you'll see in the section "Capturing an Image Using ImageX" later in this chapter.

Keep the following warning in mind: your system may not be configured to boot to a USB device, so you may need to modify the BIOS. The BIOS on some older systems doesn't support booting to BIOS, so you may have to flash the BIOS to get this capability.

Preparing a System with Sysprep

Before you can capture an image using any of Microsoft's tools, you must first prepare it by running the System Preparation Tool (Sysprep). The Sysprep tool is located in `C:\Windows\system32\sysprep`.

You cannot run Sysprep on a computer that has been upgraded from a previous operating system. You can only run it on clean installations that have been installed by choosing Custom during the installation process. If you try to run Sysprep on an upgraded system, it will refuse to run.

You launch Sysprep from the command line:

```
c:\windows\system32\sysprep\sysprep
```

You can also browse to the C:\Windows\system32\sysprep folder with Windows Explorer and double-click the Sysprep file. Figure 4.3 shows the Sysprep tool GUI with the typical selections used to prepare a system for imaging.

FIGURE 4.3

Sysprep tool

The Sysprep GUI includes two primary sections: System Cleanup Action and Shutdown Options. The available options in these sections are as follows:

Enter System Out-of-Box Experience (OOBE) This option causes the system to mimic the first boot screens you'll see when performing a normal installation. It starts by running the Windows Welcome program and initializes settings on the computer. You must select this option to prepare a computer for imaging.

Enter System Audit Mode Original equipment manufacturers (OEMs) use System Audit mode to bypass the Windows Welcome program and install additional programs and applications. Once the programs are installed, you run Sysprep again, selecting the OOBE choice. If you do not run Sysprep again, it will never enter the Windows Welcome phase but will instead continue to boot into System Audit mode.

Generalize The Generalize check box causes Sysprep to remove system-specific information from the computer. You must check this option to prepare a computer for imaging.

Quit This option quits Sysprep but doesn't shut down the computer.

Reboot This option reboots the system. It is useful with System Audit mode, but not when using the OOBE choice. If the Windows Welcome program starts before you've captured the image, you'll have to run Sysprep again.

Shutdown This option shuts down the computer and is the most common choice when running Sysprep to prepare the system for imaging. Once the system is shut down, you can use any available technique to capture the image, including using ImageX (described later in this chapter), or Windows Deployment Services (described in upcoming chapters).

You can also run Sysprep from an elevated command prompt (a command prompt run with administrative permissions). The following command mimics choosing Enter System Out-of-Box Experience (OOBE), Generalize, and Shutdown from the GUI:

```
C:\windows\system32\sysprep\sysprep /oobe /generalize /shutdown
```

Capturing an Image Using ImageX

After you've prepared your system with Sysprep, you can capture the system image using ImageX. You should have a bootable disc that includes the ImageX file. We covered the steps to do this in the section "Creating a Bootable WinPE Image" earlier.

IMAGEX IS NOT A BACKUP TOOL

You may be tempted to use ImageX to capture images of systems and use them as a system backup. However, it's not intended to be used this way and will result in inconsistent results. Microsoft's Knowledge Base article KB 935467 (http://support.microsoft.com/kb/935467) discusses some of the negative consequences of doing this on Windows Vista and the same issues apply with Windows 7. Additionally, using ImageX to back up systems may violate your software license agreement for Windows 7.

You use the ImageX /capture switch to capture an image. There are several options that are repeated with the /capture switch:

image_path   This is the path to the volume image to be captured. On a single-drive, single-partition system, this will be C:. If you have a dual-boot system with Windows XP on the C: drive and Windows 7 on the D: drive, then image_path will be the D: drive to capture the Windows 7 image.

image_file   This is the path to the new WIM file that will store the captured image. It includes the full path and image filename, and the folder specified in the path must exist or the capture will fail. You can name the file almost anything, but it must end with .wim.

image_name   This is the unique name for the image being captured that will be stored in the WIM file and needs to be in quotes. Later, you'll be able to use this name or the index number to identify the image within the WIM file.

image_description   This optional text provides additional information on the image. If it's included, it should be in quotes.

flags switch   Use the flags switch to specify which edition you are capturing. While it isn't needed if you're deploying the image with ImageX, it is necessary when you use other tools to deploy the image. The format is /flags "Enterprise", /flags "Professional", or /flags "Ultimate".

The basic syntax with these options looks like this:

```
Imagex /Capture /flags "Enterprise" image_path image_file

   "image_name" ["image_description"]
```

The drive you'll image is almost always the C: drive. However, in some instances where you have dual-boot systems, you may be imaging another drive. The folder where the image will be stored can be on any available system drive that has adequate space, including the drive that you're imaging.

As an example, the following command can be used to capture an image after booting into the WinPE:

```
Imagex /Capture /flags "Enterprise" c: D:\images\Win7.wim

 "Mastering Windows 7"
```

This command will capture the C: drive and store the image in the Win7.wim file in the pre-existing D:\Images folder with a name of Mastering Windows 7.

After you have prepared a Windows 7 system with Sysprep, you can use the following steps to capture an image of the system:

1. Boot using the WinPE media you created. But be careful: make sure that you boot to the WinPE media and not directly into the Windows 7 system. If the Welcome phase starts, you'll have to rerun Sysprep before you can capture the image.

   When the WinPE boots, it will run the wpeinit program and eventually you'll see a command prompt in the X:\Windows\System32 folder after wpeinit completes. In this case, X: is the actual drive and it represents a RAM disk created by the WinPE.

2. Enter the following two commands to create a folder named Images that will be used to store the image:

   ```
   C:
   Md Images:
   ```

3. Identify the drive letter of your bootable media. You can do this by entering the Dir command followed by a letter and a colon like this:

   ```
   Dir C:
   Dir D:
   Dir E:
   ```

   Continue doing this until you see a directory that includes the Image.exe command, and the Boot, EFI, and Sources folders.

4. Once you identify the drive holding the ImageX program, change to the drive by entering the letter and a colon. For example, on our system, the bootable media was the H: drive so we entered this command:

   ```
   H:
   ```

5. Enter the following ImageX command to capture the image of the C: drive, store it in the C:\images\win7.wim file, and name it Mastering Windows 7:

   ```
   Imagex /Capture c: C:\images\Win7.wim "Mastering Windows 7"
   ```

The display will show steady progress in the format of:

```
[ 50% ] Capturing progress: 7:40 mins remaining
```

When the process completes, you'll see a message indicating that the drive has been successfully imaged, with a total elapsed time. At this point, you'll have an image file created in the location you specified. You can reboot the system and complete the Welcome phase of Windows startup.

You can view the details of the image with the following command:

```
Imagex /info C:\images\Win7.wim
```

Applying an Image Using ImageX

You can use your bootable media with ImageX to apply a captured image to a stand-alone system. The image can be stored and applied from several different locations, including the following:

A USB Flash Drive   This includes the USB flash drive used to boot to WinPE. If the USB flash drive is large enough, this is the easiest method.

A Removable USB Hard Drive   On some systems, you may need to attach the hard drive after booting into WinPE, and on other systems, you may need to attach it before booting into WinPE.

A Drive on the Existing System   If the system has a preexisting operating system, you can copy the image file onto the system while booted into the operating system. The only drawback is ensuring that you have enough hard drive space to accept the image file and install Windows 7.

You use the Imagex /Apply command to apply an image. The /Apply command includes the following options:

image_file   This is the full path and filename of the WIM file containing the volume image.

image_number   This is the index number that identifies the image within the WIM file. You can use the Imagex /info command to identify the index number if your WIM file includes more than one image. If there is only one image in the file, it has an index number of 1.

image_name   Instead of the number, you can use the image name. If the name contains any spaces, it must be enclosed in quotes. The ImageX /info command also identifies the image name.

image_path   The path where the image will be applied. This is normally the C: drive but can be another partition for a dual-boot system.

The basic syntax with these options is as follows:

```
Imagex /apply image_file image_number or image_name imagepath
```

For example, if you have an image file named Win7.wim with a single image located in the D:\ Images path and you want to apply the image to the C: drive, you can use the following command:

```
Imagex /apply D:\images\win7.wim 1 c:
```

The following steps show how to apply an image using ImageX:

1. Boot using the WinPE media you created. When the WinPE boots, it will run the wpeinit program and eventually you'll see a command prompt in the *X:*\Windows\System32 folder after wpeinit completes. As a reminder, *X:* is the actual assigned drive and it represents a RAM disk created by the WinPE.

2. Identify the drive letter of your bootable media. You can do this by entering the `Dir` command followed by a letter like this:

   ```
   Dir C:
   Dir D:
   Dir E:
   ```

3. Once you identify the drive, change to the drive by entering the letter and a colon. For example, on our system, the bootable media was the H: drive, so we entered this command:

   ```
   H:
   ```

4. Enter the following ImageX command to apply the image:

   ```
   Imagex /apply H:\images\win7.wim 1 c:
   ```

   If your image is located somewhere else, you'll need to modify the path to the image instead of using `h:\images\win7.wim`. Additionally, if you have an image file with multiple images, you may need to use a different index number than the number 1, depending on which image you want to apply.

The display will show steady progress in the following format:

```
[ 26% ] Applying progress: 3:24 mins remaining
```

When the process completes, you can reboot the system and it will boot into the Windows 7 Welcome phase.

VIEWING THE CONTENTS OF AN IMAGE

If you want to view the contents of an image, you can use the `imagex /dir` command by specifying the path to the image and the image number, or image name. The output is extensive, so you may want to redirect it to a text file. You can issue the following command from the Deployment Tools command prompt to create a text file listing all the files and folders from the first image in the `C:\images\win7.wim` file:

```
Imagex /dir c:\images\win7.wim 1 > c:\images\win7.txt
```

Customizing Images Using Deployment Image Servicing and Management

The Deployment Image Servicing and Management (DISM) tool is included with the WAIK and can be used to perform offline maintenance of images. Offline maintenance means that you don't need to boot into the image to make changes, but can instead modify the contents of an image file that is stored within a WIM file. You can apply this modified image to a system with the changes.

For example, if you followed the previous procedures using ImageX to capture an image, you can now use DISM to modify the contents of the image without having to apply the image to a system and booting into the system. Additionally, you don't have to recapture the image. If you use DISM to open the image in read/write mode, you can save the changes with DISM.

The steps for modifying an image with DISM are as follows:

1. Mount the image using DISM. This expands the image into a folder on your hard drive. All the files and folders that are stored on the original hard drive of the captured image are accessible here.

2. Modify the image. You can do so using DISM. DISM allows you to add and remove drivers, packages, and features. Additionally, you can copy files and folders directly into the mounted image.

3. After completing the modifications, commit the image. This step rewrites the image file with your changes.

UPPERCASE OR LOWERCASE?

DISM is not case sensitive, but options are case sensitive. When entering DISM commands, you can usually enter them as all uppercase, all lowercase, or a combination of the two. It's common to show the documentation with initial caps for words, but this is just for readability. For example, the following three commands are interpreted the same by DISM:

```
DISM /Get-WimInfo /WimFile:C:\Images\Install.wim
dism /get-wiminfo /wimfile:c:\images\install.wim
DISM /GET-WIMINFO /WIMFILE:C:\IMAGES\INSTALL.WIM
```

However, there are some exceptions. For example, when working with features in an offline image, you need to use the exact case of the feature such as InboxGames, instead of inboxgames, or Solitaire instead of solitaire. If you don't follow the exact case of the feature, the command won't be recognized.

While this section covers many of the basic capabilities of DISM, there is much more you may want to dig into. You can open the Windows Automated Installation Kit (WAIK) Users Guide for Windows 7, which is installed when you install the WAIK, and take a look at the following help articles for additional information:

♦ Deployment Image Servicing and Management Command-Line Options

♦ Driver Servicing Command-Line Options

♦ Operating System Package Servicing Command-Line Options

The easiest way to locate these articles is to select the Search tab, enter the article title in the search text box, select the Search Titles check box in the lower-left corner, and click List Topics. Figure 4.4 shows this done for the Driver Servicing Command-Line Options article.

FIGURE 4.4
Viewing the WAIK
help file

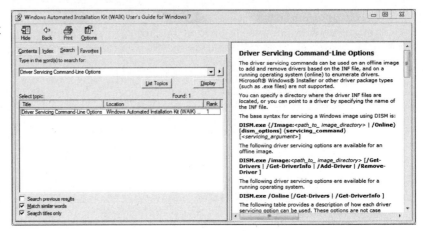

Viewing Information about an Image with DISM

When using DISM, you'll frequently use the /WimFile switch. This points to the image file with the full path in the following format:

    /WimFile:Drive:FullPath\ImageName.wim

For example, if an image file named install.wim is stored in the Images folder on the C: drive, it would take the following format. Notice that there are no spaces anywhere in this switch:

    /WimFile:C:\Images\Install.wim

The following example shows the /WimFile switch used with the /Get-WimInfo switch to retrieve information on an image file. In this example, the install.wim file from the \sources folder of the Windows 7 installation DVD is copied into the C:\Images folder.

```
DISM /Get-WimInfo /WimFile:C:\Images\Install.wim

Deployment Image Servicing and Management tool
Version: 6.1.7600.16385

Details for image : C:\Images\Install.wim

Index : 1
Name : Windows 7 STARTER
Description : Windows 7 STARTER
Size : 7,936,340,784 bytes

Index : 2
Name : Windows 7 HOMEBASIC
Description : Windows 7 HOMEBASIC
Size : 7,992,394,907 bytes

Index : 3
```

```
Name : Windows 7 HOMEPREMIUM
Description : Windows 7 HOMEPREMIUM
Size : 8,432,859,356 bytes

Index : 4
Name : Windows 7 PROFESSIONAL
Description : Windows 7 PROFESSIONAL
Size : 8,313,318,889 bytes

Index : 5
Name : Windows 7 ULTIMATE
Description : Windows 7 ULTIMATE
Size : 8,471,060,645 bytes

The operation completed successfully.
```

This output is a lot easier to digest than the ImageX XML output shown earlier. It's interesting to note that the queried `install.wim` file is about 2.2 GB when stored on a disk. However, it holds the contents of these five installation images, and each of the images will expand to about 8 GB.

All image files don't include multiple images. For example, if you captured the image using ImageX earlier, the `Win7.wim` file would have only one image with a name of Mastering Windows 7. If you copied that image to the `Images` folder on your computer, you could use the following command to view its details:

```
DISM /Get-WimInfo /WimFile:C:\Images\win7.wim

Deployment Image Servicing and Management tool
Version: 6.1.7600.16385

Details for image : C:\Images\win7.wim

Index : 1
Name : Mastering Windows 7
Description : <undefined>
Size : 9,759,693,132 bytes

The operation completed successfully.
```

Mounting an Image

The `/Get-WimInfo` is useful for viewing details about images in a WIM file, but it doesn't allow you to work with an image or view the actual contents. To work with the contents, you need to mount the image using the `/Mount-Wim` switch.

For example, you can use the following command to mount an image:

```
dism /mount-wim /wimfile:c:\images\win7.wim /index:1 /MountDir:C:\MountWin7

Deployment Image Servicing and Management tool
```

```
Version: 6.1.7600.16385

Mounting image
[=========================100.0%=========================]
The operation completed successfully.
```

This command uses the familiar /wimfile switch and also the /index and /MountDir switches. These switches, and some additional switches available with /Mount-wim, are explained in Table 4.1. Mounting an image will take some time but will show you progress as it expands the files. The directory where you'll mount the image must exist before you execute the command. You can create the directory using Windows Explorer or from the command prompt with this command:

```
md c:\MountWin7
```

TABLE 4.1:   DISM /Mount-Wim options

SWITCH	DESCRIPTION	EXAMPLE
/WimFile	Identifies the path of the image.wim file.	/WimFile:C:\Images\Install.wim
/Index	Identifies the image index number of the image to mount.	/WimFile:C:\Images\Install.wim /index:1
/Name:	Identifies the image with the name instead of the index number. If there are spaces in the name, it must be enclosed in quotes.	/WimFile:C:\Images\Install.wim /name:"Windows 7 Ultimate"
/MountDir	Identifies the location where the image file will be mounted and expanded as individual files.	/MountDir:Path
./ReadOnly	Specifies that the image will be in read-only mode and can't be committed. If not used, the command can be committed.	/ReadOnly

After you mount the image, you can use Windows Explorer to view the contents of the image. Figure 4.5 shows the mounted image from the earlier example.

At this point, you can copy any files you want to the mounted image. Additionally, you can use DISM to service drivers and applications on the image.

Servicing Drivers in an Image

DISM includes several commands you can use to view, add, and remove drivers within an image. These drivers must use the INF file format. Unfortunately, drivers that are installed as executable files are not supported using these methods.

You can use the following command to view any third-party drivers that are already included in an image:

```
dism /image:c:\MountWin7 /get-drivers

Deployment Image Servicing and Management tool
Version: 6.1.7600.16385


Image Version: 6.1.7600.16385


Obtaining list of 3rd party drivers from the driver store...


Driver packages listing:


Published Name : oem0.inf
Original File Name : prnms001.inf
Inbox : No
Class Name : Printer
Provider Name : Microsoft
Date : 6/21/2006
Version : 6.1.7600.16385


The operation completed successfully.
```

FIGURE 4.5
Viewing the
mounted image

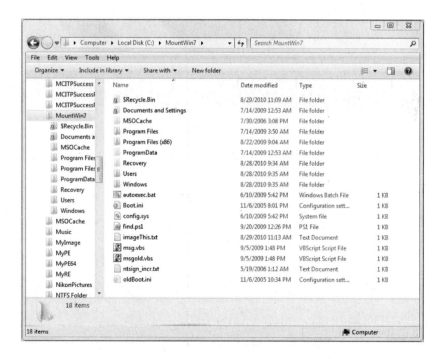

Table 4.2 shows several other available DISM commands.

TABLE 4.2: DISM driver-servicing command-line options

SWITCH	DESCRIPTION	EXAMPLE
`/Get-DriverInfo`	Displays detailed information about a specific driver package. The package is specified using the Published Name obtained from the `/get-drivers` command.	`dism /image:c:\mountwin7 /get-driverinfo /driver:oem0.inf`
`/Add-Driver`	Adds a third-party driver package to an offline image. The example shows how to add a driver package that has been copied to a folder named `Display`. DISM scans the folder and installs all the drivers in the folder.	`dism /image:c:\mountwin7 /add-driver /driver:c:\display`
`/Remove-Driver`	Removes a third-party driver from an offline image. You can use the Published Name of the driver displayed with `/Get-Drivers`.	`dism /image:c:\mountwin7 /remove-driver /driver:oem9.inf`

Servicing the Operating System in an Image

You can add and remove features and packages from an image. Packages come as cabinet (`.cab`) files or Microsoft Windows Update Standalone Installer (`.msu`) files. Table 4.3 shows common commands you can use to work on packages and features with an offline image.

TABLE 4.3: DISM operating system command-line options

SWITCH	DESCRIPTION	EXAMPLE
`/Get-Packages`	Displays information about installed packages.	`dism /image:c:\mountwin7 /get-packages`
`/Get-PackageInfo`	Displays detailed information on a specific package. You can identify the package using the Package Identity label displayed with the `/Get-Packages` command.	`dism /image:c:\mountwin7 /get-packageinfo /PackageName:<package identity>` `dism /image:c:\mountwin7 /get-packageinfo /PackageName:Microsoft-Windows-LocalPack-ZA-Package~31bf3856ad364e35~x86~~6.1.7600.16385`

TABLE 4.3:   DISM operating system command-line options   *(CONTINUED)*

SWITCH	DESCRIPTION	EXAMPLE
/Add-Package	Adds a package to the offline image. You can use this switch to add any CAB or MSU file to the image. The example adds the KB 958559 package to install Windows Virtual PC used for Windows XP Mode.	`dism /image:c:\mountwin7 /add-package PackagePath:<package path>~LBdism /image:c:\ mountwin7 /add-package /PackagePath:C:\pkg\ windows6.1-kb958559-x86.msu`
/Remove-Package	Removes installed cabinet (.cab) packages. Updates (.msu packages) can't be removed this way. You can identify the package using the Package Identity displayed with the /Get-Packages command.	`dism /image:c:\mountwin7 /remove-package PackageName:<package identity>~LBdism / image:c:\mountwin7 /remove-package / PackageName:Microsoft-Windows-LocalPack-ZA- Package~31bf3856ad364e35~x86~~6.1.7600.16385`

When you boot into Windows 7, you can enable and disable installed features via the Control Panel. Figure 4.6 shows the Windows Features dialog box. You can access this by selecting Control Panel ➢ Programs ➢ Turn Windows Features On Or Off.

You can also manipulate these features in an offline image using DISM. Table 4.4 shows some of the available commands. This is one of the few times when using uppercase and lowercase matters at the command prompt. Specifically, the features must be entered exactly as shown in the /Get-Features output.

TABLE 4.4:   DISM features' command-line options

SWITCH	DESCRIPTION	EXAMPLE
/Get-Features	Displays a list of available features within the image. It also shows whether the feature is enabled or disabled.	`dism /image:c:\mountwin7 / get-features`
/Get-FeatureInfo	Provides detailed information on a feature. Note that features must be entered using exact case as shown in the /Get-Features output. If you enter **Chess** as **chess**, it will not be recognized.	`dism /image:c:\mountwin7 /get-featureinfo / featurename:Chess`

TABLE 4.4: DISM features' command-line options *(CONTINUED)*

SWITCH	DESCRIPTION	EXAMPLE
/Enable-Feature	Enables a feature using the feature name. The feature name must be entered using exact case as shown in the /Get-Features output.	`dism /image:c:\mountwin7 /enable-feature / featurename:Chess`
/Disable-Feature	Disables a feature using the feature name. The feature name must be entered using exact case as shown in the /Get-Features output.	`dism /image:c:\mountwin7 /disable-feature / featurename:Chess`

FIGURE 4.6
Turning Windows
features on or off

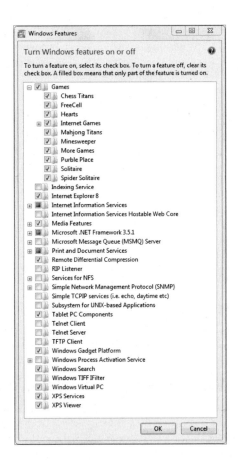

Committing an Image

Committing an image applies all the changes you've made to the mounted image to the original WIM file. For example, if you mounted an image from the `win7.wim` file into the `C:\mountwin7` folder, you can use the following command to commit the changes:

```
dism /unmount-wim /Mountdir:c:\MountWin7 /commit
Deployment Image Servicing and Management tool
Version: 6.1.7600.16385

Saving image
[=========================100.0%=========================]
Unmounting image
[=========================100.0%=========================]
The operation completed successfully.
```

The `/unmount` switch also removes the files within the mounted folder. In other words, if the image was mounted to the `C:\MountWin7` folder, after unmounting it all of the files within this folder will be deleted. If you decide you don't want to save the changes, you can unmount the image with the `/discard` switch instead of the `/commit` switch as follows:

```
dism /unmount-wim /Mountdir:c:\MountWin7 /discard
```

DISM will not dedicate system resources to unmounted images. However, if you don't unmount an image, DISM continues to track the image even through reboots of your system. It's best to unmount the image when you're done with it. You can verify that you don't have any mounted images with the following command:

```
dism /get-mountedwiminfo

Deployment Image Servicing and Management tool
Version: 6.1.7600.16385

Mounted images:

No mounted images found.

The operation completed successfully.
```

Ideally, it will show *No mounted images found*. If it identifies mounted images you aren't working with, you should investigate them and unmount them if they aren't needed.

Using Windows System Image Manager

The Windows System Image Manager (WSIM) is installed when you install the WAIK. You can access it by clicking Start ➢ All Programs ➢ Microsoft Windows AIK ➢ Windows System Image Manager. You can use WSIM to create unattended Windows Setup answer files to automate the installation of Windows 7. Instead of a user answering the questions for an installation, the answer file can provide all the information. Additionally, you can modify the default behavior of the installation with an answer file.

WSIM comes in both x86 and x64 (32-bit and 64-bit) versions. It's important to use the version that matches the image of your reference computer. For example, if you try to use the x64 version to create a catalog for an x86-based image, it will fail. However, you can use the x86 version to create catalogs for both x86- and x64-based images.

Exploring the Panes: An Overview of WSIM

When you first open WSIM, it has almost nothing in it. However, once you start creating an answer file, the different panes of WSIM start displaying some important information. Figure 4.7 shows WSIM with an image opened and an answer file started. In the figure, you can see the various panes of WSIM:

FIGURE 4.7
The WSIM panes

Distribution Share A distribution share is a set of folders that contain files you can use to customize the Windows installation. This can be a local folder that includes items that will be installed after the installation, or a network share available to the system after the installation. Windows Setup will use the path defined here to install additional applications and drivers. When you create the distribution share, it creates the three folders shown in the Distribution Share pane.

Windows Image The Windows Image pane shows the selected image and available components and packages that can be defined for the image. The figure shows an image named Windows 7 ULTIMATE added with the available components. As you can see, many components can be added. You can add components to the answer file by right-clicking them and selecting Add Setting. Different settings are added to different passes of the installation. You can add packages by right-clicking them and selecting Add To Answer File. Instead of selecting an image here, you can select a catalog file for the image if one exists.

Answer File This pane shows the answer file as you're building it. This pane starts empty, but as you add components and packages from the Windows Image section, it becomes populated. In the figure, only one component has been added: x86_Microsoft-Windows-Setup_ neutral. This has two sections: UserData (selected) and ProductKey.

Selected Components' Properties and Settings When you select a component in the Answer File pane, the available properties and settings for the component appear. You can then configure the settings as desired. For example, the AcceptEula setting has been configured with a value of True and an organization name has been added. Some properties have specific data types you can select (such as true or false) whereas other properties allow you to enter the data as free text.

Messages The Messages pane includes different messages for you while working with an answer file. For example, if you select Tools ➢ Validate Answer File, it will check for any issues. In the figure, the validation has identified that the ProductKey setting doesn't have a value and the message indicates this will be not be added to the answer file.

Understanding Catalog Files

A catalog file (.clg) is a binary file that contains the state of all the components and packages within a Windows image. If you look back at Figure 4.7, you'll see that the Windows Image pane has been expanded to show the available components for the image, and one of the components has been added to the answer file. This list is derived from the catalog file.

Figure 4.8 shows an answer file with the available packages expanded. You can right-click any of the packages and select Add To Answer File. After adding the package, you can select package components, and configure their properties. and settings sections of the answer file.

FIGURE 4.8
Viewing packages
in an image file

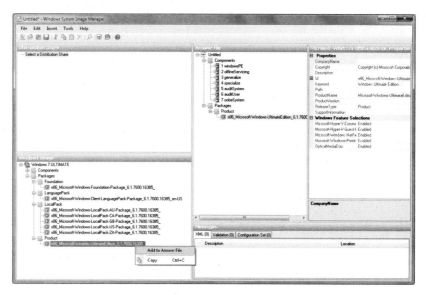

The installation DVD includes separate catalog files for each image within the `install.wim` file in the sources folder. If you're using a default image, you can simply copy one of these catalog files to your technician's computer when you copy the `install.wim` file. Alternately, you can use WSIM to create a catalog file. WSIM queries the image and creates a list of the settings in the image to create the catalog. If you update the image, you need to re-create the catalog file. For example, if you use DISM to add or remove packages, the catalog file needs to be updated to reflect these changes.

When you open an image in WSIM, it looks for the catalog file for the image. If it can't locate the catalog file, it will prompt to you create one. If you launched WSIM with administrative permissions, you can simply click Yes and it will create the catalog file.

Be careful, though. There are several known reasons why the catalog file creation will fail, including the following:

When the WIM File Is Read-Only or in a Read-Only Location   The location includes the installation DVD. You need to copy the image file to your hard drive.

When You're Trying to Create an x86 Catalog from an x86 Image on an x64 Technician's Computer   If the WAIK is installed on an x86 technician's computer, the x86 version of WSIM will run and you can use it to create both x86- and x64-based catalogs. The help file indicates that you can use the x86 WSIM to get around this problem, but it isn't available if you installed the WAIK on an x64 computer.

When You're Using It for a Nonsupported Version   For example, you cannot create a catalog file for Windows Vista RTM version.

Exploring the Components of an Answer File

The answer file has several components based on seven configurable passes of an installation. Chapter 3 presented the seven passes and they directly relate to these different components of an answer file:

◆ `windowsPE`

◆ `offlineServicing`

◆ `generalize`

◆ `specialize`

◆ `auditSystem`

◆ `auditUser`

◆ `oobeSystem`

You can look at sample unattended XML files if you've installed the WAIK. Several sample files are stored in the `C:\Program Files\Windows AIK\Samples` folder. You will need to add the `UserData/ProductKey/Key` information into the answer file or enter it manually during the installation. These files are architecture specific; in other words, some answer files are for x86-based systems and others for 64-bit systems. The section "Viewing Sample Answer Files" later in this chapter shows how you can open these files in WSIM.

Pass 1: windowsPE

Pass 1 includes many of the basic Windows preinstallation options as well as some basic setup options. Figure 4.9 shows the Setup section expanded to show many of the available options that can be added to the answer file. If you right-click over any of the items, the context menu appears.

FIGURE 4.9
Adding compo-
nents to Pass 1

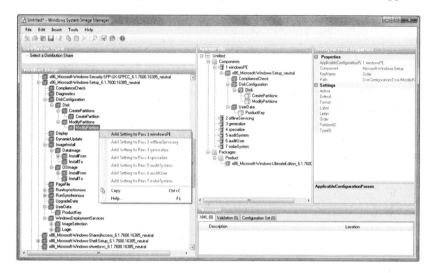

In the figure, the `ModifyPartition` component is selected, and it shows that the setting can be added to Pass 1. Most items can be added to only a single pass, but some items can be added to different passes. For example, the `ExtendOSPartition` item available in the Windows Deployment section (not shown in the figure) can be added to Pass 3, 4, 5, or 7. The good news is that you don't have to remember which passes are available for each item. WSIM only allows you to choose valid selections; invalid selections are dimmed.

Pass 2: offlineServicing

You can use the `offlineServicing` service to apply updates, drivers, or language packs to a Windows image. Any settings in the offlineServicing section of the answer file are applied after the Windows image is applied to the hard disk and before the computer reboots. This allows you to install and process any third-party device drivers you may need for special devices. There aren't many components and settings available for this section of the answer file. For example, if you have drivers that need to be available before the image is applied, you can add the `Microsoft-Windows-PnpCustomizationNonWinPE` component. You can then add the path to device drivers to this component.

Pass 3: generalize

You run the `generalize` pass only if you prepared your image with Sysprep. During this pass, the system-specific information (such as the SID and other hardware-specific settings) on the computer is removed. Even when the `generalize` pass is run, there aren't many additional settings that are commonly added to this pass. The most common setting is shown in Figure 4.10.

However, if you have any third-party drivers that are included in the image and you want them to be included in the final image, there is an important setting you must add. Figure 4.10 shows the PnpSysprep component being added. It is added to the Pass 3 generalize answer file section.

FIGURE 4.10
Adding components to Pass 3

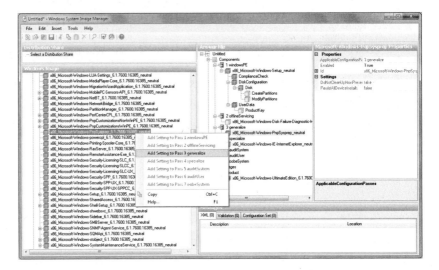

The PersistAllDeviceInstalls value can be changed from false to true to keep these third-party drivers. When you change the value to true, all the unique device drivers for a system are not removed from the installation image.

PASS 4: SPECIALIZE

This pass creates and applies computer-specific information. It runs after the first boot and creates the SID for the computer. You can configure a wide variety of settings during this pass, such as network settings, additional Windows features, and domain information.

Figure 4.11 shows a couple of the settings added to this pass. In the figure, the Internet Explorer settings are shown being added in the Windows Image components. The figure also shows some the settings available for Internet Explorer in the Answer File and Properties sections. The UnattendedJoin component, which allows you to specify details for joining a domain, has been added, along with the Windows-Defender component.

You can also configure network settings and international settings during this pass.

PASS 5: AUDITSYSTEM

Pass 5 is used only when a system is configured to boot to Audit mode from Sysprep. The auditSystem pass can be modified to add additional configurations to an image, such as adding third-party drivers by an OEM, but you may not use it in an organization.

PASS 6: AUDITUSER

Similar to Pass 5, the `auditUser` pass is used only if you boot into Audit mode after running Sysprep on a system. You can use this pass to run custom commands or configure Windows Shell options, but you may not use it for typical unattended installations.

PASS 7: OOBESYSTEM

The last pass applies settings to Windows before the Windows Welcome phase begins. You can use this pass to modify Registry settings, create user accounts, and specify language and locale settings. It also includes many settings used by OEMs. Figure 4.12 shows some of the settings added to this pass.

FIGURE 4.11
Adding compo-
nents to Pass 4

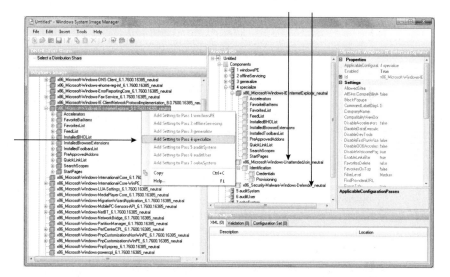

FIGURE 4.12
Adding compo-
nents to Pass 7

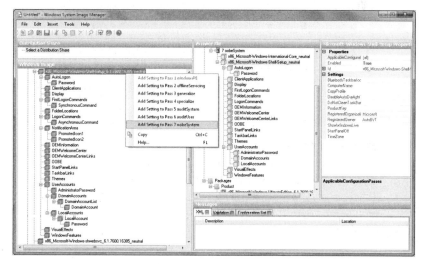

The `Windows-Shell-Setup` component includes several settings that you can add to modify the initial setup of Windows for your end users. Notice that the Windows-Shell-Setup section includes settings that can be added to all the passes except for Pass 1. You can also see that you have many different settings you can add in this section.

Creating an Unattended Answer File

This section shows you how to create an unattended answer file on a technician's computer that can be used for unattended installation. These steps are divided into five major areas:

- ◆ Adding an image to WSIM
- ◆ Adding components to the answer file
- ◆ Configuring the components in the answer file
- ◆ Testing and saving the answer file
- ◆ Viewing sample answer files

The following steps show how to create an unattended answer file on a technician's computer that can be used to boot a system into the Sysprep Audit mode without user invention. They require a copy of a WIM file on the computer's hard drive. If desired, you can copy the `install` `.wim` file from the sources folder of the installation DVD onto the hard drive or copy an image that you have captured. You can also copy the associated CLG file so that WSIM doesn't have to re-create it since this process can take quite a while.

Adding an Image to WSIM

The first step is to add an image to WSIM. These steps assume you have copied an image file onto your system's hard drive. The available components reflect what is available in the image.

1. Launch WSIM with administrative permissions by clicking Start ➤ All Programs ➤ Microsoft Windows AIK, right-clicking Windows System Image Manager, and selecting Run As Administrator.

2. Select File ➤ Select Windows Image. Browse to the location of the WIM file you want to use. Select the file and click Open. If the file has multiple images, you'll be given a choice similar to Figure 4.13. Select the desired image and click OK.

FIGURE 4.13
Selecting an image
in WSIM

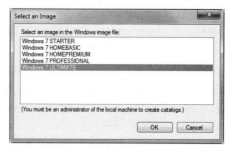

3. If you didn't copy a catalog file with the image, you'll see a prompt indicating that a catalog file isn't available. A prompt similar to Figure 4.14 will appear, prompting you to create one. Click Yes to create the catalog file. Remember that this process will fail if you're running WSIM on a 64-bit computer but trying to create a catalog for an x86 image.

4. Select File ➢ New Answer File. You'll see the Windows Image pane become populated with components. You can add these components to your answer file.

FIGURE 4.14

Prompt to create a catalog file

At this point, you have the shell of your answer file, but it doesn't have any content. Next you'll learn how to add components to the answer file and configure settings.

ADDING COMPONENTS TO THE ANSWER FILE

Once you have created the shell of your answer file, you can begin to add components. The following steps lead you through the process of adding components for basic disk configuration and Windows Welcome settings:

1. Expand the Components section in the Windows Image pane of WSIM.

2. Browse to the `Microsoft-Windows-Deployment\Reseal` component. Right-click it and select Add Setting To Pass 7 oobeSystem.

3. Browse to the `Microsoft-Windows-International-Core-WinPE\SetupUILanguage` component. Right-click it and select Add Setting To Pass 1 windowsPE.

4. Use the following steps to add settings to create the first partition:

    A. Browse to the `Microsoft-Windows-Setup\DiskConfiguration\Disk\CreatePartitions\CreatePartition` component. Right-click it and select Add Setting To Pass 1 windowsPE.

    B. Browse to the `Microsoft-Windows-Setup\DiskConfiguration\Disk\ModifyPartitions\ModifyPartition` component. Right-click it and select Add Setting To Pass 1 windowsPE.

5. Use the following steps to add settings to create a second partition:

    A. Browse to the `Microsoft-Windows-Setup\DiskConfiguration\Disk\CreatePartitions\CreatePartition` component. Right-click it and select Add Setting To Pass 1 windowsPE.

    B. Browse to the `Microsoft-Windows-Setup\DiskConfiguration\Disk\ModifyPartitions\ModifyPartition` component. Right-click it and select Add Setting To Pass 1 windowsPE.

6. Browse to the `Microsoft-Windows-Setup\ImageInstall\OSImage\InstallTo` component. Right-click it and select Add Setting To Pass 1 windowsPE.

7. Browse to the `Microsoft-Windows-Setup\UserData` component. Right-click it and select Add Setting To Pass 1 windowsPE.

8. Browse to the `Microsoft-Windows-Shell-Setup\OOBE` component. Right-click it and select Add Setting To Pass 7 oobeSystem.

At this point, the minimal components are added to the answer file and your display will look similar to Figure 4.15.

FIGURE 4.15
Answer file
in WSIM

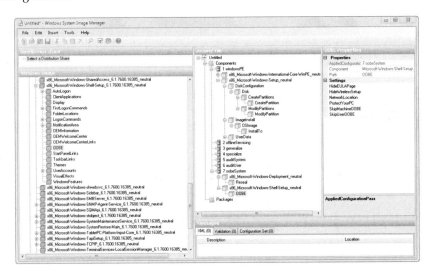

The next section shows how to configure the properties of the components that you have added to the answer file.

CONFIGURING THE COMPONENTS IN THE ANSWER FILE

You can use the following steps to configure the properties of the components of an answer file. These steps assume you have added the components to the answer file in the previous section.

1. If necessary, expand the 1 windowsPE section in the Answer File pane.

2. Select the `Windows-International-Core` component. Enter the following values in the settings section:

   InputLocale: `en-US`

   SystemLocale: `en-US`

   UILanguage: `en-US`

   UserLocale: `en-US`

3. Select SetupUILanguage within the Windows-International-Core component. Enter the following value:

   UILanguage: en-US

4. If necessary, expand the Windows-Setup section. Select the Microsoft-Windows-Setup\DiskConfiguration component. Select OnError for the WillShowUI setting.

5. Select the Microsoft-Windows-Setup\DiskConfiguration\Disk component. Enter the following values in the settings section:

   DiskID: 0

   WillWipeDisk: true

6. Use the following steps to configure the first partition. Select any of the Microsoft-Windows-Setup\DiskConfiguration\Disk\CreatePartitions\CreatePartition components. Enter the following values in the settings section:

   Extend: false

   Order: 1

   Size: 200

   Type: Primary

7. Use the following steps to configure the second partition. Select the Microsoft-Windows-Setup\DiskConfiguration\Disk\CreatePartitions\CreatePartition component. Enter the following values in the settings section:

   Extend: true

   Order: 2

   Size: <blank>

   Type: Primary

8. Modify the first partition with the following steps. Select any of the Microsoft-Windows-Setup\DiskConfiguration\Disk\ModifyPartitions\ModifyPartition components. Enter the following values in the settings section:

   Active: true

   Format: NTFS

   Label: System

   Order: 1

   PartitionID: 1

9. Modify the second partition with the following steps. Select the `Microsoft-Windows-Setup\DiskConfiguration\Disk\ModifyPartitions\ModifyPartition` component. Enter the following values in the settings section:

Active: `false`

Format: NTFS

Label: `Windows`

Order: 2

PartitionID: 2

At this point, your display will look similar to Figure 4.16.

FIGURE 4.16
Creating and modifying partitions in an answer file

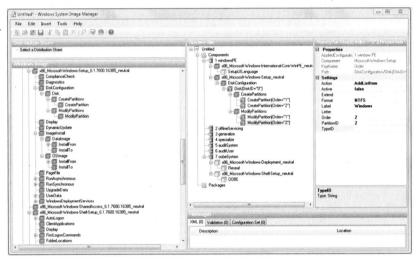

10. If necessary, expand the ImageInstall section in the 1 windowsPE section. Select the `Microsoft-Windows-Setup\ImageInstall\OSImage` component. Enter the following values in the settings section:

InstallToAvailablePartition: `false`

WillShowUI: `OnError`

11. Select the `Microsoft-Windows-Setup\ImageInstall\OSImage\InstallTo` component. Enter the following values in the settings section:

DiskID: 0

PartitionID: 2

12. Select the `Microsoft-Windows-Setup\UserData` component. Enter **true** for the AcceptEula setting.

13. Select the Microsoft-Windows-Setup\UserData\ProductKey component. Enter the following settings:

Key: <Enter your product key here>

WillShowUI: OnError

14. If necessary, expand the 7 oobeSystem section. Select the Microsoft-Windows-Deployment\Reseal component. Enter the following values in the settings section:

ForceShutdownNow: false

Mode: Audit

The Audit mode is most commonly used by OEMs. It allows you to boot skip the Welcome phase on the next boot and add additional drivers or applications.

15. Select the Microsoft-Windows-Shell-Setup\OOBE component. Enter the following values in the settings section:

HideEULAPage: true

ProtectYourPC: 3

At this point, the answer file is configured. However, it's possible that some of the settings were missed or misconfigured. You can validate the answer file before saving it to identify any possible problems. The following section shows these steps.

TESTING AND SAVING THE ANSWER FILE

The validation step within WSIM can be used to test the answer file. If you followed the previous steps to create the answer file, you can use these steps to validate it. After it's validated, you can save the file for later use.

1. Select Tools ➢ Validate Answer File. You should see a message indicating that no warnings or errors were discovered, as shown in Figure 4.17.

FIGURE 4.17
Validating the answer file

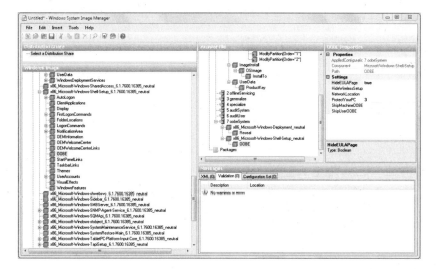

If you have any errors, double-click the error to navigate to the setting and correct the problem. After correcting the problem, validate the answer file again until you no longer have any warnings or errors.

2. Select File ➢ Save Answer File. Browse to a location on your system and save the file as `Autounattend.xml`.

You now have a basic answer file you can use to automate Windows Setup. If you copy it to a USB flash drive and boot to the installation DVD, the `autoattend.xml` file will automatically be used for the installation.

VIEWING SAMPLE ANSWER FILES

There are literally hundreds of settings that can be configured and there simply isn't enough room in this chapter to cover them all. However, the WAIK does include some sample answer files that show more of the components and settings that may interest you.

The following steps show how to add the sample answer files to the WSIM so that you can browse them to see additional settings. You need to first add an image; the image we used in step 2 in the section "Adding an Image to WSIM" earlier will work. If you still have WSIM open from the previous series of steps, click File ➢ Close Answer File first.

1. Click File ➢ Open Answer File.

2. Browse to `C:\Program Files\Windows AIK\Samples`.

3. Select one of the sample XML files such as `autounattend_sample.xml` or `Corp_autounattend_sample.xml`. Click Open.

4. You will be prompted to associate the answer file with the image within WSIM. Click Yes.

5. Expand the different elements to view them. Notice that the validation shows a problem with the key. If you double-click it, it will bring you right to the error, as shown in Figure 4.18. This sample doesn't include a product key, but it does show you where you need to enter your product key.

FIGURE 4.18
Viewing the sample answer file

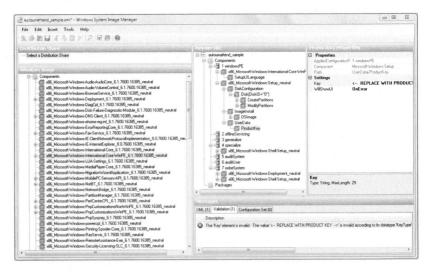

If desired, you can open additional sample answer files and view their settings.

The Bottom Line

Create a dual-boot system using a VHD.   You want to create a dual-boot system so that you can boot into two different versions of Windows 7. You plan to use the second installation to test applications for compatibility. However, you have only one drive.

Master It   You need to use a single system to install two versions of Windows 7. How can you accomplish this?

Prepare a system to be imaged.   You want to capture an image that will be deployed to multiple systems. However, before you can capture the image, it must be prepared.

Master It   What should you use to prepare the system to be imaged?

Capture an image.   After you've prepared an image, you can capture it so that it can be deployed to other computers. This can be much more efficient than installing Windows 7 individually on each computer. There are tools available within the Windows Automated Installation Kit (WAIK) that can be used to capture an image.

Master It   What tool can you use to capture an image?

> **A.**   Sysprep
>
> **B.**   ImageX
>
> **C.**   LoadState
>
> **D.**   ScanState

Modify an image offline.   There are some instances where you want to modify an offline image instead of deploying, modifying, and recapturing it. The WAIK provides tools that can be used for offline servicing of an image.

Master It   You have captured an image but want to apply additional drivers to the image. What tool can you use?

Apply an image.   After capturing an image, you can then deploy it to other systems. While you can use tools such as Windows Deployment Services (WDS) to deploy the image to multiple systems through multicasting, you can also use tools within the WAIK to deploy images to a single system at a time.

Master It   You have captured an image from a Windows 7 reference computer. You now want to apply the image to a system. What should you do?

Create an unattended answer file.   There are some times when you want to install Windows 7 without standing in front of the computer to answer all the questions. You can do this if you first create an unattended answer file that you can use to answer the questions automatically.

Master It   You want to create an unattended answer file named `unattend.xml` to install Windows 7 without user intervention. What should you use to create the `unattend.xml` file?

Chapter 5

Migrating the Existing User Data

When users get new systems, they want to have as much of their existing data and settings as possible restored on the new system. And if you can't do that, instead of being happy about the shiny new toys, they may get a little unpleasant. Thankfully, Microsoft includes some good tools you can use to restore your users' data. The Windows Easy Transfer tool can be used to transfer user state data on a system-by-system basis. You wouldn't use it for all the users in your organization, but you can use it for systems you manually migrate, such as systems used by some executives.

The Windows Automated Installation Kit (WAIK) includes the User State Migration Tool (USMT) that can be used in large organizations. The USMT includes two command-line tools: ScanState and LoadState. Each of these tools includes a rich set of options you can use to fine-tune the migration for large-scale deployments. Since they are command-line tools, they can be scripted to automate the migration.

In this chapter, you will learn to:

- ◆ Identify folders holding user state data
- ◆ Identify the best tool to use to transfer user state data for a single user
- ◆ Capture user state data
- ◆ Apply user state data
- ◆ Capture and apply user state data from the `Windows.old` folder

Exploring User Data and Settings

The first time a user logs on to almost any version of Windows, a profile is created. In Windows XP, the majority of the profile information is stored in the `C:\Documents and Settings` folder by default. In Windows 7, the majority of the profile information is stored in the `C:\Users` folder by default. The Registry also holds key profile information for the users.

When users log on, they are able to make changes to the Windows environment, such as modifying the way Windows looks and feels, adding items to the desktop, and configuring printers. The next time users log on, this profile data is accessed, giving them the same settings they had the last time they were logged on. Table 5.1 shows some of the contents of a profile.

TABLE 5.1: Data held in a profile

SOURCE	INFORMATION SAVED
My Documents	Documents stored by the user
My Pictures	Pictures stored by the user
Windows Explorer	All user-definable settings for Windows Explorer, such as whether hidden files are shown
Favorites	Links to favorite websites on the Internet
Mapped network drive	Any user-created mapped network drives
Desktop contents	Items stored on the Desktop, including both data and shortcuts
Screen colors and fonts	All user-definable computer screen colors and display text settings
Application data and Registry hive	Application data and user-defined configuration settings
Printer settings	Network printer connections
Control Panel	All user-defined settings made in Control Panel
Accessories	All user-specific program settings affecting the user's Windows environment, such as the clock and calendar

Figure 5.1 shows the profile folder for a user named Sally on a Windows 7 computer. This profile is created from the Default profile the first time the user logs on. Here the settings of Windows Explorer have been changed so that all the hidden and system files are shown. As you can see, the contents of the profile can be quite extensive.

FIGURE 5.1
User profile in
Windows 7

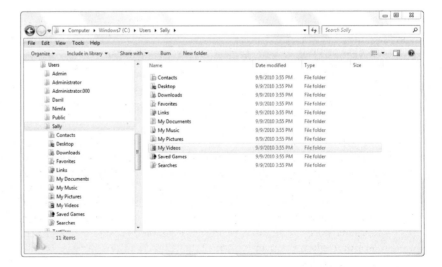

VIEWING HIDDEN AND SYSTEM FILES

You probably know how to show hidden and system files in Windows XP via the Tools ➤ Folder Options menu. However, the Tools menu isn't available by default, so this method isn't accessible by default in Windows 7. You can access the Folder Options menu by clicking Organize ➤ Folder And Search Options. From there, you'll see the familiar Folder Options. You can then click the View tab; select Show Hidden Files, Folders, And Drives; and deselect Hide Protected Operating System Files (Recommended).

Additionally, you can select the Always Show Menus check box to bring back the familiar Windows Explorer menu, including the Tools menu that includes Folder Options.

User Data

User data in Windows XP can be stored in the profile in the My Documents folder. This includes the My Music, My Videos, and My Pictures folders. Of course, users aren't restricted to only using the My Documents folder but can also store data directly on the Desktop or anywhere else on their computer. Similarly, users can store data in any of the libraries (Documents, Music, Pictures, and Videos) in Windows 7. These libraries are virtual folders pointing to the actual locations of folders on the user's system. For example, the My Documents folder within the Documents library is located in the C:\Users*Username* folder.

The migration tools have the ability to easily capture all the data stored in the user's profile, and they can also capture data stored elsewhere. For example, if a user has data stored in the C:\Data folder, the entire contents of this folder can be migrated.

Application Settings Data

The application settings data includes all the settings for any of the configurable applications. For example, if a user configures the Save options of Microsoft Word to save AutoRecover information every 10 minutes, this setting will be stored in the application settings area of the profile. Application data is typically stored in the C:\Users*Username*\AppData folder.

Windows 7 uses three locations for application settings data within the C:\Users*Username*\AppData folder:

- Local
- LocalLow
- Roaming

The Local and LocalLow folders are used for different levels of security. Some applications have a low level of integrity or trust, so they are given access to only the LocalLow folder and access is restricted. Other applications with a higher level of integrity have access to the Local folder, and the Local folder is also used for settings that are specific to the computer or are too big to roam.

Roaming profiles are stored in a central location such as a server and the user can access the same roaming profile when they log on to any computer in the network. Although the profile is stored permanently on the central server, the profile is also copied down to the local computer when the user logs on. The Roaming folder stores profile data that can be stored in a roaming profile.

Migrating User Data

Data migration tools will transfer the user's data and settings for different applications from one operating system to another. These tools do not transfer the applications themselves but only the settings and some data. If a user was running Microsoft Word on Windows XP, you can use these tools so that the user will have similar settings in Microsoft Word on their new Windows 7 system, but data migration tools don't install Microsoft Word. You use other methods to install Microsoft Word, such as including it in the new image or deploying it with Group Policy.

The two primary tools you have available are Windows Easy Transfer and the User State Migration Tool (USMT), discussed in the following sections. If your migrations require customization on a machine-by-machine basis, you can use the Windows Easy Transfer tool instead of the USMT, as described in the previous section. In large organizations, it's possible that the majority of the systems will be migrated using the USMT and some special computers with unique needs will be migrated with Windows Easy Transfer.

Working with Windows Easy Transfer

Windows Easy Transfer is a software tool you can use to transfer files and settings from one computer to another, or from one operating system to Windows 7. You can transfer files and settings to Windows 7 from several different operating systems, including the following:

- Windows XP
- Windows Vista
- Windows 7

You can transfer the data from the old computer to the new computer using an Easy Transfer Cable, via a network share, or via an external hard disk or USB flash drive, as shown in Figure 5.2. The Easy Transfer Cable is available for purchase at electronics stores and on the Web. Unfortunately, a common USB cable can't be used to transfer the data between systems.

FIGURE 5.2
Transferring files using the Windows Easy Transfer wizard

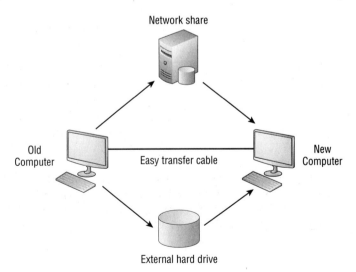

If you're transferring files from Windows XP (or Windows Vista) to Windows 7, you can download a free copy of the Windows Easy Transfer tool to run on the Windows XP computer. You can find this file on Microsoft's download site (http://www.microsoft.com/downloads) by searching for **Windows Easy Transfer XP**. You'll find both 32- and 64-bit versions of this program. You should download the version that matches the architecture of Windows XP. There is an older version of this tool that you can use to transfer files from Windows XP to Windows Vista, but you'll want to get the newer version that can be used to transfer files to both Windows Vista and Windows 7. This program can also be used to transfer files from Windows Vista to Windows 7 if you're not doing an upgrade.

The steps you'll take to run Windows Easy Transfer are as follows:

1. Download and install Windows Easy Transfer on the older computer.

2. Run Windows Easy Transfer on the older computer to capture the data.

3. Run Windows Easy Transfer on Windows 7 to migrate the data.

After the wizard runs, it creates a report that you can view. Figure 5.3 shows part of a sample report with the Program Report tab selected. It shows a listing of the program settings that were transferred.

FIGURE 5.3
Viewing a Windows Easy Transfer wizard report

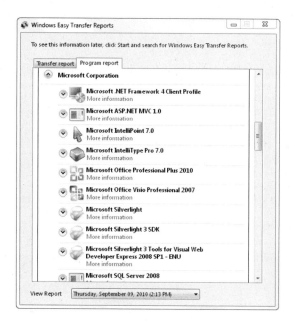

It's important to remember that the wizard doesn't transfer the applications; it only transfers the settings for the applications. While some applications will retain the transferred settings if you install them after performing the transfer, other applications will overwrite these transferred settings. In other words, it's best to install the applications before doing the transfer.

The Windows Easy Transfer tool is a wizard that allows you to choose what you will transfer. Figure 5.4 shows the first screen you'll see when you launch it. As you can see, it allows you to transfer a significant amount of data and settings.

FIGURE 5.4
Launching the
Windows Easy
Transfer wizard

When you run the wizard, it scans your system looking for profiles. If you're running it on Windows XP, it will scan the `Documents and Settings` folder looking for profiles that have been created there. If you run it on Windows Vista or Windows 7, it will scan the `Users` folder. These profiles can be quite large or relatively small, depending on what the user stores within them. When the scan is complete, you'll see a display similar to Figure 5.5.

FIGURE 5.5
Viewing the user
profiles detected
by Easy Transfer

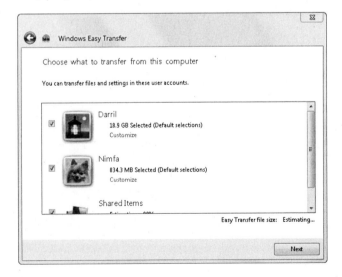

Thankfully, it's not an all-or-nothing approach; you can choose what data you want to transfer. The following section shows how to run the Windows Easy Transfer wizard on both the old and the new computer.

Capturing Data with Windows Easy Transfer

The following steps show you how to capture data on a system using the Windows Easy Transfer tool. If you are running it on Windows XP, you'll first need to download and install it. These steps show how it can be run on one computer to capture the data and then restored onto a Windows 7 computer:

1. Start the Windows Easy Transfer Wizard by clicking Start ➢ All Programs ➢ Accessories ➢ System Tools ➢ Windows Easy Transfer.

2. Review the information on the Welcome screen and click Next.

3. You'll see a prompt asking you how you want to transfer the items. You can choose an Easy Transfer Cable (if you have the special cable and the computers are connected with it), a network share, or an external hard disk or USB flash drive. For this example, choose an external hard disk (if you choose one of the other options, the steps will be slightly different).

4. You'll be prompted to choose either This Is My New Computer or This Is My Old Computer. Click This Is My Old Computer.

   The Windows Easy Transfer wizard will then scan all the existing user accounts on the system to identify what files and settings can be captured. When it's complete, you'll see a listing of all the users who have profiles on your local computer.

5. Click Customize on one of the user profiles. You'll see a display similar to Figure 5.6. You can click on any of the items to deselect or reselect them based on how much space you have and what you want to transfer.

FIGURE 5.6
Viewing the user profiles detected by the Windows Easy Transfer tool

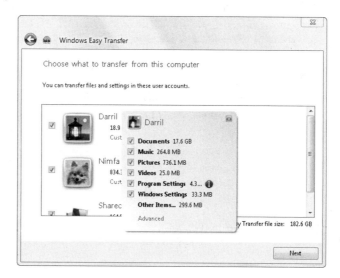

6. Click Advanced. You'll see a screen similar to Figure 5.7. Notice how you can pick specifically what will be transferred. Instead of using the wizard, you can use traditional methods to back up user data and just focus on using the wizard to transfer the settings. However, you can also use it to copy all the user data. Select the items you want to transfer and click Save.

FIGURE 5.7
Customizing the data to be transferred

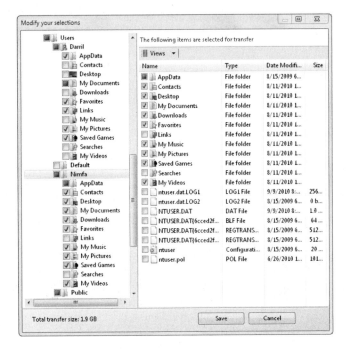

7. You'll be prompted to provide a password. Enter a password that you'll remember in the Password and Confirm Password text boxes. For a lab environment, you can use something like **P@ssw0rd**. Click Save.

8. Select your external hard drive and click Open. If desired, you can create or browse to a folder on the drive. Click Save. The wizard will begin the process of saving the files and settings to this location.

    At this point, take a break. For a transfer of about 2 GB, it may take your system about 5 minutes.

9. When the transfer finishes, the wizard will indicate the save is complete for each of the users with a green check mark by the user icon. Click Next. You'll see a screen similar to Figure 5.8. Notice that this identifies the name of the file that holds all the data and settings: Windows Easy Transfer - Items from old computer.MIG. It also identifies the location (drive M: in the figure).

FIGURE 5.8
Completing
the Windows
Easy Transfer
save process

Windows Easy Transfer

Your transfer file is complete

Open Windows Easy Transfer on your new computer

You've saved the items you want to transfer in a special transfer file named:
Windows Easy Transfer - Items from old computer.MIG
Here's where it's saved:

M:

Write down the location where you saved your transfer file because you'll need to open it on your
new computer. If you're upgrading this computer to Windows 7, open the file when your upgrade
is complete.

Next

10. Click Next and click Close. At this point, the files and settings are ready to be imported into the new computer.

Restoring Data with Windows Easy Transfer

Once you have saved the files and settings into a file, you can then use the following steps to restore them onto the Windows 7 computer:

1. Start the Windows Easy Transfer wizard by clicking Start ➤ All Programs ➤ Accessories ➤ System Tools ➤ Windows Easy Transfer.

2. Review the information on the Welcome page and click Next.

3. Select the method you used to transfer the files. In these steps, I'm using an external hard disk. If you use another method, the steps will be slightly different.

4. Select This Is My New Computer.

5. The wizard will ask if you have already saved your files to an external hard disk or USB flash drive. Ensure the external drive is connected to the new computer and click Yes.

6. Browse to the location of the Windows Easy Transfer file. It is named `Windows Easy Transfer - Items from old computer.mig` by default. Select the file and click Open.

7. Enter the password you used when creating the files and click Next.

8. You'll see a screen showing the same usernames that were detected and saved when you captured the data. By default, each of the profiles and the shared items are automatically selected. Deselect any users you don't want to migrate, or click Customize to pick items to transfer.

9. Click Advanced Options. You'll see a screen similar to Figure 5.9. You can use the options on the Map User Accounts tab to map the profile of the account on the original system to the profile of the account on the new system. This step can be useful if the account name is different. You can also create a new account using this tab. However, if an account doesn't exist on the new computer but the profile is selected to be transferred, the wizard will automatically create the account with the same username. Therefore, it's not necessary to create a new account unless you want the data to be migrated to an account with a different name.

FIGURE 5.9
Mapping old user profiles to new user profiles

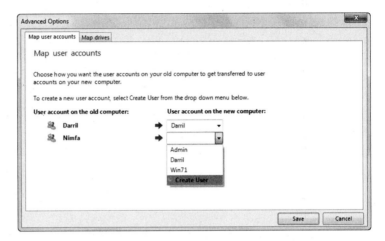

10. Click Cancel, then click Transfer and the wizard begins the transfer process.

11. When the wizard finishes, it will indicate that the transfer is complete. You can click on either of the links to view the Windows Easy Transfer Report. You can also view the report later by clicking Start ➤ All Programs ➤ Accessories ➤ System Tools ➤ Windows Easy Transfer Reports. This allows you to view the data that was transferred at any time in the future.

12. Click Close. You'll be prompted to restart the computer. Click Restart Now.

When the system reboots, the settings from the original computer will be in place. The user will immediately see the settings from their original computer, such as the wallpaper, data in their libraries, and settings in applications such as Internet Explorer. If the user has any of the same applications known to the Windows Easy Transfer tool installed in both operating systems, these settings will also be the same.

Working with the User State Migration Tool

The User State Migration Tool (USMT) is a group of command-line tools that can be used to capture and restore user accounts, profiles, settings, and data. This data is collectively referred to as *user state data*.

There are two primary components of the USMT:

ScanState   This command-line tool is normally run on the older computer or operating system to capture the user state data. When using the `Windows.old` folder that is created for some installations of Windows 7, ScanState is run after the installation of Windows 7 to retrieve the user state data from this folder.

LoadState   This command-line tool is run on the newer computer hosting Windows 7 to restore the system state data that was captured by ScanState. It can re-create all the users that existed on the original installation and migrate the profile and other data for each of them.

Since these tools are command-line tools, you can script and automate them. You can create batch files with the commands and then schedule the batch files to run on the source and target machines. Batch files allow you to perform large-scale migrations with little user interaction.

There are several XML files used with the USMT. Each of these files contains migration rules that specify what is migrated from the source to the destination computers. You don't have to modify these files for a migration. However, if you have some special needs, you do have options. Most migrations will use the files (listed here) just as they are:

MigApp.xml   This file identifies the application settings that are migrated. It can be used in both the `ScanState` and `LoadState` commands. `MigApp.xml` is included in the same folder as other USMT tools and doesn't need to be migrated. However, if you have special application settings that aren't migrated by default, you can modify this file.

MigDocs.xml   This file is used by both ScanState and LoadState to identify user data on the hard drive that will be migrated. Note that this file does not specify the migration of system files, program files, or application data. It is common to use `MigDocs.xml` with `MigApp.xml` when capturing or loading system state data. However, `MigDocs.xml` cannot be used with the `MigUser.xml` file. To clarify, the `MigDocs.xml` and `MigApp.xml` files are commonly used together, but the `MigUser.xml` and `MigApp.xml` file combination is not used as often.

One reason to modify `MigDocs.xml` is to exclude certain documents. For example, if you want to exclude MP3 files, you can modify `MigDocs.xml` by adding an `<exclude>` node. An example shows how to do this in the section "Getting Extra Mileage Out of the USMT" later in this chapter.

MigUser.xml   This file identifies the user folders, files, and file types that are migrated. It can be used in both the `ScanState` and `LoadState` commands but is not used with the `MigDocs.xml` file. Note that this file doesn't specify which user accounts and profiles to migrate, but instead identifies the data to migrate within each migrated user account and profile. You can specify which accounts to migrate within the `ScanState` and `LoadState` commands.

Config.xml   This is an optional file that you can create with the `ScanState /GenConfig:config.xml` command. This file is not needed, but you can use it if you want to change default store-creation or profile-migration behavior. It includes a list of components within XML nodes with a `migrate="yes"` clause. You can modify any of these components to `migrate="no"`.

USMT Resources for Modifying Files

The User State Migration Tool 4.0 User's Guide has additional information on modifying these XML files for a migration. This help file is named USMT.chm and it is stored in the C:\Program Files\ Windows AIK\Docs\CHMs folder after the WAIK has been installed. Here are some articles that may interest you:

◆ "Customize USMT XML Files"

◆ "Custom XML Examples"

◆ "Exclude Files and Settings"

◆ "XML Elements Library"

◆ "Config.xml File"

Using the USMT in Four Deployment Scenarios

Chapter 3, "Installing Windows 7: Meet the Panther," presented four deployment scenarios:

◆ Deploying new bare-metal computers

◆ Upgrading computers

◆ Refreshing computers

◆ Replacing computers

The bare-metal and upgrade scenarios don't require the use of the USMT. The bare-metal installation installs Windows 7 on a system that doesn't have any operating system on it. This could be a new computer that doesn't have an operating system, or a computer on which you want to remove the existing operating system. This scenario implies that it is a brand-new system for a brand new-user: there isn't any user state data to migrate. (If you did have user state data to migrate, you could perform the steps in a replace scenario.) In an upgrade, an existing computer running a compatible version of Windows Vista or Windows 7 is upgraded to Windows 7. All existing user state data is automatically migrated during this operating system upgrade.

In this section you'll see how you can use the USMT to restore the user's state data in the refresh and replace scenarios.

REFRESH SCENARIO

The refresh scenario uses the same computer but changes the operating system. For example, a computer may have been running Windows XP, and it is refreshed so that it is now running Windows 7. There are several methods of using the USMT when you do a refresh:

Wipe-and-load with a Compressed Migration Store   A wipe-and-load is where the original computer is wiped clean and includes any time the hard drive is reformatted, repartitioned, or replaced before the new operating system is installed. If you are planning a wipe-and-load, you can take the following steps with the USMT:

1. Use ScanState to collect the user state data and store it to a migration store in a compressed state to save space. It can be stored on a network share or a removable hard drive.

2. Wipe the system clean and install Windows 7.

3. Use LoadState to restore the user data.

Refresh with a Hard-Link Migration Hard-link migration is explained in more detail in the sidebar "Learning about Hard-Link Migration," but in short, it creates an additional link to the existing files prior to installing the new operating system. LoadState can then change these links to new locations understood by Windows 7.

The hard-link migration store method uses these steps:

1. Use ScanState to collect the user state data with the /hardlink and /nocompress switches and store it to a migration store. The migration store is stored on the same volume as the operating system.

2. Install Windows 7.

3. Use LoadState to restore the user data using the /hardlink switch.

LEARNING ABOUT HARD-LINK MIGRATION

You can perform a hard-link migration in some computer refresh scenarios. The hard-link migration provides significant improvement in the migration performance. When you perform a hard-link migration, the migration store is created as a full folder structure similar to the following graphic:

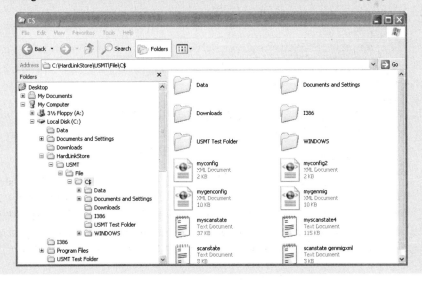

While it looks as though this is a full copy of all the folders and files that will be included in the migration, they are actually just links to the files. At this point, you have two links to each of the files and folders but only one copy of the file on the drive. If you delete only one link, the file still exists. The file is only deleted when you delete both the links.

When the hard-link migration store is restored with LoadState, the files aren't actually copied. Instead, the hard link is modified to have the data in a different location in the directory structure. In other words, if Sally's profile was stored in the C:\Documents and Settings\Sally folder in Windows XP, the hard-link migration changes the location to C:\Users\Sally in Windows 7.

The hard-link migration store takes up relatively little space. For example, the actual C:\Windows folder takes up about 1.6 GB of space on the hard drive but the C:\HardLinkStore folder shown in the graphic (which includes the \C$\Windows folder) takes up only 24 MB on disk. A hard-link migration store can't be compressed. Because the migration is compressed by default, you need to include the /nocompress switch when using the /hardlink switch.

You cannot do a hard-link migration in any of the following scenarios:

◆ You are migrating from one computer to a second computer, such as in a replace scenario.

◆ You are migrating data from one volume to another volume (such as from the C: drive to the D: drive). A hard link can only point to files on the same volume.

◆ You are formatting or repartitioning the disk that contains the hard-link migration store.

Refresh Using Windows.old If you do a clean installation (not an upgrade) of Windows 7 on a computer that has Windows XP, Windows Vista, or Windows 7 installed, the installation will detect the previous operating system and store files in a folder called Windows.old. You can then retrieve user state data from this folder using LoadState.

The high-level steps when using this method are as follows:

1. Install Windows 7 on a computer that includes another operating system.

2. Use ScanState to capture the user data from the Windows.old folder.

3. Use LoadState to restore the user data from the Windows.old folder.

REPLACE SCENARIO

There are times when the existing hardware is replaced. This could be because the hardware is older and it can't support the hardware requirements, or as part of a regular hardware upgrade within the organization. Replace scenarios are also known as side-by-side upgrades.

When the user receives a new computer, you can restore their user state data just as if you're performing a wipe-and-load. You can use these high-level steps:

1. Use ScanState to collect the user state data and store it to a migration store in a compressed state to save space. It can be stored on a network share or a removable hard drive.

2. Install the new computer with Windows 7.

3. Use LoadState to restore the user data.

Setting Up the Source Computer

If you plan on running LoadState on a computer, you'll need to copy several files onto the computer first. The source computer can be running Windows XP, Windows Vista, or even Windows 7. Since the most common migration scenario will be migrating from Windows XP to Windows 7, it's important to know how to prepare the Windows XP computer to run LoadState.

The easiest way to do this is to simply copy the appropriate folder. If you install the WAIK on a technician's computer, it will include the following two folders:

◆ `C:\Program Files\Windows AIK\Tools\USMT\x86`

◆ `C:\Program Files\Windows AIK\Tools\USMT\amd64`

The ...\x86 folder includes all the USMT files needed for a 32-bit source computer, and the ...\amd64 folder includes all the files needed for a 64-bit source computer. You can simply copy the contents of these folders to a root folder on the C: drive such as `C:\USMT`. You need to ensure that the folders within these folders are also included.

You can also install the WAIK on the source computer. Chapter 4, "Cloning the Panther: Automating Windows 7 Installation," walked you through the installation of the WAIK. As a reminder, it is available as a free download from Microsoft's download site (www.microsoft.com/downloads/) by entering **WAIK** in the Search All Download Center text box. The Windows AIK for Windows 7 download (KB3AIK_EN.iso) file should be listed on the first page. Windows XP may not have the .NET Framework 2.0 and MSXML 6.0 installed on it already, so you may see an error similar to Figure 5.10 if you try to install the WAIK. However, the WAIK includes these tools.

FIGURE 5.10
Installing the WAIK on Windows XP

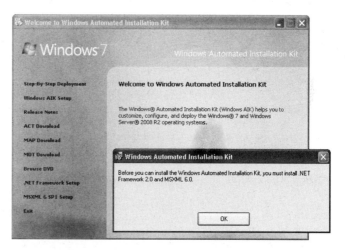

In Figure 5.10, you can see links for the .NET Framework Setup and the MSXML 6 SP1 Setup. If you get the error message, install these two components and then restart the installation. It's also possible to automate the deployment of the WAIK using one of many methods, such as assigning it computers using Group Policy or deploying it with System Center Configuration Manager (SCCM).

After you have copied the appropriate files or installed the WAIK on the Windows XP system you plan to use as the source computer, you can use the steps detailed in the following sections to begin running ScanState.

Gathering Data by Running ScanState

The ScanState command captures the user state data. It includes several options that you can use by including different switches. The basic syntax of the ScanState command is:

```
ScanState <store path> [switches]
```

The store path is the location where you want the migrated data stored. It can be a network location using a UNC path or an external hard drive accessible to the source computer. You can also specify a path on the local hard drive if desired.

You have several switches available to you when running ScanState. Table 5.2 shows some of the common switches associated with the following typical ScanState command.

```
c:\usmt>ScanState C:\USMTStore /i:migdocs.xml /i:migapp.xml /v:5

/l:MyScanState.log /o /c
```

Notice that this this command is issued from the C:\USMT> prompt, indicating the path has been changed to C:\USMT with the cd \usmt command. It assumes that the appropriate USMT files (x86 for a 32-bit source system, or amd64 for a 64-bit source system) have been copied to the C:\USMT folder.

TABLE 5.2:   Common ScanState switches

SWITCH	DESCRIPTION
/i:<file name> /i:c:\usmt\migdocs.xml /i:c:\usmt\migapp.xml	You use the /i switch to specify the path and XML filenames that include the rules for migration. It's common to use the MigDocs.xml and MigApp.xml files for the migration. These files include rules that will locate user data and application data.
/v:<level> /v:5	The /v switch enables verbose output in the log file. The default verbosity level is 0 and the highest is 13. You can use 0, 1, 4, 5, 8, 9, 12, or 13. Any level beyond 5 requires the use of a debugger to fully analyze the output.
/l:<log file name> /l:MyScanState.log	The /l switch specifies the location and name of the log file.
/o	Overwrites any existing migration store.
/c	Indicates to continue even if there are nonfatal errors. If this switch is not used, ScanState will stop and exit for any error.

The previous command is executed from the C:\USMT folder and the XML files are located in the same folder so their path doesn't need to be included. However, if you execute the command from a different path, you'll have to include the path to the XML files. For example, if the ScanState command and XML files are in a folder named USMT, and you're executing the command from the root of C: (C:\>), you'd need to use a command like this:

```
C:\>c:\USMT\ScanState C:\USMTStore /i:c:\usmt\migdocs.xml

/i:c:\usmt\migapp.xml /v:5 /l:MyScanState.log
```

USING THE /AUTO SWITCH

You can also use the /auto switch to specify the location of the XML files. The /auto switch sets the verbosity to level 13. Here's an example using this switch; Table 5.3 explains the switches used here.

```
C:\>c:\usmt\scanstate /auto:c:\usmt\ c:\USMTStore /l:myscanstate.log
```

TABLE 5.3: ScanState /auto switch

SWITCH	DESCRIPTION
/auto	Using the /auto switch without a directory path causes it to set the directory path to the location where the USMT files are installed (if they were installed rather than just copied).
	The /auto switch selects all users. You can't use the /ui or /ue switches to select specific users when using the /auto switch. The /ui and /ue switches include or exclude users and are described in the section "Identifying Users to Migrate" later in this chapter.
/auto:c:\usmt	If you specify a path with the /auto switch, it will use this path to locate and use the MigDocs.xml and MigApp.xml files.

CREATING XML FILES

The following two example commands show how you can create a Config.xml file and a general migration XML file. These are optional files, but you can use them to create a template Config.xml file, and to gain insight into what files ScanState will capture. Table 5.4 describes the use of these switches.

```
C:\>c:\usmt\scanstate /genmigxml:mygenmig.xml
C:\>c:\usmt\scanstate /genconfig:myconfig.xml
```

TABLE 5.4: ScanState switches to create XML files

SWITCH	DESCRIPTION
/genmigxml:<path> /genmigxml:mygenmig.xml	This switch causes ScanState to search the system to locate files that will be migrated. It then creates the XML file identifying and defining how all the files are migrated. This command doesn't actually create the migration store, but instead provides you with a preview of what will be migrated.
/genconfig:<path> /genconfig:mygenconfig.xml	This switch creates a Config.xml file that you can modify and then use with the /config switch.

IDENTIFYING USERS TO MIGRATE

By default all users are migrated, but you can pick specific users to migrate with the user include (/ui) switch, or pick specific users to exclude with the user exclude (/ue) switch. For example, the following command (which is shown on multiple lines but is entered on a single line) will exclude all domain and local users except the local user named TestUser:

```
C:\>c:\usmt\scanstate c:\USMTStore
/i:c:\usmt\migdocs.xml /i:c:\usmt\migapp.xml /v:5 /l:myscanstate.log
/ue:*\* /ui:TestUser
```

This second example only migrates users who have logged on in the past 30 days. It should also be entered on a single line but is shown on multiple lines here:

```
C:\>c:\usmt\scanstate c:\USMTStore
/i:c:\usmt\migdocs.xml /i:c:\usmt\migapp.xml /v:5 /l:myscanstate.log
/uel:30
```

Table 5.5 shows some of the switches you can use to identify which users to migrate.

TABLE 5.5:   ScanState switches to migrate users

SWITCH	DESCRIPTION
/all	Migrates all the users on the system. This is the default so the switch isn't needed.
/ue:[Domain\]UserName /ue:Darril /ue:Mastering\Darril /ue:Mastering* /ue:**	Excludes specified users. To exclude a local user, specify the UserName parameter only. If you want to exclude a user in a domain (such as the Mastering.hme domain), enter the domain name and the username. You can use the * wildcard character to exclude all domain users or all local users. This is needed when you're using the /ui switch.
/ui:[Domain\]UserName /ue:** /ui:Mastering\Darril /ue:** /ui:Darril	If you only want to migrate specific users, you can exclude all of them with the /ue switch (/ue:**) and then use the user include (/ui) switch to specify which users to migrate. To migrate a local user, specify the UserName parameter only. The Domain and UserName parameters can contain wildcard characters (* or ?).
/uel:NumberOfDays /uel:30 /uel:yyyy/mm/dd /uel:2010/09/10	You can use the /uel switch to only include users based on their last logon. For example, if you only want to migrate users who have logged on the past 30 days, you can use /uel:30 and users that logged on 31 or more days ago will not be migrated. You can also specify a date and only users who have not logged on since that date will be excluded.

ENCRYPTING THE MIGRATION STORE

The data in the migration store may be valuable and may need extra protection to ensure its confidentiality. You can use several methods of encryption to protect the data. The following command will encrypt the store using the default encryption method with a password key of **P@ssw0rd**. The switches are explained in Table 5.6.

```
C:\>c:\usmt\scanstate /auto:c:\usmt\ c:\USMTStore

/l:myscanstate.log /encrypt /key:P@ssw0rd
```

TABLE 5.6:   ScanState encryption switches

SWITCH	DESCRIPTION
`/encrypt` `/encrypt:<method>` `AES	AES_128	AES_192 |` `AES_256	3DES	3DES_112`	Encrypts the migration store using the specified cryptographic algorithm. The default value is 3DES but the AES methods are considered stronger and more efficient. You must also specify the `/key` or `/keyfile` option when encrypting the store.
`/key:KeyString` `/key:"my P@ssw0rd"`	Specifies the encryption key. If the encryption key has a space, it needs to be enclosed in quotes.
`/keyfile:FileName`	Specifies the location and name of a TXT file containing the encryption key.

IDENTIFYING SUPPORTED ENCRYPTION ALGORITHMS

USMT version 4.0 is included with the WAIK for Windows 7 and it supports multiple encryption algorithms, including the Advanced Encryption Standard (AES) 128, 192, and 256 bits. However, there are some scenarios when the source system does not support all these methods. The Usmtutils.exe file is stored in the same folder as the ScanState and LoadState tools, and you can use it to list the encryption options supported by USMT tools. The command is as follows:

```
usmtutils /ec
```

You'll see an output similar to this:

Following is a list of USMT supported Crypto AlgIDs available on this system:

```
3DES_112
3DES
AES_128
AES_192
AES_256
```

On some Windows XP systems, you may only see the 3DES_112 and 3DES encryption algorithms.

CREATING A HARD-LINK MIGRATION STORE

If you are doing a refresh and you want to do a hard-link migration, you can use the following command:

```
C:\>c:\usmt\scanstate /auto:c:\usmt\ /hardlink c:\HardLinkStore /l:myscanstate.
log /nocompress
```

Table 5.7 shows the switches used with the /hardlink option. Notice that you must use the /nocompress switch when using the /hardlink switch.

TABLE 5.7:   ScanState /hardlink and /nocompress switches

SWITCH	DESCRIPTION
/hardlink	Enables hard links for a noncompressed store. Use only for PC refresh scenarios. Requires /nocompress.
/nocompress	Specifies that the migration store is not compressed.

IDENTIFYING USERS AND FILES THAT WILL BE MIGRATED

You can run ScanState at the command prompt to generate a log file that will let you know what the USMT will migrate. Note that this will not actually create the migration store, but instead generates an XML file that you can explore to identify the files that will be migrated. The following example assumes that the USMT files were copied to a folder named C:\USMT on a 32-bit system:

```
C:\>c:\usmt\scanstate /genmigxml:c:\usmt\mylogfile.xml
Log messages are being sent to 'C:\scanstate.log'
Starting the migration process
Success.
ScanState return code: 0
```

After running this command, there are two important files you can view. First, the Mylogfile .xml file gives you insight into what will be migrated. For example, it will have some <include> nodes within the XML document that look something like this:

```
<include>
<objectSet>
<pattern type="File">c:\downloads\*[*]</pattern>
<pattern type="File">c:\usmt test folder\*[*]</pattern>
<pattern type="File">c:[scanstate.log]</pattern>
</objectSet>
</include>
```

These include nodes are letting you know that it discovered some non-Windows folders (C:\ downloads and C:\usmt test folder) and it will include all subfolders (using the * wildcard) and all files (using the [*] wildcard). Additionally, it will include the Scanstate.log file in the migration.

If you scroll through the file further, you'll see which user profiles will be included in the migration along with a listing of the folders within these profiles. This data is generated from the `MigXmlHelper.GenerateDocPatterns` function of USMT. For example, if you created a TestUser account, you'll see a component section identifying the user with a node similar to this:

```
<component type="Documents" context="XP1\TestUser" defaultSupported="Yes">
    ...
</component>
```

The data within the `<component>` node also identifies the folders that are associated with the user in the user profile. These folders are included in the migration.

You can also look at the `C:\Scanstate.log` file. It shows the progress of the `ScanState` command and includes a list of user accounts that will be migrated.

MIGRATING FILES ENCRYPTED WITH EFS

If any of the migrated files are encrypted with the NTFS encrypting file system (EFS), you need to specify the `/efs` switch. If EFS encrypted files are detected during the migration, but the `/efs` switch is not used, the migration will fail. Table 5.8 shows the available options with the `/efs` switch and the following command shows the typical usage:

```
C:\>c:\usmt\scanstate /auto:c:\usmt\ c:\USMTStore

/l:myscanstate.log /efs:copyraw
```

TABLE 5.8:   ScanState /efs switches

SWITCH	DESCRIPTION
`/efs:hardlink`	Creates a hard link to the EFS file instead of copying it. This is used when the `/hardlink` and `/nocompress` options are used.
`/efs:abort`	This is the default. It will cause ScanState to fail if an EFS encrypted file is detected.
`/efs:skip`	Ignores EFS files.
`/efs:decryptcopy`	Attempts to decrypt the file. If successful, the file is migrated in an unencrypted format.
`/efs:copyraw`	Copies the encrypted file. LoadState will migrate user certificates, if available, so that users will be able to access encrypted files after the migration is completed.

RUNNING SCANSTATE TO CREATE THE MIGRATION STORE

If you've copied the appropriate USMT folders and files onto the source computer, you can use the following steps to see how ScanState is used. These steps will lead you through creating a test account and test folder prior to capturing the user state data. The steps assume you've copied the contents of the USMT folder to a folder named C:\USMT.

1. Use the following steps to create a test account, a profile, and some test documents. You can use this data to observe the steps of the migration.

    A. Launch a command prompt and enter the following command to add a user:

    ```
    net user /add TestUser P@ssw0rd
    ```

    B. Log off the system and then log onto the TestUser account using **P@ssw0rd** as the password. This will create the profile.

    C. Open Windows Explorer and browse to My Documents. Right-click within the folder and create a new text document. Name it **USMT Test**.

    D. Browse to the root of C:. Create a folder named **USMT Test Folder**. Open the folder and create a new text document named **USMT Test 2**.

    E. Log off the TestUser account.

2. Log on to the Windows XP system using an account with administrative permissions.

3. Launch the command prompt. Execute the following command to create an XML file named mygenmig.xml:

    ```
    c:\usmt\scanstate /genmigxml:mygenmig.xml
    ```

4. Open Windows Explorer and browse to the root of C:. Open the file named mygenmig.xml. Browse through this file to identify which files and users will be included in the migration.

5. Return to the command prompt and execute the following command:

    ```
    c:\usmt\scanstate /auto:c:\usmt\ c:\USMTStore /l:myscanstate.log
    ```

    When the command completes, it will indicate success. You'll see an output similar to the following text, identifying the names of the user accounts that are migrated:

    ```
    Log messages are being sent to 'C:\myscanstate.log'
    Starting the migration process
    Processing the settings store
    Examining the system to discover the migration units
     XP1\Administrator (1 of 4): 100% done
     XP1\TestUser (2 of 4): 100% done
     XP1\Sally (3 of 4): 100% done
     This Computer (4 of 4): 100% done
    Selecting migration units
    Gathering data
     XP1\Administrator (1 of 4): 100% done
     XP1\TestUser (2 of 4): 100% done
     XP1\Sally (3 of 4): 100% done
     This Computer (4 of 4): 100% done
     Commit
    Success.
    ScanState return code: 0
    ```

At this point, the `C:\usmtstore\` folder will include the user state data from this command. You can copy it to a network share, an external drive, or a USB flash drive. You can later use the `LoadState` command to apply the data to the new operating system.

Applying the Data and Settings Using *LoadState*

If you've captured the user state data with ScanState, you can restore it with the `LoadState` command. However, before you can use the `LoadState` command, you need to ensure it and other required files are accessible on the target computer. The easiest way to do so is to copy the files to the C: drive in a folder named `C:\usmt`. You can use the same steps to copy the files to the destination computer as you used to copy them to the source computer. Alternately, you can copy the files onto a USB drive and use them from there. You also need a copy of the USMT store created from the `ScanState` command.

This section assumes the following:

◆ The USMT files are in the `C:\usmt` folder.

◆ The user state data is in the `C:\usmtStore` folder.

If your files are located somewhere else, you'll have to modify the commands appropriately. The basic syntax of the `LoadState` command looks like this:

```
LoadState <store path> [switches]
```

COMMON *LOADSTATE* SWITCHES

Just as the `ScanState` command has several switches you can use, the `LoadState` command also has several switches. Table 5.9 shows common switches associated with the following typical `LoadState` command:

```
c:\usmt>LoadState C:\USMTStore /i:migdocs.xml /i:migapp.xml

/v:5 /l:MyScanState.log /lac
```

TABLE 5.9:   Basic LoadState switches

SWITCH	DESCRIPTION

`/i:<file name>`
`/i:c:\usmt\migdocs.xml`
`/i:c:\usmt\migapp.xml`
	You use the /i switch to specify the path and XML filenames that include the rules for migration. It's common to use the MigDocs.xml and MigApp.xml files for the migration. These files include rules that will locate user data and application data.

`/v:<level>` `/v:5`	The /v switch enables verbose output in the log file. The default verbosity level is 0 and the highest is 13. You can use 0, 1, 4, 5, 8, 9, 12, or 13.

TABLE 5.9: Basic LoadState switches *(CONTINUED)*

SWITCH	DESCRIPTION
/l:<log file name> /l:MyLoadState.log	The /l switch specifies the location and name of the log file.
/lac[:<password>]	The local account create (/lac) switch creates the local accounts if they don't already exist. They start disabled and will have a blank password if the password is not included. If you're using a script, we don't recommend that you include the password since the password will be in clear text. Also, this is the same password that is used for all accounts.
/lae	You can enable the local user accounts that are created with the /lae switch. You must include the /lac switch when using the /lae switch.

USING THE /AUTO SWITCH

You can use the /auto switch in the LoadState command the same way you can use it with the LoadState command. Table 5.10 shows the switches used with the following command:

```
C:\>c:\usmt\loadstate /auto:c:\usmt\ c:\USMTStore /l:myloadstate.log /lac
```

TABLE 5.10: Using the LoadState /auto switch

SWITCH	DESCRIPTION
/auto	Using the /auto switch without a directory path causes it to set the directory path to the location where the USMT files are installed (if they were installed rather than just copied). If you have local users to migrate, you must include at least the /lac switch.
/auto:c:\usmt	If you specify a path with the /auto switch, it will use this path to locate and use the MigDocs.xml and MigApp.xml files.

DECRYPTING THE MIGRATION STORE

If you encrypted the migration store with the ScanState tool, you'll need to decrypt it using the /decrypt switch. The following command will decrypt the store using the default encryption method with a password key of **P@ssw0rd**. The switches are explained in Table 5.11.

```
C:\>c:\usmt\loadstate /auto:c:\usmt\ c:\USMTStore /l:myloadstate.log

/decrypt /key:P@ssw0rd
```

TABLE 5.11:   LoadState decryption switches

SWITCH	DESCRIPTION
/decrypt	Decrypts the migration store. If you specified the encryption algorithm when creating the store, you need to include it when decrypting it.
	You must specify either the /key or /keyfile option when decrypting the store to identify the correct password.
/key:KeyString /key:"my P@ssw0rd"	Specifies the decryption key. This is the same key used to encrypt the store. If the encryption key has a space, it needs to be enclosed in quotes.
/keyfile:FileName	Specifies the location and name of a TXT file containing the decryption key.

RETRIEVING DATA FROM A HARD-LINK MIGRATION

If you used the /hardlink switch to create a hard-link migration store, you can use the /hardlink switch with the LoadState command, as shown with the following command:

```
C:\>c:\usmt\loadstate /auto:c:\usmt\ /hardlink c:\HardLinkStore

/l:myscanstate.log /nocompress /lac
```

Table 5.12 shows the switches used with the /hardlink option. Notice that you must use the /nocompress switch when using the /hardlink switch.

TABLE 5.12:   LoadState /hardlink and /nocompress switches

SWITCH	DESCRIPTION
/hardlink	Enables hard links for a noncompressed store. This is only used for PC refresh scenarios.
/nocompress	Specifies that the migration store is not compressed.

RETRIEVING DATA FROM WINDOWS.OLD

If you performed a refresh and the installation created the Windows.old folder, you can use ScanState and then LoadState to retrieve and then restore the data. The Windows.old file doesn't exist before you refresh the computer, so you don't execute the ScanState command before the installation. Instead, you execute both commands after the refresh with Windows 7 running on the system.

The following is a sample ScanState command that will retrieve the data from the Windows.old folder. Even though this switch appears as multiple lines in this book, you'll enter it as a single line.

```
C:\>c:\usmt\scanstate c:\usmtstore /auto:c:\usmt\

/offlinewinold:c:\windows.old\windows

/hardlink c:\HardLinkStore /l:myscanstate.log /nocompress
```

If you have EFS encrypted files in the Windows.old folder, you can add the /efs switch with this command:

```
C:\>c:\usmt\scanstate c:\usmtstore /auto:c:\usmt\

/offlinewinold:c:\windows.old\windows

/hardlink c:\HardLinkStore /l:myscanstate.log /nocompress /efs:hardlink
```

You can then use this command to load the user state data:

```
c:\>c:\usmt\loadstate c:\usmtstore /auto:c:\usmt\ /lac /hardlink /nocompress
```

Table 5.13 shows the switches used with the /offlinewinold option. Notice that you must include the path to Windows within Windows.old as Windows.old\windows.

TABLE 5.13:   Offline Windows folder switches

SWITCH	DESCRIPTION
/offlinewinold:<windows.old path> /offlinewinold:c:\windows.old\window	This switch points to the location of the Windows.old folder. Normally this is named Windows.old, but if there are multiple Windows.old folders, they are named as Windows.old.000, Windows.old.001, and so on.
/nocompress	Specifies that the migration store is not compressed.

Getting Extra Mileage Out of the USMT

This section outlines some tips and tricks you can use to get some extra mileage out of the USMT.

MODIFY THE *MIGDOCS.XML* FILE TO EXCLUDE FILES

You can modify the MigDocs.xml file to exclude any specific types of files based on their extension. You do this by adding an exclude rule to the file. The exclude rule takes the following format. In this example, it will exclude all MP3 files but you can substitute any extension for .mp3:

```
<exclude>
    <objectSet>
        <pattern type="File">C:\* [*.mp3]</pattern>
```

```
                    </objectSet>
                </exclude>
```

The following XML text can be used by itself in a different `MyMigDocs.xml` file to migrate all data files except MP3 files, or you can just place the previous `<exclude>` node within the existing `MigDocs.xml` file.

```
<migration

  urlid="http://www.microsoft.com/migration/1.0/migxmlext/mp3files">
    <!-- This component migrates all files except

        those with .mp3 extension-->
  <component type="Documents" context="System">
      <displayName _locID="miguser.sharedvideo">MP3 Files</displayName>
      <role role="Data">
          <rules>
              <include filter='MigXmlHelper.IgnoreIrrelevantLinks()'>
                  <objectSet>
                      <pattern type="File">C:\* [*]</pattern>
                  </objectSet>
              </include>
              <exclude>
                  <objectSet>
                      <pattern type="File">C:\* [*.mp3]</pattern>
                  </objectSet>
              </exclude>
          </rules>
      </role>
  </component>
</migration>
```

You can find additional examples of how to exclude files in the "Exclude Files and Settings" article in the User State Migration Tool (USM) 4.0 User's Guide available in the help file at `C:\Program Files\Windows AIK\Docs\CHMs\USMT.chm`.

BUILDING A USB DRIVE TO SIMPLIFY MIGRATIONS

It's relatively easy to create a portable USB drive with the tools you need to perform hard-link migrations on systems that include the `Windows.old` folder. You can even include a script to copy all the needed files, and then complete the migration. All you have to do is plug in the USB and start the batch file.

First, copy the entire contents of the `C:\Program Files\Windows AIK\Tools\USMT\` folder onto the USB drive. These files are on your technician's computer after installing the WAIK. Next, create a batch file named `Migrate32.bat`, with the following lines:

```
@ECHO OFF
If exist D:\USMT\*.* xcopy D:\USMT\*.* /e /v /y C:\Windows\USMT\
If exist E:\USMT\*.* xcopy E:\USMT\*.* /e /v /y C:\Windows\USMT\
If exist F:\USMT\*.* xcopy F:\USMT\*.* /e /v /y C:\Windows\USMT\
```

```
If exist G:\USMT\*.* xcopy G:\USMT\*.* /e /v /y C:\Windows\USMT\
If exist H:\USMT\*.* xcopy H:\USMT\*.* /e /v /y C:\Windows\USMT\
If exist I:\USMT\*.* xcopy I:\USMT\*.* /e /v /y C:\Windows\USMT\
If exist J:\USMT\*.* xcopy J:\USMT\*.* /e /v /y C:\Windows\USMT\
If exist K:\USMT\*.* xcopy K:\USMT\*.* /e /v /y C:\Windows\USMT\
Cd c:\windows\usmt\x86
scanstate.exe c:\store /v:5 /o /c /hardlink /nocompress

 /efs:hardlink /i:MigApp.xml /i:MigDocs.xml

 offlinewinold:c:\windows.old\windows
loadstate.exe c:\store /v:5 /c /lac /i:migapp.xml

 /i:migdocs.xml /hardlink /nocompress
```

The `If exist...` lines detect which drive is the USB drive and then copy all of the USMT files onto the target computer. The `Cd` line changes the directory to the usmt\86 folder. The `ScanState` command captures the user state data, and then the `LoadState` command applies it. Note that the `ScanState` command spans two lines in the book, but it is entered as a single line.

If your target computer is a 64-bit system, save the file as `Migrate64.bat` and change the `Cd` line to:

```
Cd c:\windows\usmt\amd64
```

This script is derived from the "Windows XP to Windows 7 Hard-Link Migration of User Files and Settings" white paper available from Microsoft's download site (www.microsoft.com/downloads).

DELETING THE HARD-LINK STORE

If you later need to remove the hard-link store but get errors indicating that the folder is locked, you can delete it with the following command:

```
C:\>c:\usmt\Usmtutils /d c:\HardLinkStore
```

You should only delete the hard-link store once you are sure that you have migrated all the needed data.

DELETING THE *WINDOWS.OLD* FOLDER

The `Windows.old` folder can take a lot of space. Once you are done with it, you can delete it to regain space. The simplest way to delete it is using Disk Cleanup from the properties of the drive. You can access the properties by right-clicking the drive in Windows Explorer and selecting Properties. After clicking Disk Cleanup, click the Cleanup System Files button. The Previous Windows installation(s) selection will appear and you can then select it to delete the `Windows.old` folder.

While this will work, you may want to automate the process. You can use the following two lines in a script file to delete the `Windows.old` folder. The first line takes ownership of the `Windows.old` folder and all files and folders within it. The second line removes the folder, including all folders within it.

```
takeown /f c:\windows.old\* /r /a /d Y
rd /s /q c:\Windows.old\
```

The Bottom Line

Identify folders holding user state data.   User state data can be migrated from a user's old system to the new system. This gives the user a lot of the same settings and data as they had before the OS change.

Master It   You are preparing to upgrade several systems from Windows XP to Windows 7. You want to view some users' folders to determine where their documents are stored. Where are user profiles stored in Windows XP and Windows 7?

   A.   In the `\Documents and Settings\username` folder in both operating systems

   B.   In the `\Users\username` folder in both operating systems

   C.   In the `\Documents and Settings\username` folder in Windows XP and in the `\Users\username` folder in Windows 7

   D.   In the `\Documents and Settings\username` folder in Windows 7 and in the `\Users\username` folder in Windows XP

Identify the best tool to use to transfer user state data for a single user.   You may occasionally need to transfer a single user's user state data from one computer to another. For example, you may want to ensure that an executive's user state data is transferred due to some special needs.

Master It   What is the best tool to use to transfer user state data for a single user?

   A.   Windows AIK

   B.   ScanState

   C.   LoadState

   D.   Windows Easy Transfer

Capture user state data.   The first step in user state migration is to capture the user state data. The USMT includes tools used to capture this data.

Master It   You have copied the USMT to the `C:\USMT` folder on a source computer. You want to use these tools to capture user state data. What command should you use to capture user state data on a source system?

Apply user state data.   The last step in migrating user state data is to apply the user state data to the new system. The USMT includes tools used to apply the data.

Master It   You have captured user state data and stored it on a removable hard drive. You have installed Windows 7 on a new computer and copied the USMT tools into the `C:\USMT` folder. You now want to apply the captured user state data to the new computer. What command should you use to apply the captured state data onto a target computer?

Capture and apply user state data from the Windows.old folder.   User state data can be retrieved from the Windows.old folder after Windows 7 has been installed. You can even apply user state data after the Windows 7 installation if you didn't capture the data before the installation.

Master It   You performed a refresh of a PC that originally had Windows XP. You performed a clean installation of Windows 7 without modifying the partitions and a copy of the Windows.old folder was created. You also installed the USMT tools into the C:\USMT folder. You now want to apply the user state data from the Windows.old folder to the Windows 7 installation. What command(s) should you use?

Chapter 6

Windows Deployment Services: The Basics

When looking to perform installations of Windows images in the past, many organizations have turned to third-party solutions that require additional licensing. Microsoft has included a network-based image deployment solution called Windows Deployment Services (WDS) in every release of the server operating system since Windows Server 2003 Service Pack 2.

WDS allows administrators to capture and deploy operating system images using the hardware features of the computer being worked with. This makes it very useful for deploying operating systems to computers that don't have a DVD drive, such as budget PCs or netbooks. WDS can be used as a standalone solution, or it can be used to extend the functionality of the Microsoft Deployment Toolkit (light-touch deployment) and Microsoft System Center Configuration Manager (zero-touch deployment). The best bit is WDS requires no additional license purchases.

In this chapter, you will learn to:

◆ Understand how WDS works

◆ Install and configure WDS

◆ Add boot and installation images

Understanding WDS

There are many ways to install an operating system. An administrator can manually install an image. The manual installation is slow and requires a lot of effort to customize. By now you are aware that you can use the Windows Automated Installation Kit (WAIK) to create an image and deploy it using a boot image. That boot image must be stored on either a USB stick or a DVD. That requirement can cause a problem; the computer might not have a DVD drive or you might not have a USB stick or writeable media when you need them.

The History of WDS

Microsoft provided a basic network deployment solution in Windows Server 2000 and Windows Server 2003 called Remote Installation Services (RIS). It was difficult to manage and slow. As a result, many organizations chose not to use it, preferring third-party imaging solutions that had to be purchased, such as the ubiquitous Ghost. Many of those organizations failed to understand the licensing requirements of these solutions and left themselves vulnerable to prosecution for license violations.

The story changed starting with the release of Service Pack 2 for Windows Server 2003. It introduced Windows Deployment Services (WDS) as a replacement for the RIS role. The new network-based operating system deployment solution used boot images and installation images. Client computers used a feature of the hardware to download a boot image and then pick and install an installation image. WDS has evolved and matured with the releases of Windows Server 2008 and Windows Server 2008 R2. It can be used as a stand-alone solution where administrators and end users can install an image containing the operating system, applications, and their configurations. It can also be used to extend the functionality of the Microsoft Deployment Toolkit (MDT). MDT also uses boot images, and you can store them on a WDS server to boot up client computers without any media. Microsoft System Center Configuration Manager 2007 also makes use of WDS to allow computers to boot up on the network without any media.

WDS provides a solution where you can boot up a computer on the network using a boot image that is stored on the WDS server. An administrator or user can log into a WDS client and select an installation image to be deployed. WDS administrators can add device drivers to the WDS server so that they can be automatically installed using Plug and Play during an image installation. WAIK unattended installation answer files can be used to completely automate the installation of the Windows image. There is even support for multicast deployments in Windows Server 2008 and Windows Server 2008 R2. This is everything you could ask for in a network-based operating system deployment solution. And you get all of this without having to spend anything extra on licensing. This makes WDS a must-know solution.

How Does WDS Work?

WDS is an operating system deployment solution that allows new bare-metal or existing computers to boot up from a network-stored Windows PE boot image, run a WDS client, choose a Windows Imaging (WIM)-based installation image, and install it.

That installation image must be created. You can use any of the solutions that create a WIM file, such as WAIK, or even use the default installation images on the Windows 7 media. WDS, much like cloning solutions such as Ghost, will allow you to capture an image from a generalized template computer. The new WIM file will be captured and stored on the WDS server, available to be deployed to other computers.

Boot Up with PXE

WDS depends on a technology that was created by Intel called Pre-boot Execution Environment (PXE). PXE allows computers to boot up using their network cards instead of a hard disk, floppy drive, or USB device.

The computer that is to be captured or deployed is booted up using PXE. This requires the following:

The hardware is capable of supporting a PXE boot.   The computer must have a network card that is Net PC/PC98 compliant. It is the network card that is providing the boot-from-network functionality. Computers have provided this support for many years. It is very unlikely that a Windows 7–capable computer won't have support for a PXE boot.

The BIOS is configured to allow a PXE boot.   Your computer may have the option for booting from PXE disabled. You will see a prompt to press a key, such as F12, to boot from the network during the machine's POST if it is enabled. You should enable the boot from network option in the BIOS of any machine that you will deploy operating system images to using WDS.

The computer will start the PXE client. This will broadcast on the network. It requires responses from two services:

DHCP   The computer is booting up using bare metal. It will require a network configuration to communicate with the WDS server. This IP configuration will be provided by a DHCP server. This means that the broadcast domain (or subnet) that the client is booting up on must have a DHCP server that can respond to the client with a valid IP configuration for the current network.

PXE Server   The PXE is a component of the WDS server. It is made up of one (by default) or more (provided possibly by third parties) providers that will respond to PXE clients. This will initiate the next phase of the bootup process.

The PXE server is what is interesting here. The broadcast sent by the client (Figure 6.1) is in the form of a DHCPDISCOVER packet with PXE options on User Datagram Protocol (UDP) port 67. It should be noted that UDP 4011 will also be used if the PXE server is running on the same server as DHCP because both services cannot share UDP 67.

FIGURE 6.1
The PXE client
broadcasts on the
network.

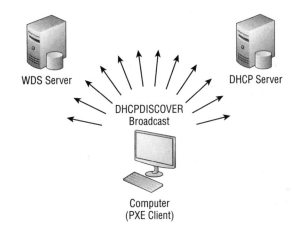

WDS Server

DHCP Server

DHCPDISCOVER
Broadcast

Computer
(PXE Client)

This packet will be ignored by DHCP servers. The PXE server will respond with a DHCPOFFER including the following (see Figure 6.2):

◆   The IP address of a PXE boot server

◆   A PXE boot menu

◆   A prompt for the user sitting at the PXE client to press F8

◆   A timeout for the user to respond to the prompt

DOWNLOADING A BOOT IMAGE USING TRIVIAL FTP

The PXE boot menu, which is configured using the settings in the PXE server DHCPOFFER, will be presented to the user sitting at the client machine. A list of possible boot images will be presented if there is more than one suitable boot image. The process will continue when the user sitting at the client responds to the boot menu.

FIGURE 6.2
The DHCP and
WDS servers
respond to the
broadcast.

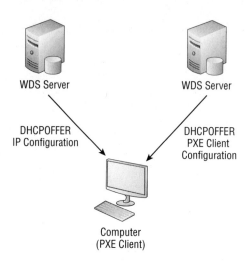

The PXE client will use Trivial FTP (TFTP) to download the boot image that you have chosen from the WDS server (Figure 6.3). TFTP is usually a pretty slow protocol for file transfers because it requires each data packet from the server to be acknowledged by the client. This could be very noticeable on slower networks. Windows Server 2008 introduced TFTP windowing to improve this file transfer performance. This allows a larger block of data to be sent in a window.

FIGURE 6.3
The PXE client
downloads the
boot image.

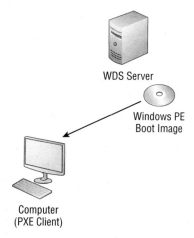

BOOTING UP THE WDS CLIENT

The boot image will download and boot up. The WDS client will now start up. This will allow the user to authenticate with the WDS server. If the WDS client is configured to deploy an image, then the user will select an installation image to be downloaded by the WDS client and installed (Figure 6.4).

FIGURE 6.4
The installation image is downloaded and installed by the WDS client.

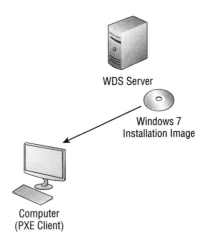

WDS Server

Windows 7
Installation Image

Computer
(PXE Client)

The installation image is installed, similarly to how a manual installation of Windows is installed, resulting in a machine running the Windows 7 operating system. Without an answer file, someone will have to answer some questions about the configuration of the machine. With a WAIK-generated answer file, the installation will be automated.

A WDS administrator can create a boot image with a WDS client that is intended to capture an image. A template machine is installed and customized, generalized with Sysprep, and shut down. The machine is booted up using the PXE client and the administrator selects the capture boot image. This will capture the generalized machine and copy the resulting image to the WDS server. This new image can be tested and then deployed to other machines using WDS.

Now that you've seen how WDS works, we'll look at how to design and install it in the next section.

DEPLOYING OTHER OPERATING SYSTEMS WITH WDS

An organization that is planning on deploying Windows 7 is likely to want to continue to deploy other operating systems such as Windows XP or Windows Vista. This is possible with WDS. They may even consider deploying server operating systems such as Windows Server 2003, Windows Server 2008, or Windows Server 2008 R2.

Windows XP and Windows Server 2003 use an older installation system than the one that was introduced with Windows Vista and it's still used by subsequent operating systems such as Windows 7. But that doesn't prevent you from deploying those legacy operating systems with WDS. The process is quite similar to how you would deploy those operating systems with Ghost or similar cloning tools. You create a template machine, generalize it with Sysprep, shut the machine down, and use WDS to capture an installation image that can be deployed by WDS.

Windows Vista, Windows Server 2008, and Windows Server 2008 R2 all use the same mechanisms as Windows 7, even if there may be minor unattended answer file differences. The great thing about Microsoft deployment technologies such as WAIK, WDS, Microsoft Deployment Toolkit, or System Center Configuration Manager is that much of the knowledge and skills is shared across the whole portfolio of solutions.

Deploying WDS

The process of installing WDS is pretty simple. The key to success is designing the solution to suit your environment and the needs of your organization.

Designing a WDS Solution

There are three considerations when you design a WDS solution:

◆ Broadcast domains

◆ DHCP

◆ WDS server

The computer that you are installing an image on uses DHCP traffic to get configurations from DHCP and the PXE server running on the WDS server. DHCP is based on broadcast traffic and this traffic is normally constrained within a broadcast domain. A broadcast domain is a subnet or VLAN that is designed not to allow noisy broadcast traffic into another subnet or VLAN. For example, a PXE client in a 192.168.1.0/24 VLAN will not be able to send a DHCPDISCOVER packet to a DHCP server in the 192.168.2.0/24 VLAN, as illustrated in Figure 6.5.

FIGURE 6.5
DHCP traffic limited by broadcast domain

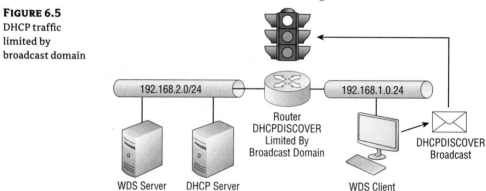

There are a few options. The first is to place the WDS and DHCP servers in the same broadcast domain (subnet or VLAN) as the computers that are to be built. That's not a realistic solution in any but the simplest networks where there is just a single subnet. Larger organizations will need a more elegant solution that doesn't require servers to be wastefully dotted around every network. The solution that is recommended by Microsoft as the most reliable will involve working with the network administrators. Network appliances that are used to create and segregate VLANs have a feature called an *IP helper table*. An IP helper will forward DHCP and PXE broadcast traffic from a selected VLAN and forward it to configured IP addresses. The DHCP server(s) will be configured with the necessary DHCP scopes for each VLAN that will be supported, as shown in Figure 6.6.

The precise configuration for the IP helper table is as follows:

UDP 67: DHCP: The DHCP traffic will be forwarded from the client VLAN to the IP addresses of the appropriate DHCP and WDS servers.

UDP 4011: PXE: The PXE traffic from the client VLAN will be forwarded to the IP address of the WDS server.

You may find yourself working in an existing network where DHCP is fully functional across many VLANs and you need to quickly add WDS functionality. It might not be possible to get the IP helper table updates, either for engineering, political, or timing reasons. An alternative solution is to add knowledge of the WDS server to each DHCP scope that will be used by WDS clients. The options in question are as follows:

66: This will direct the PXE client to the WDS server.

67: This will tell the PXE client which boot file should be downloaded.

Microsoft does state that the DHCP options approach for making the WDS server findable by PXE clients will work but that the IP helper approach is preferred.

It is possible that an organization will have more than one PXE server on the network. For example, desktop administrators may choose to use WDS to deploy images to personnel computers and server administrators may choose to use a manufacturer's solution for deploying images to servers. How will PXE clients know which PXE server to work with if both PXE servers are on the same network? It is possible to configure a response delay in WDS. This will, as you can see in Figure 6.7, allow a WDS server to co-exist with another PXE server in a single server VLAN.

FIGURE 6.6
Using DHCP relays to span VLANs

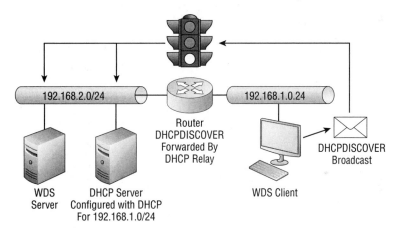

FIGURE 6.7
WDS co-existing with another PXE server

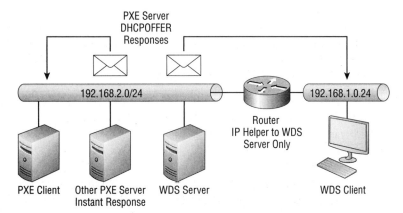

The router between the personnel computer VLAN and the server VLAN is configured with an IP helper to forward DHCP traffic to the DHCP server and the WDS server. The PXE server that is responsible for server installations is not configured. This means that the WDS server can respond to PXE clients in the personnel computer VLANs and the other PXE server is completely unaware of them.

You can see that servers will also be PXE clients so they can use the other PXE server for server image installations. The other PXE server will respond as normal to their DHCPDISCOVER broadcasts. However, the WDS server is configured with a delay. This means that the PXE client has already been serviced by the other PXE server by the time the WDS server can respond.

As you can see, the planning of WDS revolves around the network of the organization that you are working with. You will plan the location of your servers and the configuration of your network devices with the assistance of your network administrators.

WDS Requirements

We have already mentioned some of the requirements but we will remind you of them and cover the rest before we look at installing the first WDS server. Here are the requirements for WDS:

Operating System WDS is included with Windows Server 2003 with Service Pack 2, Windows Server 2008, and Windows Server 2008 R2. We will be focusing on the latest version, Windows Server 2008 R2, because it has the most features.

Active Directory The WDS server must be a member of a domain or be a domain controller in the domain. The latter is not recommended in a non–small business server network. A benefit of this requirement is that the WDS server can authenticate and authorize access to image deployment resources. Note that a Windows Server 2008 R2 WDS server does not have this Active Directory requirement.

DHCP The PXE clients must be able to get an IP address that allows them to communicate with the WDS server.

DNS Name resolution will be required, so you must have DNS operational.

NTFS Volume The image store is where the boot and installation images will be located. This must be on an NTFS volume on the WDS server.

Credentials You must have local administrator rights to install WDS on the server. Enterprise Administrator rights in the Active Directory forest are required to authorize the WDS server as a DHCP server so it can respond to PXE clients. Domain users will be able to access WDS deployment services from a PXE client. Note that authorization for Windows Server 2008 R2 WDS servers is optional.

So far we have looked at how WDS works and how to design a WDS installation, and we have summarized the prerequisites. We will examine the process of installing WDS next.

Installing WDS

Installing WDS is quite easy. In Windows Server 2003 you just have to add a Windows component in Control Panel. In Windows Server 2008 and Windows Server 2008 R2 you will use the Server Manager administrative tool. Windows Server 2008 also allows you to use a command-line tool called servermanagercmd. Windows Server 2008 R2 allows you to use the Server Manager PowerShell *cmdlets* (pronounced *command-lets*) to add the Windows Deployment Services role.

SERVER MANAGER

You can learn more about the Server Manager administrative tool in Chapter 2 of *Mastering Microsoft Windows Server 2008 R2* (Sybex, 2010). That chapter goes into great depth about the process of installing and configuring Windows Server 2008 and Windows Server 2008 R2.

This chapter will feature an example network where we have installed a server called deploysrv in a domain called deploy.com. The machine has two volumes: Windows Server 2008 R2 is installed on the C: drive. The D: drive is where the image store will be located. This is formatted with NTFS.

You have two ways to install WDS on Windows Server 2008 R2. The first option is to use Server Manager. Navigate into Roles and click the Add Roles link. This will launch the Add Roles Wizard. Navigate to the Select Server Roles screen, shown in Figure 6.8, and select Windows Deployment Services.

FIGURE 6.8
Select the Windows Deployment Services role.

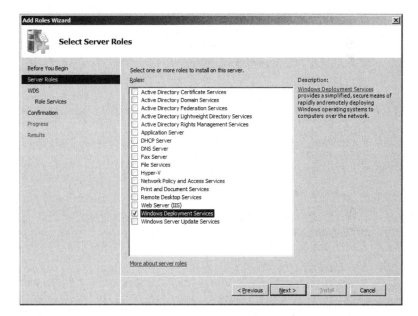

The Select Role Services screen (Figure 6.9) gives you granular control over the components of a role that will be installed. There are two WDS role services:

Transport Server   This role service provides networking functionality to the Deployment Server role, such as multicasting.

Deployment Server   The Deployment Server role service provides the bulk of the functionality of WDS. It depends on the Transport Server role service and cannot be installed without it.

Complete the wizard and the WDS role will be installed. A reboot is not normally required.

FIGURE 6.9

Add the WDS role services.

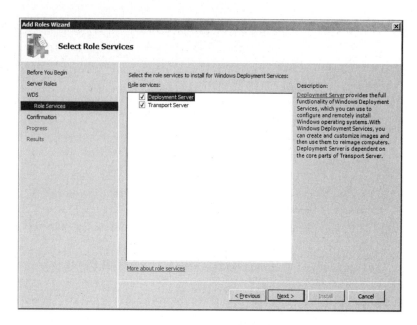

To speed things up, you can complete the previous steps using two PowerShell cmdlets. Start up the PowerShell interface. The first command will add the Server Manager module:

```
import-module servermanager
```

This will give you access to the Server Manager cmdlets. The next command will enable the Windows Deployment Services role:

```
add-windowsfeature wds
```

WDS is installed (using any of the previous methods) but it is not yet active. The server needs to be configured.

Configure the WDS Installation

The WDS role is installed, but you must configure it before you can proceed with adding any images or clients.

You will do the server configuration using the Windows Deployment Services console, which is found in Administrative Tools. Expand Servers in the navigation pane on the left and you will find your new WDS server, which has an exclamation mark icon beside it (Figure 6.10).

Right-click the server in question and select Configure Server. This will launch the Windows Deployment Services Configuration Wizard, shown in Figure 6.11. Pay attention to this screen, making sure that you have met every requirement. Desktop administrators or consultants will have to work with network and domain administrators.

The Remote Installation Folder Location screen allows you to choose the location of the image store on your WDS server. We recommend that you do not use the C: drive of your WDS server. A D: drive will allow you to expand your data without impacting the health of the operating system. You can see in Figure 6.12 that we've entered the location of **D:\RemoteInstall**.

FIGURE 6.10
The unconfigured
WDS server

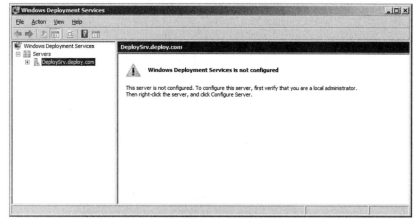

FIGURE 6.11
A reminder of the
WDS requirements

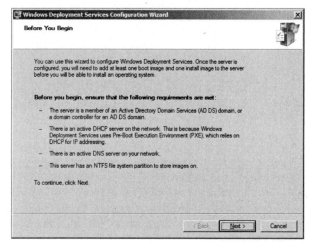

FIGURE 6.12
Specify the image
store location.

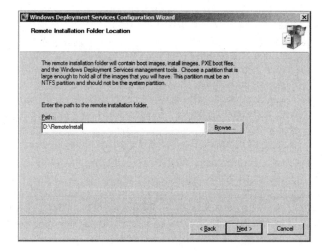

The PXE Server Initial Settings screen (Figure 6.13) allows you to configure if WDS will respond to PXE clients, and if it does, how it will respond. There are three options:

Do Not Respond To Any Client Computers This is pretty self-explanatory. WDS will ignore all PXE clients when this option is selected. You will probably have WDS configured to ignore all PXE clients until the WDS server is configured.

FIGURE 6.13
PXE Server Initial
Settings

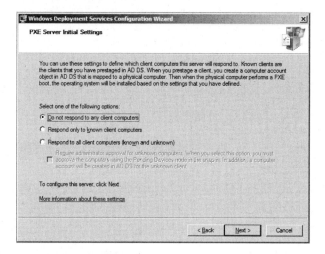

Respond Only To Known Client Computers This option will configure WDS to only work with hardware that is authorized within the domain. WDS uses the network card MAC address and a GUID to uniquely identify computers. Any computer that is built by WDS will have a computer object in the domain and the unique identifier will be stored as an attribute. You can also provision computer objects in the domain with one of these identifiers for new computers that do not yet have an operating system. This option gives you total control over which machines can access your services, but it does come at a significant administrative overhead. We will cover this subject in more detail in Chapter 7, "WDS from the Client's View."

Respond To All Client Computers (Known And Unknown) This option will allow any computer on the network to connect to WDS and use its services. This is probably the option that will be most popular because it allows easy deployment of operating systems, potentially even for end users, with zero administrative overheard. You might like to retain a little control over this process when a new computer arrives on the network. The Require Administrative Approval For Unknown Computers suboption will affect computers that do not have computer objects with a populated GUID/MAC attribute. The PXE client will sit in a pending state until an administrator approves the computer in the Windows Deployment Services console. The user will be prompted to call a help desk, at which point their request can be approved (or not) and the PXE client will continue the process.

Don't worry; you will be able to change the PXE server response configuration at a later point to suit the state of your deployment server and the security policies of the organization.

The wizard will offer you the option to add images to the server at this point. You could choose to do that now, but we'll skip this step in this example. (See the "Image Management" section later in this chapter.) Clear the checkbox and end the wizard.

You might remember that a pre–Windows Server 2008 R2 WDS server must be authorized as a DHCP server on your network. This will allow it to respond to PXE clients when they send out their `DHCPDISCOVER` packet. This authorization process will require Enterprise Administrator rights in the Active Directory forest that the WDS server is a member of. You will need to get assistance if you do not have these rights. You will be asked to explain the requirement, so you need to be able to explain how WDS will respond to PXE clients sending out a `DHCPDISCOVER` and how this will not interfere with normal DHCP operations.

You can log into a machine that has the DHCP role installed and launch the DHCP console. Alternatively you can launch the console on a computer that has the Remote Server Administration Tools installed. Right-click on DHCP in the navigation menu and select Manage Authorized Servers. This will open the screen shown in Figure 6.14.

Click the Authorize button. This opens the dialog box shown in Figure 6.15. Here you can enter the name or IP address of the WDS server that you want to authorize.

FIGURE 6.14
The Manage Authorized Servers screen

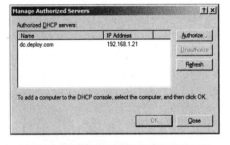

FIGURE 6.15
Authorize the WDS server.

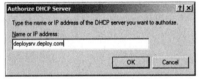

You will be presented with another screen that shows the name and IP address of the server you have entered. This allows you to confirm your selection. You will be returned to the Manage Authorized Servers screen, where you should see your freshly authorized WDS server (Figure 6.16), nearly ready to respond to PXE clients. All that remains is to customize the WDS server and add some images.

FIGURE 6.16
The WDS server is authorized to respond.

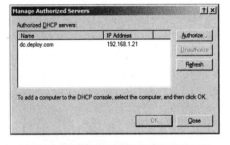

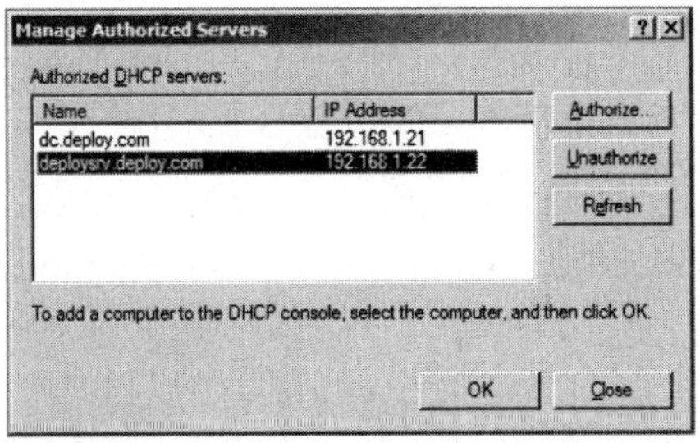

Image Management

WDS uses the same types of images that you use in a manual installation of Windows 7 (and Vista, Windows Server 2008, and Windows Server 2008 R2), as you saw in Chapter 4, "Cloning the Panther: Automating Windows 7 Installation."

Boot Image The boot image is the stripped-down version of Windows, called Windows PE, that starts up and allows the Windows installation image to be installed on the hardware. In the case of a WDS deployment, the boot image will run a WDS client, and it will require a network card driver (to talk to the WDS server) and may require an additional storage controller driver (to gain access to the hard disk on the computer). The boot image will be stored in the WDS image store and will be downloaded by the PXE client using TFTP. The default boot image can be copied from the Windows 7 media kit.

Installation Image The installation image contains the operating system that will be deployed. It can also contain additional software and configurations. WDS stores installation images in the WDS store, and they are downloaded to the computer being prepared by the WDS client. WDS can use the default installation image from the media kit, and it can create a customized installation image from a generalized template machine.

We'll discuss how to add these images to WDS, how to organize them, and how to optimize disk usage in this section.

Managing Boot Images

The process of adding and managing images in WDS is much easier than you might expect if you have only worked with WAIK before this. A lot of the complexity is hidden behind the GUI. We're going to look at managing boot images in WDS.

ADDING A BOOT IMAGE

You will need to create a starting point by adding a boot image to your WDS server. The easiest place to find a boot image is in your Windows 7 media kit. You can load your DVD or mount an ISO file to copy the boot.wim file from the \Sources folder in the Windows 7 installation media.

WHICH BOOT IMAGE?

You might aim to deploy 64-bit editions of Windows 7 because it allows you to use 4 GB of RAM or more in your computers. But you may find that you have to deploy some 32-bit installations because of legacy hardware or application/driver compatibility issues.

Some legacy hardware will have 32-bit processors. This means that you will have to use 32-bit boot images for them.

Boot images contain Windows PE. We recommend that you always use the latest version of Windows PE. For example, you shouldn't try to use a boot image from a Windows Vista media kit to deploy Windows 7.

You will manage your images in the Windows Deployment Services console. Navigate to Windows Deployment Services ➤ Servers ➤ *<ServerName>* ➤ Boot Images. Right-click on Boot Images and select Add Boot Image. This will open the Add Image Wizard, shown in Figure 6.17. The boot image on the Windows 7 media kit has been selected in our example.

FIGURE 6.17
Adding a
boot image

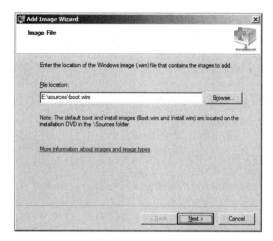

The Image Metadata screen (Figure 6.18) allows you to give the boot image a name and a description. Try to be as descriptive as possible. This boot image will be used to deploy Windows installation images so you might consider entering something like **Install Windows 7** or **Deploy Windows 7** in the Image Name field.

FIGURE 6.18
Boot image
metadata

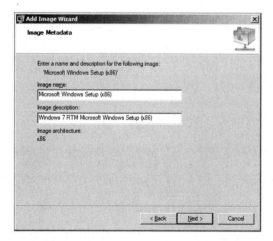

The boot image is copied into the image store once you proceed past the Summary screen. You can see in Figure 6.19 that the boot image is now available for management and for PXE clients to download. You can see that the image name that you entered in the Image Metadata screen is used to identify the boot image in the console.

FIGURE 6.19
The new
boot image

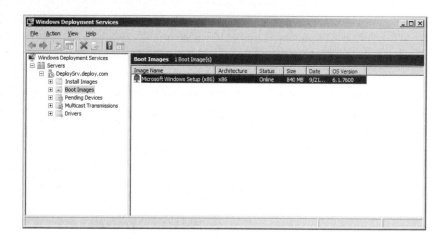

You can edit the properties of the boot image to change the name or description as required.

ADDING DRIVERS TO THE WDS SERVER

A boot image will require drivers to use the network card in the computer that is being prepared. It may also need a storage controller driver. Like with Windows 7, Windows PE will have a number of included drivers that can be loaded as required. You may find that many older machines will not require you to add any drivers. However, you may find that you need to use newer drivers to resolve driver fault issues, or to provide support for newer devices that do not already have a driver included with Windows PE. The drivers that you import here will also be provided to the device installation process during the deployment of an installation image.

We have some very good news here. There is no need to use Deployment Image Servicing and Management (DISM) for this. You can do all of your driver management in the Windows Deployment Services console.

You will need to download your drivers and extract them. The latter can sometimes require a little bit of work. For example, some manufacturers prefer to include drivers in an executable that is not extractable using normal means. You can run the installer program, find where the files are extracted by the installer, and copy them for later use. You need to find the folder that contains the Windows 7 drivers as well as the SYS and INF files.

You will need access to the drivers while managing the WDS server. Copy all the drivers you want to add to WDS to a location on the network that gives you this access. Launch the Windows Deployment Services console and browse to Drivers in the navigation pane. Right-click on Drivers and select Add Driver Package to add new drivers to the WDS server. This will launch the Add Driver Package Wizard, shown in Figure 6.20. WDS refers to a device driver as a *driver package*. You have two ways to specify driver packages in this wizard:

Select Driver Packages From An .inf File   Select this option if you want to add a single driver package to WDS. You will click Browse and navigate to the location where the driver package is located. This option is useful if you want to update a single driver package in scenarios where you are troubleshooting or when a manufacturer publishes an update with a bug fix.

Select All Driver Packages From A Folder   This is the option you will use when you want to do a bulk import of driver packages. You click the Browse button and navigate to a folder where the driver packages are located (possibly in subfolders). This option is useful when you are adding a new model of supported computer in the organization or when you are first setting up WDS.

FIGURE 6.20
Add Driver Pack-
age Wizard

In this example, we have copied a set of 32-bit drivers into a folder called `D:\ISO\Drivers\x86` and we have chosen the Select All Driver Packages From A Folder option to add them all.

WDS IN A VIRTUAL LAB

There is a very good chance that you will develop your skills and processes for WDS in a virtualized lab environment. Virtual machines may not have hardware, but they do require a type of driver in the form of integration components (Microsoft's Hyper-V) or additions (VMware). The required driver installation files are sometimes found in ISO files on the host machine. For example, on a Hyper-V host you can mount `C:\Windows\system32\vmguest.iso` and copy the contents of the cabinet files found in `\support\<architecture>\`.

The lab used in this chapter is running on a Hyper-V host server and the drivers shown have been copied from the integration components ISO file.

Figure 6.21 shows the Available Driver Packages screen in the Add Driver Package Wizard. This screen presents every driver that was found in the chosen folder. You can decide to exclude some drivers by clearing the check boxes beside them. View detailed information about a specific driver by double-clicking on it in the Package Details box.

FIGURE 6.21
Choose which of
the found drivers
you want to add.

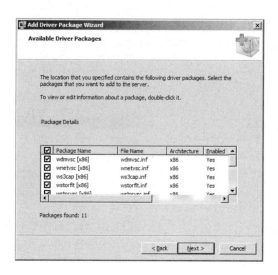

The drivers will be imported after a Summary screen. After the import you have the option to add the driver packages to a *driver group*. Driver groups are used in WDS to organize the driver packages and to make it easier to work with large numbers of them. Drivers groups are also used to make driver packages available for installation. Figure 6.22 shows the Driver Groups screen, which has three options:

Select An Existing Driver Group You can add the drivers to an existing driver group, such as the default DriverGroup1 or any other driver group that you have previously created.

Create A New Driver Group Named You can specify the name of a new driver group to be created. The new driver packages will be added to this new driver group.

FIGURE 6.22
Adding new driver
packages to a
driver group

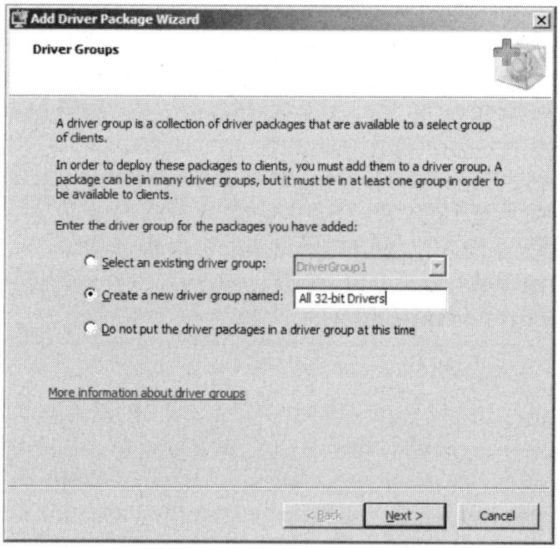

Do Not Put The Driver Packages In A Driver Group At This Time The final option is pretty self-explanatory. You might have added many drivers that you want to put into many different driver groups. You can do that at a later point in the Windows Deployment Services console. You will need to add the driver packages to a group at some point so that they can be made available for installation.

In this example, we are adding all the driver packages to a new package group called All 32-bit Drivers.

The final screen (Figure 6.23) in this wizard asks if you want to associate any filters with this driver group to control which machines the associated driver packages will be attempted to be installed on. This is useful because it will control wasted effort. You can clear the check box to skip this step. It is always possible to edit the filters at a later point by editing the properties of the driver group.

FIGURE 6.23
Modifying the package group filters

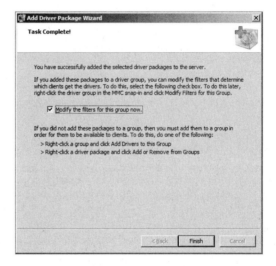

Figure 6.24 shows the Filters tab of the drivers group. This will automatically appear if you do decide to edit the filters, as is the default option in the previous screen. You can click the Add or Edit button to create new or modify existing filters. These filters will be used to check if the hardware in question is appropriate for these driver packages. For example, you may have OEM-specific drivers from a manufacturer and you want to ensure that the driver packages are not accidentally installed on another brand of machine, thus causing a support issue. You can create filters based on the following:

◆ BIOS vendor

◆ BIOS version

◆ Chassis type

◆ UUID

◆ Operating system version

◆ Operating system edition

◆ Operating system language

FIGURE 6.24
Editing the driver
packages filters

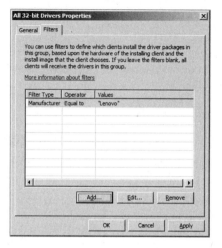

This means that even though you might have a huge library of drivers in WDS, you can maintain very tight control in how they are automatically installed on machines.

You can see the added driver packages and two new driver groups that were added in Figure 6.25. Driver packages are associated with driver groups rather than being contained within them. You can see all the driver packages in the All Packages in the Windows Deployment Services console. You can safely delete a driver group without deleting the associated driver packages. It is possible to create more driver groups and even associate a driver package with more than one driver group. For example, you might choose to create driver groups like the following:

◆ Architecture, such as 32-bit and 64-bit

◆ Vendor, such as HP, Dell, or Lenovo

◆ Type, such as network or storage

Design your driver groups and test the design in a proof of concept. Document the design and the processes involved. It is something that you will want to keep pretty simple because unwanted complexity will lead to inconsistencies and administrative overhead. Added driver packages can be enabled, disabled (making them unavailable for installation), and deleted.

You are now at a stage where you can add these drivers to your boot images.

FIGURE 6.25
The added driver packages and driver groups

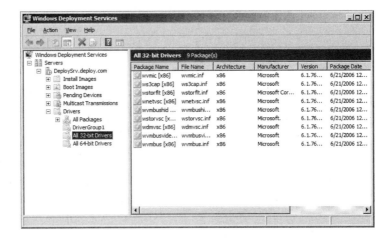

ADDING DRIVERS TO BOOT IMAGES

If you were working with WAIK you would probably have to search through the included documentation or use your favorite search engine to find the correct DISM commands to add the drivers to your boot image. This is not the case with WDS.

Navigate to the boot image that you want to update, right-click on it, and select Add Driver Packages To Image. This opens the Add Driver Packages To Boot Image Wizard (Figure 6.26).

FIGURE 6.26
Choose driver packages to add to the boot image.

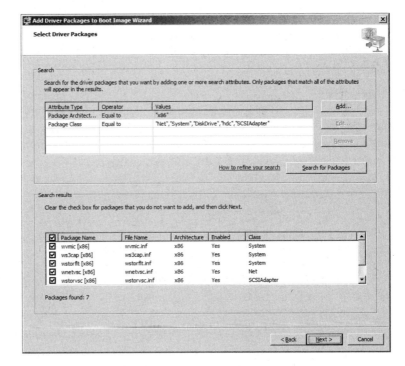

You may have many drivers added to a production WDS server. The search tool will help you filter the drivers to only those that are suitable to add to a boot image. Helpfully, the search criteria are set up by default to include the network, system, and storage drivers that you will need, and the correct architecture for the boot image that you have selected. All you have to do is click Search For Packages and the appropriate driver packages will be found. You can choose to add all or only selected driver packages to your boot image. Remember that your boot image will grow in size if you add more driver packages to it.

WDS will mount the boot image and inject the driver packages for you when you complete the wizard. No command prompt or scripting black magic is needed. However, we must admit that doing some of that DISM black magic can make a bigger impression than a few WDS wizard clicks will if you are working as a contractor or as a consultant on a client site. The injection of the drivers to the boot image will take some time, even with just a few driver packages. This will be the first of many progress-bar engineering opportunities for you in your deployment project to take a break or work through your email.

The wizard will report on the success/failure of your driver import when it is completed. You can refresh the console's view of your server once the import is completed to see the updated boot image details, including the size of the WIM file and the date/time of the last update.

CREATING A CAPTURE IMAGE

The boot image that we have just talked about will be used to deploy installation images on computers. You can choose to use the default installation image from the Windows 7 media, but it is likely that you will want to add extra software, such as Microsoft Office 2010, or customize the image configuration in some way that is not possible with an unattended answer file. If so, you will need to create a custom image. WDS will allow you to boot up a generalized template machine with a *capture image*. A capture image is a specialized boot image that is used to create a new installation image file and store it in the image store of the WDS server. We will now look at creating a capture image.

We have more good news. You have already done most of the work! A capture image is created from an existing boot image. That means that any driver work you have previously done won't have to be repeated. You will create a new capture image by right-clicking on an existing boot image and selecting Create Capture Image. The Create Capture Image Wizard will start (Figure 6.27).

The default details in the Image Name and Image Description fields will be derived from those same details in the source boot image. You should customize them to make it clear that this is a capture image rather than a normal (deployment) boot image.

The Location And File Name field is used to specify where the new WIM file for the capture image will be created. We're going to show you a little shortcut. The wizard will lead you to think that you should create the new WIM file in a temporary location and then add it again in a later step. We feel like that is a bit of wasted effort. Instead, we recommend that you simply create the new capture image file in the image store location for boot images. That will eliminate the additional step. You should create 32-bit images in `\Remoteinstall\Boot\x86\Images` and 64-bit images in `\Remoteinstall\Boot\x64\Images`. We have entered `D:\Remoteinstall\Boot\x86\Capture.wim` in Location And File Name.

FIGURE 6.27
Creating a new
capture image

FIGURE 6.27
Creating a new
capture image

The source boot image will be used as a template for the new capture image file. The new
capture image WIM file will be added in the location that you have specified. This process will
provide more time to consider the wonders of progress bar engineering.

The screen in Figure 6.28 will appear when the image creation has completed successfully.
Clear the Add Image To The Windows Deployment Server Now check box if you have followed
our advice on where to create the image. This option is used when you have created the capture
image in another location and want to add it to the correct location.

FIGURE 6.28
The capture image
task is complete.

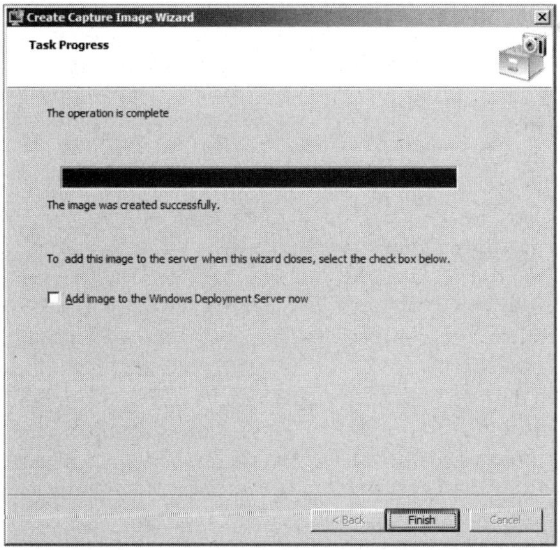

Returning to the Windows Deployment Services console, you can right-click on your server in the navigation pane and select Refresh. Browse into Boot Images and you should see your new capture image. This is a new WIM file that is independent of the source boot image and consumes disk space. You will need to remember to update this capture image with any new driver packages that you add from this point on. Remember that you may also need to have 32-bit and 64-bit capture images.

CREATING A DISCOVER IMAGE

You should now be aware that WDS normally uses PXE to download a boot image for deploying installation images to a PC. You may have legacy hardware that is capable of running Windows 7 but does not have a network card with adequate PXE support. You could purchase replacement network cards, but that might be considered an unwanted expense and may require too much effort. Luckily, you can create bootable media called a *discover image* that will let you connect to a WDS server and download an installation image on the computer.

There are two prerequisites for creating and using WDS discover images:

WAIK   The latest version of Windows Automated Installation Kit needs to be installed (you should always have WAIK installed somewhere in a Windows 7 deployment project) so that bootable media can be created.

Media   You will need media such as a USB stick or DVD (and DVD writer) to store the discovery image on.

You will create the discover image by right-clicking on an existing (template) boot image and selecting Create Discover Image. The Create Discover Image Wizard will be launched, as seen in Figure 6.29.

FIGURE 6.29
Creating a discover image

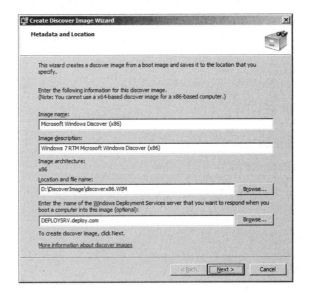

As with the other boot images, you will have to enter an image name and description. You should try to use names and descriptions that are meaningful and will be useful, considering that you may have many boot images in the future.

This wizard will create a WIM file. Unlike with the other boot images, you do not want this boot image to be available to download via PXE. You should create it outside of the image store. We are creating the new WIM file as D:\DiscoverImage\discoverx86.wim. The discover image will need to know what the name of the WDS server will be. You should enter the name. In our case it is deploysrv.deploy.com.

Once again, you will have to wait for a while. Eventually the new WIM file will be created in the location that you specified and you can move on to the next step in the process.

You now have a WIM file but you need to create some physical bootable media. You will carry out the remaining steps using the WAIK Deployment Tools command prompt. The first step is to create a copy of WindowsPE in a folder. You do this by running the CopyPE command:

```
CopyPE <architecture> D:\Winpe
```

You will substitute x86 or x64 for <architecture>. For example, the following command will create an x86 WindowsPE:

```
CopyPE x86 D:\Winpe
```

The next command will copy the new discover image WIM file into the WindowsPE folder.

```
Copy /y D:\DiscoverImage\discoverx86.wim D:\Winpe\ISO\Sources\boot.wim
```

If you are planning to boot from USB, then you will now create an ISO file. You can do that by running the oscdimg command:

```
Oscdimg -n -bD:\winpe\ISO\boot\etfsboot.com D:\Winpe\ISO
D:\DiscoverImage\discoverx86.iso
```

You can burn the ISO file to a DVD and use the DVD to boot up computers that cannot boot using PXE.

If you are planning to boot from a USB stick, then you will need to prepare it using the following diskpart commands:

```
Diskpart
List disk
```

Identify the USB drive. In this example, it is disk 1:

```
select disk 1
clean
create partition primary
select partition 1
active
format fs=fat32
assign
exit
```

The USB drive is now capable of being bootable. It just needs a copy of WindowsPE. You can copy your customized WindowsPE onto it by using xcopy. The USB drive is the E: drive in this example:

```
xcopy D:\Winpe\iso\*.* /s /e /f E:\
```

You now have the ability to create all the boot images you will need in a WDS solution. In the next section we will explore adding an installation image.

Managing Installation Images

An installation image is a WIM file that contains the files that are necessary to deploy the Windows 7 operating system and any additional programs, files, or settings. WDS can deploy the Microsoft-supplied Windows 7 images, or you can use a capture image to create a custom image of a generalized template computer. Normally you will deploy a machine using a Microsoft installation image, customize it, generalize it, and capture it. You would test this new image and then use that for future deployments. In this section we are going to look at how you will add installation images, how they are stored by WDS, and how you can secure them. Chapter 7, "WDS from the Client's View," will show you how to create custom images.

MANAGING IMAGE GROUPS AND SINGLE-INSTANCE STORAGE

Think about how you might use WDS in a medium to large organization. Many CIOs dream and preach about a *standard desktop image*. It is a nice idea but it lasts about 5 minutes in the real world. In reality, there is usually a core standard image, with some variations. The standard image is created, with Office, a PDF reader, some antivirus software, and a few other bits and pieces. But once you start talking to a few teams or departments in the business, you soon find that department A needs application X, team B needs applications X and Y, and division C needs application Z. You could deploy your standard image and install those applications by hand. That would not be very successful. In reality, if there are enough computers to justify it, you will likely create variations of the standard desktop image to suit each of the custom requirements of the business.

Think about this for a few moments. Imagine you are using one of the third-party cloning solutions on the market. They are using sector-based disk images. Every one of those images, maybe 10 GB in size or more, will be stored on a shared folder and replicated on the WAN to various branch offices. That is a lot of wasted disk space and bandwidth. Microsoft uses file-based WIM files for imaging. This allows WDS to do some clever single-instance storage optimization and is made possible using *image groups*.

Image groups can be used for single-instance storage. The idea is that you use them to group together very similar installation images. For example, you may have a number of Windows 7 with Service Pack 1 installation images. Some have a copy of Microsoft Visio installed. Some have a copy of Microsoft Project installed. And others have a line-of-business application installed. Most of the files in those images are actually the same: they are the Windows operating system files and the rest of the standard desktop image. The image group will store those duplicated files just once. You may have one file that is 10 GB or more and the rest will be quite small. This optimization will save considerable disk space and will save bandwidth if you replicate the images to other WDS servers in the organization.

There are some guidelines for using image groups. The images that are contained should be based on very similar operating systems. Here are some group recommendations:

Versions   There should be one image group for every version of Windows. This means you would have unique image groups for Windows Server 2008 R2, Windows Vista, and Windows 7.

Service Packs   A release of a service pack is a change of the operating system build and binaries. For example, there would be unique image groups for Windows 7 RTM and Windows 7 with Service Pack 1.

Architecture   32-bit and 64-bit operating systems have different binaries. This means you would need different image groups for Windows 7 x86 and Windows 7 x64.

Pre–Windows Vista   Each localized version of a pre–Windows Vista operating system, such as Windows XP, will require a unique image group because the binaries are different.

You can create an image group by right-clicking on Install Images in the navigation pane and selecting Add Image Group. Make sure you use a name that is very descriptive of the contained installation images. You would want to include all the previous information that is used to decide if a new image group is required or not. You can also create an image group when adding a new installation image to your WDS server.

ADDING INSTALLATION IMAGES

You can add a new installation image by browsing to Install Images, right-clicking, and selecting Add Install Image. Figure 6.30 shows the Add Image Wizard. Here you have the option to add the install image into an existing image group or to create a new one. We don't have any image groups yet in our example, so we are going to create one called Windows 7 x86 Ultimate Edition.

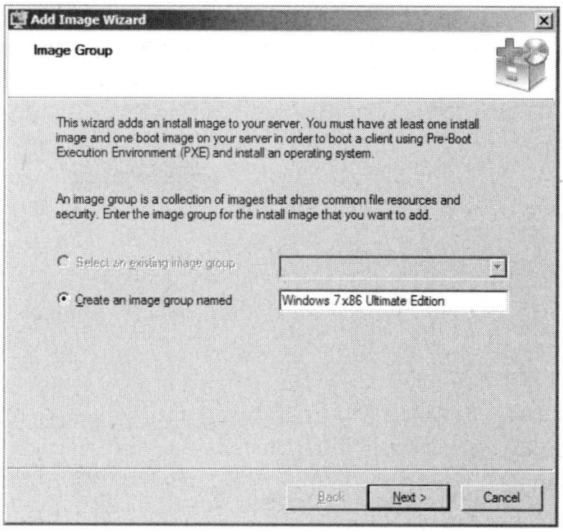

FIGURE 6.30
Create an image group for the installation image.

The next screen (Figure 6.31) is where you will tell the wizard which WIM file contains your desired installation image. We are importing the `install.wim` file from the Windows 7 DVD (`Sources` folder).

The Available Images screen (Figure 6.32) shows you each of the available images that are contained within the selected WIM file. You can deselect any image that you do not want to import. We are only going to import the Ultimate edition of Windows 7.

The wizard will verify that that installation image is valid and then import it into WDS.

FIGURE 6.31
Choose a WIM file
to import.

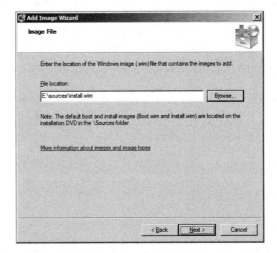

FIGURE 6.32
Select an installa-
tion image from
the WIM file.

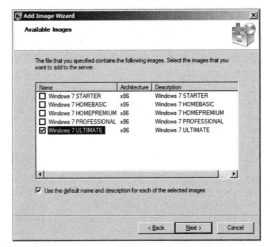

SECURING INSTALLATION IMAGES

You might ask yourself now: do you want everyone with an authorized computer to be able to access any installation image on your WDS server? Remember that some images might have specially licensed software. You can't let that get out of control. It is possible to restrict access to installation images. That's what we will look at now.

SECURING BOOT IMAGES

A common question is "How can I secure access to my boot images?" Unfortunately there isn't a way to do that. There is no logon during the PXE bootup. The PXE client simply downloads a list of available boot images and presents them to the end user. It is possible for an end user to download a boot image and use it to do something unexpected or unauthorized to their Windows installation, bypassing the security mechanisms.

There are some solutions but they are not as elegant as the mechanism that is used to secure the installation images.

You could decide not to put any enabled boot images on the WDS server. Instead, you could create DVD or USB boot media from the boot images using WAIK. This means that you would require some media for building or rebuilding computers. Of course, there is nothing to stop determined users from bringing in their own boot media. Any Windows 7 or Windows Vista DVD comes with a copy of Windows PE, and the tools you use to create customized boot images are free to download and use.

Another solution would be to encrypt the hard disks on your computers by policy. This could be done using BitLocker on the Ultimate or Enterprise editions of Windows 7. A user might be able to boot up their computer with some boot media but they will not be able to access the contents of the hard disk to bypass the administrative restrictions of the Windows installation.

You can control which domain-based groups (recommended) or users (not recommended) will have access to your installation images. This uses the traditional Windows security dialog box. You can do this for an image group (affecting all contained images) or for a specific installation image. You can access this dialog box by editing the properties of the image installation image, or by right-clicking on an image group and selecting Security.

By default, Authenticated Users has the following permissions on an installation image:

◆ Read & Execute

◆ Read

Also, by default Authenticated Users has those two permissions in addition to List Folder Contents. This means any domain-authenticated user can download and install those images on a computer that is authorized to use WDS.

You can restrict access in either of the following ways:

◆ Granting access to desired security group(s) by copying the previous permissions.

◆ Removing access to Authenticated Users. Do not click Deny because this will prevent access for everyone.

By now, if you are following the example, you will have done quite a bit of work to load content into your WDS server. It might be a good time to peek under the covers to see what is happening in the image store.

Exploring the WDS Image Store

The WDS image store is located in the `Remoteinstall` folder that you specified during the initial configuration of WDS. This contains the files and data that make up your WDS server. You will see a number of folders in `Remoteinstall` if you browse it with Windows Explorer.

Boot   This is where all of the boot image files are stored. The WIM files are contained within the `\<architecture>\Images` folders. You may notice some BCD files. Each boot image has an associated BCD file. This Boot Configuration Data (BCD) file contains the bootup parameters that used to be stored in the `boot.ini` file in pre-Vista versions of Windows. You can find more information about the BCD file here: `http://technet.microsoft.com/library/dd299773(WS.10).aspx`.

Images   This is where the installation images are kept. There is a subfolder for each image group. You will notice that each image group has one large read-write memory (RWM) file and one or more small WIM files. The RWM is the single instance store for your image group. This is where the install image contents are stored. The WIM file contains metadata for the installation image.

MGMT   This is the Auto-Add devices database, which is an ESE (Extensible Storage Engine) database, and it is used to automatically add computers to Active Directory.

Stores   This is where driver packages are processed and stored.

Templates   Here you will find a template unattended file for joining legacy operating systems to a domain.

Tmp   This is a temporary working location for WDS.

WdsClientUnattend   This is where the WDS client unattended answer files are stored.

WDSUTIL

Like the rest of Windows Server 2008 and Windows Server 2008 R2, the Windows Deployment Services console only reveals a certain amount of the management features in the GUI. WDSUTIL is a command-line utility that gives you total control over your WDS server. You can learn more about this utility here:

`http://technet.microsoft.com/library/cc771206(WS.10).aspx`

By now, you have installed your WDS server, added boot images, added drivers, and added and secured your first installation image. All that remains is to provide some PXE and WDS clients.

Modifying PXE Client Response Policy

You configured how the WDS server would respond (if at all) to PXE clients during the initial configuration of the service. You probably set it up to ignore PXE clients until your machine was ready. You now are at a stage where you need to start testing. That means you will need to allow some form of access to PXE clients. Right-click on the WDS server in the navigation pane of the Windows Deployment Services console and select Properties. Then click the PXE Response tab in the dialog box that appears (Figure 6.33).

FIGURE 6.33

Modifying the
WDS server PXE
response

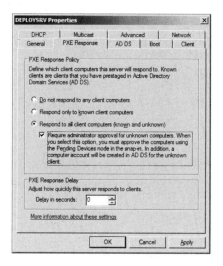

The now-familiar options are presented. You should not push your new WDS server into full-blown production without doing lots of testing. The Respond To All Client Computers (Known And Unknown) option has been selected. This is being tightly controlled by also selecting the associated suboption to require administrative approval for the PXE client connection. This will mean that you can use any machine for your testing, without having to edit Active Directory computer objects. But you will also prevent unwanted access by colleagues or users by requiring that the PXE client connection be approved in the Windows Deployment Services console.

Chapter 7 will continue the WDS story. There you will learn how to use WDS, customize deployments, capture images, control PXE client access, monitor the performance of WDS, and troubleshoot issues.

The Bottom Line

Understand how WDS works.   WDS is an operating system image deployment solution that is based on the ability to boot up a computer using PXE.

Master It   What are the requirements for installing and using WDS to deploy Windows installation images?

Install and configure WDS. You will use the components of the server operating system to add the WDS component or role.

Master It What two ways can you use to install the WDS role on a Windows Server 2008 R2 machine?

Add boot and installation images. You can add boot images and installation images to your WDS server to allow Windows 7 deployment operations.

Master It You want to add a variety of Windows 7 Professional images to your WDS server. You need to keep the amount of storage space to a minimum. You have a standard desktop image but you have been forced to create several variations to allow for 32-bit and 64-bit architectures, as well as departmental customizations. How will you accomplish your goals?

Chapter 7

WDS from the Client's View

Chapter 6, "Windows Deployment Services: The Basics," introduced you to Windows Deployment Services (WDS). In this chapter you will start working with client machines to access the services that WDS provides.

When looking to perform installations of Windows images in the past, many organizations have turned to third-party solutions that require additional licensing. Microsoft has included a network-based image deployment solution called Windows Deployment Services (WDS) in every release of the server operating system since Windows Server 2003 Service Pack 2.

WDS allows administrators to capture and deploy operating system images using the hardware features of the computer being worked with. This makes it useful for deploying operating systems to computers that don't have a DVD drive, such as budget PCs or netbooks. WDS can be used as a stand-alone solution, or it can be used to extend the functionality of the Microsoft Deployment Toolkit (light-touch deployment) and Microsoft System Center Configuration Manager (zero-touch deployment). The best part is that WDS requires no additional license purchases.

In this chapter, you will learn to:

◆ Use and customize the PXE client

◆ Create a customized installation image

◆ Automate WDS

Employing the PXE Client

Chapter 6 introduced you to the PXE client. Here's a quick refresher. The client computer that will be working with a WDS server will boot up using a PXE client in order to get a network configuration, connect to a WDS server, and download a WDS client. In this section you will learn how to use the PXE client and see how it works by default. You will then learn how to customize the PXE client so that it functions according to the needs of your organization.

The PXE client is a feature that is normally provided by the network adapter in a computer. It is used to boot up a computer, and it will obtain a DHCP IP configuration and connect the computer to a WDS server. This allows the PXE client to download the WDS client, after which you can either install a new operating system image on the PC or capture the existing installation, which can be copied to the WDS server for later deployment.

You are now going to see how the PXE client works without any customization. We will deploy an operating system to a computer that has no operating system. You'll also see how to configure the way WDS will respond to PXE clients.

Booting a PXE Client

It is likely that any hardware that can support Windows 7 will have a PXE-capable network adapter. If not, you can create a discover image in the WDS console by right-clicking on a suitable boot image and selecting Create Discover Image. You would boot up the computer using this discover image. However, you will probably not need to do this.

Real World Scenario

USING A VIRTUAL LAB

Tara is a network administrator who is working in a deployment project. She wants to learn about the available deployment technologies and will require a number of machines to work on. Tara chooses to use a hardware virtualization solution such as Hyper-V because it allows her to create many virtual machines (VMs) on a single piece of hardware. She can easily revert snapshots of lab machines to a previous clean state if she wants to repeat a test or correct a mistake. She can quickly deploy new machines without waiting for hardware to be delivered or configured.

Tara learned that she needed to configure her virtual machines with static MAC (or Ethernet) addresses to learn more about PXE response. That is because WDS will use the MAC address to identify computers. Virtual machines with dynamic MAC addresses will constantly change and be unable to authenticate.

Tara uses Microsoft's Hyper-V for the virtual lab. The VMs were set up to use the emulated legacy network adapters instead of the synthetic network adapter. This was contrary to the usual recommendation for VM configuration on Hyper-V. This is because the legacy network adapter supports booting up using PXE whereas the better-performing synthetic network adapter does not.

Thanks to this virtual lab solution, Tara was quickly able to learn about the technologies and even develop the final production solution on a small amount of hardware. Her boss was impressed with how efficiently she was able to deploy a production environment with very few mishaps.

You may have noticed in the past when you power up a computer that there is a prompt to press a key to boot the machine up on the network. Using this prompt is how you start the PXE client. If this prompt does not appear, you can go into the BIOS and enable it to appear. The exact instructions and the key to press are hardware specific, so you should consult your hardware vendor, their support site, or their supplied documentation.

Pressing that key will bring you to a screen similar to that shown in Figure 7.1. What you are seeing is the machine requesting the DHCP-supplied IP configuration and a PXE server configuration. You can also see the MAC address of the network adapter and the GUID of the machine that you are working on. This information may be useful later, as you will soon see.

This process may time out. Some of the possible causes of this include the following:

◆ There is no DHCP server with a configured DHCP scope for the network that the machine is on.

◆ DHCP is not functioning correctly.

   ◆ The WDS server is not configured.

   ◆ WDS is not functioning correctly. Check the IP Helper.

   ◆ An enterprise administrator has not authorized the WDS server in the DHCP console.

   ◆ The PXE response settings are not configured.

   ◆ A segmented network is not configured to forward the DHCP traffic as required (see Chapter 6).

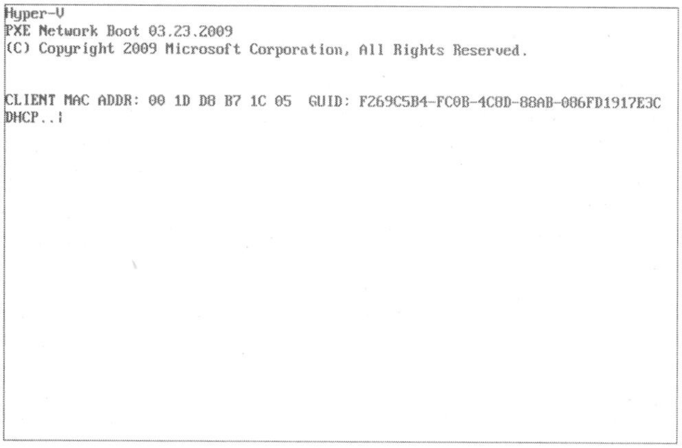

FIGURE 7.1
The client
requesting IP
configuration

```
Hyper-V
PXE Network Boot 03.23.2009
(C) Copyright 2009 Microsoft Corporation, All Rights Reserved.


CLIENT MAC ADDR: 00 1D D8 B7 1C 05  GUID: F269C5B4-FC0B-4C8D-88AB-006FD1917E3C
DHCP..i
```

Configuring PXE Response

You were asked how you wanted to configure the PXE response during the initial configuration of WDS. Here are the possible settings:

Do Not Respond To Any Client Computers   The WDS server will not respond to any requests by PXE clients. Your WDS server may be configured this way during the initial configuration of the service. You will need to change this setting before you test the WDS server or before you put it into production.

Respond Only To Known Client Computers   This means that only machines that have Active Directory computer objects with a configured GUID or MAC address will be serviced by WDS. This is how you might configure WDS in a secure environment.

Respond To All Client Computers (Known And Unknown)   You might choose this configuration when you are using WDS in an open environment that is subject to frequent hardware change. This option could be further controlled by requiring an administrator to authorize each connection by an unknown computer.

There is a related suboption for Respond To All Client Computers (Known And Unknown) that lets you require administrative approval for any PXE client request.

You can control all these settings in the WDS console. Right-click on the server in question, select Properties, and navigate to the PXE Response tab, shown in Figure 7.2.

FIGURE 7.2

The PXE
Response tab

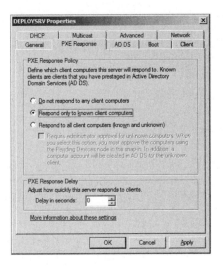

Let's assume that you want to restrict access to your WDS server to just a few machines. The Respond Only To Known Client Computers setting will allow you to do this. WDS will only respond to PXE clients that have an associated computer object in Active Directory. This computer object must have the `netbootGUID` attribute configured with either the MAC address or the GUID of the computer that is being worked with. This is the downside of this complete-control approach. Any new machine that you wish to prepare using WDS will require you to manually create a computer object and to populate the `netbootGUID` attribute with the MAC address or GUID of the machine. This process is referred to as *prestaging* the machine. Any previously existing machines that were prepared using something other than WDS will require you to populate the `netbootGUID`.

You have two ways that you can edit this computer object attribute. The first is to use the Active Directory Users and Computers console. Enable the Advanced Features option in the View menu and navigate to where the computer object is located. Right-click on the computer object, select Properties, and go into the Attribute Editor. You can double-click the `netbootGUID` attribute to edit it.

Alternatively, you can use scripting (such as Visual Basic or PowerShell) to edit this attribute. This approach will be useful if you need to prestage a lot of machines. Microsoft shares some Visual Basic scripts for manipulating and accessing the `netbootGUID` attribute here: `http://support.microsoft.com/kb/302467`.

So what do you enter in the `netbootGUID` attribute? You saw the MAC address and GUID of a machine when you started a network boot (earlier in Figure 7.1). You can enter either of these in this attribute to associate the computer object with the machine. Doing so allows this machine to access the PXE server (on the WDS server) when Respond Only To Know Client Computers is enabled. Let's see how this works.

The machine in Figure 7.1 has a MAC address of 00 1D D8 B7 1C 05. The GUID is F269C5B4-FC0B-4C8D-88AB-086FD1917E3C. The GUID is 32 characters if you strip away the hyphens. WDS also expects to find a 32-character string in the `netbootGUID` attribute. That means you can enter **F269C5B4FC0B4C8D88AB086FD1917E3C** to associate this computer object with the machine. Alternatively you can enter the MAC address of the network adapter.

The MAC address is only 12 characters (without the hyphens) so it won't be usable without some help. You can pad out the `netbootGUID` attribute if using the MAC address by adding twenty 0 characters on the left. This pads the MAC address up to 32 characters. For example, you would enter **00000000000000000000001DD8B71C05** for this machine.

MULTIPLE NETWORK ADAPTERS AND PXE

Some machines may have multiple network adapters, and this fact may cause some confusion when you are trying to boot up the machine on the network. You need to ensure that the primary network card for PXE boots is the one that is connected to the PXE-enabled network. This is also the network adapter that you need to associate with the computer object in Active Directory if you are prestaging the machine.

The result will look something like what is shown in Figure 7.3, where you can see that the MAC address has been entered. You'll notice that it is displayed in a format similar to the GUID you observed in Figure 7.1. This machine will now be able to access the PXE services of this WDS server.

FIGURE 7.3
A prestaged
computer account

You can choose to configure PXE Response with the option Respond To All Client Computers (Known And Unknown) when the prestaging process becomes too much to manage. For example, you may have an environment where hardware is constantly changed or your organization is replacing a lot of hardware for the Windows 7 deployment project. You will not need to prestage computer objects if you choose this option. Note that the `netbootGUID` attribute will be populated by WDS.

A BENEFIT OF THE *NETBOOTGUID* **ATTRIBUTE**

The netbootGUID attribute associates a machine with a computer account in Active Directory. Because it is associating a computer name with that machine, you can rebuild a machine using WDS and the machine will retain the computer name from the associated computer account.

At this point you should be able to power up your test machine that you want to boot up with the PXE client. You will have to be quick. By default you will have a few seconds to respond to a prompt that asks you to press **F12** to continue the PXE boot, referred to as a network service boot (as shown in Figure 7.4). The PXE boot will be aborted if you fail to respond to this prompt quickly enough.

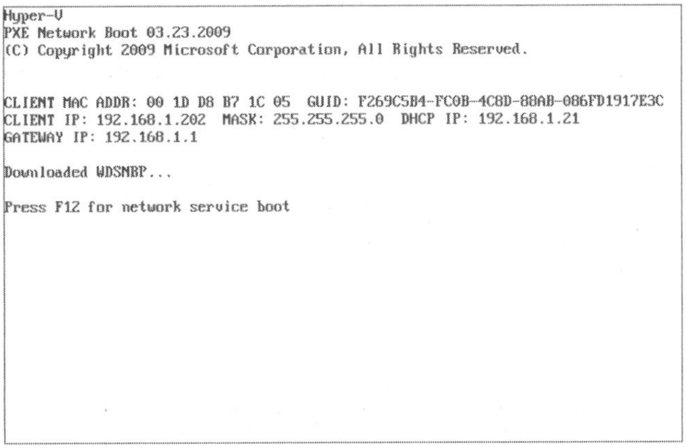

FIGURE 7.4

Press F12 to continue the network service boot.

```
Hyper-V
PXE Network Boot 03.23.2009
(C) Copyright 2009 Microsoft Corporation, All Rights Reserved.


CLIENT MAC ADDR: 00 1D D8 B7 1C 05  GUID: F269C5B4-FC0B-4C8D-88AD-086FD1917E3C
CLIENT IP: 192.168.1.202  MASK: 255.255.255.0  DHCP IP: 192.168.1.21
GATEWAY IP: 192.168.1.1

Downloaded WDSNBP...

Press F12 for network service boot
```

There is a middle ground between manually prestaging computer objects and providing unlimited access to PXE services. You can enable the Respond To All Client Computers (Known And Unknown) option and combine that with the Require Administrator Approval For Unknown Computers option. Any machine that has a previously unknown MAC address or GUID will not be rejected as would happen with the Respond Only To Known Client Computers option. Instead, the process would work as follows:

1. A user will acquire a new machine and boot it up.

2. The user will initiate a network boot.

3. WDS will check to see if the machine has a computer account with a matching netboot-GUID attribute.

4. If it does, then the PXE boot will continue as normal. If the machine does not have an associated computer account, then the network service boot will be halted until an administrator approves it.

5. The user is prompted to press F12 and then to call support with the IP address of the WDS server and a request ID.

6. An administrator uses this information to approve or reject the PXE boot request.

7. If approved, the PXE boot will continue as normal. WDS will later populate the computer account's `netbootGUID` attribute.

Figure 7.5 shows the screen that informs users that their PXE or network service boot must be approved by an administrator. Users are given two pieces of information that the administrator will need in order to approve the session. The first is a request ID. This uniquely identifies the connection request and allows the administrator to deal with many simultaneous requests. The contacting server IP address identifies the WDS server that the administrator will have to either log into or manage remotely.

CONFIGURING CONTACT DETAILS FOR ADMINISTRATORS

If you configure WDS to require administrative approval for any connecting PXE client, you must consider how the end users can initiate a help desk call. Your organization might have shared the phone number or email address via a website or a global address list. But how exactly do users access those if they are trying to install an operating system on their computer?

A useful solution to this chicken-and-egg problem is to configure the WDS server to display the administrator contact details on the PXE client. You can do this by running the WDSUtil command on the WDS server:

```
WDSUtil /set-server /AutoAddPolicy
/message:"To contact your network administrator please dial 9999"
```

This will display the contact message to the end user when the WDS server requires administrative approval for the client.

FIGURE 7.5
The network service boot must be approved.

```
Hyper-V
PXE Network Boot 03.23.2009
(C) Copyright 2009 Microsoft Corporation, All Rights Reserved.


CLIENT MAC ADDR: 00 1D D8 B7 1C 07  GUID: 5E6CF96B-A62B-4405-8A37-12BBC14BECEE
CLIENT IP: 192.168.1.202  MASK: 255.255.255.0  DHCP IP: 192.168.1.21
GATEWAY IP: 192.168.1.1

Downloaded WDSNBP...

Press F12 for network service boot
Architecture: x64

The details below show the information relating to the PXE boot request for
this computer. Please provide these details to your Windows Deployment Services
Administrator so that this request can be approved.

Pending Request ID: 3

Message from Administrator:

Contacting Server: 192.168.1.22.
```

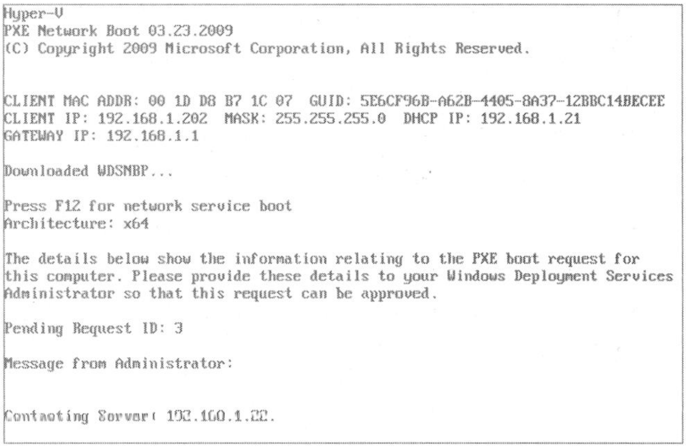

With that information, the administrator can launch the WDS console and browse into Pending Devices. Figure 7.6 shows a machine that is waiting for administrator approval or rejection. You can right-click on a pending device to perform an action. There are three choices.

Approve The network service boot request will be approved and the PXE boot will continue as normal.

Name And Approve The network service boot request will be approved. However, the administrator will provide the name of the computer account as well. This can be a new (unique) computer object name, or the administrator can select a previously created computer object. The administrator also has the opportunity to pick a specific OU location for the new computer object.

Reject The network service boot request will be rejected, preventing the machine from downloading the PXE client and being able to access the WDS services. A message briefly appears on the monitor of the machine before it attempts to boot up with alternative boot devices that are configured in the BIOS.

If you are working in an isolated lab, you will probably want to set the PXE response policy to Respond To All Client Computers (Known And Unknown) without any further controls.

NETWORK SERVICE BOOT REJECTIONS ARE REMEMBERED

WDS records the rejection of network service boots in an Auto-Add Devices database. This means that all future requests to boot up using PXE will be ignored by this WDS server. The DHCP request on the machine will time out if no alternative WDS server is available. Eventually the following error will appear: "ProxyDHCP: No reply to request on port 4011."

You can use the WDSUTIL command to manage any records of rejected network service boot requests. You can view all rejected devices by running this command:

    Wdsutil /Get-AutoAddDevices /DeviceType:RejectedDevices

The following will delete all rejection records on the current WDS server:

    Wdsutil /Delete-AutoAddDevices /DeviceType:RejectedDevices

Note that you can substitute PendingDevices or ApprovedDevices for the RejectedDevices. No way is available for deleting individual rejections.

Luckily, you probably won't have to do that very often. By running the following command, you will see (under Auto-Add Policy) that, by default, device approvals are retained for 30 days and others (including rejections) are retained for 1 day:

    Wdsutil /Get-Server /Show:Config

You can alter the other approvals (or rejections) retention by running this command:

    WDSUTIL /Set-Server /AutoAddPolicy /RetentionPeriod /Others:<time in days>

Selecting a Boot Image

At this point the client machine's connection request to the PXE (WDS) server has been approved. A PXE client is downloaded to the client machine. The PXE client will allow you to select a boot image from the WDS server. You can see in Figure 7.6 that the previously created setup and capture images are available to be selected using the keyboard. If there is only one boot image, this screen will not appear and the single boot image will be downloaded automatically.

FIGURE 7.6
Selecting a
boot image

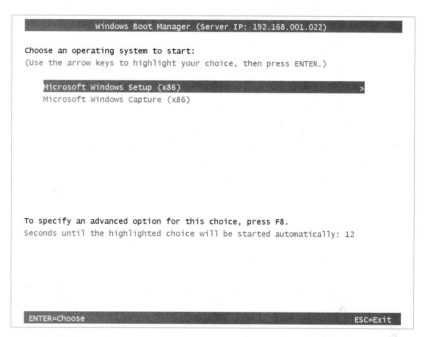

Use the cursor keys to navigate between boot images in this screen. Normally you will press **Enter** to select the image. If you experience trouble with the boot image, you can press **F8** to select a boot mode such as Safe Mode, Safe Mode With Networking, and so on.

Once you've selected a boot image, the boot image will be downloaded and it will start up. Plug and Play will figure out which of the included drivers need to be started. The boot image will get an IP address and then start interacting with the user.

The first screen asks the user who is sitting at the PC to enter the Locale and Keyboard Or Input Method. These entries should match the regionalization of the keyboard being used.

A logon box will appear. This is where users will authenticate themselves using their Active Directory credentials. WDS will use this information to determine whether it should authorize the users.

A list of available installation images is presented to the user once they have been authorized. You can see this screen in Figure 7.7.

From this point on, the user experience is very similar to installing Windows 7 using a DVD. A big difference is that Windows 7 is being installed over the network. In fact, the installation runs in what is known as Windows Deployment Services mode.

FIGURE 7.7
Choose an
installation image.

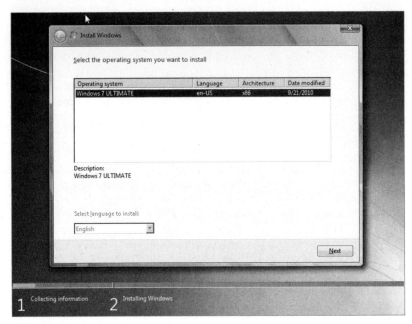

Customizing the PXE Boot Process

You may have noticed that you had to make a few clicks during the PXE bootup process. And you also had to be very quick to hit that F12 key or the network service boot would fail. This can be quite annoying, especially if you are building several machines at once and can't watch each and every monitor.

The good news is that you can customize how the PXE client works. You can make some changes by accessing the properties of your WDS server in the WDS console and browsing to the Boot tab (Figure 7.8).

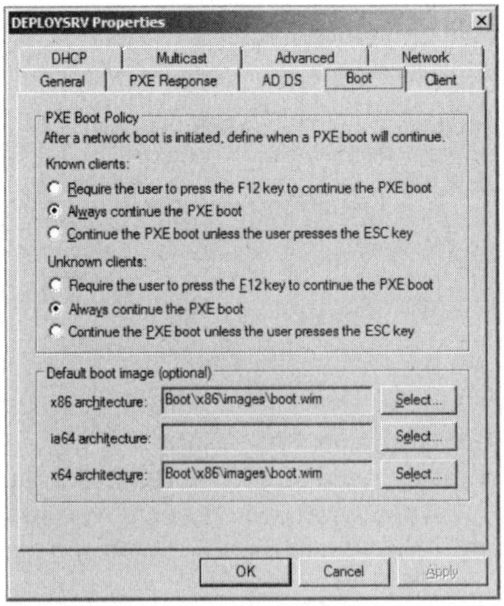

FIGURE 7.8
Customizing the
PXE boot process

You can customize the PXE Boot Policy for known and unknown clients. Here are the possible settings:

◆ Require The User To Press The F12 Key To Continue The Boot (default setting)

◆ Always Continue The PXE Boot

◆ Continue The PXE Boot Unless The User Presses The ESC Key

The default option requires you to press the F12 key almost immediately after the prompt appears. That can be quite frustrating after several near misses. The other options make the process a little less annoying.

You can select what the default boot image will be when the menu appears, assuming that there is more than one boot image. You can select different boot images for the 32-bit, 64-bit, and Itanium architectures. The boot image will appear (if there is more than one boot image) and a countdown clock of half a minute will start to tick. You only need to interact with this menu if a nondefault boot image is required. That means you can completely automate the PXE bootup process once the initial network boot is started during the power-on self-test (POST) of the machine.

Now you have the knowledge and the means to deploy the Microsoft-provided Windows 7 installation images over the network using WDS. That's a big improvement over installing an operating system using a DVD. But now it is time to look at how you can create and deploy a customized Windows 7 installation image.

Creating a Customized Installation Image

One of the biggest benefits of learning how to use the Windows deployment solutions is that you can deploy a customized image. This process allows you to create an image that contains preinstalled software with all your configurations. This approach eliminates a huge amount of time in the deployment process.

You will now learn how to prepare a reference (also referred to as a template or gold) machine, use WDS to capture an image, and add that image to your WDS server for deployment to other machines.

Prepare a Reference Machine

The goal here is to prepare a typical machine with Windows 7, install any software that is required by all recipients of the new image, and configure the operating system and software.

You can use WDS to deploy a normal installation of Windows 7. After that you will install all the software that you want to be included in the new image. This stage is where things can get a little interesting. Organizations will adopt different strategies, including, but not limited to, the following:

Minimal Customizations   Only a small number of applications will be installed, such as a software distribution client. This client would be able to automatically install software on a policy basis once the image is deployed to a machine and it boots up.

Moderate Installation   An identified set of software that is standard across the entire organization might be installed on the reference machine. This image will be deployed to every machine. Any customizations can be installed afterward using manual or automatic mechanisms.

One-Size-Fits-All   This option is not likely to be chosen in anything but the smallest organizations. A single image will be deployed to all computers. It will contain all required software.

Customized Images   You might want to create images for individual teams, departments, offices, or divisions. Each image will contain all the software required for the recipient machines.

You can make configurations to the operating system and software. However, it would probably be best if you did so using Active Directory Group Policy where possible. Group Policy allows changes to be implemented more easily and provides more granular control.

You will need to generalize the reference machine once it is ready for image creation. As with all the Windows deployment solutions, you use Sysprep to accomplish this. (Unlike with Windows XP and earlier operating systems, you do not need to copy this utility onto the machine. It is preinstalled and kept up-to-date by service pack installations.) You can find Sysprep in C:\Windows\System32\Sysprep. Run sysprep.exe when you are ready to generalize the machine. Doing so opens the window shown in Figure 7.9. By default, Enter System Out-Of-Box-Experience (OOBE) is specified and the Generalize check box is selected. Be sure to configure what the machine should do once the generalization is complete. The default is to reboot. We do not recommend using the default, even if you do intend to start the WDS capture client right away. The reason is that you might miss the POST prompt to start a network boot and the machine will start to configure the generalized operating system. This will force you to generalize it once again. Instead, we recommend configuring the machine to shut down after the generalization. You can power it up and start a network boot when you are ready.

FIGURE 7.9
Generalizing the machine using Sysprep

HOW MANY TIMES CAN YOU RUN SYSPREP?

Microsoft does not recommend that you run Sysprep more than once on an image. In other words, they don't like it when you generalize a machine, capture an image, deploy that image, generalize it again, and capture it again. However, Microsoft does support running Sysprep up to three times on a single image.

The next step will be to create an installation image from this reference machine.

Create an Image

You learned how to create a capture image in Chapter 6. You will now use this capture image to boot up the reference machine and capture the generalized image.

Power up the reference machine and boot it up on the network. Choose the capture boot image when the PXE client starts. The boot image will download over the network and start. You can skip the welcome screen to get to the Directory To Capture screen, shown in Figure 7.10.

FIGURE 7.10

Configure what you want captured.

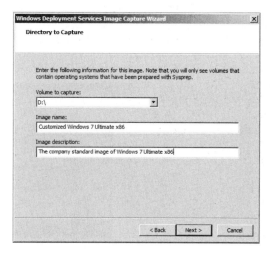

You have to enter three pieces of information. You should select the volume letter that you want to capture using WDS. This highlights a limitation of WDS; you can only capture and deploy a single volume. You might notice something odd here. The volume we are capturing is shown as D:, even though it is the C: drive when the reference machine is booted up. There is a handy solution you can use if you are a little confused about the volume that you are capturing.

1. Start a command prompt in Windows PE by pressing Shift+F10.

2. Navigate the volumes (cd) and list their contents to see which volume letter it is that you need to select. You can do this using DiskPart and by running the list volume command.

3. Enter the image name and description as you want them appear in the WDS console and to users when they are deploying images to their machines. You can change the name and description later in the console.

   The New Image Location screen (Figure 7.11) is where you configure the location of the new image that is to be created and if and how you want the image to be uploaded to the WDS server.

4. Click Browse to select a location to create the new installation image in and to name the file. You can create the new image on the same volume that you are capturing if there is sufficient space. You will need an additional local (not network-based) volume or drive if there is not enough space.

5. Optionally select the option to upload the new image to the WDS server. If you do want to do this, click the Connect button to authenticate with the WDS server. Once you have entered valid credentials, you can select an Image Group to add the new image to. This will use single instance storage (as discussed in Chapter 6) to reduce the amount of disk space that is needed to store the image. Make sure you choose an image group that matches the operating system, edition, and architecture of your new image.

FIGURE 7.11
Configure the storage of the new installation image.

Now you can put your feet up while the capture image does the work for you. The image is captured and will be uploaded to your WDS server if configured. The image will then be available for further configuration (such as access permissions) and deployment to other machines using the same process as described earlier for the Microsoft-supplied installation image. Remember that you will need to refresh the WDS console (if it was open already) to see the new installation image.

Using Unattended Answer Files with WDS

You saw earlier how you could customize the PXE client to minimize your interaction with it. In Chapter 4, "Cloning the Panther: Automating Windows 7 Installation" you learned how to use Windows System Image Manager (WSIM) to create answer files to automate Windows PE and the installation image installation. We have some good news. You can reuse those techniques to automate the WDS boot image and the deployment of the installation image.

Preparing WSIM

WSIM is the tool that is used to create unattended answer files. It uses a catalog file which is created from the WIM file that will be deployed. As discussed in Chapter 6, the WIM files that are stored on the WDS server do not actually contain any files, thanks to the single-instance storage mechanism. This means you need to export the installation image from WDS so that WSIM can use it to create a catalog.

You can export an installation image by right-clicking it and selecting Export Image. In this example, we are exporting the new customized image as `D:\Wim\StdWin7UltimateX86.wim`.

Automating the Boot Image

There can be up to three boot image unattended answer files on the WDS server, one for each possible boot image architecture (x86, x64, or Itanium). These answer files will do everything that you would otherwise have to do manually:

◆ Configure the regionalization for the WinPE pass

◆ Provide domain credentials to gain access to the WDS server

◆ Create a partition

◆ Modify a partition

◆ Select an image to deploy

To automate the boot image, take the following steps:

1. Use WSIM to create an answer file that will be associated with the boot images of your WDS server.

2. In the Windows Image pane, right-click and choose Select Windows Image. Open the previously exported image. In this case the file is `D:\Wim\StdWin7UltimateX86.wim`. WSIM will need to create a catalog file for the image if it is the first time that WSIM has opened it. Note that this process could take a little while.

SAMPLE UNATTENDED ANSWER FILES

You can find a number of sample answer files in the WAIK folder (the default location is `C:\Program Files\Windows AIK\Samples`). Microsoft has also shared some sample answer files here:

`http://technet.microsoft.com/library/cc732280(WS.10).aspx`

---

3. Choose File ➢ New Answer File to create a new empty answer file, whose contents you can edit in the Answer File pane.

   You will be adding a few components from the Windows Image pane to the Answer File pane and editing the settings in the right-hand pane of WSIM. A possible set of details for an unattended execution of the boot image is shown in Table 7.1.

TABLE 7.1:   Boot image unattended answer file details

COMPONENT	SETTING NAME	SETTING VALUE
x86_Microsoft-Windows-International-Core-WinPE_neutral	InputLocale	en-us
x86_Microsoft-Windows-International-Core-WinPE_neutral	SystemLocale	en-us
x86_Microsoft-Windows-International-Core-WinPE_neutral	UILanguage	en-us
x86_Microsoft-Windows-International-Core-WinPE_neutral	UILanguageFallback	en-us
x86_Microsoft-Windows-International-Core-WinPE_neutral	UserLocale	en-us
x86_Microsoft-Windows-International-Core-WinPE_neutral\SetupUILanguage	UILanguage	en-us
x86_Microsoft-Windows-Setup_neutral\DiskConfiguration\Disk	DiskID	0
x86_Microsoft-Windows-Setup_neutral\DiskConfiguration\Disk	WillWipeDisk	True
x86_Microsoft-Windows-Setup_neutral\DiskConfiguration\Disk\CreatePartition	Extend	True
x86_Microsoft-Windows-Setup_neutral\DiskConfiguration\Disk\CreatePartition	Order	1
x86_Microsoft-Windows-Setup_neutral\DiskConfiguration\Disk\CreatePartition	Type	Primary
x86_Microsoft-Windows-Setup_neutral\DiskConfiguration\Disk\ModifyPartition	Active	True
x86_Microsoft-Windows-Setup_neutral\DiskConfiguration\Disk\ModifyPartition	Extend	True
x86_Microsoft-Windows-Setup_neutral\DiskConfiguration\Disk\ModifyPartition	Format	NTFS
x86_Microsoft-Windows-Setup_neutral\DiskConfiguration\Disk\ModifyPartition	Label	Windows

TABLE 7.1:   Boot image unattended answer file details   *(CONTINUED)*

COMPONENT	SETTING NAME	SETTING VALUE
x86_Microsoft-Windows-Setup_neutral\ DiskConfiguration\Disk\ModifyPartition	Letter	C
x86_Microsoft-Windows-Setup_neutral\ DiskConfiguration\Disk\ModifyPartition	Order	1
x86_Microsoft-Windows-Setup_neutral\ DiskConfiguration\Disk\ModifyPartition	PartitionID	1
x86_Microsoft-Windows-Setup_neutral\ WindowsDeploymentServices\ImageSelection\ InstallImage	Filename	Install.wim
x86_Microsoft-Windows-Setup_neutral\ WindowsDeploymentServices\ImageSelection\ InstallImage	ImageGroup	Windows 7 x86 Ultimate Edition
x86_Microsoft-Windows-Setup_neutral\ WindowsDeploymentServices\ImageSelection\ InstallImage	ImageName	Customized Windows 7 Ultimate x86
x86_Microsoft-Windows-Setup_neutral\ WindowsDeploymentServices\ImageSelection\ InstallTo	DiskID	0
x86_Microsoft-Windows-Setup_neutral\ WindowsDeploymentServices\ImageSelection\ InstallImage	PartitionID	1
x86_Microsoft-Windows-Setup_neutral\ WindowsDeploymentServices\Login\Credentials	Domain	deploy.com
x86_Microsoft-Windows-Setup_neutral\ WindowsDeploymentServices\Login\Credentials	Password	<password of user>
x86_Microsoft-Windows-Setup_neutral\ WindowsDeploymentServices\Login\Credentials	Username	<username of user>

4. Validate the answer file (using the Validate Answer File on the Tools menu) and then save it. You should note that an answer file may still have issues when you use it even if the validation shows none. For example, you could enter an invalid product key. The location for WDS client answer files is the WDSClientUnattend folder in the RemoteInstall folder. For example, we will save WDSClientUnattend.xml in D:\RemoteInstall\ WDSClientUnattend.

5. You can associate this WDS client unattended answer file with boot images of a specific architecture via the properties of the WDS server in the WDS console. Navigate to the Client tab, shown in Figure 7.12.

6. Select the option Enable Unattended Installation.

7. Click the Browse button to find and select the unattended answer file(s) in the WDSClientUnattend folder.

You have now configured the WDS client to work without any human interaction.

FIGURE 7.12
Adding unattended WDS client answer files

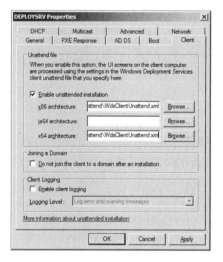

Automating Image Installation

The previous section described how to get your boot image to run in an unattended manner. This solution would choose which installation image would be deployed. The installation will execute as normal, requiring some human interaction. You can use WSIM once again to create an answer file for the operating system installation.

The process for creating a WDS Windows 7 unattended answer file is similar to what we covered in Chapter 4. The big difference is that you will not need to add the Windows PE pass components. That's because this pass is handled by the WDS client unattended answer file.

Once you have created the answer file, you will need to save it on the WDS server. For example, you could save it in a new folder as D:\RemoteInstall\InstallUnattend\Customized Windows 7 Ultimate x86.xml.

You can associate this answer file with your desired installation images by browsing to an installation image and opening its properties, as shown in Figure 7.13. Select the option Allow Image To Install In Unattended Mode. You will then click Select File and browse to and select the answer file you have saved to the WDS server. From now on, any deployments of this installation image will be controlled by this answer file. It will require no more human interaction if you have configured it correctly.

FIGURE 7.13
Enable the unattended installation of an installation image.

Monitoring, Logging, and Troubleshooting WDS

There are a lot of pieces to WDS, and from time to time, things will not work as expected. It is important to understand how to identify issues and know how to resolve them.

Monitoring WDS Performance

The effectiveness of WDS depends on the physical network. It is likely that many issues you encounter are caused by something in the network. For example, a machine's network adapter might not synchronize speed and flow control with a switch port. This would cause PXE client, boot image, and installation images to download very slowly. Network monitoring might reveal this and an enterprise monitoring solution, such as System Center Operations Manager with a third-party network management pack, would alert administrators to the issue as soon as it occurred.

SYSTEM CENTER OPERATIONS MANAGER AND WDS

Microsoft's enterprise monitoring solution is System Center Operations Manager (SCOM or OpsMgr); the current version is OpsMgr 2007 R2. OpsMgr uses product expertise in the form of management packs to monitor individual products. Microsoft provides a management pack for WDS, which you can download from:

`www.microsoft.com/downloads/en/details.aspx?FamilyId=5883D85E-3B50-4C4F-BEF4-355FCEA4B035`

You can use a number of counters in Performance Monitor on the WDS server to identify performance bottlenecks. Table 7.2 details some of these counters.

TABLE 7.2:   WDS Performance Monitor counters

COUNTER GROUP	COUNTER	DESCRIPTION	PURPOSE
WDS TFTP Server	Active Requests	The number of current TFTP session requests.	Determine whether the WDS server can handle the TFTP requests.
WDS TFTP Server	Transfer Rate/ Second	Total amount of TFTP data being downloaded from the WDS server per second.	Identify the amount of TFTP traffic and whether the network can handle it.
WDS Server	Active Requests	Total number of currently active requests, including RPC and multicast.	Determine whether the WDS server is able to handle the workload.
WDS Server	Requests/Second	The number of requests received in the last second.	Identify the amount of new client requests.
WDS Server	Processed/Second	The number of requests processed in the last second.	Used with Requests/Second to identify whether the WDS server is processing the workload.
Network Interface	Bytes Sent/Sec	The amount of data transmitted by the WDS server.	Determine whether the network is capable of handling the required traffic.
Physical Disk	Avg. Disk Sec/Read, Avg. Disk Sec/ Write, and Current Disk Queue Length	Monitor the physical disk performance on the WDS server.	Determine whether the physical disk on the WDS server is overloaded with requests.
Process	Page Faults/Sec	High amounts of page faults are an indicator of insufficient RAM.	Monitor the server over time to determine trends. Unusual spikes indicate that the WDS server requires more memory.
Processor	% Processor Time	High CPU utilization will affect the overall performance of the WDS server.	Determine whether you need to have a specialized WDS server (not sharing other roles), add more WDS servers, or add more processor(s) to the existing server.

WDS Logging

Trying to troubleshoot without any intelligence on a problem is like navigating in the dark; you will only get to where you need to be by luck. If you are having problems, then you should enable logging to get WDS to record fault information. You can use this information to analyze the issue, seek help on the Internet or from Microsoft or other experts, and resolve the problem. You can enable logging on the WDS server and on the WDS client.

LOGGING ON THE WDS SERVER

You can enable WDS logging in the Application log and the System log (in Event Viewer) by running the following command:

```
WDSUTIL /Get-Server /Show:All /Detailed
```

You can use /Verbose or /Progress instead of /Detailed to change the amount of data being recorded.

You can enable tracing for individual WDS components by editing the Registry. Start by enabling tracing for WDS. To do this, change the value of EnableFileTracing (REG_DWORD) found at HKEY_LOCAL_MACHINE\SOFTWARE\Microsoft\Tracing\WDSServer to **1**. You will then enable tracing for the required individual components by setting the associated Registry value to have a value of **0**, as shown in Table 7.3. This is because tracing is disabled by default.

TABLE 7.3: Enable tracing for WDS components

WDS COMPONENT	REGISTRY VALUE
Windows Deployment Services Dynamic Driver Provisioning Service (Windows Server 2008 R2 only)	HKEY_LOCAL_MACHINE\SYSTEM\CurrentControlSet\services\ WDSServer\Providers\WDSDDPS\TraceDisabled
Windows Deployment Services Multicasting	HKEY_LOCAL_MACHINE\SYSTEM\CurrentControlSet\services\ WDSServer\Providers\WDSMC\TraceDisabled
Windows Deployment Services PXE	HKEY_LOCAL_MACHINE\SYSTEM\CurrentControlSet\services\ WDSServer\Providers\WDSPXE\TraceDisabled
Windows Deployment Services TFTP	HKEY_LOCAL_MACHINE\SYSTEM\CurrentControlSet\services\ WDSServer\Providers\WDSTFTP\TraceDisabled

Windows Server 2008 R2 has additional tracing, which you can enable using the Registry values in Table 7.4 with the following settings:

◆ 7F0000: Includes packet tracing and protocol tracing

◆ 3F0000: Excludes packet tracing

◆ 3E0000: Excludes packet tracing and protocol tracing (default setting)

TABLE 7.4: Enabling additional WDS tracing on Windows Server 2008 R2

WDS COMPONENT	REGISTRY VALUE
Windows Deployment Services TFTP	HKEY_LOCAL_MACHINE\SYSTEM\CurrentControlSet\services\WDSServer\Providers\WDSTFTP\TraceFlags
Windows Deployment Services Multicasting	HKEY_LOCAL_MACHINE\SYSTEM\CurrentControlSet\services\WDSServer\Providers\WDSMC\TraceFlags

Tracing will consume resources and will affect performance. You should only enable tracing when you need to analyze a problem. Be sure to undo your changes when you have finished troubleshooting.

The resulting trace logs can be found at %windir%\tracing\wdsserver.log.

LOGGING ON THE WDS CLIENT

Sometimes issues will happen on the client and nothing will appear in logs on the WDS server. You can enable trace logging on the WDS client to identify the cause of these issues. You can turn on logging by running the following command on the WDS server:

```
DSUTIL /Set-Server /WDSClientLogging /Enabled:Yes
```

You can then set the logging level with this command:

```
WDSUTIL /Set-Server /WDSClientLogging /LoggingLevel:<LoggingLevel>
```

The possible logging levels are as follows:

◆ None

◆ Errors

◆ Warnings

◆ Info

You can find the client logs on the WDS server in Event Viewer. Browse to Applications and Services Logs ➤ Microsoft ➤ Windows ➤ Deployment-Services-Diagnostics. The Admin log will contain any errors and the Operational log will contain informational messages. Note that there is a code to identify the architecture of the clients:

◆ Architecture 0 is x86.

◆ Architecture 9 is x64.

◆ Architecture 6 is Itanium.

Some logging can also take place on the WDS client, depending on when the error occurs.

Any issues during the execution of the Windows PE boot image, before disk configuration, will be logged to X:\Windows\Panther. You can access this location while the boot image is still running by pressing Shift+F10 to launch the command prompt.

Issues that take place in the boot image after the disk configuration will be logged to `$Windows.~BT\Sources\Panther`, usually on the C: volume, and can also be accessed using the command prompt.

Any issues that occur on the first boot after the installation image is installed will be logged to `\Windows\Panther`, usually found on the C: volume of the machine.

Now you have the means to determine what is happening if any problems are reported with your WDS deployment implementation.

Troubleshooting WDS

Any troubleshooting of WDS should start with analyzing the performance of the server and capturing logs to get as much information as possible. There are a number of issues that are commonly reported. We will now describe how you can resolve these issues.

A 64-bit PXE client does not see 64-bit boot images.   Sometimes an x64 machine will not be able to see or download x64 boot images on the WDS server. This is because the BIOS is not correctly reporting the architecture of the machine. You can overcome this by forcing WDS to recognize the correct architecture by running this command on the WDS server:

```
WDSUTIL /set-server /architecturediscovery:yes
```

A 64-bit PXE client is correctly identified but still won't boot.   Make sure that you have added and created x64 boot images with the appropriate x64 drivers. If the x64 boot image is still not working, then you can configure WDS to use an x86 boot image as the default boot image for x64 machines.

The WDS Capture wizard does not display the drive you want to capture.   Ensure that the required storage drivers are included in the capture boot image. If they are, then it is possible that you have forgotten to run Sysprep to generalize the reference machine. You will need to reinstall the operating system, configure the machine, and generalize it.

The boot image cannot access network resources.   Press Shift+F10 to open a command prompt. Check that the machine has a valid IP by running the `ipconfig` command. If it does not, then it is likely that the boot image does not have a valid network driver. Use `ping` to verify that you can access the default gateway, a domain controller, and the WDS server. Any failures should be investigated in cooperation with the network administrators.

Download and startup of the boot image is slow in a nonmulticast environment.   You may need to adjust the TFTP block and window size. Microsoft provides step-by-step instructions for this task here: `http://technet.microsoft.com/library/cc731245(WS.10).aspx`.

The Bottom Line

Use and customize the PXE client.   A user or administrator can start the PXE client of a capable machine once it is enabled in the BIOS and a special key or key sequence is entered during the POST of the machine when it starts up.

> **Master It**   The WDS PXE client requires the person who is sitting at the client machine to observe and quickly respond to a prompt to press F12. Failure to do so causes the PXE client to time out and exit. You are receiving complaints about this and have been asked to disable this prompt. How will you accomplish this?

Create a customized installation image.   You can create customized installation images and deploy them using WDS.

Master It   A junior administrator is working in a lab to learn how WDS works. She has created a reference machine. A capture boot image was created with all the required drivers. The administrator has booted up the machine with the capture boot image but is unable to create a new image. What could be the cause?

Automate WDS.   Although WDS is not a light-touch or a zero-touch operating system deployment solution, it is possible to automate much of what it does.

Master It   How can you automate image operations in WDS?

Chapter 8

Tweaking Your WDS Server

In Chapter 6, "Windows Deployment Services: The Basics," you learned what Windows Deployment Services (WDS) is and how to prepare the server. We followed that up with Chapter 7, "WDS from the Client's View," in which you read about deploying operating system images to clients, creating custom images, and automating deployments. In this chapter we are going to focus on using some advanced WDS features. Our topics will include machine naming policies, computer object placement in organizational units (OUs), and optimizing bandwidth utilization by performing multicast deployments.

In this chapter, you will learn to:

◆ Implement a machine naming policy using WDS

◆ Manage domain membership of WDS clients

◆ Understand how multicast WDS image deployments work

Using WDS to Name Machines

What is the most difficult part of deploying a desktop operating system? Choosing the applications to include in an image (if any) might seem difficult, but that tends to be a pretty straightforward process because you just find the common denominator in the usage requirements and look at the licensing requirements. Choosing a deployment solution can also be straightforward. Once again, licensing comes into play and you just figure out how manual or automated the process needs to be. Believe it or not, the thing that may cause the most intense discussions in your project will be how you will name your machines. In this section we will briefly discuss naming standards for machines before looking at how you can implement that policy using WDS.

Developing a Naming Standard

A machine is given a computer name when it is deployed. The computer name is the name that makes the machine unique on the network, and it is this name that you as an administrator will use to manage the machine in your Windows environment, such as Active Directory, where it will be the computer object name. You could use the default random string that the Windows 7 setup provides. However, the default Windows 7 setup generated name can be a bit difficult to use when you are performing manual tasks such as network troubleshooting, security, or centralized software deployment. It is quite long and very random, offering no memorable structure, and the end user will find it difficult to communicate the name when talking to the help desk. You might want to use something that is still short enough to communicate, unique, and memorable.

This means that you will have to generate a new name. To make it memorable and unique, you will need some form of machine naming standard. This standard consists of a set of rules that will be used to name the machine.

One of the perks of working as an IT consultant is that you get to visit a wide variety of IT infrastructures over the years. Some are spectacular and allow you the opportunity to learn something new that you can reuse later in your career. Some are spectacular disasters and allow you the opportunity to learn the pitfalls that you should avoid. This also gives you the chance to see how organizations implement machine naming standards. There are many approaches and we will have a look at a few of them now.

Random Computer Names   Extreme security consultants (these are the folks who believe a demon is hiding behind every cubicle) love the idea of random computer names. The reason is that a potential attacker who is unfamiliar with a network cannot associate a user or an application with a name. That's the theory anyway. It's believed that social attacks are the most common type being employed at the moment. That's where an attacker pretends to be someone that they are not and uses conversation and human observation to gain an entry point into an organization. It's easy to associate a computer with an executive because they're either using it in the airport (where it can be stolen) or it's the one sitting in the very nice office. Applications can be identified using social engineering by calling into a help desk and pretending to be a salesperson and asking a few questions. The security consultant's favored approach may delay the attacker but security by obscurity is not a defense. Education and real network security are the real mechanisms that should be employed.

The real benefit of a random computer name is that you don't have to do anything to have one; the Windows 7 setup does this by default. Unfortunately, the name is pretty useless for human communications. Imagine an end user who needs someone on the help desk to remotely connect to their PC. The help desk may need to know the name of the machine. Some long, random name will be difficult to communicate over the phone. The user will either need to start an instant messaging session or send an email so that they can copy and paste the name. This process is not efficient.

Memorable Names   Some organizations (typically small or medium) choose to use memorable computer names. For example, some networks are full of computers that are named after football players, past and present. Others feature computer names that are inspired by the cast of long-running cartoon shows. Such a naming convention can provide the nerdy IT department with a laugh but the HR manager might not be pleased to have a laptop that is called *Grimey*. Seriously, though, these computer names are memorable and they are easy to communicate. Unfortunately for those of us who might be nerds, the names are not very professional and this sort of naming standard is not scalable in larger organizations.

Named After the User   It is not unusual to see networks where the computer name follows the name of the primary user of that machine. For example, a user called Joe Elway may have a user account called JElway. The computer for this user may be called JElway-PC. The computer name is going to be unique because the username is unique. The name is easy to communicate; in fact, the help desk engineer who gets a call from a user can probably guess the name of the machine. This system may work for many organizations. Where it fails is that you cannot always predict who the end user of a PC is going to be. For example, if IT is building 2,000 PCs in a "factory" (a dedicated room or lab dedicated to the nonstop building of PCs), then they won't know who the user will be. They just stack up PCs and those PCs are shipped out. Maybe the organization is very organized and has barcode asset tags and very tight asset control and shipping to allow this process, but this would be the exception. The username-based approach would also be inappropriate for an organization where the PC is used by many people, such as a call center, or it doesn't have an assigned user at all, such as a kiosk.

Structured Name It is possible to build a computer name using some form of algorithm that is structured, easy to communicate, meaningful, and easy to remember. It may look like a pretty random string to the uninitiated but once you know the structure (for that organization), you can read a lot of information from the computer name when you see it. The idea is to break the computer name down into a number of components. Each component describes something about the machine, such as its role or its primary location. Some part of the computer name will require a unique component. This can either be a random string or an incremental counter.

This type of computer name can be approached in many ways. Imagine a multinational organization that has two offices in Ireland, one in Dublin and one in Cork. There will be a number of Linux and Windows PCs. One naming standard may use the country (Ireland), the office location (Dublin or Cork), the operating system (Linux or Windows), and the type of machine (PC or server). For example, the first Windows machine might be called IEDBWPC001. That 10-character string tells us a lot about the machine. It is a Windows PC (WPC) in the Dublin (DB), Ireland (IE) office. There might also be a machine called IECKLPC099. That would be a Linux PC (LPC) in the Cork (CK), Ireland (IE) office. This can be expanded internationally. For example, CASFWPC125 might be a Windows PC in the San Francisco, California office. Of course, the same organization could also call a machine something like US-CA-Win-PC-125.

This is by no means a complete listing of your naming standards options. But why is this relevant to this chapter? It just so happens that WDS allows you to automatically implement a naming standard. You can define a rule on your WDS server to ensure that all computers that are built by it are named according to that rule. And that is what we will discuss next.

Naming a Computer Using WDS

Chapter 4, "Cloning the Panther: Automating Windows 7 Installation," introduced you to how you can use an unattended answer file, created using the Windows System Image Manager (WSIM), to control the naming of a computer. You can continue to use that system with WDS by associating an unattended answer file with an installation image (see Chapter 7). The problem with that approach is that it requires various WSIM administrators to work together to implement a single naming standard. Otherwise your organization will end up with no standard at all. Alternatively, this approach can be useful because you might deliberately want to have different naming standards. For example, a university may have one or more shared WDS servers that are shared by different faculties. Each faculty could have their own naming standards and installation images. These naming standards could be implemented in the unattended answer files that are associated with the installation images. So the Computer Science faculty could have a Windows 7 image with an unattended answer file that implements their naming standard. The Humanities faculty would also have their own installation image with their own unattended answer file.

Most organizations will want something that is simpler, where a single policy that is consistent can be defined. WDS allows this by implementing a policy on a per-WDS server basis. Every machine that has an operating system deployed by a WDS server with this policy configured will be subject to the naming standard and named accordingly.

CONFIGURING A WDS CLIENT NAMING POLICY

The naming standard on a WDS server is referred to as a *client naming policy*. This policy is defined once per WDS server. You can do this by opening the properties of your WDS server in the WDS console and navigating to the AD DS tab. This tab, shown in Figure 8.1, does a little more work, which we will look at later, but for now, we are going to focus on the Client Naming Policy section.

FIGURE 8.1
The AD DS tab and the default client naming policy

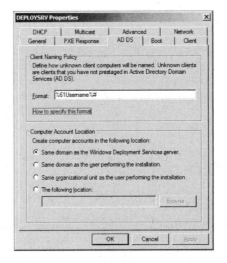

WDS is configured with a client naming policy, which you can see in the Format field. The default policy is to name computers as `%61Username%#`. That is a code or a set of instructions that tells WDS how to build the computer name. You can find instructions for this code by clicking on the How To Specify This Format link in the dialog box. The possible variables that you can use are as follows:

%Username   This variable instructs WDS to use the username of the WDS client user as a basis for the computer name. For example, if the user `helpdesk` is used to log into the WDS client and initiate an installation of an image, then the `%Username` variable will be replaced with `helpdesk`. That would be rather unhelpful because all computers could end up using that as a core component of the computer name.

%First   This variable uses the forename of the user who logs into the WDS client to install the image.

%Last   WDS will substitute the surname of the WDS client user when this variable is used.

%MAC   The MAC or Ethernet address of the network adapter that is used to install the image will be substituted for this variable.

These variables could be combined. For example, if you use %First%Last and deploy an image using the Joe Elway user account, then the computer name will be JoeElway. You could also set the client naming policy to something like %First%Last-PC. The computer might then be called JoeElway-PC. That is because -PC is a constant and not a variable. The username of Joe Elway might be JElway. You could end up with JElway-PC if you set the client naming policy to %Username-PC.

Computer names are typically short. They are limited to 15 characters if you want the machine to join a domain. It is possible that you have users with very long names that would not be appropriate. You can control how many characters will be used from a variable.

For example, if you wanted to use six characters from the surname, you would enter %6Last. For example, deploying an image with a client naming policy of %1First%6Last-PC with the user Rebecca Handleman would result in a computer being called RHandle-PC.

What if Robert Handleman joins the company and tries to build a PC for himself using WDS? Computer names must be unique. Using this client naming policy his machine should also be called RHandle-PC. That will cause a problem.

A numeric counter would solve this problem by making the computer name unique. You can do this by using the %[n]# variable. This approach allows you to add an incremental counter of n digits. For example, %1First%6Last-PC-%2# will allow an incremental counter of two digits. Rebecca's PC would be called RHandle-PC-1 and Robert's PC would be called RHandle-PC-2. This could continue up to RHandle-PC-99. You can increase this counter by allowing for more digits. For example, a %4# variable will allow for up to 9,999 machines.

THE DEFAULT WDS COMPUTER NAMING POLICY

The default computer naming policy in WDS is set to %61Username%#. That sets the computer name to use the first 61 characters of the user's username. The name will be truncated to the first 15 characters of the username.

Imagine that your client naming policy is %1First%6Last-PC-%4#. That means that your computer names could be between 12 and 15 characters. This policy could cause problems if you are scripting based on computer name length or if you have third-party applications that need a predictable length of computer name. You can do this by padding the incremental counter with zeroes. For example, instead of having a counter of 1, you could have a counter of 0001. You can do this by using %0[n]#. For example, %1First%6Last-PC-%04# could give you RHandle-PC-0001 to RHandle-PC-9999. The computer name will always be a predicable length.

You have a lot of options by using and/or combining these variables to create a computer naming policy. How will WDS use it?

 **Real World Scenario**

AN EXAMPLE COMPUTER NAMING POLICY

Imagine that the company Deploy.com is a multinational organization with offices in three different countries:

◆ San Francisco, USA

◆ New Orleans, USA

◆ Beijing, China

◆ Shanghai, China

◆ Dublin, Ireland

◆ Galway, Ireland

A WDS server is set up in each office to deploy Windows 7 images. The head office IT department has designed a naming standard that will contain information describing the country, city, operating system (Windows or Linux), and role of each machine (PC or server). There will be up to 999 PCs in each office and the computer name must be a fixed length.

A constant (not a variable) will be used to define the description of the computer. A variable will be used to ensure that the computer name is unique. The computer naming policy will be defined on each WDS server as follows:

◆ San Francisco: USSFWPC%03#

◆ New Orleans: USNOWPC%03#

◆ Beijing: CHBJWPC%03#

◆ Shanghai: CHSHWPC%03#

◆ Dublin: IEDBWPC%03#

◆ Galway: IEGAWPC%03#

This means that computers built by WDS will be named as follows:

◆ San Francisco: USSFWPC001–USSFWPC999

◆ New Orleans: USNOWPC001–USNOWPC999

◆ Beijing: CHBJWPC001–CHBJWPC999

◆ Shanghai: CHSHWPC001–CHSHWPC999

◆ Dublin: IEDBWPC001–IEDBWPC999

◆ Galway: IEGAWPC001–IEGAWPC999

A Linux machine may be built (using some Linux deployment solution) and named as CHBJLPC001 in the Beijing office.

This computer naming policy describes the location and role of the computer while providing for a short and easily communicated computer name.

How WDS Implements the Client Naming Policy

WDS will use the client naming policy to configure the name of a computer as it is being built. For example, you could deploy a number of machines such as IEDBWPC001, IEDBWPC002, IEDBWPC003, and IEDBWPC004 using an IEDBWPC%03# computer naming policy.

If there is a %# variable, the counter will simply increment to generate the next available machine. For example, you could manually build IEDBWPC005 and join it to the domain. The next machine built by WDS won't actually be IEDBWPC005. WDS will simply move on to IEDBWPC006 if that is available.

WDS will join the computers to a domain. The computer object that is created has an attribute called netbootGUID. WDS will store the MAC address or GUID of the machine's hardware (physical or virtual) in this attribute. This means that the computer name is linked to the hardware, as long as the MAC/GUID does not change or the computer object is not removed.

You could decide to rebuild IEDBWPC002 by deploying an image to it using WDS. WDS will determine the MAC or GUID of the machine. If that value is found in an existing computer object's netbootGUID, WDS will know to reuse the computer name.

This functionality makes the most of the available numbers you can use in a computer name and links a computer name to hardware. This can be very useful. You may implement a software distribution or computer management solution that is based on computer name. A user can rebuild their PC and still retain the same management policies because WDS will reuse their old computer name if the MAC/GUID is unchanged.

Manage Domain Membership Using WDS

You may have noticed something to do with computer accounts while reading about client naming policy in the previous section. WDS will join to a domain the computers that it builds. You can control exactly how this is done.

Specifying Computer Account Location   You can manage how WDS joins computers to Active Directory by opening the properties of the WDS server in the WDS console and navigating to the AD DS tab, shown earlier in Figure 8.1. The computer account location policy can be configured, once per WDS server, with one of four possible settings:

Same Domain As The Windows Deployment Services Server   This is the default policy. WDS will join the newly built machine to the same Active Directory domain as the WDS server. The computer object will be created in the default location, which is usually the Computers container. This location might not be appropriate. The user may be a member of a different domain in the forest and their computer should be in the same domain as they are. Or administrators may want to create computer objects in an organizational unit (OU) so that they can inherit configured Group Policy Objects.

Same Domain As The User Performing The Installation   With this policy enabled, the computer will be joined to the same domain as the user who logged into the WDS client. This policy can be beneficial in a multidomain organization. The computer account will be created in the default location for that domain, which is usually the Computers container. This strategy may not be desired if there are policies that must be inherited

Same Organizational Unit As The User Performing The Installation   The new computer object will be created in the same OU as the user who logged into the WDS client. If this is an end user, this strategy can be effective. The computer object is created where it will inherit the appropriate policies and where delegated administration has been set up. However, this approach will not be useful if an administrator is building the computer because the computer object will be created in an administrative OU rather than in a user's OU. It would also be inappropriate if you use dedicated OUs for computer objects.

The Following Location   This policy allows you to specify a domain (in the forest) and OU/container where the new computer object will be created. This is useful if you plan to have one location for all computer objects that will be created by a WDS server. However, a very large site may have different OUs or domains for users and computers. This policy will only allow you to select one location that must suit every machine that the WDS server will be used to prepare.

There is no one policy that will suit everyone. You should evaluate your organization's requirements for computer account location and then choose the policy that best meets those needs.

The WDS server will require some rights to create or manage computer accounts in the specified Active Directory locations. You can do this in Active Directory Users And Computers by right-clicking the required OU and selecting Delegate Control. You will specify Computers under Object Types and enter the computer name of the WDS server. Select Create A Custom Task To Delegate. Click Create Selected Objects In This Folder and select Computer Objects. Grant the Full Control permission. The WDS server will have rights to create computer objects in the OU when you complete the wizard.

 Real World Scenario

AN EXAMPLE OF COMPUTER ACCOUNT LOCATION

Imagine that the company Deploy.com is a multinational organization with offices in three different countries:

◆ San Francisco, USA

◆ New Orleans, USA

◆ Beijing, China

◆ Shanghai, China

◆ Dublin, Ireland

◆ Galway, Ireland

The company has built a single-domain Active Directory called deploy.com. An organizational unit architecture has been set up as follows:

◆ [domain] Deploy.com

◆ [OU] The Company

◆ [OU] The Company ➤ San Francisco

◆ [OU] The Company ➤ San Francisco ➤ Users

◆ [OU] The Company ➤ San Francisco ➤ Groups

◆ [OU] The Company ➤ San Francisco ➤ Computers

◆ [OU] The Company ➤ New Orleans

◆ [OU] The Company ➤ New Orleans ➤ Users

◆ [OU] The Company ➤ New Orleans ➤ Groups

◆ [OU] The Company ➤ New Orleans ➤ Computers

This pattern continues to provide OUs for the remaining offices in the company. A WDS server is deployed in each office. Any computer objects that are created should be joined to the Computers child OU for the relevant location.

The computer account location policy will be configured to use the setting The Following Location. Each WDS server will be configured to join computers to the relevant Computers OU for its location. For example, the New Orleans WDS server will create computer objects in the The Company ➤ New Orleans ➤ Computers OU.

This approach ensures that computer objects are created in an OU where delegated Active Directory administrators will have permissions to access them and that the computers will inherit policy that is relevant to their logical location in the company.

Advanced Domain Controller Settings

In extremely large Active Directory environments, you may need to control which domain controllers the WDS server will work with. You can manage the domain controller settings by opening the properties of the WDS server in the WDS console and navigating to the Advanced tab, shown in Figure 8.2.

By default, the WDS server will use any domain controller that it discovers by normal methods. This is perfectly valid in most environments. In some scenarios, such as where there is a massive load on production domain controllers, you may need to configure the WDS server to use specific domain controllers that won't impact on line-of-business services.

You can select the Windows Deployment Services Should Use The Following Services option and then select a specific domain controller and global catalog replica that WDS should use.

FIGURE 8.2
Advanced domain
controller settings

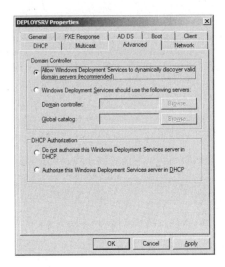

Using WDS for Multicast Deployments

Any project designed to deploy Windows 7 in an organization will probably require that entire teams, departments, or offices be migrated in as short a time as possible. That means you could have dozens or even hundreds of machines all trying to download an image from a WDS server at the same time. Even a handful of WDS clients could congest the network. This congestion would slow down the image deployment. Worse still, it could negatively affect the other production systems on the network and prevent people from doing their jobs. Windows Server 2008 added the ability to do a multicast deployment to resolve this issue.

Normally, network conversations are one-to-one (sender-to-recipient) transmissions. In such a transmission, a sender sends each packet out once for each recipient. If a stream of data contains 1,000 packets and there are 100 recipients, then the sender transmits 100,000 packets. There will be 100 simultaneous conversations and the network might become congested. In a *multicast* transmission, a sender transmits each packet on the network to multiple simultaneous recipients. One packet is sent out at a time and each recipient listens for that packet. Using the previous example, the sender will transmit 1,000 packets. Each of the 100 recipients will listen to the transmission and pick up the data. There is much less data transmitted at once and the network is much less likely to be congested by the transmission.

In this section you will read about why multicast is important to WDS administrators, how multicast works, and how to set up a multicast deployment.

Why Multicast Deployments Are Needed

Imagine that you are working on a Windows 7 deployment project. You are using WDS to deploy a 7 GB installation image to a number of machines. Because a deployment is quick, the organization has decided that you can do this one team at a time during the workday. You start working on the first team where there are 20 machines to be updated. You go to each machine, start up the WDS client, and start a deployment. All 20 machines are installing at the same time. That's when your phone starts to ring.

Figure 8.3 illustrates what has happened. Twenty WDS clients have simultaneously started downloading a single 7 GB installation image over the network. This is the default configuration for WDS and it will flood the network, resulting in the following:

◆ The deployment will take much longer because each client has a one-to-one session with the WDS server and the installation image will take longer to download. The cumulative effect will cause all 20 machines to take much longer to install than they should have. That means the users of those machines cannot work for longer than expected.

◆ The network congestion will affect other users' ability to use network services such as file shares, SharePoint servers, email, and so on.

◆ Your hearing will be affected when your boss screams through the phone at you.

FIGURE 8.3
A default nonmulticast deployment

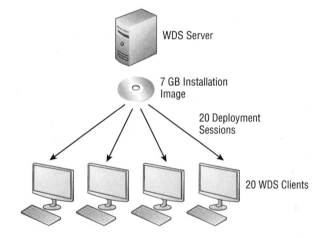

Imagine if this was a much bigger deployment. A larger enterprise might decide to upgrade hundreds of machines at once. The network would not be able to handle this load and the WDS server might also struggle.

If you are deploying an identical installation image to a number of machines, wouldn't it make sense if the WDS server could transmit it once on the network and all the clients received the transmission at the same time? Doing so would drastically reduce the impact on the network. In this scenario, around 1/20th of the original amount of data would be transmitted. That is the idea behind a multicast deployment.

How WDS Multicast Works

The basic idea of a multicast is that a server with data (the WDS server with an installation image) will transmit data once on the network and a number of listening clients (WDS clients) receive the data. This greatly reduces the workload on the server and the amount of congestion on the network. You can see how Figure 8.4 compares with Figure 8.3.

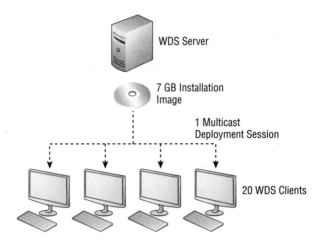

FIGURE 8.4
A multicast
deployment

That option sounds pretty easy, but it's not quite that simple. There are a few considerations:

Multicast IP Address Range A multicast client will require a special IP range. You can configure a WDS server to obtain these IPv4 or IPv6 addresses from DHCP. You can also set up the WDS server to provide configurations to WDS clients from a range of IPv4 or IPv6 addresses that are configured on the WDS server. If you have multiple WDS servers in a site, you must ensure that they have nonoverlapping IP ranges if the WDS server will provide the IPv4 and IPv6 configurations.

WDS Clients with Differing Network Connections It is likely that a WDS server will have to work with clients that have connections of different speeds. For example, there may be machines with 10 Gbps, 1 Gbps, and 100 Mbps network cards. A multicast deployment of an installation image will, by default, run at a single speed that suits all of the multicast WDS clients. In other words, the deployment will run at the speed of the slowest client (also known as the *master client)*. That may mean that many 10 Gbps clients will download an installation image at 100 Mbps if a single slow WDS client joins the multicast session.

WDS allows you to limit how clients on slow network connections will delay clients on faster network connections. You can configure a multicast to run at different speeds. Clients can be divided up into three sessions (slow, medium, and fast) or two sessions (slow and fast). You can even specify a minimum supported connection speed in Kbps that a WDS client must meet in order to join the session.

WDS Clients Not Starting at the Same Time It is possible that some WDS clients will start up later than others. For example, you might start a multicast deployment for 100 computers. You cannot boot up all 100 machines into the WDS client at the same time. That means that the multicast deployment will start before all of the clients are ready. WDS gives you two solutions to this.

By default, the late WDS clients will join the existing session and download the image. They are joining the middle of the session and will be missing the first part of the image. Eventually the WDS server will reach the end of the transmission. All of those WDS clients that received the complete image will continue with their installation. The WDS server will not hang up. It knows that there are existing WDS clients that have a partial image. It will restart the multicast transmission from the start. Each of the late WDS clients will complete their download of the installation image. They will sign off and start their installation as the missing part of the image is downloaded. Eventually all WDS clients will complete their download and the WDS server can terminate the multicast. That means there may be more than one multicast of the installation image. It is much better than the default one-to-one behavior of WDS, but it is not as efficient as it could be in a large simultaneous deployment.

WDS supports scheduled multicasts. The WDS clients can be started up in advance. The WDS clients will wait for the multicast to start. The scheduled cast can be triggered to start when one of three possible conditions is met. An administrator can manually start it. It can start once a minimum number of WDS clients join the multicast, or it can be started at a specified date or time.

Disk Space on the Client   WDS client behavior is slightly different in a multicast deployment. In a normal nonmulticast deployment, the WDS client expands the installation image as it is downloaded. In a multicast deployment, the complete image is downloaded to the local disk of the WDS client before it can be expanded. In this way, a WDS client can join an existing WDS session and download a partial image before the missing piece can be retransmitted by the WDS server.

The requirements for multicast deployments are as follows:

Network Appliances   The devices on the network, such as switches and routers, must support multicast transmissions. Internet Group Membership Protocol (IGMP) snooping should be enabled on all devices that reside between the WDS server and the WDS clients. (See the section "Network Flooding with IGMP Snooping Disabled" later in this chapter.) This will optimize the multicast transmission by ensuring that the multicast packets are sent only to the relevant multicast clients. If you do not enable IGMP snooping, the multicast will actually be a broadcast that is sent to all machines on the network.

Boot Image   If you are deploying Windows 7, you will probably be using a boot image that is created from the Windows 7 media or the latest version of the Windows Automated Installation Kit. The boot image will have support for multicast deployments. You may decide to support older operating systems using the knowledge in this book. If so, be aware that you must use a boot image that is created from Windows Vista or later.

Creating a Multicast Deployment

You now know some of the theory behind a WDS client. It is time to see how to put this theory to use. We will look at setting up the behavior of multicast on the WDS server. You can do this by editing options on the Multicast tab in the properties of the WDS server in the WDS console, shown in Figure 8.5.

Here you can configure how IPv4 or IPv6 addresses are assigned to WDS multicast clients. By default, the WDS server will manage a predefined range of IP addresses (select the Use Addresses From The Following Range radio button). You need to ensure that there is no IP range overlap between servers if more than one WDS server can service a subnet or subnets. You can choose to allow DHCP to manage the allocation of IP addresses (select the Obtain IP Address From DHCP radio button).

FIGURE 8.5

FIGURE 8.5
WDS server multi-
cast configuration

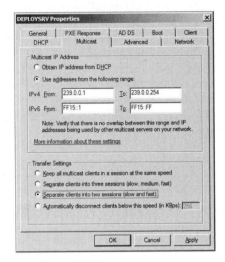

The Transfer Settings area allows you to manage how WDS multicast will deal with clients with different network connection speeds. You have four options here:

♦ The default, keep all clients in a single multicast session at the same speed

♦ Divide clients into slow, medium, and fast sessions

♦ Divide clients into slow and fast sessions

♦ Automatically disconnect WDS clients that have a connection speed that is less than defined (in Kbps)

You will choose one of the Transfer Settings options based on how many client network speeds you have and how many simultaneous streams you want. For example, if you have 100 Mbps and 1 Gbps clients, then will want to support slow and fast sessions. If you add additional clients with 10 Gbps network cards, you might want to support slow, medium, and fast sessions.

You need to create a multicast transmission in the WDS console (under Multicast Transmissions) and associate it with an installation image if you want to perform multicast deployments. Any WDS client requesting that installation image will then initiate or join a multicast session. You can create a multicast transmission by right-clicking and selecting Create Multicast Transmission.

The Create Multicast Transmission wizard will appear. The first screen asks you to name the transmission. Provide a meaningful name that will make sense to you and others at a later time.

The Image Selection screen allows you to associate an installation image with the multicast transmission. You can navigate between image groups and select the installation image that you want to deploy via multicast.

Figure 8.6 shows the Multicast Type screen. On this screen you can switch between the default Auto-Cast option (where the multicast starts as soon as any WDS client requests it) or the Scheduled-Cast option. The Scheduled-Cast option allows you to control the start of a multi-cast. In this way, you can make the most of multicast functionality and available bandwidth. By default, if you select Scheduled-Cast, WDS clients will join the multicast but nothing will happen until an administrator approves starts the session. There are two suboptions for Scheduled-Cast that allow the session to start automatically.

Start When The Number Of Clients That Have Requested The Image Is This option allows an administrator to set a threshold. A minimum number of WDS clients must join the multicast before it starts.

Start At A Later Time WDS administrators can define a date and time when the multicast session can start.

FIGURE 8.6
Configuring the multicast type

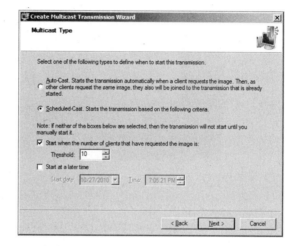

You can choose to not select any Scheduled-Cast suboptions, select one at a time, or combine them as required.

The new multicast transmission will appear in the WDS console under Multicast Transmissions. It will have a status of Waiting while no WDS clients are connected to it.

Note that you cannot edit the properties of a multicast transmission. You will have to delete it and re-create it if you want to make any changes. You can have more than one multicast transmission, thus providing support for different installation images.

Now you can boot up your WDS clients. Log into the WDS client and select the image that is associated with the new multicast transmission. If you selected the Scheduled-Cast option, the image download will not start right away. Instead, you will be told that the WDS client is waiting for the server, as shown in Figure 8.7.

Back in the WDS console, you can navigate into your new multicast transmission object to see which WDS clients are connected (you might need to refresh the screen). Here you have a few options. You can instruct a WDS client to bypass multicast and start a normal download. You can also disconnect the client to abort the image download.

You can right-click on a multicast transmission to manually start the session. You can do so even if the transmission has not yet met any defined start conditions.

FIGURE 8.7
A WDS client waiting for a scheduled multicast

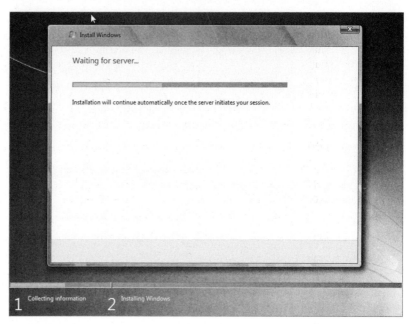

The multicast session will appear as Active once it starts. The detail for each WDS client's session can be seen within the multicast transmission object. Here you get information that can be used to monitor progress and troubleshoot the multicast transmission:

◆ Identifying information (MAC address and IP address)

◆ Image download progress (Status)

◆ The amount of time that the WDS client has been connected to the multicast transmission

◆ Data transfer rate

◆ WDS client CPU utilization

The image will be expanded and installed once it is downloaded to the clients.

Troubleshooting a Multicast Deployment

Two problems can commonly occur with a multicast deployment.

SLOW MULTICAST IMAGE DOWNLOAD

The most common complaint will be that a multicast transmission is very slow. You should use the multicast transmission client information in the WDS console. Doing so gives you a quick overview of what is happening.

The most obvious thing to do is to check the network. Things like dodgy switch ports or other network activity could affect the speed of an image download. Microsoft recommends that you use switches instead of hubs, and that you use CAT5 or CAT5e cabling or better. Check with your network administrator colleagues or the network monitoring systems to see if anything stands out.

You may have a mix of clients with different connection speeds. If so, make sure that you have set up the multicast configuration (WDS server properties) to divide up the transmission into slow/fast or slow/medium/fast sessions.

Sometimes a single faulty machine can cause a large multicast to run slowly. This machine will have a slow connection and will become the master client, thus reducing the download for everyone else in its session. You can identify the master client by running this command:

```
Wdsutil /Get-AllMulticastTransmissions /Show:Install /Details:Clients
```

This code will return information on each of the clients. Search for an attribute called `Master Client` where the value is set to `Yes`. This is the machine that is causing the session to be slow. Note the `ClientID` value for this machine. This value is what you will use to identify the machine. You can disconnect this machine in the console or by running this command:

```
Wdsutil /Disconnect-Client /ClientID:<ClientID of the master client>
```

The role of master client will switch to the next slowest machine. Check the download rates to see if they have improved. If not, you will need to identify and disconnect the new master client.

NETWORK FLOODING WITH IGMP SNOOPING DISABLED

Without IGMP snooping enabled on network devices, the multicast will effectively become a broadcast and can flood the network. The obvious answer would be to enable IGMP snooping. This might not be possible. If that is the case, you can limit the life of the multicast packets on the network using a Registry edit on the WDS server. Microsoft suggests that you set the time-to-live (TTL) for the multicast packets to 32. On Windows Server 2008 you do so by editing `HKEY_LOCAL_MACHINE\SYSTEM\CurrentControlSet\Services\WDSServer\Providers\Multicast\Profiles`. On Windows Server 2008 R2, you do so by editing `HKEY_LOCAL_MACHINE\System\CurrentControlSet\Services\WDSServer\Providers\WDSMC\Protocol`.

The Bottom Line

Implement a machine naming policy using WDS.   You can automate the naming of machines that are built using WDS.

Master It   Users will build their own computers using WDS. You have been asked to name computers using the first two letters of the user's forename and the first six characters of their surname. Some users may have up to 10 PCs. The computer name should be 10 characters long. What client naming policy will you use?

Manage domain membership of WDS clients.   It is possible to control where new computer objects are created when WDS prepared machines are joined to a domain.

Master It   You receive a call from a branch office help desk engineer. They are delighted to see that machines that are rebuilt will retain their original computer name. She asks you how this is accomplished. What will you tell her?

Understand how multicast WDS image deployments work. WDS can optimize the usage of network capacity for large-scale deployments by using a multicast transmission.

Master It A colleague has set up a multicast transmission for 100 clients. He has gone home with an illness and you have taken over the deployment task. You notice that the deployment is taking longer than expected. What will you do?

Chapter 9

Microsoft Deployment Toolkit 2010

In Chapter 4, "Cloning the Panther: Automating Windows 7 Installation," we showed you how to deploy Windows 7 images using the Windows Automated Installation Kit (WAIK). As you learned in that chapter, manually deploying Windows 7 is doable but not very intuitive or easily repeatable. Microsoft Deployment Toolkit 2010 (MDT) was designed to remove the complexity of manually creating, deploying, and maintaining your images by implementing friendly and concise wizards. Another great strength of MDT is that it's script driven for full flexibility, allowing you to tailor MDT's behavior to fit any environment. Microsoft provides a portal of sorts where you can easily download the latest and greatest deployment tools. From this portal you can download tools MDT will use (along with other useful applications like MAP and ACT that MDT does not need but that might be helpful to you).

MDT 2010 is the first version to employ PowerShell cmdlets, which help you automate your most common management tasks by making them easily scriptable. If these benefits are not enough to get you interested in MDT 2010, consider that it is completely free.

There are four deployment scenarios we'll be referring to throughout this chapter: refresh, replace, bare metal, and upgrade. In a refresh scenario, you are using the same hardware but changing (refreshing) the operating system. A replace scenario is where you actually replace the hardware with newer hardware so the end user receives a completely new system. A bare-metal scenario typically refers to purchasing new hardware.

In this chapter, you will learn to:

◆ Set up a technician machine/deployment server (install the MDT 2010 Update 1)

◆ Create an image containing an operating system, drivers, packages (patches), and applications

◆ Deploy an image using the MDT client wizard

Setting Up Your Deployment Server

The machine on which you install MDT will be called either a technician machine (when you're installing MDT on a desktop OS) or a deployment server (when you're installing MDT on a server class operating system). Whether you have a technician machine or a deployment server, the steps for installing, configuring, and using MDT are identical. But before you dive in and start installing MDT to create your technician machine/deployment server, consider these three things:

- Your technician machine/deployment server must meet the minimum hardware requirements.
- MDT requires additional software that needs to be installed before MDT will be usable.
- You should know which OSs you can install MDT on and which OSs MDT can deploy.

In this section we'll focus on setting up the technician machine/deployment server, including the hardware and software requirements, and explain which operating system would work best on the deployment server and why.

 Real World Scenario

TAKE CONTROL

Working with OS deployment puts you in a seat where you need control. You must spend time figuring out naming for folders, scripts, task sequences, applications, and so on. The naming convention does not need to be perfect, but it must be logical and easy to understand. One case we recall was a company that had drivers for more than 20 different models of PCs. The company imported every single driver into the root folder Out-Box Drivers. That approach almost worked for 2 or 3 months—then they had problems. They added new drivers for a new model, but what they did not know was that the vendor removed support in the new driver for older models, although the Plug and Play (PNP) number was the same. The only solution was to do what they should have done from the beginning: pick just the drivers they needed and put them in a nice, clean folder structure. Somehow, it always comes back when you try to cheat...

Hardware Requirements

The Microsoft bare minimum hardware requirements are fairly low, and if you install MDT 2010 on a Windows Server 2008 R2 you have already passed all the minimum requirements since Windows Server 2008 R2 has higher requirements than MDT has, and we highly recommend that you install MDT 2010 on Windows Server 2008 R2. If you install MDT 2010 on another operating system, the minimum hardware requirements are the following:

- 1.4 GHz processor
- 512 MB of RAM
- 2 GB, or enough hard drive space to store your images

Moving past the minimum requirements, think about this—installing MDT on a server doesn't burden the server. Even creating images for deployment doesn't take a lot of juice. But when clients connect across the network and start pulling those big image files from the hard drive—that's where the server is going to take a performance hit. A server has four subsystems you must take into account: the processor, memory, disk performance, and network interface. The most important subsystems for a deployment server are disk performance and the network interface. The processor and memory are not as heavily utilized by MDT's deployment process. We suggest spending your money on high disk performance and (depending on how many machines you plan to deploy concurrently) possibly multiple network interfaces. We recommend the following, at minimum, for your minimum hardware:

◆ 1.4 GHz processor or better

◆ 2 GB of RAM or more

◆ 2 disk sets (RAID 1 for your OS and RAID 5 for your data) with at least 150 GB of disk space to store your images

◆ A gigabit network card (multiple NICs if you plan on deploying a lot of machines at the same time, but that will require that you use teamed NICs)

Software Requirements

The installation of MDT 2010 requires installing the Windows Automated Installation Kit 2.0 (WAIK), also referred to as the Windows Automated Installation Kit for Windows 7. MDT utilizes the WAIK's tools for capturing, applying, and maintaining images.

There are two versions of MDT 2010 Update 1: one 32 bit and one 64 bit. You select the version that matches your OS version. The WAIK is both 32 and 64 bit at the same time if you download it from Microsoft Download. But from within the Deployment Workbench you will see that there are two downloads: one 32-bit and one 64-bit. When you download the WAIK from Microsoft Download, it is a complete package that works on many operating systems; it also has Windows Deployment Services included for Windows Server 2003. When you download the WAIK from within MDT 2010 Update 1, you get only the parts that you need (WinPE, WSIM, and the tools). That's why it's in most cases faster to first install MDT and then use the Components tab to download the rest of the tools you need.

USE INFORMATION CENTER'S COMPONENTS NODE FOR FASTER MDT DOWNLOAD

We recommend that you first install MDT 2010 Update 1 and then, from the Components node, download and install the WAIK toolkit. When you choose this route, downloading will be faster, since you download just the parts from the kit that are needed. If you download the complete kit, you will notice that there are no 32- and 64-bit versions. The full download version is both 32 and 64 bit, so you will save time downloading the WAIK from the Components node, discussed in the section "Meeting the Deployment Workbench" later in this chapter.

The WAIK 2.0 has software requirements as well: .NET Framework 2.0 or later and MSXML 6.0 or later have to be installed *before* you can install the WAIK. Not to worry; the required software for the WAIK is included in the WAIK download, so you won't have to waste time searching for it. And if you choose to set up a deployment server using Windows Server 2008 or later, both the .NET Framework and MSXML are built in.

Supported Operating Systems

The operating system of a technician machine may be either Windows Vista SP1 or Windows 7. The OS of a deployment server can be Windows Server 2003 SP2 (the Windows AIK documentation states 2003 SP1, but that's incorrect), Windows Server 2008, or Windows Server 2008 R2. We recommend an OS that supports Server Message Block (SMB) 2.0 (Vista, Windows 7, or Windows Server 2008 R2). SMB 2.0 will speed up the deployment process since it handles larger file transfers better than SMB 1.0.

Installing MDT on a server class OS such as Windows Server 2008 R2 allows you to easily integrate Windows Deployment Service (WDS) and MDT or Configuration Manager and MDT (we'll cover MDT and integration scenarios in Chapter 11, "Fine-Tuning MDT Deployments"). Even though MDT 2010 can be installed on client class and older server class OSs, we strongly recommend installing MDT on the latest server operating system, which will give you better performance, better scalability, and more flexibility.

The following operating systems are supported by MDT 2010 Update 1 for deployment:

◆ Windows XP (SP3)

◆ Windows Server 2003 R2

◆ Windows Vista (all SPs)

◆ Windows 7

◆ Windows Server 2008 (all SPs)

◆ Windows Server 2008 R2

The version of Windows Pre-Installation Environment that MDT supports is WinPE 3.0, which is included in the WAIK 2.0. (WinPEs were covered in Chapter 4.)

Installing MDT 2010 Update 1

Once you have chosen the operating system (Server 2008 R2, we hope) for your deployment server, ensured that you have met the hardware requirements, downloaded and installed the WAIK and its associated components (if needed), and downloaded MDT 2010 Update 1 from Microsoft, you're ready to install MDT. Installation of MDT couldn't be simpler. The installation is wizard driven and should take no more than 5 minutes. Follow these steps to install MDT:

1. Double-click `MicrosoftDeploymentToolkit2010_x86.msi` or `MicrosoftDeploymentToolkit2010_x64.msi` (depending on your architecture).

2. Click Install to see the "Welcome to the Microsoft Deployment Toolkit 2010 (5.1.1642.01) Setup Wizard" page, and click Next.

3. Accept the End-User License Agreement by putting a check mark in the "We accept the terms in the License Agreement" box, and click Next.

4. On the Custom Setup page, accept the default installation location, `C:\Program Files\ Microsoft Deployment Toolkit\`, as shown in Figure 9.1. You can also determine the amount of hard drive space required to install MDT by clicking the Disk Usage button shown in Figure 9.1. The Disk Usage button displays the Disk Space Requirements page,

which lists your hard drives, the amount of space available on each, and the amount of space needed to install MDT. The Disk Space Requirements page shows that only 75 MB is required for the installation. We recommend storing your deployment shares on a drive separate from the OS and ensuring that you have plenty of hard drive space; you may be surprised at how much this install will consume.

FIGURE 9.1

The Custom
Setup page

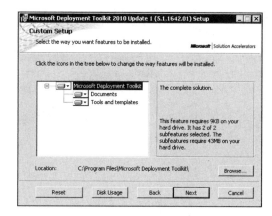

5. When you have configured your location and ensured that you have enough hard drive space, click Next and then click Install.

6. As the installation completes, you will see the "Completing the Microsoft Deployment Toolkit 2010 (5.1.1642.01) Setup Wizard" page. Click Finish to complete the installation of MDT 2010 Update 1.

Meeting the Deployment Workbench

The Deployment Workbench (Figure 9.2) is the tool you'll use to work with MDT. The Deployment Workbench allows you to import operating systems, applications, drivers, and packages to create reference images or to deploy reference images or default images. After you have installed MDT, you'll find the Deployment Workbench in Start ➤ All Programs ➤ Microsoft Deployment Toolkit.

In this section, we will explain what all the different parts in the workbench really mean and what they are used for. We'll also introduce you to some of MDT's wizards, like the New Deployment Share Wizard, the Import Operating System Wizard, the New Task Sequence Wizard, and the Update Deployment Share Wizard. In Figure 9.2 you can see that we have high-lighted the Getting Started topic under Information Center. The process flow you see is what's considered to be a best practice and it is simple.

1. *Import source files to management computer.* Set up MDT, then add the operating system(s) you will deploy together with patches, language packs, device drivers, and applications.

2. *Create task sequence and boot image for reference computer.* A reference image is what you get when you install the OS along with patches, language packs, and some applications.

FIGURE 9.2
The Deployment
Workbench

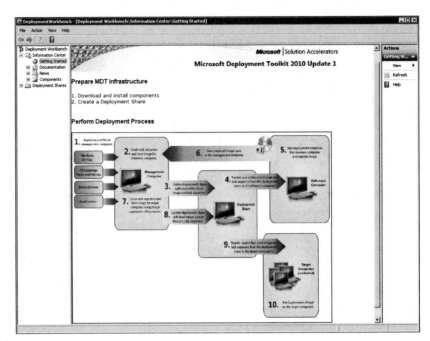

3. *Update deployment share with source files, boot images, and task sequence.* Updating the deployment share will also create the boot image needed to install Windows on the reference machine (this can be a virtual machine—in fact we recommend that you create reference images on virtual machines).

4. *Transfer source files, boot images, and task sequence from the deployment share to the reference computer.* Boot the reference machine. You can use WDS and PXE boot, or you can use the ISO file to boot from (or create an ISO and boot from that).

5. *Run the deployment wizard on the reference computer and capture the image.* Install the reference computer using the wizard and, once again, we suggest that you use a virtual machine.

6. *Send captured image back to the management computer.* If you select Capture And Sysprep, once you've installed the OS with your applications and patches, the task sequence will, in the end, run Sysprep and capture the image and store it in the location you selected in the wizard.

7. *Create task sequence and boot image for target computer, using image captured in number 5 as source.* Create a new task sequence, this time for deployment to real machines. Before you can create the task sequence, you need to import the captured image as a custom image. You might also create a new deployment share to separate your lab, test, and reference image content from the production deployment. You don't have to, but we recommend that you do.

8. *Update deployment share with boot image, source files, and task sequence.* If you have a separate deployment share or the production deployment share is located on another computer, you need to update it so it will receive your new custom image and your new task sequence.

9. *Transfer source files, boot images, and task sequence from the deployment share to the reference computer.* Boot the real machine using PXE (if that has been set up), or boot on the ISO image/media to deploy your real machine that should go into production.

10. *Run Deployment Wizard on the target computers.* Deploy the machine using the deployment wizard; this time you should select the new task sequence, the one for production use.

Exploring the Active Parts of the Deployment Workbench

Now that we have covered the Getting Started node, let's explore the remaining ones.

◆ The Documentation node gives you direct links to Quick Start guides to assist in planning your deployment, choosing light-touch versus zero-touch deployment scenarios and troubleshooting guides. These all point to MDT's help file (`Microsoft Deployment Toolkit Documentation Library.chm`).

◆ The News node contains links to common documents on Microsoft's TechNet site, like "Windows Optimized Desktop Scenarios" and "Streamline Migration to Windows Vista and Windows 7."

◆ The Components node shows which tools are available for download, such as WAIK 2.0, MAP, and ACT 5.6, among others. You can also find out what has been downloaded but not yet installed and what has been downloaded and installed. Since the WAIK toolkit is needed, it will also show up as required if it hasn't been installed, and you can download and install it from here. As mentioned earlier, we recommend that you download and install the WAIK toolkit from the Components node. From here, the download will be faster, since it's just going to download the parts from the kit that are needed.

Creating and Populating a Deployment Share

The deployment share (DS) is the shared folder your MDT clients (target machines) will connect to and download images from. The deployment share can reside on the deployment server or across the network on another server. In fact, you could store everything needed to deploy an image to a target machine on a single DVD or even a USB **stick** (depending on the size of your image). This type of deployment is referred to as a *media deployment*. The cool thing about a media deployment is that you can deploy an image with no network connectivity at all (media deployments are covered in Chapter 11). In this section, we'll show you how to create a deployment share using the default settings. Don't worry too much about using the default settings when you create a deployment share; there are plenty of places later where you can override any default setting. We'll go into more depth on overriding the default settings in Chapter 11.

Creating a Deployment Share

You will almost certainly need two deployment shares. The first one (the *lab share*) is where you create reference images and the other one (the *production share*) is where you create real deployment shares. Although you could combine both of these onto a single share, in most cases it is easier to have two separate deployment shares. The lab deployment share would only contain the operating system, packages, and applications that are supposed to be in the reference image.

The production deployment share would contain the captured reference image, applications that are not inside the reference image, drivers, and in some cases, packages and patches. One other reason to use two shares is that there is normally a big difference in the way you customize the settings; the settings for creating reference images are not the same as for creating production deployment. Now, let's create a deployment share that handles both reference images and production deployment.

When you have done this and you get a better understanding of how MDT works and what you can do, you should create a separate deployment share. Just repeat the steps and use another name and folder, such as MDTPrd (short for MDT Production). When you've finished, you can copy the sequences, the captured operating systems, applications, and drivers using copy and paste between these two deployment shares. Now you have a clean one for production and one that will be a bit "not so clean" where you can play around and test. The following steps will guide you through the process of creating a Deployment Share:

1. Create a deployment share from within the Deployment Workbench by right-clicking the Deployment Shares node and choosing New Deployment Share. This launches the New Deployment Share Wizard's Path page, shown in Figure 9.3.

FIGURE 9.3
The Path page

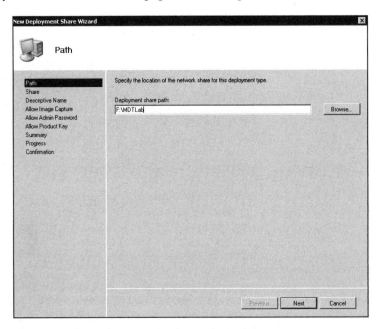

2. Choose the drive and folder where you would like your deployment share created. You can either browse to a folder or simply type over the existing path. No need to create the folder first—MDT will do that for you. Then click Next.

3. The next page of the New Deployment Share Wizard is the Share page shown in Figure 9.4. Type the name you would like to share the folder as in the Share Name field and click Next.

HIDING SHARES

Putting a $ at the end of the share name makes this a hidden share. So when users browse the shared folders on the deployment server, they won't see this folder. For those users who like to poke around network shares just to see what's out there, this shared folder will not be easily found.

FIGURE 9.4

Entering a name on the Share page

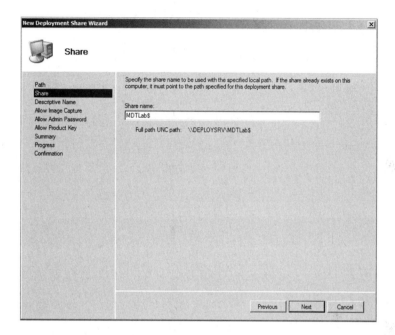

4. The Descriptive Name page shown in Figure 9.5 allows you to give your shared folder a description, which appears with the shared folder name when you view the shared folders for that server. To quickly view the shared folders of a server, open a command prompt and type the following:

```
net share
```

5. The results are shown in Table 9.1. Once you've chosen your description, click Next.

TABLE 9.1:   Shared folders information

SHARE NAME	RESOURCE	DEFAULT DESCRIPTIVE NAME
C$	C:\	Default share
MDTLab$	F:\MDTLab	MDT Lab share

TABLE 9.1:   Shared folders information   *(CONTINUED)*

SHARE NAME	RESOURCE	DEFAULT DESCRIPTIVE NAME
F$	F:\	Default share
IPC$		Remote IPC
ADMIN$	C:\Windows	RemoteAdmin

FIGURE 9.5
The Descriptive
Name page

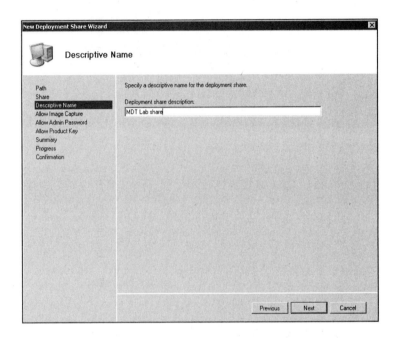

6. The Allow Image Capture page shown in Figure 9.6 by default is configured to ask if an image of the target machine should be captured. Capturing is used when you want to create a reference image, and since this deployment share is going to be able to handle both reference images and deployment images we need to be able to capture an image. If you later create a new deployment share for production only, you should answer that question with a no instead.

    You should only use the capture feature when the purpose is to create a reference image and not for backup (if you need a backup when doing a refresh, replace, or upgrade, the deployment wizard will ask you when deploying the new OS). Accept the default setting or remove the check mark and click Next.

7. The next page is the Allow Admin Password page shown in Figure 9.7. The default is to *not* ask users to set the local administrator password. Okay, wait a minute—in what corporate environment do you let users set the local administrator password? None that we've ever worked in. We think what they mean is the *technician* who is performing the

installation would be able to set the local admin password (when prompted). But in most environments this is a predetermined password that can be set in an unattended answer file so there would be no need to prompt for the admin password during deployment. One reason you might use this setting is if you have branch offices with a local IT staff that requires different admin passwords on their workstations. Barring that, leave it unchecked. When you've finished with this page, click Next.

FIGURE 9.6
The Allow Image Capture page

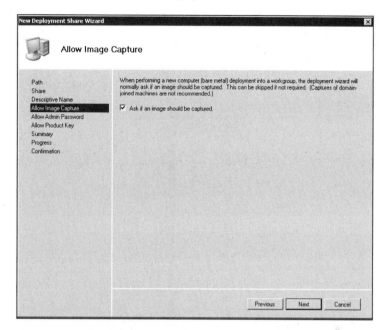

FIGURE 9.7
The Allow Admin Password page

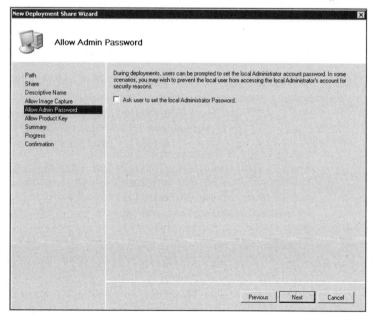

8. The Allow Product Key page shown in Figure 9.8 allows you to prompt during installation for a product key. If you're an Enterprise customer, there's no need to worry about product keys; only non-Enterprise clients need to enter a product key. (There are a couple of ways to "bake" your product key into the deployment process, so no one needs to enter this key repeatedly. We'll cover baking your product key into your image in Chapter 11.) Choose the option that is correct for you, and then click Next to go to the Summary page.

FIGURE 9.8
The Allow Product
Key page

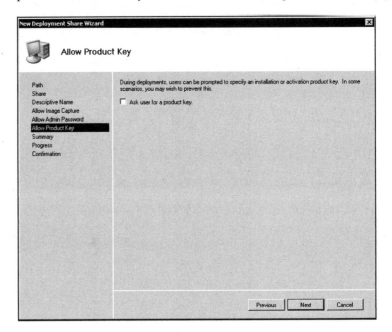

9. The Summary page shown in Figure 9.9 displays the choices you have made in the New Deployment Share Wizard. If you would like to make changes, click the Previous button until you are on the page you'd like to change. Click Next on this page to kick off the creation of the deployment share, which is displayed on the Progress page (this is pretty quick). Then the Confirmation page appears, as shown in Figure 9.10.

10. There are three buttons on the Confirmation page, two of which are new with MDT 2010. The View Script button reveals the PowerShell commands that were run to create the deployment share. The PowerShell commands to create a deployment share look like this:

```
Add-PSSnapIn Microsoft.BDD.PSSnapIn
new-PSDrive -Name "DS001" -PSProvider "MDTProvider" -Root
"F:\MDTLab" -Description "MDT Lab share"
-NetworkPath "\\DeploySrv\MDTLab$" -Verbose
 | add-MDTPersistentDrive -Verbose
```

When building your own scripts, you can copy from this page (on any MDT wizard) and paste into a Notepad text file to combine commands.

FIGURE 9.9
The Summary page

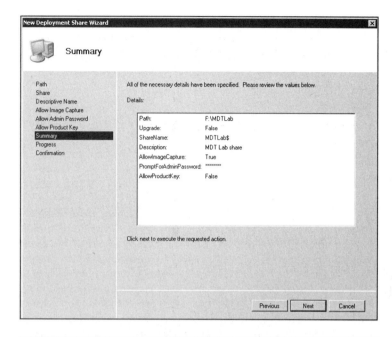

FIGURE 9.10
The Confirmation
page

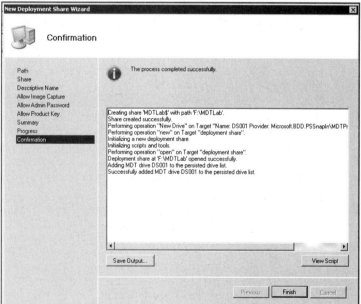

The Save Output button will dump everything you see on the Confirmation page into a text file. Click the Finish button to complete the New Deployment Share Wizard.

> **CONSISTENCY BETWEEN WIZARDS**
>
> Microsoft did an awesome job keeping the wizards of MDT consistent. The Summary, Progress, and Confirmation pages all work the same on each wizard.

Populating the Deployment Share

After you have created a deployment share, it will appear in the Deployment Workbench, as shown in Figure 9.11. Under your deployment share you'll see six nodes: Applications, Operating Systems, Out-of-Box Drivers, Packages, Task Sequences, and Advanced Configuration. In this section we'll discuss each of these nodes (except Advanced Configuration—we'll save that for Chapter 11).

Upon creation of the deployment share, a new folder is created and shared. You can see this in Windows Explorer. Figure 9.12 shows the folder and its subfolders. Most of these folders will be empty until you import operating systems, applications, drivers, and packages (patches) and create task sequences. We'll peek into those folders momentarily.

A deployment share is like a repository of components; you fill it with parts that you need during deployment or when you need to create a reference image. You'll need to import each component into the Deployment Workbench so that they can be used. First let's look at the components you can add to the repository; they include operating systems you'd like to deploy, applications, drivers, and packages (patches and language packs). For example, you could import Windows 7, Windows XP SP3, and Windows Server 2008 into the Operating Systems node. Then you could import Microsoft Office 2010, Adobe Reader, QuickBooks Pro, and a slew of other applications into the Applications node. Finally, you could import the drivers and patches for all operating systems (except for XP and Windows Server 2003, including R2—they do not support imported patches or language packs in the Packages node).

FIGURE 9.11

New deployment share

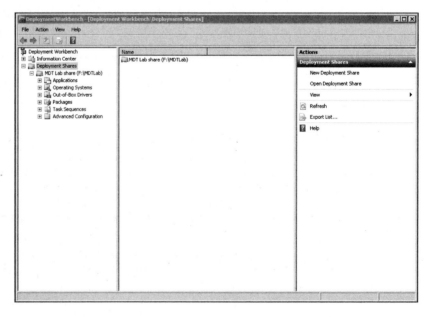

FIGURE 9.12
Deployment
share folders

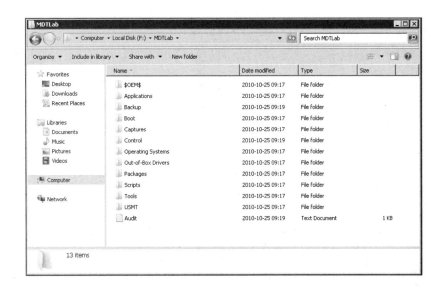

Now comes the fun part—you can bind these different components together. That is where task sequences come into play. A task sequence controls exactly what happens during the deployment and the order in which it occurs (for now we'll cover only "standard" task sequences—other types of task sequences are covered in the later section, "Creating a Task Sequence"). A standard task sequence will contain at least one OS and possibly applications, drivers, and patches. You could create a task sequence to deploy Windows 7, Office 2010, Adobe Reader, and all drivers and patches related to Windows 7. Or a task sequence could deploy Windows 7, Office 2007, and QuickBooks along with all the drivers and patches related to Windows 7. The point is, for a standard task sequence you only need one operating system (from the ones you have imported into MDT), any applications you choose, and drivers and patches for a fully functional deployment process. And here is the cool part: you can create as many task sequences as you choose, using the same components but in different groupings. To import the components, we'll begin with an operating system; then we'll cover applications, drivers, and patches. If you're looking at the Deployment Workbench and are curious about the Advanced Configuration node, rest assured it is covered in Chapter 11. Let's get started.

IMPORTING OPERATING SYSTEMS

Importing operating systems into MDT is a wizard-driven process. The supported OSs that can be imported are Windows XP SP3 and later (for a complete listing of the supported OSs, refer back to the section "Supported Operating Systems" earlier in this chapter). You can import three types of images: a full set of source files, a custom image (WIM files you have created), and Windows Deployment Service (WDS) images. The first operating system we are going to import is a full set of source files. To import your first OS, follow these steps:

1. Right-click the Operating Systems node and choose New Folder; name the folder
   Windows 7 (that way, it will be more organized if you start adding other OSs later on).

2. Open the Operating Systems node and right-click the `Windows 7` folder and choose Import Operating System.

3. The OS Type page (Figure 9.13) shows the three types of images you can import. Accept the default selection, Full Set Of Source Files, and click Next.

FIGURE 9.13
The OS Type page

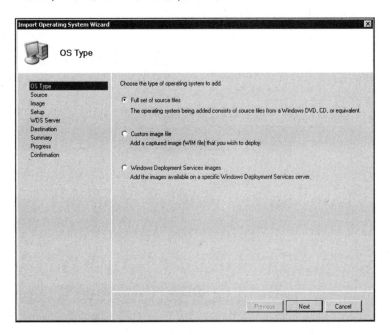

4. On the Source page (Figure 9.14), click the Browse button to navigate to your full set of source files, which can be from either the root of a Windows 7 DVD or a folder where you have copied the entire Windows 7 DVD (the D: drive in Figure 9.14). Once you have browsed to your full set of source files, click Next.

5. The Destination page shown in Figure 9.15 prompts you for the name of the folder to be created in the `F:\MDTLab\Operating Systems` folder. This folder will not appear in the Deployment Workbench; to view the newly created folder you'll need to use Windows Explorer and browse to your deployment share's `Operating Systems` folder (ours was on the F: drive). Accept the default name of "Windows 7 x86" or enter any you prefer, and then click Next.

6. The Summary page displays the details of the Import Operating System Wizard just as it did in the New Deployment Share Wizard. To make any changes, click the Previous button to reach the page you'd like to change, then click Next.

7. The Progress page is displayed, and when the process finishes the Confirmation page appears. Once again you have the View Script button (showing the PowerShell commands run to import an OS), and the Save Output button that will dump the contents of the Confirmation page to a text file. Importing image files can take a while, depending on the size of the image and the speed of your server. Click Finish on the Confirmation page and you're back in the Deployment Workbench with the Operating Systems node highlighted. The new OS is displayed in the details pane, as shown in Figure 9.16.

FIGURE 9.14

The Source page

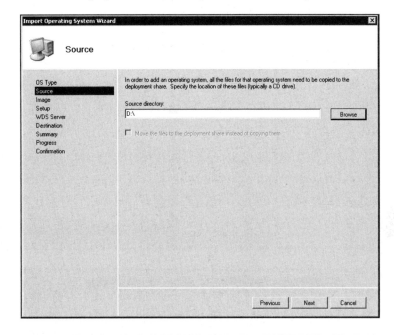

FIGURE 9.15

The Destination page

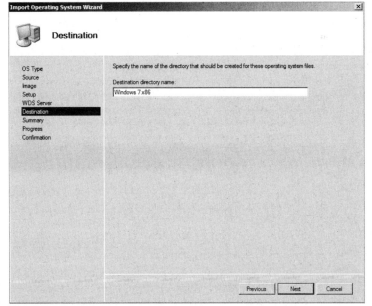

FIGURE 9.16
The workbench
with imported OSs

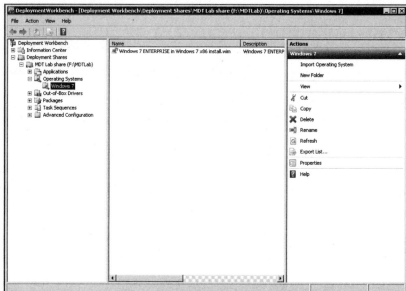

ORGANIZING YOUR DEPLOYMENT WORKBENCH

With MDT 2010, you can create folder structures to help organize everything in your Deployment Workbench. You can also use it to move around objects, using drag and drop, but we prefer copy and paste. When you copy and paste or drag and drop it does not affect the underlying file system behind the scenes; the folder structure you see in the deployment workbench is logical, not physical. The purpose of this is to make it possible to organize a large number of files and folders without consuming as much space as it would if the structure were physical. It also gives us the opportunity to work with the content as an object from a programmatic point of view.

Additionally, if you have multiple deployment shares, you can use the Deployment Workbench to connect to all of them at the same time and move objects between them. That ability is really nice. Just remember to use F5 to update the screen whenever you start moving things around.

IMPORTING APPLICATIONS

Applications are the next component we'll cover. The folder structure you create for your applications could be department based. Computers in the Research department may need different software installed than a computer going to the Marketing department. Within a department you may want to group applications by job title. Or you can create the folder structure based on the manufacturer; it all depends on how you would like to manage it. An application could also be located in different folders, since it's just going to be a copy of the object, not the application itself. Figure 9.17 shows a sample folder structure in the Distribution Workbench for your applications. Create folders in the Deployment Workbench's Applications node the same way you created folders in the Operating Systems node (right-click the Applications node and choose New Folder, give it a name, click Next twice, and click Finish on the Confirmation page).

FIGURE 9.17
Sample Applications folder structure

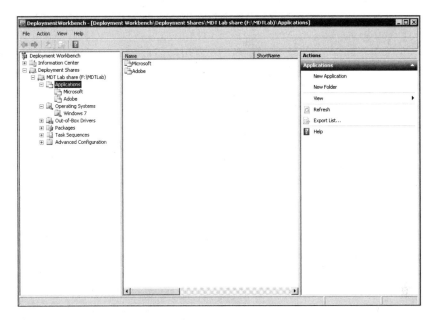

To import an application, follow these steps:

1. Right-click the node where you would like to put it (remember, cut and paste works so moving things around later is a piece of cake) and choose New Application to launch the New Application Wizard.

2. On the Application Type page, select the application type.

   There are three types of applications that can be imported, as shown in Figure 9.18: Application With Source Files, Application Without Source Files Or Elsewhere On The Network, and Application Bundle. The second option allows you to specify a command to run on the target machine or input a universal naming convention path where the application resides (*Server name**Shared folder name*). Use the third option when you want a list of applications to be installed in a specific order. The list acts as a set of dependencies for which application must be installed first, second, third, and so on. For the purposes of this exercise, choose the first option, Application With Source Files, and click Next.

3. On the Details page, you can supply information about the application, including the publisher, application name (this is the name that appears in the Deployment Workbench so you can name it whatever you like), version, and language of the application, as shown in Figure 9.19. It is important that you try to be consistent here. The name in the workbench is going to be built by a combination of Publisher, Application Name, and Version. Type in **Microsoft** as the Publisher, **Microsoft Office Pro Plus** as the Application name, and **2010** as the version, and then click Next.

4. On the Source page (Figure 9.20), you have to tell the New Application Wizard where the source files for the application are stored. Browse to the folder that contains your application's source files and then click Next. In our case it's the D: drive.

FIGURE 9.18
The Application
Type page

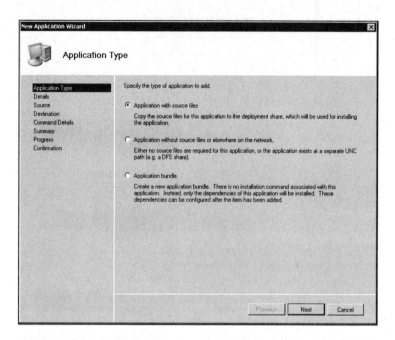

FIGURE 9.19
The Details page

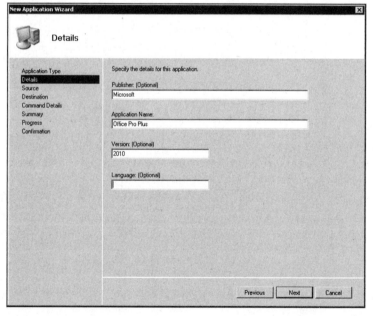

5. On the Destination page (Figure 9.21), you will see the suggested folder name (which has been built based on the name you used earlier in this wizard). Accept the name "Microsoft Office Pro Plus 2010" and click Next.

FIGURE 9.20
The Source page

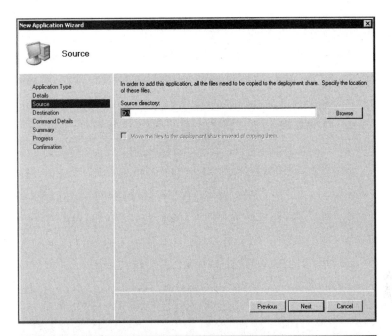

FIGURE 9.21
The Destination
page

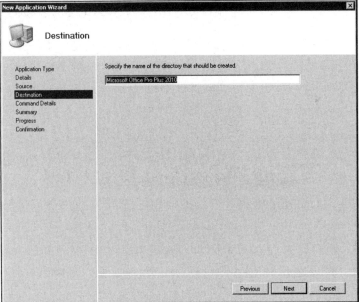

6. On the Command Details page (Figure 9.22), you will need to provide the silent command
   to install this application. The command line to run silent or quiet can be tricky (the command line is unique for each application), but if you can get the application to install on a
   test machine from the command line silently, that is the command you will use to install

the application. (Our suggestion is to search the Internet for the application with words like "silent" or "unattended" or even "quit"—or you can visit http://appdeploy.com.)

Since you're adding Microsoft Office Pro Plus 2010 in this example, the command to install it is setup plain and simple. Well, that's not completely true. Microsoft Office 2010 is recognized by MDT and therefore you can make this installation silent in two ways. One is to add /config and point to the config.xml file, and the other way is to run setup.exe admin to create an MSP file that you should then store in the Updates folder inside the application. Both these options are available once the application has been imported to the workbench. We will get back to that in just a moment. For now, just type setup.exe as the command line and click Next.

FIGURE 9.22
The Command Details page

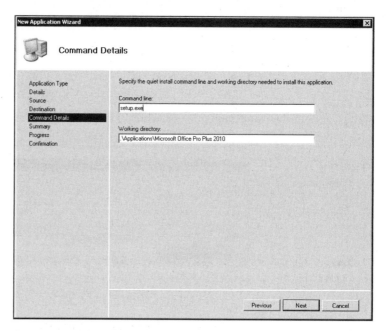

7. On the Summary page, you will see all the information that will be added for this application: if it is okay, just click Next. Otherwise go back and change the incorrect information. When you click the Next button, the Progress page appears and then the Confirmation page. Click Finish to complete the New Application Wizard. Your application will appear in the Deployment Workbench as shown in Figure 9.23.

Now, the application is imported into the Deployment Workbench, but since this is Microsoft Office 2010 and you did not enter a complete silent install command line, you need to open the application to make some adjustments before it is really silent.

8. Browse to the application called Microsoft Office Pro Plus 2010, right-click, and select Properties.

9. As you can see, there is a special tab called Office Products; click on that tab.

Now you have two options. The first option is to use the XML file. If that is your choice, use the drop-down list at the top where it says Let Office Setup Decide and select ProPlus.

Now you can specify which options you would like to use, as shown in Figure 9.24. The other option is to run the OCT (Office Customization Tool) to configure all kinds of settings inside Office. This method is what most people do, but it is a bit off the record for this chapter. To make this simple, use the first option if you just want Office 2010 to be installed in the simplest way possible. Don't forget to edit the command line on the Details tab to /config ProPlus.WW\config.xml, as shown in Figure 9.25.

FIGURE 9.23
Application imported into the Deployment Workbench

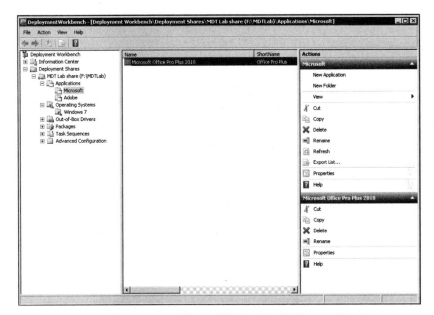

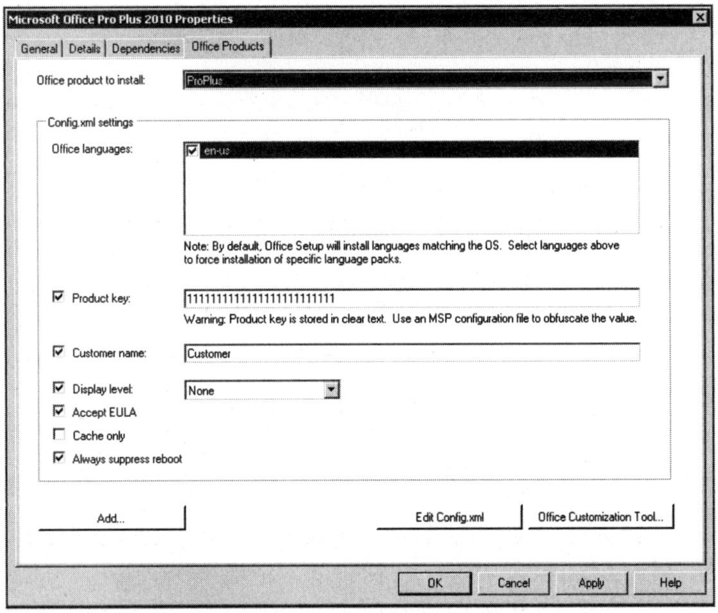

FIGURE 9.24
Office product settings

FIGURE 9.25
Office command-
line settings

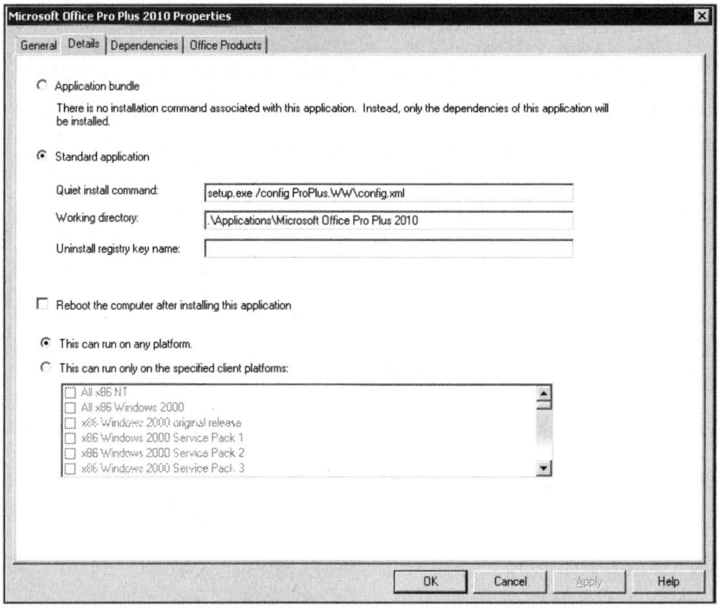

IMPORTING DRIVERS

Now it's time to add third-party (out-of-the-box) drivers. Take the following steps:

1. Create a folder structure on your hard drive.

   We created an F:\Drivers folder and copied the drivers and their accompanying files (INF, SYS, and catalog files) into that folder. (You might want to keep all the drivers stored and organized in the file system; sometimes you need to reimport them, or you might have deleted a driver in the workbench). In the workbench, you can create your folder structure to help organize drivers for specific types of machines. We like to organize based on model types, as shown in Figure 9.26.

DRIVERS IN LAB DEPLOYMENT

Drivers may not be needed when you create a reference image in a virtual machine, but they are needed when deployed in production. The reason behind this is that basically all virtualization uses generic emulated drivers and they are included in Windows 7 and WinPE from the beginning. Now, the same could be true for physical hardware—and it is at least for old computers—but you will most likely install Windows 7 on brand-new computers and you will need drivers to make them work correctly. Also, the only drivers you really need in a lab deployment share are the drivers that are needed to access the share (network) and access the hard drive (storage).

FIGURE 9.26
Drivers folder
structure in the
workbench

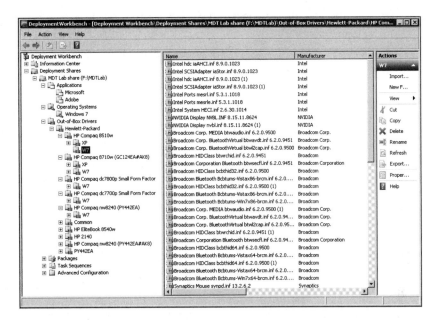

2. In the workbench, right-click the folder where you would like to import the drivers and then select Import Driver.

3. The Import Driver Wizard launches with the Specify Directory page, as shown in Figure 9.27. Browse to the folder where you copied your drivers (and their associated files). Clicking Next takes you to the Summary page (this should look familiar by now).

4. Click Next on the Summary page and the Progress page is displayed; you'll then see the Confirmation page.

5. Click Finish to complete the Import Driver Wizard.

The drivers will appear in the Deployment Workbench folder from which you launched the Import Driver Wizard. But cut and paste works the same here as it did in the Applications and Operating Systems nodes.

A common problem with drivers is that the INF file is not always correct. Sometimes a driver that is a 32-bit-only driver is marked as a 32- *and* 64-bit driver and that's not good. The problem is, that driver will be sent down to Windows and injected during deployment, but that machine will blue-screen in the worst case. In MDT 2010 Update 1, Microsoft has added some logic to be able to verify that the driver really is a 32- and 64- bit driver; and if it's not, the Deployment Workbench in MDT will flag the driver during import so that the correct override check box will be marked on the driver in the workbench. This little feature is one of the best, and it will save you hours of work. Figure 9.28 shows how the workbench handles drivers that are not correct.

FIGURE 9.27
The Specify Directory page

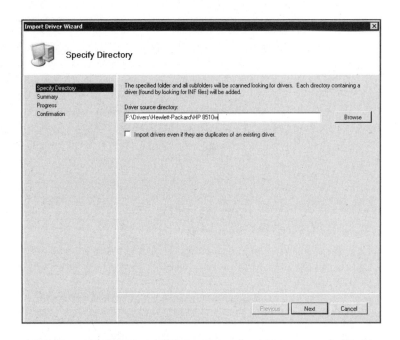

FIGURE 9.28
Incorrect INF files during import

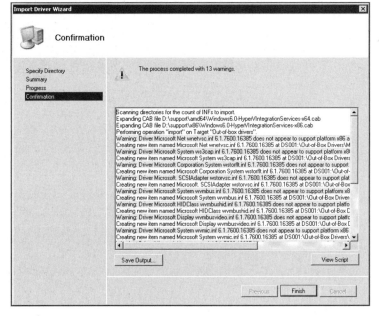

IMPORTING PACKAGES

Wow, importing packages—is it Christmas? The wording is a little misleading; what Windows really means is importing operating system *patches* and *language packs*. The Windows team refers to patches as packages, so the MDT team adopted the same terminology. First download and store your patches (or language packs) locally from Microsoft. Then take the following steps to import them:

1. In the Distribution Workbench, right-click the folder you would like to import your patches into and choose Import OS Packages. The Import Package Wizard launches with the Specify Directory page (this is identical to the Specify Directory page you saw when importing drivers).

2. Browse to the folder where you downloaded the patches (CAB or MSU files) and click Next. The Summary page is displayed. Click Next and the Progress page appears; you'll then see the Confirmation page.

3. Click Finish to complete the Import Package Wizard. The packages (patches) will appear in the Deployment Workbench, as shown in Figure 9.29.

FIGURE 9.29
Imported packages in the Deployment Workbench

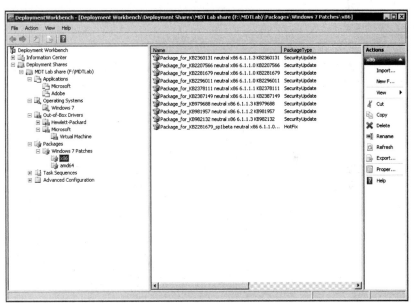

The Packages node is really useful, but it is not used for all kinds of patching. You use it when you create reference images, when the image has to be controlled, and so on. Packages are patches, updates, tools, and language packs. There are two ways to patch Windows when deploying using MDT. You can either download all the patches from http://catalog.update.microsoft.com and import them to the Packages node; that way, you will be in total control over all patches that are installed in the OS and WinPE. Or you can specify WSUSServer=http://WSUSServerName in the CustomSettings.ini file. The last option is what we prefer since that works well over time. You also need to enable the two Windows Update tasks in the task sequence you create: by default these are always disabled. There are two reasons to download patches and import them into packages. You either have a patch that applies to WinPE or you have a patch that is so critical you want that patch to be installed before the operating system starts for the first time.

Now that you've imported all the components you need at the moment to the workbench, it's time to put them to use. In the next section, you'll learn how to put the components together by creating a task sequence.

Creating a Task Sequence

Task sequences (TSs) drive the deployment process. The TS will determine which operating system is deployed along with which applications, drivers, and patches. The operating system, applications, drivers, and patches are each considered tasks within the deployment. The TS dictates not only what is deployed, but also the order in which the tasks are performed. To create a new TS from within the Distribution Workbench, take the following steps:

1. Right-click Task Sequences and choose New Task Sequence. The New Task Sequence Wizard launches and the General Settings page is displayed, as shown in Figure 9.30.

FIGURE 9.30
The General
Settings page

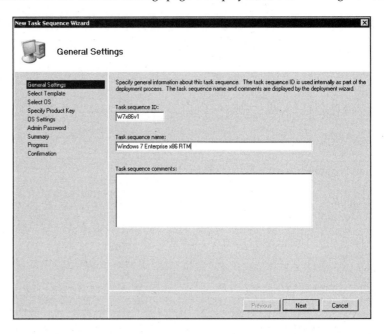

2. On the General Settings page, type a task sequence ID, name, and comments. Then click Next.

3. On the Select Template page (Figure 9.31) is a drop-down list of task sequence templates. Choose the best one for your situation. Table 9.2 gives a short description of each template and what it does. (We've chosen the Standard Client Task Sequence.)

FIGURE 9.31
The Select
Template page

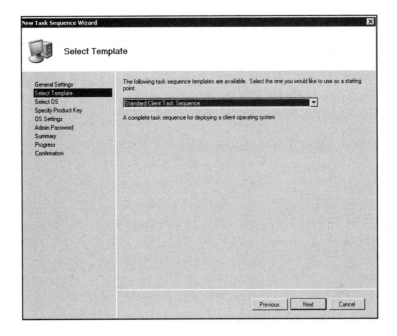

TABLE 9.2:   Default task sequence templates

TASK SEQUENCE TEMPLATE NAME	DESCRIPTION
Sysprep and Capture TS	Performs Sysprep on a reference machine, then reboots into WinPE and uses ImageX to capture an image of the machine.
Standard Client TS	Deploys a desktop operating system, applications, drivers, and packages to a target client.
Standard Client Replace TS	Backs up the target machine, and prompts you to save user settings and data (it can also perform an optional secure wipe of the machine if configured, which is covered in the next chapter). This TS does not deploy any image.
Custom Task Sequence TS	Does not deploy an operating system. Mostly used to deploy applications, roles, and features.
Litetouch OEM TS	Stages a setup to the disk so that it can be shipped to an OEM for cloning.
Standard Server TS	Deploys a server operating system, applications, drivers, and packages to a target server (including roles like DNS, AD, and DHCP).
Post OS Installation TS	Performs installation tasks after the operating system is deployed to a target machine.

4. Click Next to display the Select OS page (Figure 9.32). Expand the folders to find the OS you would like to deploy from this task sequence—we chose W7 Enterprise—and then click Next.

FIGURE 9.32
The Select OS page

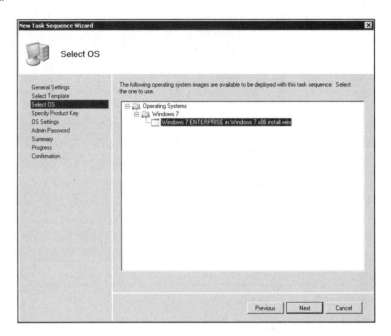

5. On the Specify Product Key page, choose one of the three selections (Figure 9.33): "Do not specify a product key at this time"; "Specify a multiple activation key (MAK key) for activating this operating system"; or "Specify the product key for this operating system." The first selection works if you are simply testing deployment methods or if you are an Enterprise customer whose product key is baked into your answer file. Also choose this option if you create a reference image. The second option allows you to type a MAK key for activating the target machines after deployment (MAK keys are covered in great detail in Chapter 13, "Taking Advantage of Volume Licensing"). The third option lets you type in a product key that will be used for all deployments that use this task sequence. Once you've made your selection, click Next.

6. On the OS Settings page (Figure 9.34), type your full name, organization, and Internet Explorer home page. Then click Next.

7. On the Admin Password page shown in Figure 9.35, you can specify a password for the local administrator account that will be created on the target machine after the installation of the OS. Either supply a password to be used or choose to *not* specify a password at this time and the password will be blank. If you would like the wizard to prompt you for a password during deployment time, you need to modify customsettings.ini, which causes MDT's client wizard to prompt the technician during deployment for the local admin password. If SkipAdminPassword=NO is set in CustomSettings.ini, the wizard will stop and ask for the local password.

FIGURE 9.33
The Specify Product Key page

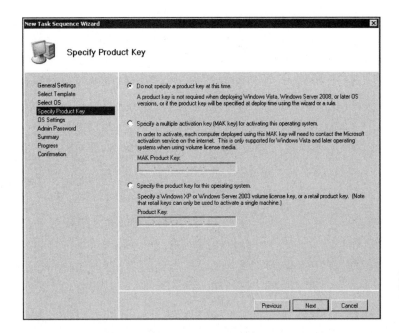

FIGURE 9.34
The OS Settings page

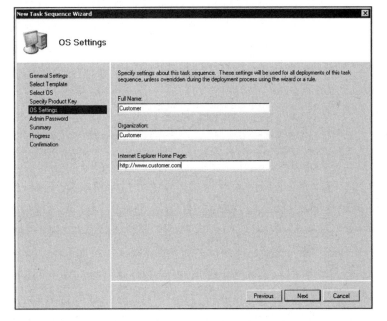

FIGURE 9.35
The Admin Pass-
word page

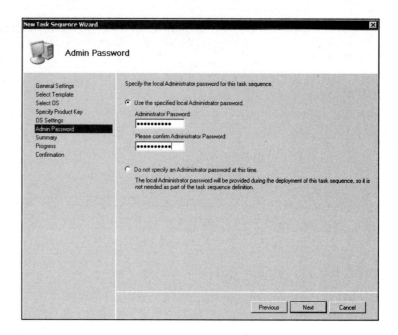

8. Click Next to display the Summary page. Review the details of the TS you are about to create, make changes if necessary, and click Next. The Progress page appears and then the Confirmation page. Click Finish to complete the New Task Sequence Wizard.

You're almost ready for deployment. You have imported all the components into the Deployment Workbench and put them together in the task sequence. Now it's time to update your deployment share. This is where the fun begins.

Updating the Deployment Share

Updating the deployment share is where the gears of MDT begin to turn. The process of updating the deployment share performs three important tasks:

1. The tools MDT uses for deploying images to target machines are copied from the WAIK.

2. WinPE image files (WIMs) are created containing custom MDT settings and scripts.

3. The WinPE image files are added to ISO files (we'll show you those files in a moment), which you can burn to CD or DVD.

Before you update the deployment share, you need to tweak it a bit. You'll modify the scratch space in WinPE to make it bigger. The reason behind this is that the scratch space is used when you inject drivers during deployment. The default size is 32 MB, and many of the larger graphics drivers do not fit into that space. To modify this, right-click on your deployment share and select Properties, and then click the Windows PE x86 Settings tab. Now modify the scratch space size to 128 MB, and repeat this on the Windows PE x64 tab (Figure 9.36).

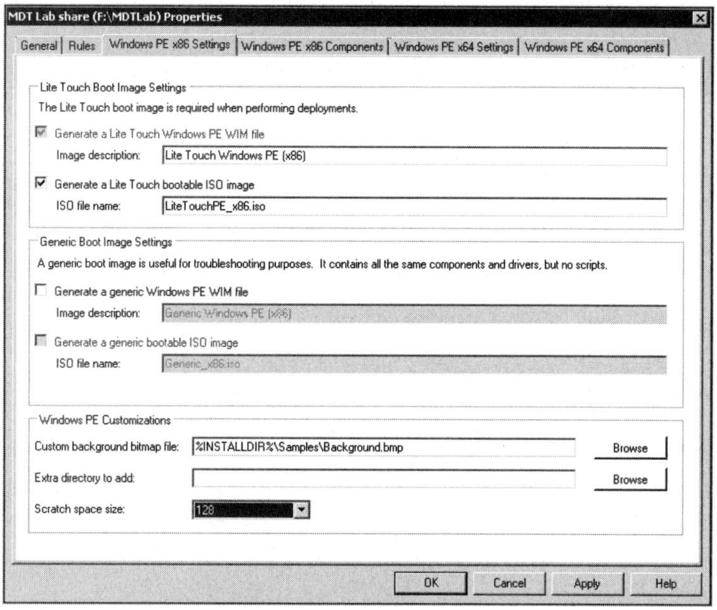

FIGURE 9.36
Modifying the
scratch space

To update the deployment share, take the following steps:

1. Right-click your deployment share name in the Deployment Workbench and choose Update Deployment Share.

2. The Update Deployment Share Wizard opens to the Options page, as shown in Figure 9.37. The default option, "Optimize the boot image updating process," is fine for the first time you update the deployment share. The "Compress the boot image contents to recover space used by removed or modified content" option can also be selected to reduce the size of your WinPE images (smaller WinPE means faster boot time). The downside of compressing WinPEs is that it will take longer to update the deployment share. Accept the default option, "Optimize the boot image updating process," and click Next on the Options page; the Summary page appears.

3. Review your selections and click Next.

4. The Progress page is displayed, showing you every step that is being performed. When that completes successfully, you'll see the Confirmation page; click Finish to close the Update Deployment Share Wizard.

Once you have updated the deployment share, you'll have two new WIM files and two new ISO files in your deployment share \boot folder (F:\MDTLab\Boot in this example, as shown in Figure 9.38). Notice the name of your WinPE is LiteTouchPE_x86.wim or LiteTouchPE_x64 .wim. The WIM files are then added to LiteTouchPE_x86.iso and LiteTouchPE_x64.iso. The LiteTouchPE_x86.xml and LiteTouchPE_x64.xml files are the instructions for MDT to build the WinPE WIM image files.

FIGURE 9.37
The Options page

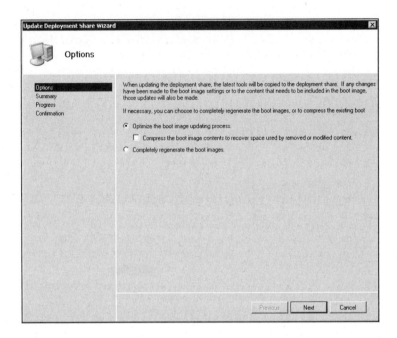

FIGURE 9.38
The Deployment
Share\Boot folder
contents

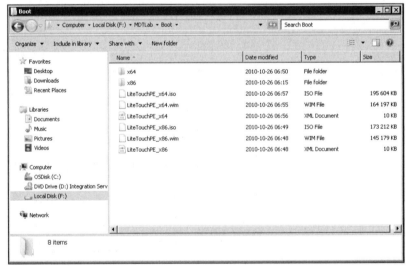

As time marches on and you import new OSs, applications, drivers, and packages or create new task sequences or make changes to your deployment share properties (covered in Chapter 10), you might need to update the deployment share again. You need to update the deployment share so that it will create new boot media only when either of the following conditions is true:

◆ You add drivers and they need to be in the boot image

◆ You modify bootstrap.ini or anything else that affects the boot image

The second and all subsequent updates can be optimized if you choose the "Optimize the boot image updating process" option as you did earlier. If the WinPE image files have not been modified, the MDT update process will not waste time re-creating something that hasn't changed (like the old MDT did). This will significantly speed up your update process. If you want the WinPE WIM and ISO files to be re-created (due to possible corruption or because they simply won't boot properly), you can choose the second option, "Completely regenerate the boot images," which takes a little longer to update the deployment share because it is regenerating the WinPE image files.

You're now ready to deploy your very first image to a target machine. Be sure the target machine has networking functionality and can connect to MDT server's deployment share.

Deploying Your First Image

Boot the target machine with the custom MDT WinPE (LiteTouch_x86.iso or LiteTouch_x86. wim) created by updating your deployment share. The MDT client wizard launches automatically and walks you through the deployment process. In this section we'll explore the default client wizard settings.

The MDT client wizard opens to the Welcome Windows Deployment page (Figure 9.39). There are three options to choose from: Run The Deployment Wizard To Install A New Operating System, Run The Windows Recovery Wizard, and Exit To Command Prompt. There is also a Configure With Static IP Address button. Before you make your selection, let's talk about how this target machine gets an IP address and related information (subnet mask, default gateway, and so forth).

FIGURE 9.39
The Welcome Windows Deployment page

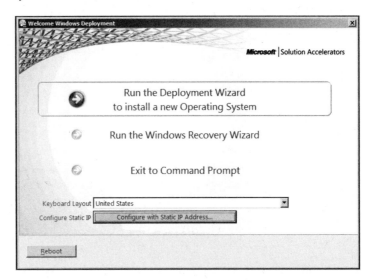

The target machine by default is a Dynamic Host Configuration Protocol (DHCP) client, which works fine if you have a DHCP server configured with a valid scope and proper network connectivity to this machine. If DHCP is not an option for you and you need to set a static IP address, subnet mask, default gateway, DNS server, DNS suffixes, or WINS server, click the

Configure With Static IP Address button. The Configure Static IP Network Settings dialog box is shown in Figure 9.40. Click Finish when you are done configuring your static IP information and you'll be back at the Welcome Windows Deployment screen (if you click the Configure With Static IP Address button again after configuring it once, all fields will be blank and you will have to reconfigure your static information again—so no peeking after you're done).

FIGURE 9.40
The Configure
Static IP Network
Settings page

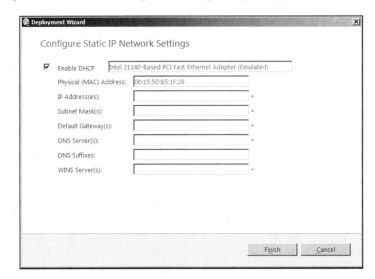

Now back to the three options. Running the Windows Recovery Wizard launches a custom WinPE that contains tools that search for all files needed to boot the target machine after an operating system has been deployed. If any files are missing or corrupted, the Windows Recovery Wizard will replace the files. The option Exit To Command Prompt will do exactly that—it will end the MDT client wizard and dump you to a command prompt. The Run The Deployment Wizard To Install A New Operating System option begins the deployment process (this is the one you should choose to deploy an image to a target machine). Take the following steps:

1. Enter user credentials to connect to MDT's deployment share in the Specify Credentials For Connecting To Network Shares screen shown in Figure 9.41 and click OK.

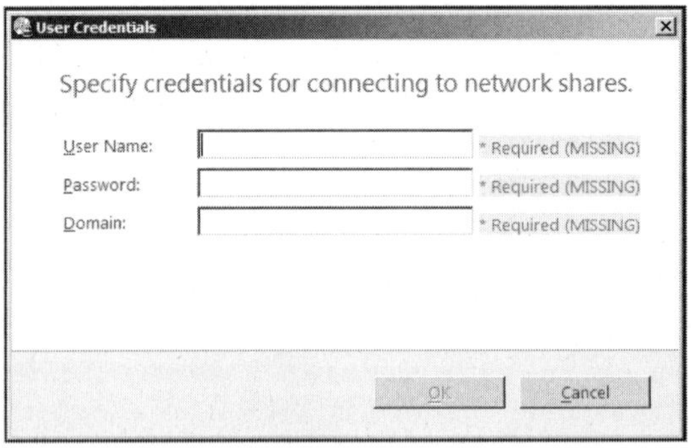

FIGURE 9.41
The User Creden-
tials page

2. Select your task sequence, as shown in Figure 9.42. If your task sequence does not appear, check which MDT WinPE you booted the target machine with. A 32-bit (x86) WinPE will only display 32-bit task sequences and a 64-bit (x64) WinPE will only show 64-bit task sequences. Select your task sequence and click Next.

FIGURE 9.42
Task sequence
selection

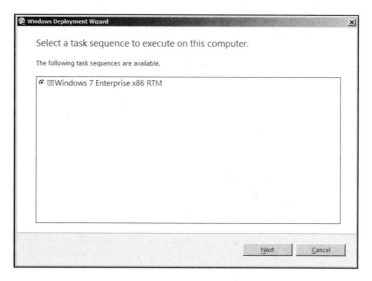

3. Accept the default computer name or enter one in the Configure The Computer Name screen shown in Figure 9.43. Then click Next. The Join The Computer To A Domain Or Workgroup screen lets you choose whether you would like the target machine to join a workgroup or domain environment, as shown in Figure 9.44. Accept the option you want (in this example, we've chosen the default setting of joining a workgroup) and click Next.

FIGURE 9.43
Configuring the
computer name

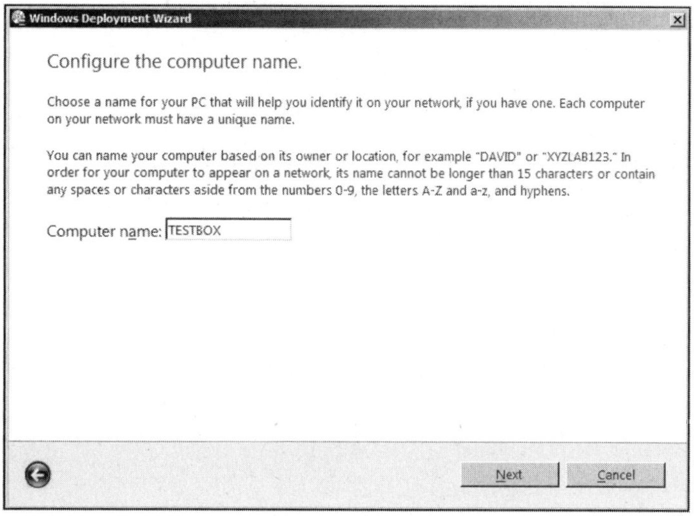

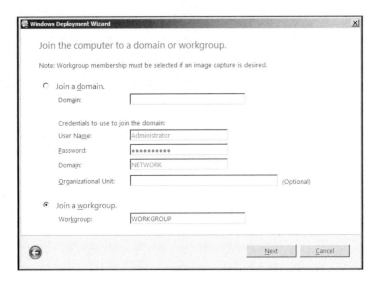

4. The Specify Whether To Restore User Data page (Figure 9.45) can be used when performing a refresh or replace scenario. This page allows you to restore the user's data and settings (IE favorites, My Documents, and Outlook settings, to name a few) from an existing machine that you previously gathered the user's data and settings from and stored on a server. To restore the user's data and settings, specify the UNC path (\\ServerName\ SharedFolderName) in which you stored it. When the deployment of Windows 7 is complete, the user's settings and data will be placed on the new Windows 7 machine. The user's data and settings are covered in great detail in chapter 5, "Migrating the Existing User Data." For purposes of this walkthrough, choose the default option, Do Not Restore User Data And Settings, because you are deploying to a new computer and you have no data to restore. Click Next to continue.

FIGURE 9.45
Specifying
whether to
restore user set-
tings and data

> **Windows Deployment Wizard**
>
> Specify whether to restore user data.
>
> ○ Do not restore user data and settings.
>   This is not a replacement computer, so there are no user data and settings to restore.
>
> ○ Specify a location.
>   Restore user data and settings from a network location created from a different machine.
>
>   Location:
>   [   ]
>   (Full network path to previously saved USMT data files).
>
>   Next   Cancel

5. Choose the language in which to perform the installation, the time and currency format, and the keyboard layout on the Language And Other Preferences page shown in Figure 9.46 and click Next.

FIGURE 9.46
Setting the language and other preferences

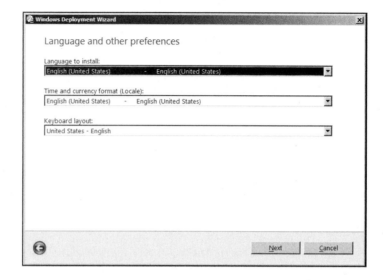

6. The time zones are displayed on the Set The Time Zone page shown in Figure 9.47; select your time zone and click Next.

7. Choose which applications you would like to install from the Select One Or More Applications To Install page (Figure 9.48). You have added only one application so far, which is why that's the only one you see. Put a check mark in the box next to Microsoft Office Pro Plus 2010 and then click Next.

FIGURE 9.47
Setting the time zone

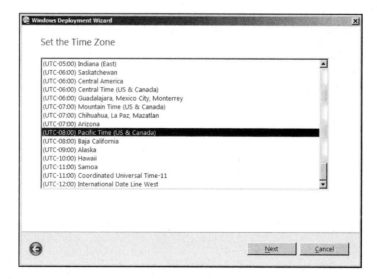

FIGURE 9.48
Selecting applications to deploy

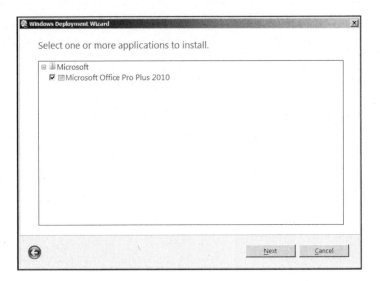

8. The first option on the Specify Whether To Capture An Image page (Figure 9.49) allows you to capture an image of this reference computer for creating a reference image of the installation once it's completed. This option will first install Windows with its application and then prepare the machine with Sysprep. When it's done, it will copy the WIM file back to the deployment server. The Prepare To Capture The Machine option copies the files needed to prepare the machine with Sysprep but does not actually run Sysprep or capture an image of the machine. The last option, Do Not Capture An Image Of This Computer," is used if you want to do a normal deployment. Select Do Not Capture An Image Of This Computer and click Next.

FIGURE 9.49
Specifying whether to capture an image

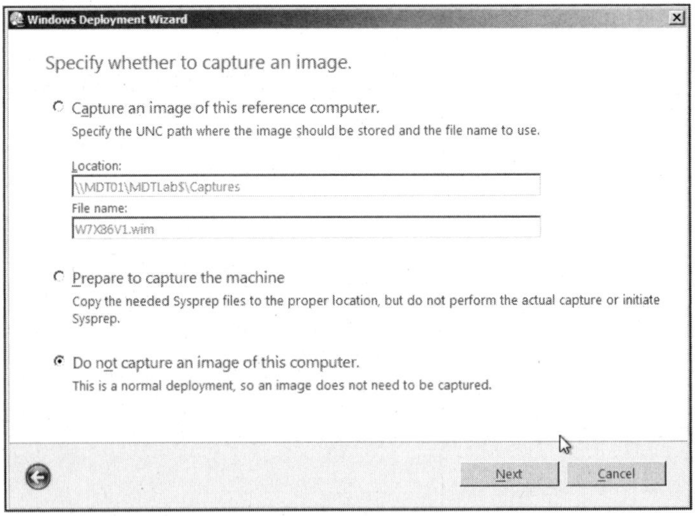

9. The Specify The BitLocker Configuration page (Figure 9.50) lets you choose whether or not you would like to enable BitLocker on the target machine. If you choose to enable BitLocker, you can also specify where to store the BitLocker encryption key. Choose the option you prefer (for this example, choose the default setting, Do Not Enable BitLocker For This Computer) and click Next.

FIGURE 9.50
Specifying the
BitLocker settings

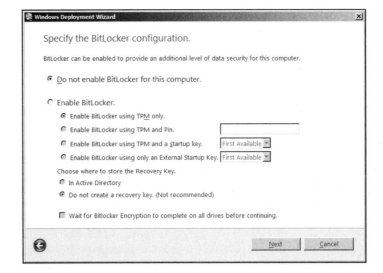

10. The Ready To Begin page shown in Figure 9.51 is the last page in the client wizard. Clicking Details will display your selections. After reviewing your settings, if you need to change any setting click the blue circle with the back arrow in the bottom-left corner. If everything looks good, click Begin and let it rip. The deployment begins and displays the Installation Progress bar that shows each stage of the installation, as shown in Figure 9.52.

FIGURE 9.51
Details of the
deployment

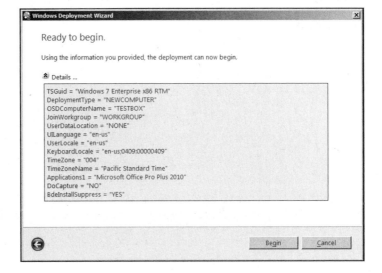

FIGURE 9.52
Progress bar

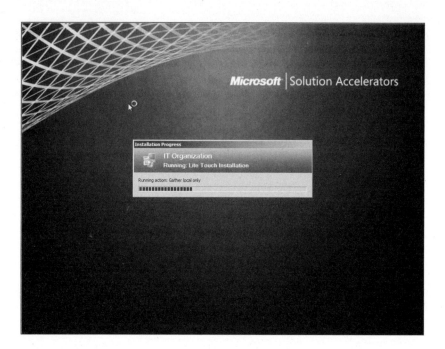

If the Installation Progress bar seems to freeze, you may need to move it and look underneath for error messages. When an error in the deployment occurs, the message is sometimes hidden under the Installation Progress bar. Next you'll see the Installing Windows page appear (behind the Installation Progress bar), as shown in Figure 9.53.

FIGURE 9.53
Installing
Windows

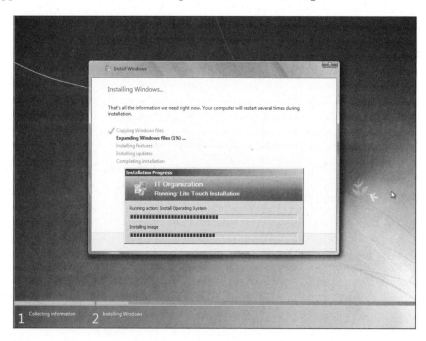

11. The target machine will reboot and prompt for a product key if you have not given it one up to this point (unless you are an Enterprise client who doesn't require a product key). Enter your product key and choose whether you would like to activate the OS (activation is covered in Chapter 13, "Taking Advantage of Volume Licensing") automatically when the target machine has completed the installation. Click Next to complete the installation.

You should now have a new Windows 7 machine, complete with Microsoft Office 2010, drivers, and patches. In the next chapter we'll dive a little deeper into the deployment share properties, various task sequences, and their properties and show you how to automate MDT's client wizard.

The Bottom Line

Set up a technician machine/deployment server (install MDT 2010 Update 1). The technician machine/deployment server is the computer on which you install MDT. If you install MDT on a desktop OS (Windows Vista SP1 or Windows 7), it is called a technician machine. If you install MDT on a Server OS (Windows Server 2003 R2, Windows Server 2008 or R2), it is referred to as a deployment server.

Master It You have chosen to create a deployment server; which operating system should you use? What is the required software that will need to be installed? Which architecture of WAIK and MDT should be installed?

    A. Server 2003 R2; .NET Framework 2.0, MSXML 6.0, WAIK, and MDT 32-bit

    B. Server 2008, WAIK, and MDT 64- bit

    C. Server 2008 R2, WAIK, and MDT 32-bit

    D. Server 2008 R2, WAIK, and MDT 64-bit

Create an image containing an operating system, drivers, packages (patches), and applications. MDT's greatest strength is in how easy it is to create an image that you can deploy to a bare-metal machine that will install an operating system, applications, drivers, and patches.

Master It Create an image in MDT that will deploy Windows 7, Office 2010, and all necessary drivers and is fully patched.

Deploy an image using MDT client wizard. MDT client wizard launches automatically when you boot using one of the custom WinPEs created by updating your deployment share. By default there will be two WinPEs created: `LiteTouchPE_x86` and `LiteTouchPE_x64`. MDT's client wizard walks you through the deployment process.

Master It Boot the `LiteTouchPE_x64` custom MDT WinPE that is generated for you. The MDT client wizard launches and you choose to install an OS, but when the Task Sequence page is displayed there are no task sequences to choose from. What is the problem?

Chapter 10

MDT's Client Wizard

In Chapter 9, we covered the basic MDT configuration. In this chapter, we will customize MDT a bit. The most important thing to remember is that MDT has the capability to do almost everything (except make coffee)—you just need to figure out how to use the rule set. In this chapter, we will go through most of the nodes in the Deployment Workbench, customize `CustomSettings.ini`, and similar tasks. Here you will learn how to make some of the pages in the wizard "silent": for example, if you deploy the operating system at the same location over and over again, there is no point of providing the same time zone information every time. We will also add rules and logic to the deployment to make it more automated. Now things are getting fun.

In this chapter, you will learn to:

◆ Customize your deployment share, applications, operating systems, drivers, and packages

◆ Create custom task sequences

◆ Automate the MDT Deployment Wizard to show only the pages you want displayed during deployment

Customizing the Deployment Share

A *deployment share* is a shared folder that target machines connect to during the deployment process. From the deployment share, files that are needed for the deployment process such as scripts are copied to the target machine. In Chapter 9, "Microsoft Deployment Toolkit 2010," we created a deployment share on a Windows 2008 R2 Server named DeploySrv, the deployment share name was MDT Lab, and it had a local path of `F:\MDTLab`. The shared folder name was `MDTLab$`, which is a hidden share name. The network path (UNC) was `\\DeploySrv\MDTLab$`. We'll refer to the local path, shared folder name, and UNC path throughout this chapter. There is a lot more to your deployment share than we covered in the last chapter, and we want to show you everything so you can decide which settings you want to customize.

We'll start by opening the properties of the deployment share. You can do that by right-clicking the deployment share and choosing Properties. You don't *need* to customize the installation; you could just go ahead and deploy, but every company is slightly different. Every user would have to spend 30–40 minutes the first time they fired up their new computer, but you could instead configure most settings according to your company standard, and save a lot of money.

The properties dialog box of a deployment share contains six tabs: General, Rules, Windows PE x86 Settings, Windows PE x86 Components, Windows PE x64 Settings, and Windows PE x64 Components. The General tab, shown in Figure 10.1, displays fields for the description, comments, network (UNC) path, and local path of the deployment share. The platforms supported by default are x86 (32-bit) and x64 (64-bit). This explains why when you updated the deployment share for the first time, a 32-bit and 64-bit custom WinPE containing the MDT scripts LiteTouchPE_x86.wim and LiteTouchPE_x64.wim were created in the F:\MDTLab\Boot folder. Along with the WIM files, ISO files were created named LiteTouchPE_x86.iso and LiteTouchPE_x64.iso (which you could easily burn to a CD that you could use to boot the target machine).

If you select x86 only as your supported platform by de-selecting the x64 check box on the properties page of the deployment share, then only the LiteTouchPE_x86.wim and LiteTouchPE_x86.iso will be created. And if you choose only x64 as a supported platform, the LiteTouchPE_x64.wim and LiteTouchPE_x64.iso alone are created.

Using the properties dialog box, you can customize WinPE by configuring the corresponding tabs. If you chose x86 as a supported platform, you use the tabs Windows PE x86 Settings and Windows PE x86 Components. The configuration parameters for the x64 WinPE are on the Windows PE x64 Settings and the Windows PE x64 Components tabs.

FIGURE 10.1

The General tab, deployment share properties

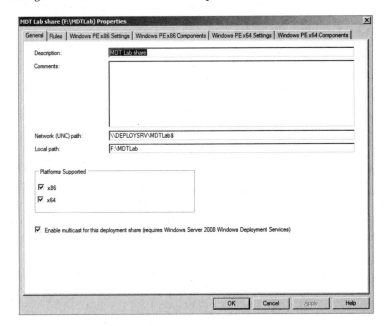

We'll get back to these tabs in just a second, but first let's look at the last setting on the General tab: "Enable multicast for this deployment share (requires Windows Server 2008 Windows Deployment Services)." By default this setting is deselected, and there is good reason for that. MDT doesn't know if you have a Windows Deployment Services (WDS) server. As you can see from the name of this setting, MDT requires a WDS server. Normally (with this setting deselected), MDT distributes images using unicast (using the SMB 2.0 protocol if using Windows Server 2008 or higher as the deployment server, otherwise SMB 1.0) packets on the network. For an image to be deployed to a target machine, the image files (usually between 2 GB and 5 GB in size) need to be sent to each computer. Now, if you deploy a small number of machines at the same time, things will most likely work nicely, but when the number of machines deployed at the same time increases, you will load up the network and your switches and routers will look like a Christmas tree.

There is one other big difference between unicast and multicast: When using multicast, the image is first copied down to the computer before being installed. The great thing about that is that if you have networking issues, this method will be more resilient. A multicast transfer will try to reconnect for a much longer period of time than a unicast session will. For example, with multicast you can unplug the cable during the multicast phase (do not try this in real deployment scenarios) and then plug it in again and the image will still be deployed; with unicast, you will most likely be forced to redeploy the machine. With multicast you will have a lower number of packets passing through switches and routers since it will be basically one stream of packets, and that will also lessen the burden on the deployment server. The problem is that MDT 2010 alone cannot provide multicasting—only WDS can. When you select "Enable multicast for this deployment share," you'll need to set up a WDS on the server that will host the deployment share. We covered installing and configuring a WDS server in Chapter 6, " Windows Deployment Services: The Basics." We recommend you use multicast, if possible. For now, you can leave it unchecked but when everything is working the way you want it to, please go back and check Enable Multicast and re-generate new boot images to start using multicast.

From that point forward, when you deploy an image from the MDT server the image will be handled by WDS, which can distribute it via the multicast protocol.

Before we move onto the Rules tab, let's go back to the supported platforms and look at your configuration options. The Windows PE x86 Settings and Components tabs have settings identical to those on the Windows PE x86 Settings and Components tabs. It's just that the x86 settings and components determine the settings for the x86 WinPE (`LiteTouchPE_x86.wim`) and the x64 settings and components determine the settings for the x64 WinPE (`LiteTouchPE_x64.wim`). For this reason we'll cover only the options from one set of these tabs, the Windows PE x86 Settings and Components tabs.

On the Windows PE x86 Settings tab, shown in Figure 10.2, in the Lite Touch Boot Image Settings pane, the Generate A Lite Touch Windows PE WIM File is selected and you can't deselect this option. It wouldn't make a lot of sense to choose to support x86 clients and then *not* create a `LiteTouchPE_x86.wim`, right? What you *can* change is the image description and whether or not the `LiteTouchPE_x86.iso` is created. If you are adding your `LiteTouchPE_x86.wim` file to a WDS server, there may be no need to create the `LiteTouchPE_x86.iso`, which would result in the update of the deployment share finishing more quickly. You can also edit the ISO filename if you have selected Generate A Lite Touch Bootable ISO Image.

In the Generic Boot Image Settings pane, you can choose to create a generic Windows PE WIM file and ISO image. Choosing the generic boot image creates a WinPE file named `Generic_x86.wim` or `Generic_x64.wim` along with the accompanying ISO files (you would find these in the `F:\MDTLab\Boot` folder) that do not contain the MDT scripts. The WIM and ISO files created from the Lite Touch Boot Image Settings create the WinPE image that contain the scripts needed for the MDT client wizard. If you mounted the `LiteTouchPE_x86.wim` file to a folder, you would find these scripts in the `<mountfolder>\Deploy\Scripts` folder (mounting WIM files was covered in Chapter 4, "Cloning the Panther: Automating Windows 7 Installation," in the "Creating Your First Image" section).

The Windows PE Customizations pane allows you to change the background bitmap that is displayed when you boot a WinPE image, add an extra directory to the WinPE image, and set your scratch space size. First let's change the default custom background bitmap file The default background is displayed in Figure 10.3.

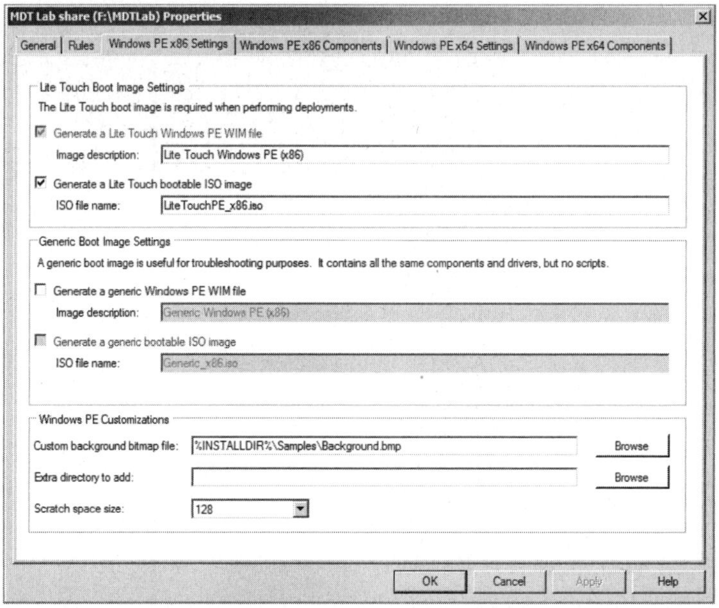

FIGURE 10.2
The Windows PE
x86 Settings tab,
deployment share
properties

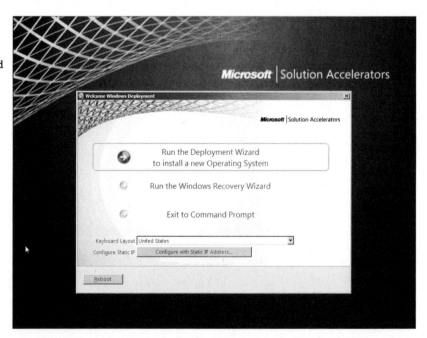

FIGURE 10.3
Default back-
ground for the
MDT client wizard

In the Custom Background Bitmap File box, browse to the bitmap file you would like for your new background. The new file will be copied into the new `LiteTouch_x86.wim` file in the `Windows\` `System32` folder when you select Update Deployment share (that is the process that will create the WinPE .wim files) and rename to `Winpe.bmp`. A new background is shown in Figure 10.4.

FIGURE 10.4
Custom
background

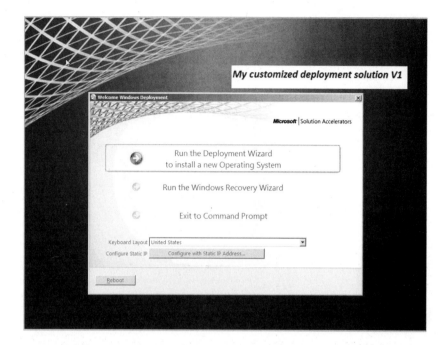

FIGURE 10.4
Custom
background

WHY CUSTOMIZE THE BACKGROUND

It might seem inefficient to spend time modifying the background image, but there are some real-world reasons. We have seen deployment issues regarding different boot images where the IT department updates new versions of the boot images when they put in new drivers for new models and/or change rules in boot strap.ini. Other technicians might not be aware of the fact that the boot images have been updated to reflect the new environment changes and they might still try to use the old boot images. That will almost certainly result in error messages and a blocking issue; for example, the installation will not continue. One way to avoid this issue is to update the image every time you create new boot images; that way it will be very easy to see what version they are using as boot images and if there is a problem during a deployment, you can eliminate a number of problems by just asking what version they are using to boot from and they would easily see that directly on the screen.

The Extra Directory To Add field allows you to add folders and files to `LiteTouchPE_xXX` `.wim`. At first glance you might think, "I'll just browse to a folder that contains tools I like to have handy in my `WIM` file and the folder will appear at the root of my `WIM` file (X:)." But that's not what happens. The folder itself does not get added; only the files within the folder are added to the root of the `WIM` file. Well, that's fine if you just have one tool to add but a bit messy if you have a few tools you'd like to keep handy in the `WIM` file. If you add a folder with a subfolder that contains the tools, then the second folder does get added to the `WIM` file. That is, if you browse to `C:\Tools` to add it as an extra folder, only the contents of the folder are added. But when you browse to `C:\Extra\Tools` (where the `Tools` folder contains the additional tools), the `Tools` folder is added to the root of the `WIM` file.

The Scratch Space Size box provides an area in RAM that acts as a temporary storage location for files. During the deployment process, tasks are performed that require hard disk space. There isn't any hard disk space until `DiskPart.exe` creates and formats a volume. Until there is hard disk space, the scratch space is used. MDT uses the scratch space for logging and configuration files. It also uses the scratch space to inject drivers when deploying Windows Vista and above. As you probably know, drivers tend to be a bit larger than 32 MB which is the default scratch space size. So on a production deployment share, you must change the scratch space to 128 MB to be able to inject some of the drivers.

The Windows PE x86 Components tab is shown in Figure 10.5. Here you'll find options related to driver injection, feature packs, and optional fonts to be included in `LiteTouch_x86.wim`.

FIGURE 10.5

The Windows PE x86 Components tab, deployment share properties

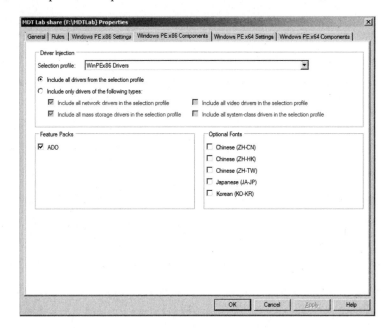

In the Driver Injection pane, you can choose a selection profile from the drop-down list. Selection profiles must be created before you can use them here (creating selection profiles is covered in Chapter 11, "Fine-Tuning MDT Deployments"). In WinPE you only need drivers to be able to access the deployment share, so follow these steps:

1. Create two folders under `Out-Of-Box Drivers` using the Deployment Workbench by browsing to the `Out-Of-Box Drivers` folder, right-click, and select New Folder. Call one of the new folders `WinPEx86` and the other `WinPEx64`.

2. Browse to Advanced Configuration\Selection Profiles and create two selection profiles, one called WinPEx86 Drivers (which only includes `Out-Of-Box Drivers\WinPEx86`) and the other called WinPEx64 Drivers (which only includes `Out-Of-Box Drivers\WinPEx64`).

3. Return to the Windows PEx86 Components tab and select the "WinPEx86 Drivers Selection" profile and then do the same for Windows PE x64 Components tab. This way, you will only include the drivers that are needed for booting WinPE. Doing so will make the WinPE image smaller, more stable, and faster to load. Otherwise, the image would include all network drivers and storage drivers you have in the `Out-Of-Box Driver` folder. It would also mean that regenerating the boot image would take a long time every time you added or removed a driver.

In the Feature Packs pane notice that ADO is selected by default. ADO stands for ActiveX Data Objects, which is a COM object that provides communications to data sources such as the MDT database (which we cover in Chapter 11).

The Optional Fonts options are pretty self-explanatory; the listed fonts can be added to `LiteTouchPE_xXX.wim` by simply putting a check mark in the accompanying box and regenerating `LiteTouchPE_xXX.wim`.

There is one more reason to select only the platform that you will be deploying to. If you are only going to be deploying, say, 32-bit images, you can speed things up by deselecting x64 as a supported platform. That way, when you update your deployment share only one set of WinPE WIM and ISO files is generated. Let's get back to the Rules tab now in the deployment share's properties dialog box.

The Rules tab, shown in Figure 10.6, displays a list of settings that determine the behavior of the MDT client wizard. The Rules tab displays the settings that are stored in the `CustomSettings.ini` file in `MDTLab/Control`. These settings are a combination of the `CustomSettings.ini` template found in `CustomSettings.ini` in `C:\Program Files\Microsoft Deployment Toolkit\Templates` and the answers you provided when running the New Deployment Share Wizard.

FIGURE 10.6

The Rules tab, deployment share properties

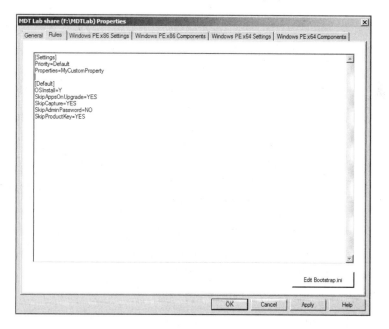

When you compare the `CustomSettings.ini` template with your deployment share's `CustomSettings.ini` displayed in the Rules tab, you can see that the template settings have been modified: `SkipCapture=YES` is now set to `NO` and the `SkipAdminPassword=NO` is set to YES. What do these settings mean and what can they be set to? The following list describes each setting and explains where the setting originated from and how it can change the behavior of the MDT client wizard:

[Settings], `Priority=Default`, and [Default]   The first section, [Settings], points to which section the MDT client wizard should begin reading during the deployment process. Under the [Settings] section, the `Priority=Default` setting points to the [Default] section heading, so this is where the MDT client wizard will begin reading the settings during the deployment process.

OSInstall=Y   This setting allows the target machine to receive an operating system. If this setting is not listed, then deployment of an OS is allowed to any target machines. If this setting is set to N, then no OS will be deployed. There are built-in task sequence (TS) templates that do not deploy OSs but that perform other functions like the Sysprep And Capture TS and the Post OS Installation TS.

SkipAppsOnUpgrade=YES   This setting is from the **CustomSettings.ini** template. During the deployment of an OS, the MDT client wizard presents the Select One Or More Applications To Install page, which lists applications you've added to the MDT Deployment Workbench. When technicians are performing the installation, they can select applications to be installed after the OS is installed successfully. Setting this to YES will prevent the page from being displayed. Setting it to NO presents this page during deployment. Please note that the `SkipAppsOnUpgrade` property applies to upgrades only and therefore is not commonly used. For normal deployments (bare-metal, refresh, or replace scenarios), the property for the Select One Or More Applications To Install page is `SkipApplications=YES/NO`.

SkipCapture=NO   If set to **YES**, this setting will tell the MDT client wizard to not ask if you would like to create a reference image (Sysprep & Capture). The reason you'd select Prepare is that for some reason you don't want the wizard to do the Sysprep step for you; instead you would like to perform that step manually.

SkipAdminPassword=YES   During the creation of the deployment share you saw the option Ask User To Set The local Administrator Password. You accepted the default setting to not ask the user to set the local administrator password, which resulted in `SkipAdminPassword=YES`. This setting causes the MDT client wizard to skip this page during the deployment process. If you would like this page to be displayed during deployment, set `SkipAdminPassword` to NO.

SkipProductKey=YES   Enterprise clients do not need to worry about entering a product key but all non-Enterprise clients will need to do so. Upon creation of the deployment share, you saw the option Ask User For A Product Key. You accepted the default to not ask the user to enter a product key, which resulted in `SkipProductKey=YES`. If you prefer this page to be displayed during deployment (so someone can type in a product key), `SkipProductKey=NO` will do just that.

At this point you may be thinking, "Okay, I understand where these settings came from and how they were modified when the deployment share was created, but what happens when you leave the settings as `SkipAdminPassword=YES` and `SkipProductKey=YES`? How does the local

Administrator account get a password? And where does the product key come from?" Well, you could supply them in the Rules tab; the entries would look like this:

```
[Settings]
Priority=Default

[Default]
OSInstall=Y
SkipAppsOnUpgrade=YES
SkipCapture=NO
SkipAdminPassword=YES
AdminPassword=P@ssw0rd
SkipProductKey=YES
OverrideProductKey=11111-22222-33333-44444-55555
```

Before we move on, we'll talk a bit about the password for the local Administrator account. If you leave SkipAdminPassword=YES and you do not supply a local administrator password in the properties of the deployment share Rules tab, then whatever password you supplied in the task sequence you created will be used. You'll learn more when we get to the properties of the task sequences. In the section "Automating the MDT Deployment Wizard" later in this chapter you'll learn how to automate the pages of the MDT client wizard even further.

Before we leave the Rules tab, let's look at the Edit Bootstrap.ini button in the bottom-right corner. Clicking this button displays the following:

```
[Settings]
Priority=Default

[Default]
DeployRoot=\\DeploySrv\MDTLab$
```

The settings from the Bootstrap.ini file were generated just like the CustomSettings.ini file. The template Bootstrap.ini found in the C:\Program Files\Microsoft Deployment Toolkit\Templates folder was copied to the deployment share and then modified when you created your deployment share to include the network path (UNC) of your deployment share. This file is read by the MDT client wizard to locate the root of the deployment share. When you click the Edit Bootstrap.ini button, you are actually looking at the contents of your Bootstrap.ini file in F:\MDTLab\Control.

That wraps up everything you can configure for LiteTouchPExXX.wim in the deployment share properties dialog box. Next you'll see the properties for the OS you added (Windows 7 Enterprise Edition) in Chapter 9.

Operating System Properties

To open the properties of the OS you added in Chapter 9, you'll need to expand the Deployment Share/Operating Systems/W7 node in the Deployment Workbench (in the last chapter we moved our OS into the W7 folder). Right-click Windows 7 Enterprise in Windows 7 x86 install.wim and choose Properties; the result is displayed in Figure 10.7.

FIGURE 10.7
Operating system
properties

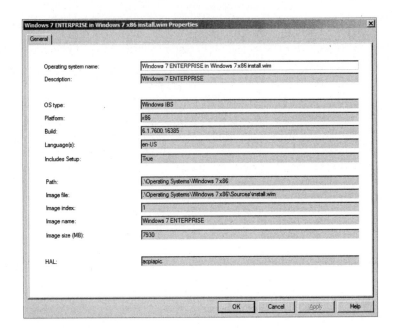

The properties of the operating system cannot be edited from here, so let's walk through the properties first and then you'll learn how you can edit them if needed:

Operating System Name   The name you gave the OS when you added it to the Deployment Workbench.

Description   The OS description you supplied.

OS Type   Shows Windows IBS (Image-Based Setup).

Platform   Displays either x86 or x64 (or ia64).

Build   Shows the complete build number.

Language(s)   Displays the language.

Includes Setup   Set to true or false, determines whether Setup.exe is included in this image.

Path   Displays the folder that was created within the deployment share to store the OS.

In Chapter 9 you imported your OS into the F:\MDTLab\Operating Systems\Windows 7 x86 folder). The . (dot) represents the root of the deployment share, or in this case, F:\MDTLab. So .\ Operating Systems\Windows 7 x86 really represents the F:\MDTLab\Operating Systems\ Windows 7 x86 folder.

Image File   Shows the image file or WIM you added (Install.wim, in this case).

Image Index   Displays the index number. A single WIM file could have multiple WIM files within it. Here you can see 1 as the index number and, since the Enterprise version of Windows 7 by default only contains one install image, it makes sense.

Image Name   Shows the name of the image inside the WIM file.

Image Size (MB)   Contains the size of the image file in megabytes.

HAL   Shows the hardware abstraction layer (HAL) or ACPI APIC (with this evolution of the OS, the HAL has become more generic and less of an issue with deployment).

As you know, the process of importing an OS takes some time to complete. So if you have added an OS and now want to make a change to one of these settings, you have to open the OperatingSystems.xml file in F:\MDTLab\Control. Or if you don't mind waiting, you could delete the OS and add it again, this time making your changes. Editing the XML file is not a lot of fun; Listing 10.1 shows its contents.

LISTING 10.1   OperatingSystems.xml

```
<?xml version="1.0" encoding="utf-8"?>
<oss>
  <os guid="{e97ff94c-1b21-4a66-86ec-0d708c73683e}" enable="True">
    <Name>Windows 7 Enterprise in Windows 7 x86 install.wim</Name>
    <CreatedTime>9/27/2009 11:03:58 PM</CreatedTime>
    <CreatedBy>DEPLOY\Administrator</CreatedBy>
    <LastModifiedTime>9/27/2009 11:03:58 PM</LastModifiedTime>
    <LastModifiedBy>DEPLOY\Administrator</LastModifiedBy>
    <Description>Windows 7 ENTERPRISE</Description>
    <Platform>x86</Platform>
    <Build>6.1.7600.16385</Build>
    <OSType>Windows IBS</OSType>
    <Source>.\Operating Systems\Windows 7 x86</Source>
    <IncludesSetup>True</IncludesSetup>
    <SMSImage>False</SMSImage>
    <ImageFile>.\Operating Systems\Windows 7 x86\Sources\install.wim</ImageFile>
    <ImageIndex>1</ImageIndex>
    <ImageName>Windows 7 ENTERPRISE</ImageName>
    <Flags>Enterprise</Flags>
    <HAL>acpiapic</HAL>
    <Size>7930</Size>
    <Language>en-US</Language>
  </os>
```

Microsoft has a wonderful *free* XML editor called XML Notepad, and it is slightly easier to use than Notepad, the built-in editor. Once you download and install XML Notepad, you can open any XML file by right-clicking the file and choosing Edit With XML Notepad. The same OperatingSystems.xml opened by XML Notepad is shown in Figure 10.8.

To change an attribute (such as the OS name, description, or image name), double-click the attribute and change it to whatever you like. For example, if you want to change Windows 7 Enterprise to read W7E, you highlight Name in the Tree View tab at the top left, then double-click on Windows 7 ENTERPRISE in windows 7 x86 install.wim, type **W7E**, and save your changes. The next time you open the Deployment Workbench you'll see W7E as the name; if you already have the Deployment Workbench open, refreshing the screen (by pressing F5) displays any changes you made in OperatingSystems.xml.

FIGURE 10.8
Editing Operating-Systems.xml via XML Notepad

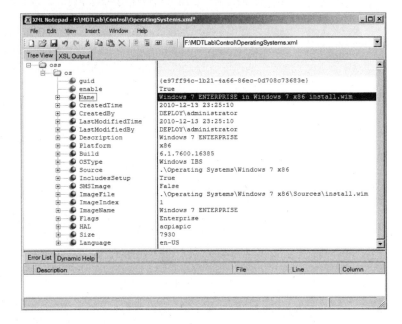

A note of caution here: We do not recommend changing the following attributes in this manner: OS Type, Platform, Build, Language(s), Includes Setup, Image Index, Image Size, or HAL. These are all attributes that were built into the **Install.wim** file and should not be changed. The Path and Image File attributes should be changed from within the Deployment Workbench or by moving (using copy and paste) Operating Systems from one folder to another.

Application Properties

Applications you add to the Deployment Workbench appear under the Deployment Workbench/Deployment Shares/*Name of your deployment share*/Applications node. There are two ways to view the properties of an application. You can right-click the application name and choose Properties, or you can double-click the application name. The properties dialog box of an application has three tabs: General, Details, and Dependencies. (If the application is a Microsoft Office 2007 or Office 2010 application, it will have a fourth tab called Office Products.) The General tab is shown in Figure 10.9.

The General tab displays the Name, Comments, Display Name, Short Name, Version, Publisher, Language, and Source Directory attributes. When you added the application by running the New Application Wizard, you were asked a series of questions. If you answered the questions or filled in the boxes, the information you supplied then is displayed on the General tab.

The Source Directory field specifies where the target machine should look for application files (like Setup.exe or Install.exe) to install after the OS deployment has completed successfully. `Applications\Microsoft Office Pro Plus 2010\` points the target machine to the root of the deployment share (`\\DeploySrv\MDTLab$\`). From the root it will then look in the `\Applications\Microsoft Office Pro Plus 2010` folder, so the complete path is `\\DeploySrv\MDTLab$\Applications\Microsoft Office Pro Plus 2010`.

FIGURE 10.9

General tab, application properties

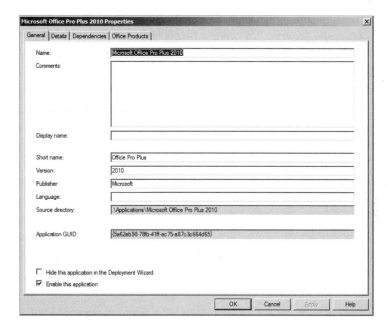

At the bottom of the General tab are two selections: Hide This Application In The Deployment Wizard and Enable This Application. The first option prevents the application from being listed on the Select One Or More Applications To Install page of the MDT Deployment Wizard. If you have applications that you do not want listed during the deployment process but you do want to install, add the application on the Rules tab of the deployment share properties (`CustomSettings .ini`). You'll see how to do this in the last section of this chapter, "Automating the MDT Deployment Wizard." The Enable This Application option is selected by default, but if you have an application that you're not ready to deploy, you can deselect this option. Applications that have been disabled or set to hide will not appear on the list of available applications to install during the deployment process. Changing these settings (enabling an application or choosing to no longer hide an application) does not require you to update your deployment share, so feel free to test these settings out. Just change the option of your choice and then launch `LiteTouchPE_xXX` again and your new setting will take effect.

The Details tab, shown in Figure 10.10, allows you to choose either an application bundle or a standard application. (We'll discuss the Application Bundle option last.) A standard application is one you would like to install, and you must complete the Quiet Install Command and Working Directory fields. The Quiet Install Command is the command that performs the installation in quiet or silent mode. A quiet or silent mode is also called unattended mode sometimes; it means that the installation of the application does not require any kind of user input. Working Directory is where the MDT Deployment Wizard will look for the application's source files.

The last setting for a standard application is Uninstall Registry Key Name. The key name identifies applications that are already installed on the target machine so that no attempt is made to install the application if it already exists on the machine. To find the value you need to enter in this field, check the Registry of a machine that currently has the application installed.

FIGURE 10.10

Details tab, application properties

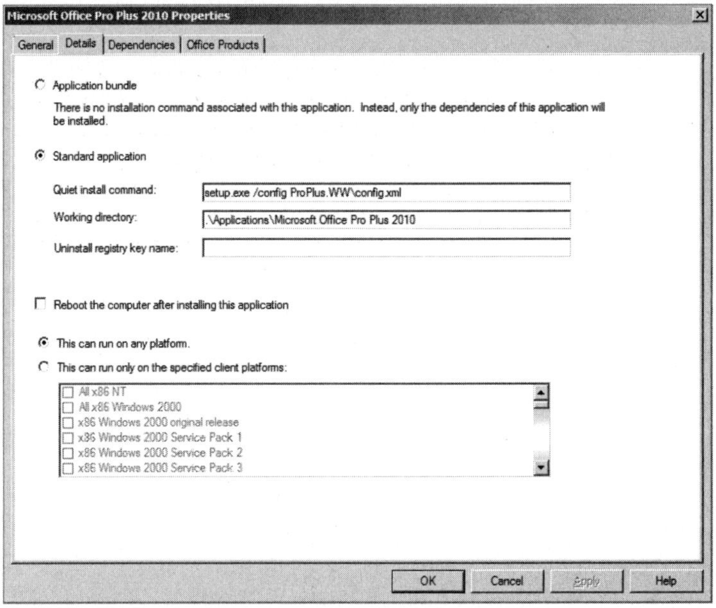

For example, let's say you want to find the uninstall key for Microsoft Office. On a machine that has Microsoft Office installed, open the Registry (click the Start button and type **Regedit** in the Search Programs And Files box and press Enter) and drill down to HKEY_LOCAL_MACHINE\ Software\Microsoft\Windows\CurrentVersion\Uninstall. Under the Uninstall key, you'll need to find the subkey that pertains specifically to Microsoft Office.

The first thing you'll probably notice is you're looking at a bunch of GUIDs. So to find the GUID that belongs to Microsoft Office, highlight each GUID until you find the one that has a display name of "Microsoft OfficeOffice 64-bit Components 2010" (the machine we tried this on is running Windows 7 64-bit). When you find the correct display name, copy the information by right-clicking the GUID and choosing Copy Key Name. This will put the key name, HKEY_LOCAL_MACHINE\SOFTWARE\Microsoft\Windows\CurrentVersion\Uninstall\ {90120000-002A-0000-1000-0000000FF1CE}, into your Clipboard. Now open Notepad and press Ctrl+V; then just copy and paste the GUID {90120000-002A-0000-1000-0000000FF1CE}, including the curly brackets, into the Uninstall Registry Key Name field.

This setting is not important in all installation scenarios. A bare-metal machine would not have any applications installed, so it would be a waste of time to configure this setting if you are only performing bare-metal installations. But if you are creating a task sequence using the Post OS Installation task sequence to install applications on machines that already have an OS, this setting may come in handy. You might have seven applications that always need to be installed on your users' desktop machines, and a quick fix for a missing application would be to run the MDT Deployment Wizard and choose the Post OS Installation task sequence. This task sequence should be configured with the appropriate uninstall keys for all seven applications. When the task sequence runs, only the applications that do not currently have an uninstall key in the Registry would be installed.

CONTROLLING APPLICATION REBOOTS

If an application needs to reboot the machine before it can continue or complete successfully, you'll want to put a check mark in the Reboot The Computer After Installing The Application box. *Never* allow an application to reboot during the MDT deployment process. You must allow the MDT to control when reboots occur or you will lose control of your installation and the MDT Deployment Wizard will have problems knowing where and how to continue. It will more or less be lost. When it gets lost, your deployment will fail.

The last two settings on the Details tab pertain to which operating systems this application should be installed on. You can choose This Can Run On Any Platform (the default). Or you can select This Can Run Only On The Specified Client Platforms. You must then select the platforms (down to the service pack level) that you would this application to be installed on.

Finally, the Application Bundle radio button at the top of the Details tab lets you set up dependencies for applications to be installed in a specific order. You configure that order on the Dependencies tab.

The Dependencies tab, shown in Figure 10.11, lists the other applications that need to be installed successfully before this application can be installed. Click Add and the Select An Item box appears, as shown in Figure 10.11. In the Select An Item box, expand the folders to browse to the application you want and click OK. The application will then be listed on the Dependencies tab.

FIGURE 10.11
Dependencies tab, application properties

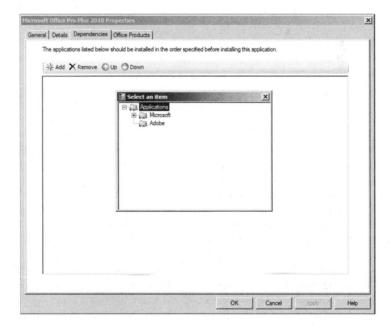

Driver Properties

In Chapter 9 we talked about importing drivers. You learned that you can just right-click the Out-of-Box Drivers node (or a folder you created within that node) and choose Import Drivers. You supply the folder and path to the drivers you want imported and that's it. Looking at the properties of a driver after they have been imported into the Deployment Workbench reveals two tabs: General and Details.

The General tab shows the driver name, comments, and platforms supported (x86 or x64). At the bottom of the page is the Enable This Driver option. By default, after you add a driver it is enabled, but if you choose to disable a driver, you must remove the check mark from the Enable This Driver box. On the General tab (see Figure 10.12), you can input comments to help you remember why you are installing the driver or anything else you would like to comment on.

FIGURE 10.12

The General tab, driver properties

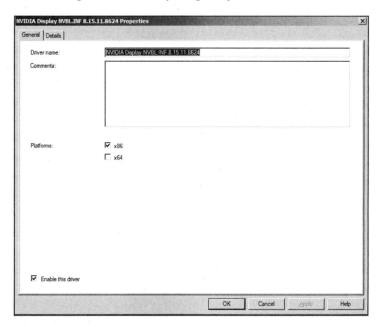

The Details tab, shown in Figure 10.13, displays the manufacturer, version, driver date (of creation), driver type (class), INF path (path to the information file supplied by the vendor), supported OS versions (if they are listed in the INF file for the driver), a hash to determine whether a driver has been tampered with, and the list of supported PNP IDs. The driver shown in Figure 10.13 has only two supported PNP IDs, but drivers can have more. Beginning at the top of the list of PNP IDs will be the most specific ID for that device; then they become more generic as you get to the bottom of the list. For example, the PNP ID of PCI\ VEN_8086&DEV_2A07F&CC_0700 will tell you this is an Intel driver (VEN_8086 is Intel).

The option at the bottom of the Details tab, This Driver Is WHQL Signed, is very important because it indicates whether the driver has a Windows Hardware Quality Lab signature.

Figure 10.13

The Details tab, driver properties

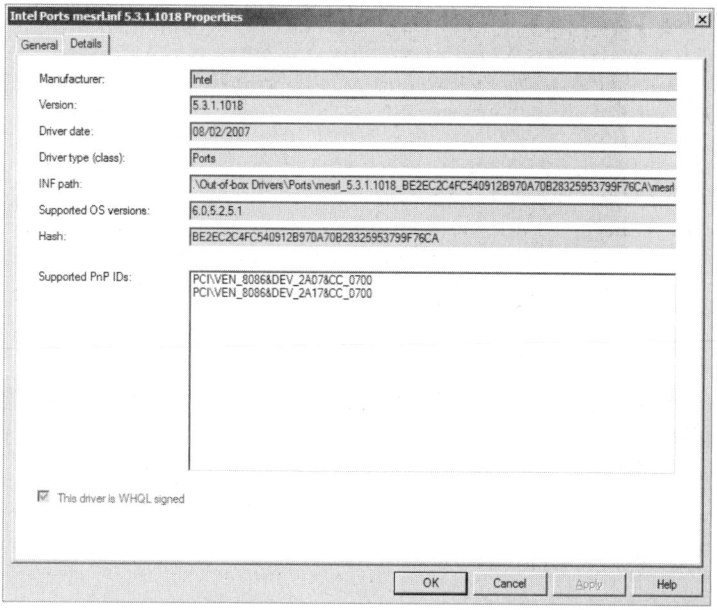

Package Properties

A package's properties dialog box has only one tab, General, as shown in Figure 10.14. This tab doesn't have a lot of settings that you can edit. Most of the information is retrieved from the package (or patch) itself:

Package Name   The name Microsoft gave the package

Comments   Allows you to add comments

Display Name   The name you will see in the Deployment Workbench; can be edited here

The next 10 fields of information are grayed out and cannot be edited:

Type   Shows the type of package; the one in the example is a SecurityUpdate package.

Processor Architecture   Displays the architecture the package is supported on; the example shows that the package is for a 32-bit OS.

Language   Shows the language of the package; Neutral represents English.

Keyword   Contains the searchable keyword (if you were to Google or Bing the KB article (Microsoft Knowledge Base Article).

Public Key Token   Pertains to the signature of the package.

Version, Product Name, and Product Version   These options are self-explanatory.

Package Path   Displays the physical path in which the MDT Deployment Workbench stored your package, along with the name of the package.

Package Guid   Displays the internal GUID used by MDT. You normally don't use this GUID for patches, but for language packs you could install a language pack using the GUID number with the property called LanguagePacks001={GUID Number} in, for example, CustomSettings.ini.

Two options appear at the bottom of the tab:

Hide The Package In The Deployment Wizard (Only Applicable For Language Packs)
Choose this option only when you are deploying language packs and you do not want to see a list of language packs to install during the MDT Deployment Wizard.

Enable (Approve) This Package   This option, when selected (the default), enables the package; deselecting this option disables the package.

FIGURE 10.14
Package properties

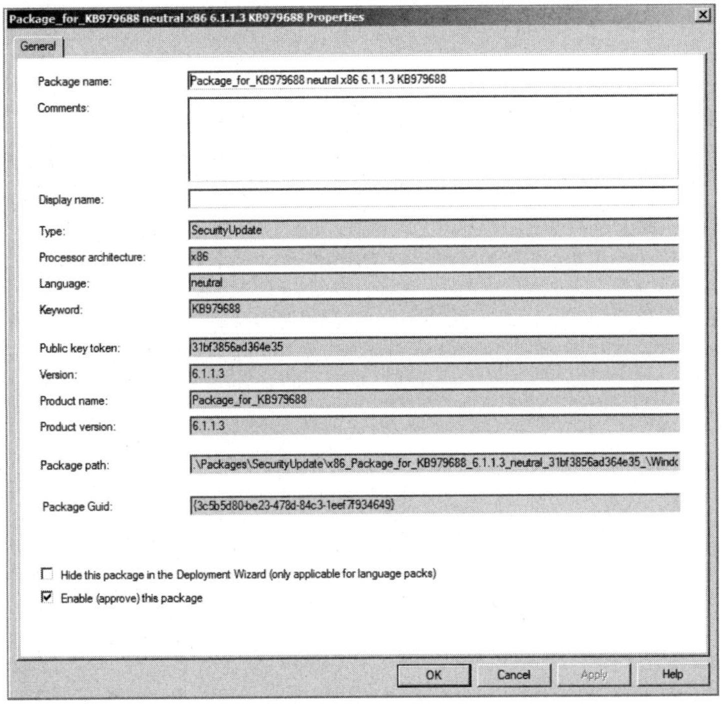

If you're having issues with packages being installed during the deployment, it is a good idea to disable all packages and then reenable them one at a time to determine which one is causing the issue. In most cases, you shouldn't use this method to add patches; it is much easier to let Windows do that for you at deployment time. If you would like to control which Windows Server Update Services (WSUS) server should be used, you can modify WSUSServer=http:// SERVERNAME in CustomSettings.ini. You also need to enable the two Windows update tasks in the task sequence, since they are disabled by default.

Task Sequence Properties

The task sequence might be considered the heart and soul of MDT. The properties dialog box has three tabs: General, Task Sequence, and OS Info. You will do most of your customization on the Task Sequence tab, but sometimes you'll want to edit the `unattended.xml` template directly (if you are deploying an operating system that is Windows Vista or newer). The most common reason is that there is a setting that does not exist as a property in MDT; in that case you must use the OS Info tab.

General Tab

The General tab is shown in Figure 10.15. Its components are as follows:

Task Sequence ID You supplied this ID when you created the task sequence. Notice you cannot edit the task sequence ID in the properties dialog box. Editing the `TaskSequences.xml` file in `F:\MDTLab\Control` allows you to make any changes you need. We recommend that if you are using a task sequence based on a template and you haven't customized the TS significantly, simply delete the TS and re-create it.

Task Sequence Name, Comments, and Task Sequence Version You can edit any of these settings in the properties dialog box.

FIGURE 10.15
The General tab, task sequence properties

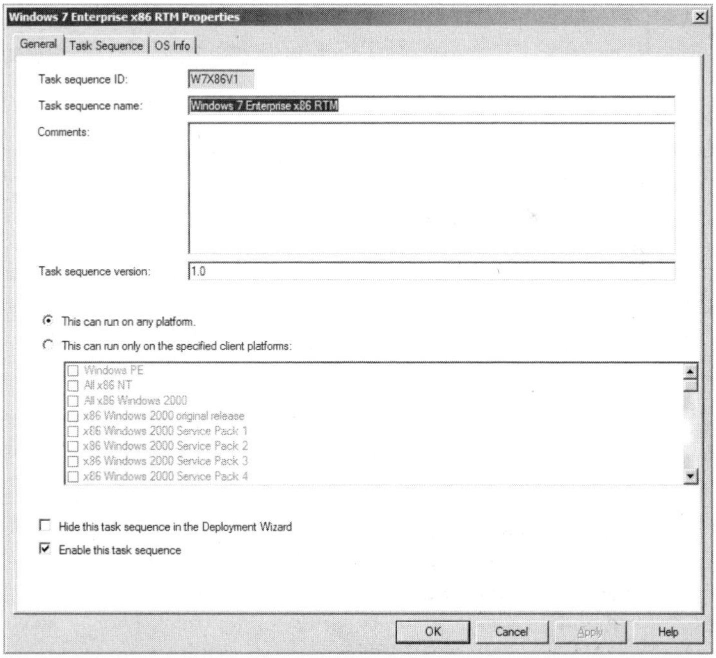

The next few options should look familiar to you by now:

This Can Run On Any Platform   This setting is selected by default, but if you would like to ensure this TS only runs on a specific platform, select the next option, This Can Run Only On The Specified Client Platforms, and choose all the platforms from the options available (notice you can choose as many as you like).

Hide This Task Sequence In The Deployment Wizard   Selecting this option means this task sequence will not be displayed in the MDT Deployment Wizard. To be able to use this TS, you must specify that you would like to use it in CustomSettings.ini or elsewhere.

Enable This Task Sequence   Task sequences by default are enabled; if you would like to disable this task sequence, remove the check mark from this box.

Task Sequence Tab

The Task Sequence tab, shown in Figure 10.16, shows all tasks that will be performed during a deployment and the order of the tasks. A lot of this information is created when you answer the questions in the New Task Sequence Wizard you launched by right-clicking the Task Sequence node and choosing New Task Sequence. The tasks displayed in the task sequence properties can be modified. You can also add a new task by clicking Add on the menu bar or delete an existing task by highlighting the task and clicking Remove. You can also rearrange the tasks by highlighting a task and clicking either the Up or Down icon on the menu bar.

FIGURE 10.16

The Task Sequence tab, task sequence properties

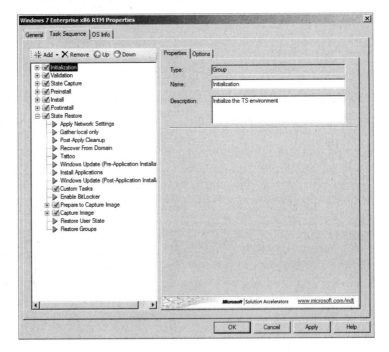

In this exercise, you'll create a new partition scheme. You want to have two partitions on your target machine: one for the operating system and one for storing data files. (There will be one more partition; MDT will create a 300 MB partition by default. That partition is used to host the boot files to make BitLocker work correctly.)

1. In the list of tasks, expand Preinstall, then New Computer Only, and highlight Format And Partition Disk, as shown in Figure 10.17. On the Properties tab, notice the Type and Name fields both contain Format And Partition Disk. You can add a Description if desired.

FIGURE 10.17
Format and partition disk attributes

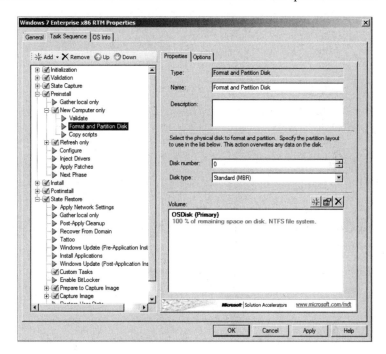

2. Select the physical disk you want to format and partition (disks are numbered beginning with 0 whereas partitions are numbered starting at 1).

   In this example the target machines all have only one hard drive, so Disk Number 0 should be fine. For Disk Type you choose either Standard (MBR) or GPT. What's the difference between the two? Standard MBR (master boot record) is the type of disk used since the DOS days; you can have a maximum of three primary partitions and one extended partition. GPT (GUID Partition Table) was introduced with Windows Server 2003 SP1. GPT, which is supported on Windows Vista and later OSs, allows for 128 basic volumes on a single disk and allows for basic volumes larger than 2 TB.

3. Click on the existing disk and modify the size to 72 GB.

4. Click the gold star button to create a new partition; give it the name **DataDisk**. For Partition Type choose Primary (Primary and Extended are the only two choices); for the size select Use A Percentage Of Remaining Free Disk and set it to 100% Format NTFS (FAT32 is the other option). Selecting Quick Format speeds things up. The setting selections used in this example are shown in Figure 10.18.

5. Click OK.

FIGURE 10.18
New partition properties

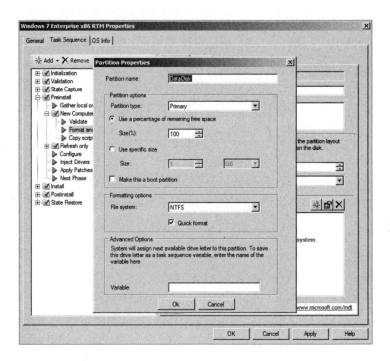

Choosing Disks from the Add drop-down allows you to add Format And Partition Disk and Enable BitLocker options. Images have only one option: Install Operating System. Settings have three: Apply Network Settings, Capture Network Settings, and Recover From Domain. Add Roles allows you to add server and client roles and features, as well as configure some of the server roles via the Configure DHCP, DNS, ADDS, and Authorize DHCP tasks. If you would like to add a role that is not listed, choose the Install Roles And Features option. You'll see a screen similar to the following graphic. Make sure you put the task in the correct phase; for example, it is not possible to install an application before the operating system has been installed.

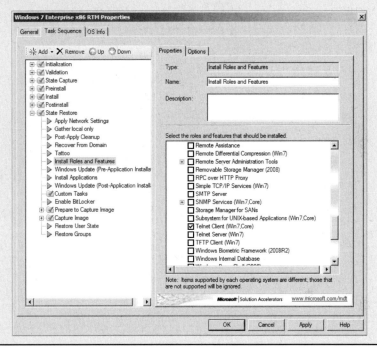

Task sequences show the phases that installation goes through when you're deploying an operating system. Which tasks are performed depends on the scenario (bare metal, refresh, replace). The phases of setup are Initialization, Validation, State Capture, Preinstall, Install, Postinstall, and State Restore. Beginning with the Validation phase, let's walk through each one and see what its purpose is and how you can tweak it should you so choose.

Initialization   Gathers local information. It will basically get all the information about the local system and the network environment—things like the MAC address, IP address, make, and model.

Validation   Validate is the first task shown in Figure 10.19 and allows you to configure the minimum hardware requirements for this task sequence. You can set the minimum amount of memory, processor speed, and amount of hard disk space (to ensure the image will fit on the target machine), and ensure that the current OS is client or server (choose from the drop-down list). Next, ZTIBIOSCheck.wsf runs to check if the BOS is incompatible; it will check if the BIOS is listed in ZTIBIOSCheck.xml. Finally, the next phase is set to State Capture.

FIGURE 10.19
Validation settings

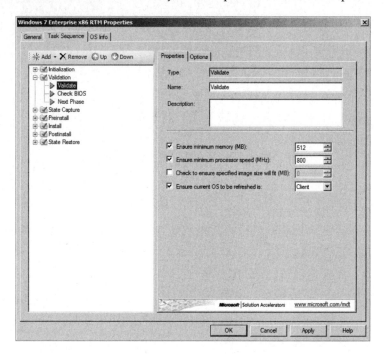

State Capture   This phase includes three subphases: Non-Upgrade And Refresh Only is listed twice. Under Non-Upgrade, the Generate Application Migration File task runs the ZTIAppXmlGen.wsf script, which runs the User State Migration Tool's (USMT) ScanState to create an XML file. This XML file contains user data (documents) that are associated with any currently installed applications. The Capture User State task runs the ZTIUserState.wsf script, which runs USMT's ScanState to capture the local user's settings and data. The Capture Groups task sequence runs ZTIGroups.wsf, which captures any local group memberships of the local user accounts. In the first Refresh Only task, the Disable BDE Protectors task runs ZTIDisableBDEProtectors.wsf, which will suspend BitLocker if it is currently enabled on the target machine. The Apply Windows PE task runs LTIApply.wsf, which applies the WinPE image to the local hard drive. And the only setting under the second Refresh Only subphase is Restart Computer, which reboots the target machine. Now the machine is booting WinPE from the local hard drive.

Preinstall   Here the first task, Gather Local, gathers only local hardware information. Then under the subphase New Computer, only the Validate task runs, checking to make sure the target machine meets the minimum hardware requirements (you can edit these options the same way you edited the Validate task earlier in the Validation phase). The Format And Partition Disk task allows you to set the partition instructions for creating and formatting partitions on the target machine. The Copy Scripts task runs LTICopyScripts.wsf, which copies scripts to the target machine. The scripts that are copied are listed here:

```
LiteTouch.wsf
ZTIUtility.vbs
ZTIGather.wsf
ZTIGather.xml
Wizard.hta
Credentials_ENU.xml
Credentials_scripts.vbs
WizUtility.vbs
Wizard.css
Wizard.ico
BackButton.jpg
plusicon.gif
minusico.gif
DeployWiz_Definition_ENU.xml
DeployWiz_Initialization.vbs
DeployWiz_Validation.vbs
Summary_Definition_ENU.xml
Summary_scripts.vbs
LTICleanup.wsf
LTIGetFolder.wsf
ZTINICConfig.wsf
ZTINICUtility.vbs
ZTIBCDUTILITY.VBS
ZTIDataAccess.vbs
LTISuspend.wsf
```

Next, the Configure task runs ZTIConfigure.wsf, which updates the information that has been gathered during the Gather task and then processed using the rules you have set up in Unattend.xml (unattend answer files were covered in Chapter 4, "Cloning the Panther: Automating Windows 7 Installation"). The Inject Drivers task installs drivers that you specify. You can create a selection profile that contains drivers and choose only that selection profile; within that selection profile you can choose "Install only matching drivers from the selection profile" or "Install all drivers from the selection profile." Selection profiles are covered in depth in Chapter 11. The Apply Patches task applies all packages that pertain to the OS you are deploying. Next Phase is set to Install.

Install   The Install phase is pretty simple; the task Install Operating System installs the OS you specified when you create the task sequence and allows you to choose the disk and partition you want to install the OS to. The Next Phase task sets the phase to Postinstall.

Postinstall   This phase's Copy Scripts task runs LTICopyScripts.wsf again and copies the scripts. The Configure task runs ZTIConfigure.wsf, which in turn runs ZTIConfigure.wsf, adding settings to Unattend.xml. The Postinstall Inject Drivers action is needed for legacy operating systems (to update Sysprep.inf and the device path value in the offline registry).

Since we are deploying Windows 7, it will do nothing. The Next Phase task sets the phase to State Restore, and the last task, Restart Computer, reboots the target machine.

State Restore This last phase contains two subphases: Prepare To Capture Image and Capture Image. Let's cover the tasks first and then we'll come back to the subphases.

Apply Network Settings This task allows you to configure your target machine's network configuration, as shown in Figure 10.20.

FIGURE 10.20
Apply Network Settings task

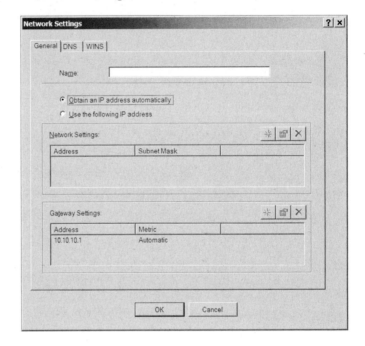

General Tab On the General tab of your Network Settings dialog box, you can choose to allow your target machines to get an IP address from a DHCP server by selecting Obtain An IP Address Automatically. Or you could specify an IP address (but you wouldn't really want to configure the same IP for more than one machine, right?) by choosing Use The Following IP Address. You can also add the IP address of your default gateway or a list of gateway IP addresses.

DNS Tab Here you can choose Obtain DNS Server Automatically (get it from DHCP) or specify an IP address (or a list of IP addresses) of a DNS server by choosing Use The Following DNS Servers. You can supply a DNS suffix, register the connection's address in DNS, and use the connection's DNS suffix in DNS registration.

WINS Tab This allows for an IP address of a WINS server (a list of WINS servers IP addresses is supported as well). You can also choose Enable LMHOSTS Lookup and enable or disable NetBIOS Over TCP/IP.

Gather Local Only This is the next task, which gathers local data again.

Post-Apply Cleanup   This task runs LTIApply.wsf, which cleans up after the installation of the OS completes successfully. The temporary account that is created for the installation is deleted. When deploying Windows Vista or higher, the C:\Drivers folder is deleted since all the drivers have now been injected into the OS.

Recover From Domain   This task will attempt to rejoin the target machine to a domain if this step failed during the deployment. There are three settings for the Recover From Domain task: Auto Recover (Rerun Join Domain) (this is the default); Manual Recover (Allow User To Join Domain), which if selected causes the task sequence to pause during the deployment process to allow the user to join the target machine to the domain; and No Recover (Stop Script Execution), which stops the whole show if the target machine is not successfully joined to a domain during the deployment process.

Tattoo   This task runs ZTITatoo.wsf, which tattoos the machine with identification and version information.

The Windows Update (Pre-Application Installation)   This task runs ZTIWindowsUpdate .wsf, which installs all drivers, updates, and service pack updates from the Windows Update/Microsoft update site or a WSUS server if you have one configured.

Install Applications   This task allows you to choose to install one or more applications. If deploying multiple applications, these must be configured in either the deployment share properties' Rules tab or selected during the Deployment wizard. If deploying a single application, you can also use the drop-down list in the Task Sequence action (you must have added the application to the Application node of the Deployment Workbench in order to choose it from this drop-down list).

Windows Update (Post-Application Installation)   This task runs ZTIWindowsUpdate .wsf again (this time it is looking for updates to your applications that have been installed).

Enable BitLocker   This task allows you to configure your BitLocker settings and specify whether you would like to store your recovery key in Active Directory.

The Restore User State   This task runs ZTIUserState.wsf to run USMT's LoadState in order to restore the user's settings and documents that were stored earlier by the ScanState that was run in the State Capture phase.

Restore Groups   This task runs ZTIGroups.wsf to restore the local group memberships of local accounts that were found when the State Capture phase was run earlier.

The subphases that we skipped earlier are as follows:

Custom Tasks   Allows you to add any task you choose.

Prepare To Capture Image   Runs LTISysprep.wsf, which prepares a computer using Sysprep to get it ready to create an image.

Capture Image   We need to spend a bit of time on this subphase. Under the Capture Image subphase, you'll see the following:

    Apply Windows PE (XP) is the task that runs LTIApply.wsf, which copies WinPE to the local hard drive.

    Add Mass Storage Drivers To Sysprep.inf For XP And 2003 runs ZTIDrivers.wsf, which modifies Sysprep.inf with the proper driver information for installation.

Execute Sysprep runs `LTISysprep.wsf` to execute Sysprep.

Apply Windows PE edits the boot configuration database (BCD) to point the target machine to boot into WinPE, getting it ready to capture an image of the target machine (remember, you cannot capture an image of a machine that is currently running an operating system—you must boot the machine into WinPE).

Restart Computer reboots the target machine into the WinPE.

Gather Local Only runs to gather local data again.

Create WIM runs `ZTIBackup.wsf`, which creates an image of the local machine using ImageX.

The OS Info Tab

The last tab on the task sequence properties dialog box is the OS Info tab. On this tab you'll see the operating system description, build number, and platform. These options cannot be changed from here, and neither should you change them by editing the XML file. Clicking the Edit Unattend.xml button opens the `Unattend.xml` file that was created during this process. The `Unattend.xml` file is opened in Windows System Image Manager (WSIM). You can make changes to this XML file, but we recommend making a backup copy before you start editing it.

To make a backup copy, go to Windows Explorer, open your MDTLab folder, and then open the folder that has the same as your task sequence ID (ours was W7X86V1). Here you will find your `Unattend.xml`. Make a copy in the same folder and change the name to **Unattend.xml.old**.

Automating the MDT Deployment Wizard

In Chapter 9, in the section "Deploying Your First Image," we walked you through the MDT Deployment Wizard using the default settings. Before we start automating the MDT deployment process, review the default MDT Deployment Wizard pages:

Welcome Windows Deployment

Specify Credentials For Connecting To Network Shares

Select A Task Sequence To Execute On This Computer

Configure The Computer Name

Join The Computer To A Domain Or Workgroup

Specify Whether To Restore User Data

Language And Other Preferences

Set The Time Zone

Select One Or More Applications To Install

Specify Whether To Capture An Image

Specify The BitLocker Configuration

Ready To Begin

Earlier in this chapter we showed you the deployment share's properties' Rules tab. That is where you want to start automating the MDT deployment process. Take the following steps:

1. In the Deployment Workbench, right-click your deployment share and choose Properties.

2. Select the Rules tab. Click the Edit Bootstrap.ini button. As you saw earlier, there is not a lot of text in this file—just the network (UNC) path of your deployment share:

```
[Settings]
Priority=Default

[Default]
DeployRoot=\\DeploySrv\MDTLab$
```

3. There is only one setting you are going to automate here, and it is getting rid of the Welcome Windows Deployment page. Add SkipBDDWelcome=YES like this:

```
[Settings]
Priority=Default

[Default]
DeployRoot=\\DeploySrv\MDTLab$
SkipBDDWelcome=YES
```

4. Close Bootstrap.ini and save your changes.

    All other settings will be entered on the Rules tab (which you now know is displaying CustomSettings.ini in the F:\MDTLab\Control folder), but working in the Rules tab is easiest. We don't like to automate every setting because authentication information (username, password, and domain) are stored in clear text; therefore, we like to present that dialog box during deployment. If the person attempting to deploy an image from your MDT server cannot authenticate properly to the MDT server, then maybe there is a reason for that. So leave Specify Credentials For Connecting To Network Shares so the dialog box appears during deployment and someone must enter valid credentials to continue the deployment.

5. Enter the following lines in the Rules tab:

```
[Settings]
Priority=Default

[Default]
_SMSTSORGNAME=DeploymentDr
OSInstall=Y
SkipTaskSequence=YES
TaskSequenceID=W7X86V1
SkipComputerName=YES
OSDComputerName=%SerialNumber%
SkipUserData=YES
SkipLocaleSelection=YES
KeyboardLocale=En-US
UserLocale= En-US
```

```
UILanguage= En-US
SkipTimeZone=YES
TimeZoneName=Eastern Standard Time
SkipApplications=YES
Applications001={9823f34e-3168-4e2b-8657-ec7b6aa1a6ec}
SkipCapture=YES

SkipAppsOnUpgrade=YES
SkipAdminPassword=YES
AdminPassword=Swordfish1
SkipProductKey=YES
OverrideProductKey=11111-22222-33333-44444-55555
SkipBitLocker=YES

SkipDomainMembership=NO
JoinDomain=Deploy
DomainAdmin=Deploy\AccountJoinToDomainName
DomainAdminPassword=Swordfish1
MachineObjectOU=ou=Workstations,dc=deploy,dc=com

SkipSummary=YES
SkipFinalSummary=YES
```

You'll end up with a deployment that prompts for user credentials to connect to the deployment share, then silently runs the task sequence with the W7X86V1 ID, assigns the serial number of the target machine as its name, installs an English version of the OS, changes the time zone to Eastern Standard Time, and installs the application you added to the Deployment Workbench. The local administrator password will be set to Swordfish1, the product key will be set to 11111-22222-33333-44444-55555, and BitLocker will be disabled. The target machine will be joined to the Deploy domain with a computer object created in the Deploy.com\Workstations OU (you'll need to create the Workstations OU).

There are tons of other options based on your deployment needs that can be automated. For a full listing of all automated settings, look in the Help menu of the Deployment Workbench under Help Topics and search for "Providing Properties for Skipped Windows Deployment Wizard Pages" and "Property Definitions."

The Bottom Line

Customize your deployment share, applications, operating systems, drivers, and packages.
Updating your deployment share by default creates both 32-bit and 64-bit custom MDT WinPE image files (LiteTouchPE_x86.iso and LiteTouchPE_x64.iso). You can customize the platforms that are supported to reduce the amount of time it takes to update your deployment share.

Master It You are planning on deploying 64-bit images only. How can you configure your deployment share to create the custom MDT WinPE image files needed for 64-bit deployment and not waste time creating the image files needed for 32-bit deployment?

Create custom task sequences. Task sequences drive the installation by controlling which tasks are performed and the order in which those tasks are performed. You can customize task sequences at any time by editing a previously created task sequence. To edit a task sequence from within the Deployment Workbench, right-click your task sequence and choose Properties. Or you could also double-click the task sequence to open its properties.

Master It You have created a custom task sequence by first selecting the default Standard Client Task Sequence template and editing it. You now need to do two things: add an application to be installed via this task sequence and change the password for the local administrator account for any target machines that install Windows 7 using this task sequence. What are the steps for further customizing the task sequence to include these new requirements?

Automate the MDT Deployment Wizard to show only the pages you want displayed during deployment. The MDT Deployment Wizard utilizes two files to determine which pages are displayed during the deployment process and which pages are hidden. These files are the `CustomSettings.ini` and the `Bootstrap.ini` found in your `F:\MDTLab\Control` folder. You can view both files from within the Deployment Workbench by right-clicking your deployment share and opening the properties. The `CustomSettings.ini` file is displayed on the Rules tab. You can view the contents of `Bootstrap.ini` by clicking the Edit Bootstrap.ini button at the bottom-right corner.

Master It You are a non-Enterprise client and all deployments require a product key that is mandated by management. You want the product key 11111-22222-33333-44444-55555 automatically supplied so no one has to type it in every time a deployment occurs. In addition, you want to hide the Welcome Windows Deployment page. Which file do you have to edit (`CustomSettings.ini` or `Bootstrap.ini`) and what entries do you need to provide?

Chapter 11

Fine-Tuning MDT Deployments

The Microsoft Deployment Toolkit (MDT) is suitable for deploying workstations and servers in a large environment. It provides the ability to scale out the environment using linked deployment shares, which can leverage Distributed File System Replication (DFS-R). Using selection profiles, you can distribute portions of the configuration in MDT to, for example, a custom installation DVD. You can also define the settings from the Customsettings.ini file in a database that can be queried based on the computer, its location, a role, or a make and model.

Leveraging these techniques can help you build a highly flexible and scalable deployment solution.

In this chapter, you will learn to:

- ◆ Use selection profiles to create flexibility

- ◆ Use linked deployment shares

- ◆ Create stand-alone media from which you can deploy the operating system

- ◆ Create and fill the MDT database

Discovering Selection Profiles

Selection profiles are part of the advanced configuration within the Deployment Workbench. Selection profiles allow you to make a selection of folders present in the Deployment Workbench. You can later use this profile during the creation of linked deployment shares so you can specify which content will be replicated to that linked deployment share. You can also use selection profiles while including the proper device drivers and packages for use within Windows Preinstallation Environment (Windows PE), which helps you define specific Windows PE images for specific configurations. Finally, you can use selection profiles within the task sequence and when creating deployment media.

By default, the selection profiles in Table 11.1 are available.

TABLE 11.1:   Default selection profiles

NAME	DESCRIPTION
Everything	All folders are selected.
All Drivers	All driver folders are selected.
All Drivers And Packages	All driver and packages folders are selected.

TABLE 11.1: Default selection profiles *(CONTINUED)*

NAME	DESCRIPTION
All Packages	All packages are selected.
Nothing	Nothing is selected.
Sample	Used as an example; packages and task sequences are selected.

In addition to the default selection profiles, you can create your own, which you can use in your custom deployment solution. Here are the steps you should follow:

1. Start the Deployment Workbench and browse to Deployment Shares ➢ *<your deployment share name>* ➢ Advanced Configuration ➢ Selection Profiles.

2. Click New Selection Profile in the Actions pane.

3. In the New Selections Profile wizard on the General Settings page, provide a selection profile name and (optionally) some comments so that you can determine later why you created the profile. Click Next to continue.

4. On the Folders page, select the folders you want to include in your selection profile. As you can see, all the folders and subfolders from your deployment share are available for selection. Choose the appropriate folder by placing a check mark in front of the folder name. Click Next to continue.

5. On the Summary page, review the details provided and click Next to execute the creation of the selection profile. You can follow the creation progress on the Progress page.

6. After the selection profile is created, verify that the outcome is "The process completed successfully." You can also save the status presented on the screen to a log file by selecting Save Output and providing a name to save the output to. Also notice that you can view the PowerShell script that was used to create the selection profile by selecting View Script. You can later use this script as a basis to create selection profiles automatically.

7. Click Finish to end the wizard, and verify that you see your new selection profile listed in the workbench.

MAKING SELECTION PROFILES WORK FOR YOU

Selection profiles can help you distinguish between different types of operating systems and their related dependencies, such as drivers. If you group your Windows 7 drivers in a selection profile, you can later use that profile in your task sequence when injecting drivers. Selection profiles can also be used to ensure that only the necessary drivers—the network drivers and the mass storage adapter drivers—are injected into your boot image. You can create a selection profile containing only these drivers and use that profile while creating the boot image.

After you have created a selection profile, you can change its settings by right-clicking on the profile and selecting Properties. You can then modify the included folders in the selection profile, rename the selection profile, or add additional comments.

You also have the ability to copy selection profiles to other linked deployment shares. However, copying selection profiles within their own folder doesn't work at this time.

Creating a Linked Deployment Share

By using several linked deployment shares, you can create a scalable deployment solution by placing these linked deployment shares in the neighborhood of the clients you are going to deploy.

Understanding Linked Deployment Shares

By using linked deployment shares, you can synchronize content from a source deployment share to a target deployment share. Using selection profiles allows you to create deployment shares servicing certain scenarios. You can, for example, create a deployment share only suitable for installing servers within your organization and place that deployment share in your server VLAN.

By using Distributed File System Replication (DFS-R), you can replicate the contents of equally configured linked deployment shares automatically. If you also replicate the contents of the MDT database, you are able to build a highly scalable deployment solution.

The target deployment share server doesn't need to have the WAIK and MDT installed. It will just host a file share containing the necessary files. WDS is needed, though, if you want this server to perform PXE boot services to its clients.

1. On the server where you want to create the target deployment share, create a folder and share it with the share name you prefer. Also make sure that the share is accessible by the source deployment server by providing correct share and NTFS permissions.

2. Start the Deployment Workbench and browse to Deployment Shares ➢ *<your deployment share name>* ➢ Advanced Configuration ➢ Linked Deployment Shares.

3. Select New Linked Deployment Share from the Actions pane on the right; the New Linked Deployment Share wizard will start.

4. On the General page, provide the UNC path to the share you just created on the target server. You can optionally provide comments explaining the purpose of the linked deployment share you are about to create.

5. By default, the Everything selection profile is selected, but you can modify this when necessary so that only a subset of the source deployment share is copied to the target deployment share.

6. Specify whether you want the New Linked Deployment Share wizard to either merge or replace the selected content into the target deployment share. Click Next.

7. On the Summary page, review the settings and click Next to create the relationship.

8. Verify on the Confirmation page that the process completed successfully.

9. Click Finish to end the New Linked Deployment Share wizard, and verify that the new linked replication share is listed in the workbench.

You also have the ability to save the status presented on the screen to a log file by selecting Save Output and providing a name to save the output to. Also notice that you can view the PowerShell script that was used to create the linked deployment share by selecting View Script. You can later use this script as a basis to create linked deployment shares automatically.

USING LINKED DEPLOYMENT SHARES TO DISTINGUISH BETWEEN TEST AND PRODUCTION

Linked deployment shares in combination with selection profiles can help you distinguish between your MDT test environment and the MDT environment that you want to make available for mass deployment. If you receive a new hardware device, you can test the driver installation in your MDT test environment and later include the drivers and applications in your MDT production selection profile. You can use this selection profile to fill the linked deployment share that you use for production deployment.

Maintaining Linked Deployment Shares

Linked deployment shares can be synchronized again after you have modified the settings or content on your master deployment share. To synchronize the linked deployment share, follow these steps:

1. Open the Deployment Workbench connected to your master deployment server and navigate to Deployment Shares. Then select the master deployment share—in this example, the MDT Deployment Share, which resides locally (D:\DeploymentShare)—and navigate to Advanced Configuration ➤ Linked Deployment Shares, as shown in Figure 11.1.

2. Select the linked deployment share that you want to synchronize, and select Replicate Content from the Actions pane.

FIGURE 11.1
Navigate to Linked Deployment Shares.

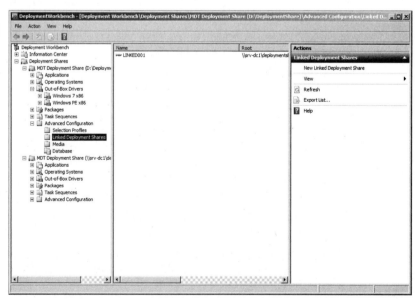

3. The Replicate To Linked Deployment Share wizard launches and displays its progress on the Progress page.

Just like in the previous series of steps, you also have the ability to save the status presented on the screen to a log file by selecting Save Output and providing a filename to save the output to. Also notice that you can view the PowerShell script that was used to create the linked deployment share by selecting View Script. You can later use this script as a basis to replicate linked deployment shares automatically.

Here is the view script information after updating the linked replication share, which you can execute directly in a PowerShell command prompt or save to a PowerShell script file (PS1). The output when running this script is presented in Figure 11.2.

```
Add-PSSnapIn Microsoft.BDD.PSSnapIn
New-PSDrive -Name "DS001" -PSProvider MDTProvider -Root "D:\DeploymentShare"
Update-MDTLinkedOS -path "DS001:\Linked Deployment Shares\LINKED001" -Verbose
```

FIGURE 11.2

PowerShell output

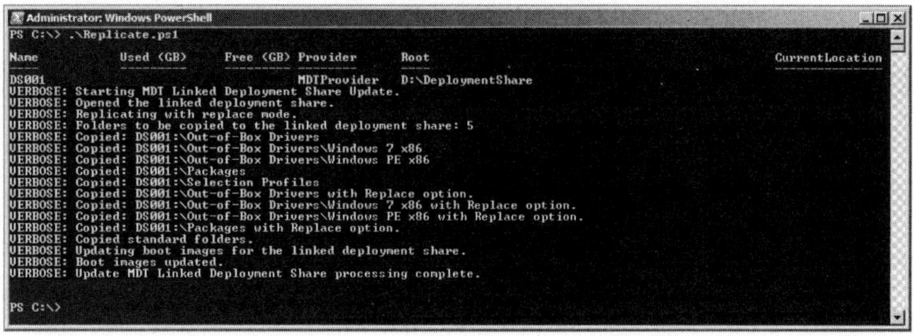

While you could use PowerShell in combination with Task Scheduler to create a replication schedule, using DFS-R will make your deployment solution more robust.

USING DFS-R AS A REPLICATION MECHANISM

DFS-R is the replacement for File Replication Services (FRS) and has been available within Windows Server since 2003 R2. DFS-R features a replication engine that is capable of keeping folders synchronized between servers across connections with limited bandwidth. DFS-R uses Remote Differential Compression (RDC) as a compression algorithm so that only changed file blocks are replicated instead of the entire file.

Follow these steps to set up DFS Replication on Windows Server 2008 R2:

1. Open the DFS management node from Server Manager.

2. Select Replication and, from the Actions pane, select New Replication Group.

3. Make sure that Multipurpose Replication Group is selected on the Replication Group Type page and click Next.

4. Provide a name and optionally a description for the replication group. If you have a multiple-domain environment, select the domain in which you are going to create your replication group. Click Next.

5. On the Replication Group Members page, indicate which servers should become members of the replication group. Make sure you select your MDT server here, and at least one server to which you want to replicate your content. Click Next.

6. If you selected only one server besides your MDT server on the Replication Group Members page, specify Full Mesh as the topology. If you selected two or more servers besides your MDT server, choose Hub And Spoke. Click Next.

7. On the Replication Group Schedule And Bandwidth page, indicate whether you want to replicate constantly or only during specified hours. You can also specify how much bandwidth should be used for replication, ranging from 16 Kbps to 256 Mbps, or you can choose the Full Bandwidth setting. If you plan to replicate on specified days and times, you can create a detailed schedule that specifies when you want to replicate using what bandwidth, as shown in Figure 11.3. Click Next when finished.

FIGURE 11.3
DFS-R replication
schedule

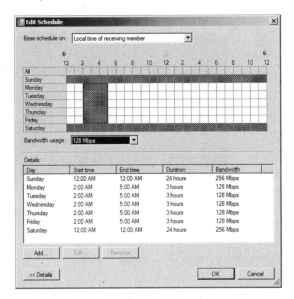

8. On the Primary Member page, select your MDT server, which contains the source of the to-be replicated content. Click Next.

9. On the Folders To Replicate page, click Add to add the folders that you want to synchronize. On the Add Folder To Replicate page, select the D:\DeploymentShare folder. Select the option Use Custom Name to provide a custom name for that folder. Or you can choose the Use Name Based On Path option if you want to use the name of the folder which you want to use. To modify the NTFS permissions, click Permissions. To replicate the boot images as well, add the \RemoteInstall\Boot folder. Click Next.

10. On the Local Path Of Deployment Share Or Other Members page, specify the local path on the receiving server where the content you just selected should be replicated to. Choose another name for the folder so that you can distinguish between the source and

the destination. You have to provide the local path separately on every destination server in order to enable the membership. Click Next.

11. On the Review Settings And Create Replication Group page, check over the settings displayed and click Create to create the new replication group.

12. Click Close on the Confirmation page to finish the wizard. The replication group you just created should now appear under the Replication icon in the DFS management node.

REMOVING HARD REFERENCES TO THE DEPLOYMENT SHARE

When using DFS-R as a replication mechanism, there is one challenge that you need to address. Because the exact content of the master deployment share is replicated, you must use a variable instead of a hard reference to the WDS server. This variable will be used in the `CustomSettings.ini` file. The WDS server you are using when booting an MDT-generated boot image will be available in the `%WDSServer%` variable. You should therefore change the `DeployRoot` value in your `Bootstrap.ini` file to `%WDSServer%`. Also check if you made any references in your `CustomSettings.ini` that you want to replace with this `%WDSServer%` variable. Make sure that you update your deployment share so that these changes are integrated into the boot image and replicated to the DFS-R receiving members.

Because refresh and replace scenarios do not leverage the WDS server, the `%WDSServer%` variable will not work. When you need to support these scenarios as well, you should use the `DefaultGateway` definition in your `bootstrap.ini`. An example is provided in Listing 11.1, where for each gateway another deployment server is defined.

LISTING 11.1   Sample `bootstrap.ini` using the `DefaultGateway` variable to determine the MDT server

```
[Settings]
Priority=DefaultGateway,Default
[192.168.0.254]
DeployRoot=\\SRV-MDT1\deploymentshare$
[192.168.1.254]
DeployRoot=\\SRV-MDT2\deploymentshare$

[Default]
SkipBDDWelcome=YES
```

When you don't use WDS as a mechanism to boot your MDT boot images, you can still have multiple replicated MDT shares. In this scenario you should not provide a `DeployRoot` property in your `bootstrap.ini`. Having no `DeployRoot` property in your bootstrap.ini will be detected by the MDT scripts which will prompt the user to provide the details for the server to connect to. You can also use a `LocationServer.xml` file, which you should include as an extra file in your boot image (which will be included during boot image creation, ending up in the `\Deploy\Control` folder). This XML file specifies the available MDT shares within your organization. MDT will then provide the user with a selection screen.

> **ADDING EXTRA FILES TO YOUR BOOT IMAGE**
>
> You can add extra files and folders to your boot image by specifying a custom folder to include when boot image creation takes place. You can specify this folder for the x86 and x64 Windows PE images when you request the properties of the deployment share. On the Windows PE x86 Settings or the Windows PE x64 Settings tab, you will find the Extra Directory To Add option in the Windows PE Customizations section. Point this setting to a folder that contains a structure that will be applied to the root of the Windows PE image. If you want to have files added to the Control folder as mentioned earlier, you should create the \Deploy\Control folder structure in your directory which you provide at the "to add folder" option.

The following example shows a LocationServer.xml configuration where you can choose between booting from the deployment share in Amsterdam HQ or in Amersfoort. The weight value determines how often the server is used compared to the total use, or weight, specified. In this case, the SRV-MDT1 server is selected two out of six times and the SRV-MDT2 server is selected four out of six times.

```xml
<?xml version="1.0" encoding="utf-8" ?>
<servers>
    <QueryDefault></QueryDefault>
    <server>
        <serverid>1</serverid>
        <friendlyname>
          Amsterdam HQ, the Netherlands
        </friendlyname>
        <Server1>\\SRV-MDT1\DeploymentShare$</Server1>
        <Server2>\\SRV-MDT2\DeploymentShare$</Server2>
        <Server weight="2">\\SRV-MDT1\DeploymentShare$</Server>
        <Server weight="4">\\SRV-MDT2\DeploymentShare$</Server>
    </server>
    <server>
        <serverid>2</serverid>
        <friendlyname>
          Amersfoort, the Netherlands
        </friendlyname>
        <UNCPath>\\SRV-DC1\DeploymentShare$</UNCPath>
    </server>
</servers>
```

Securing Linked Deployment Shares

You can connect to a deployment share in one of two ways. The first method is to specify a user ID, password, and domain in the bootstrap.ini file. These credentials are then used in Windows PE to make a connection to the deployment share and from that point a deployment can be started. Keep in mind that if you use this method, you should use an account with least privilege rights. Also keep in mind that when using MDT in a refresh scenario, the contents of `bootstrap.ini` are sent over the network in clear text, making it easy for someone with a network sniffer to record the settings in that file. When you are using an MDT database, you should also give the specified account the `db_datareader` rights within that database.

The second option is to not specify these settings in the `bootstrap.ini` file and allow the MDT wizard to prompt the user who booted into Windows PE for a username and password. Based on the NTFS and Share Security settings that you specified on the deployment share, access is granted to the user who wants to perform the installation.

Deploying from DVD

Rather than working with deployment shares, you can put all the needed software used to deploy the machine on MDT local deployment media. This media can be a DVD, USB hard disk, or any other portable device. You build the media from the Deployment Workbench and determine what to include when you choose a selection profile. Follow these steps:

1. Open the Deployment Workbench and browse to Deployment Shares ➤ *<your deployment share name>* ➤ Advanced Configuration And Media.

2. From the Actions pane, select New Media to start the New Media wizard.

3. On the General page, provide the path where the media should be created (make sure this path, including the folder, exists), and choose a selection profile to specify what should be included in the local deployment media. Click Next to continue.

4. Click Next on the Summary page. The New Media wizard will now start and display its progress on the Progress page.

You can save the status presented on the screen to a log file by selecting Save Output and providing a name to save the output to. You can also view the PowerShell script used to create the local deployment media by selecting View Script. You can later use this script as a basis to create local deployment media automatically. Click Finish to close the Create New Media wizard.

After the New Media wizard has run, you will find its output in the folder that you specified in the Create New Media wizard. After you update the media, the folder contains an ISO file. You can use this file to burn a DVD, or you can mount it to virtual machines in your virtual environment. Whether ISO files are created or not is an option that you specify in the media's properties. When you don't plan to use the ISO, disabling its creation will save a lot of time when the Update Media Content wizard runs.

The folder will also include a directory structure containing the content specified in the selection profile. You can use this directory structure to create a bootable USB drive, for example. Before you do, you should prepare your USB drive as follows:

1. Insert the USB drive into your computer.

2. Start a command prompt and type **diskpart.exe**.

3. In diskpart, type list disk and determine the disk number associated with your USB drive.

4. Type the following in diskpart:

```
Select Disk x (where x is the number you determined in step 3)
clean
create partition primary
active
format fs=NTFS quick
assign
exit
```

You can now copy the contents of the Content subfolder to the bootable USB drive, which you can use to boot into the Deployment Wizard.

USING THE MEDIA OPTION IN AN OEM PRELOAD SCENARIO

Local deployment media can be used in an OEM preload scenario. In this scenario, the installation of the OS takes place offline by the OEM. Only the steps necessary while connected to the internal network are performed onsite. To do this, you create a task sequence based on the LiteTouch OEM Task Sequence template.

When the OEM starts the created media, it is presented with the OEM Preinstallation Task Sequence For Staging Environment task sequence, which copies the contents of the bootable media to the local hard disk of the computer. The hard disk can then be duplicated by the OEM's hard disk duplication method.

When a machine equipped with a hard disk cloned from the task sequence's output is booted in the internal network, the last part of the installation is performed. Because all media is available locally on the hard disk, the deployment takes place much faster than when deploying from an MDT share on the network.

Working with the MDT Database

Within MDT 2010, you have the option to create a database that can serve as a centralized repository for the settings that you specify in the `CustomSettings.ini` file. Instead of putting the settings in the `CustomSettings.ini` file, you configure the INI file to query the database for the settings to use.

The settings you specify depend on the following:

◆ The settings specified when you defined the computer in the database

◆ The location where the computer resides

◆ The make and model of the computer

Creating the MDT Database

Before you start creating the MDT database, you must have a SQL Server available. You should have the `sysadmin` or `dbcreator` server roles.

USING SQL EXPRESS

You can use the free version of SQL Server, SQL Express, for your MDT database—the MDT database doesn't need all the features of the paid version. Keep in mind, though, that when using SQL Express, the name of the instance you use is SQLEXPRESS. If you use a named instance, you should enable the SQL Browser so that the named instance can be found on the network.

Start by opening the necessary ports on the firewall to enable access to the SQL Browser service:

1. Open Windows Firewall from the Control Panel and select Allow A Program Or Feature Through Windows Firewall.

2. Select Allow Another Program, and click Browse to browse to `Sqlbrowser.exe`, which you'll find in the `\Microsoft SQL Server\90\Shared` folder.

3. On the Allowed Programs And Features screen, ensure that SQL Browser Service EXE is enabled for the network profile you are using—in our example, Domain (since our SQL Server is domain joined).

Now you can create the MDT database using the New DB Wizard:

1. Open the Deployment Workbench and navigate to Deployment Shares ➤ *<your deployment share name>* ➤ Advanced Configuration ➤ Database.

2. From the Actions pane, select New Database to launch the New DB wizard.

3. Fill in the name of the SQL Server that will host the MDT database and provide the name of the instance if the database is available in an instance other than the default one. Optionally, provide another port number if your SQL Server operates at a port other than the default port (port 1433).

   Also select how you want to connect to your SQL Server, either by using Named Pipes, which is the default, or by using TCP/IP Sockets. Click Next.

4. On the Database page, select the option to create a new database and provide a name for the new database. Click Next.

5. When using the Named Pipes option, you must specify a share name to which a connection will be made to ensure that authentication will work. You could, for example, specify a `logs$` or any other share you created. Click Next. If you didn't select Named Pipes, then you have the TCP/IP option for which the difference is detailed in the section, "Using TCP/IP or Named Pipes."

6. On the Summary page, verify the information and click Next.

7. On the Confirmation page, click Finish to complete the New DB wizard.

USING TCP/IP OR NAMED PIPES TO ACCESS THE MDT DB

While accessing the MDT database with Windows PE, you cannot use integrated security using an Active Directory username and password if you are connecting to the database using TCP/IP. If you want to use TCP/IP, you must define a local SQL user with a corresponding password. When using named pipes, Windows PE will first make a network connection to the SQL Server, and based on that authentication, the database can be used. That's why you must supply a share name when configuring Named Pipes as the access method.

Using the MDT Database

After the database is successfully created, you will notice that the database node in the Deployment Workbench is extended with the following information:

- Computers
- Roles
- Locations
- Make and Model

DEFINING COMPUTERS

By using the Computers portion of the MDT database, you can uniquely identify computers in your organization. You must provide one of the following items: AssetTag, UUID, Serial Number, or MAC Address.

For each uniquely identified computer, you provide its own settings, which you would typically supply in `CustomSettings.ini`. namely to install MDT applications, install ConfigMgr Packages, and configure roles. You can also specify which users or groups should be included as local administrators. These settings are retrieved in the task sequence running on the computers by calling the `ZTIGather.wsf` script. To define a new computer in the MDT database, follow these steps:

1. Open the Deployment Workbench and navigate to Deployment Shares ➤ <your deployment share name> ➤ Advanced Configuration ➤ Database ➤ Computers.

2. Select New from the Actions pane; a new window opens.

3. Provide one of the following values: Asset Tag, UUID, Serial Number, or MAC Address. This value will uniquely identify your machine. Optionally, you can supply a description for your machine.

4. On the Details tab, you can enter custom values that would normally reside in `CustomSettings.ini`. These custom values are detailed in Table 11.2.

TABLE 11.2:   Computer details

SECTION	SECTION SETTINGS USED FOR...
ADDS Settings	Configuring domain controller (DC) installation–related settings, such as the path to store the Active Directory (AD) database, the domain's NetBIOS name, and the DC that will be used to replicate content.
BitLocker	Configuring BitLocker–related settings, like the startup pin to use, the Trusted Platform Module (TPM) owner password, and whether the recovery password should be written to AD.
DHCP Server Settings	Configuring the DHCP role, such as the number of DHCP scopes to configure, the name for the scope, and the Starting IP Address for the scope.
Disk Settings	Configuring disk-related settings, like the number of partitions to create, the size of the partition, and its volume label.
Display Settings	Configuring display settings, such as the resolution, the refresh rate, and the color depth.
DNS Server Settings	Configuring the DNS Server role, like the DNS zone, the AD partition to store the DNS information, and whether to enable scavenging.
Domain And Workgroup	Configuring the computer to either join a workgroup or a domain, and if in a domain, which user to use to do the domain join, and in which OU the computer should become a member.
Identification	Configuring the computer name and the registrar's name and organization.
Miscellaneous	Configuring miscellaneous settings, like the administrator password, the home page, and the product key.
NIC Settings	Configuring settings related to the NIC, such as whether to enable DHCP, the name of the network adapter, and whether to enable or disable LMHOSTS.
OS Roles	Configuring settings related to Windows Server 2003 or Windows Server 2008 roles and features.
Regional And Locale Settings	Configuring settings related to regional settings, like the time zone, the user interface language, and the keyboard layout.
SMS 2003 OSD	Configuring settings related to using packages from SMS 2003. This setting is available only for backward compatibility. MDT 2010 does not support SMS 2003 Operating System Deployment Feature Pack.

TABLE 11.2: Computer details *(CONTINUED)*

SECTION	SECTION SETTINGS USED FOR...
User Data	Configuring settings that can be used by the USMT.
Wizard Control	Configuring the pages that are presented to the user performing the installation. Here you can enable or disable pages.
Custom	Defining some extra options, like which role services should be installed, the number of the partition, and the disk to which the image should be deployed.

5. On the Applications tab, select the applications defined in MDT that must be installed for this computer.

6. On the ConfigMgr Packages tab, select the ConfigMgr packages that need to be installed for this computer.

7. On the Roles tab, select to which role (a specific configuration) the computer should belong (you'll learn more about defining roles in the next section).

8. On the Administrators tab, define which users or group should be added to the Administrators group.

DEFINING ROLES

Roles in the MDT database can be assigned to multiple computers. For example, you can define a role that reflects computers for the finance department, containing all the applications needed for finance department staff and specific OU settings. Here are the steps:

1. Open the Deployment Workbench and navigate to Deployment Shares ➤ *<your deployment share name>* ➤ Advanced Configuration ➤ Database ➤ Roles.

2. Select New from the Actions pane; a new window opens.

3. On the Identity tab, give the role a name.

4. On the Details tab, provide the same values as described in Table 11.2.

5. On the Applications tab, select the applications defined in MDT that must be installed for this computer.

6. On the ConfigMgr Packages tab, select the ConfigMgr packages that need to be installed for this computer.

7. On the Administrators tab, define which users or group should be added to the Administrators group.

DEFINING LOCATIONS

Locations can be defined based on the gateway used by the client. You determine on which location a client resides, and specify custom settings based on that.

1. Open the Deployment Workbench and navigate to Deployment Shares ➤ *<your deployment share name>* ➤ Advanced Configuration ➤ Database ➤ Locations.

2. Select New from the Actions pane; a new window opens.

3. On the Identify tab, provide a name for the location, such as **Building 1, 3rd floor**.

4. On the Details tab, provide the values described in Table 11.2.

5. On the Applications tab, select the applications defined in MDT that must be installed for this computer.

6. On the ConfigMgr Packages tab, select the ConfigMgr packages that need to be installed for this computer.

7. On the Roles tab, specify which roles the location defined is a member of.

8. On the Administrators tab, define which users or group should be added to the Administrators group.

DEFINING MAKE AND MODEL

By defining make and model, you can install hardware applications for specific models or create specific network adapter settings.

1. Open the Deployment Workbench and navigate to Deployment Shares ➤ *<your deployment share name>* ➤ Advanced Configuration ➤ Database ➤ Make And Model.

2. Select New from the Actions pane; a new window opens.

3. On the Identify tab, provide a make (which is the manufacturer) and the model (which is the configuration type).

4. On the Details tab, provide the same values described in Table 11.2.

5. On the Applications tab, select the applications defined in MDT that must be installed for this computer.

6. On the ConfigMgr Packages tab, select the ConfigMgr packages that need to be installed for this computer.

7. On the Roles tab, specify which roles the location defined is a member of.

8. On the Administrators tab, define which users or group should be added to the Administrators group.

MODIFYING *CUSTOMSETTINGS.INI* TO USE THE DATABASE

After setting up the database, you need to configure your `CustomSettings.ini` so that it will query the database for the specified values. You can use the Configure DB wizard (Figure 11.4) to generate the INI file.

FIGURE 11.4
Configure
DB wizard

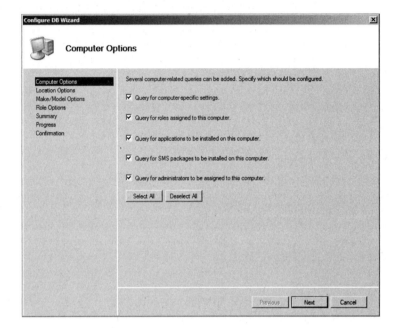

1. Open the Deployment Workbench and navigate to Deployment Shares ➤ *<your deployment share name>* ➤ Advanced Configuration ➤ Database.

2. Select Configure Database Rules from the Actions pane to launch the Configure DB wizard.

3. On the Computer Options page, select the settings that should be queried on the database about individual computers:

   ◆ Query For Computer-Specific Settings

   ◆ Query For Roles Assigned To This Computer

   ◆ Query For Applications To Be Installed On This Computer

   ◆ Query For ConfigMgr Packages To Be Installed On This Computer

   ◆ Query For Administrators To Be Assigned To This Computer

4. On the Locations Options page, select the settings that should be queried on the database about locations:

   ◆ Query For Location Names Based On Default Gateways

   ◆ Query For Location-Specific Settings

♦ Query For Roles Assigned For This Location

♦ Query For Applications To Be Installed For This Location

♦ Query For ConfigMgr Packages To Be Installed For This Location

♦ Query For Administrators To Be Assigned For This Location

5. On the Make/Model Options page, select the settings that should be queried on the database about the defined make and model combinations:

♦ Query For Model Specific Settings

♦ Query For Roles Assigned To Computers With This Make And Model

♦ Query For Applications To Be Installed On Computers With This Make And Model

♦ Query For ConfigMgr Packages To Be Installed On Computers With This Make And Model

♦ Query For Administrators To Be Assigned To Machines With This Make And Model

6. On the Role Options page, select the settings that should be queried on the database about the defined roles:

♦ Query For Roles Specific Settings

♦ Query For Applications To Be Installed For This Role

♦ Query For ConfigMgr/SMS Packages To Be Installed For This Role

♦ Query For Administrators To Be Assigned For This Role

You can view the settings in the Control folder on your deployment share in CustomSettings .ini. The file should look similar to the example in Listing 11.2.

LISTING 11.2 CustomSettings.ini after the Configure DB wizard completes

```
[Settings]
Priority=CSettings, CPackages, CApps, CAdmins, CRoles, Locations, LSettings,
LPackages, LApps, LAdmins, LRoles, MMSettings, MMPackages, MMApps, MMAdmins,
MMRoles, RSettings, RPackages, RApps, RAdmins, Default
Properties=MyCustomProperty
[Default]
OSInstall=Y
SkipAppsOnUpgrade=YES
SkipCapture=NO
SkipAdminPassword=YES
SkipProductKey=YES
[CSettings]
SQLServer=srv-sql01.vansurksum.local
Database=MDT
Netlib=DBNMPNTW
SQLShare=logs$
```

```
Table=ComputerSettings
Parameters=UUID, AssetTag, SerialNumber, MacAddress
ParameterCondition=OR
[CPackages]
SQLServer=srv-sql01.vansurksum.local
Database=MDT
Netlib=DBNMPNTW
SQLShare=logs$
Table=ComputerPackages
Parameters=UUID, AssetTag, SerialNumber, MacAddress
ParameterCondition=OR
Order=Sequence
[CApps]
SQLServer=srv-sql01.vansurksum.local
Database=MDT
Netlib=DBNMPNTW
SQLShare=logs$
Table=ComputerApplications
Parameters=UUID, AssetTag, SerialNumber, MacAddress
ParameterCondition=OR
Order=Sequence
[CAdmins]
SQLServer=srv-sql01.vansurksum.local
Database=MDT
Netlib=DBNMPNTW
SQLShare=logs$
Table=ComputerAdministrators
Parameters=UUID, AssetTag, SerialNumber, MacAddress
ParameterCondition=OR
[CRoles]
SQLServer=srv-sql01.vansurksum.local
Database=MDT
Netlib=DBNMPNTW
SQLShare=logs$
Table=ComputerRoles
Parameters=UUID, AssetTag, SerialNumber, MacAddress
ParameterCondition=OR
[Locations]
SQLServer=srv-sql01.vansurksum.local
Database=MDT
Netlib=DBNMPNTW
SQLShare=logs$
Table=Locations
Parameters=DefaultGateway
[LSettings]
SQLServer=srv-sql01.vansurksum.local
Database=MDT
```

```
Netlib=DBNMPNTW
SQLShare=logs$
Table=LocationSettings
Parameters=DefaultGateway
[LPackages]
SQLServer=srv-sql01.vansurksum.local
Database=MDT
Netlib=DBNMPNTW
SQLShare=logs$
Table=LocationPackages
Parameters=DefaultGateway
Order=Sequence
[LApps]
SQLServer=srv-sql01.vansurksum.local
Database=MDT
Netlib=DBNMPNTW
SQLShare=logs$
Table=LocationApplications
Parameters=DefaultGateway
Order=Sequence
[LAdmins]
SQLServer=srv-sql01.vansurksum.local
Database=MDT
Netlib=DBNMPNTW
SQLShare=logs$
Table=LocationAdministrators
Parameters=DefaultGateway
[LRoles]
SQLServer=srv-sql01.vansurksum.local
Database=MDT
Netlib=DBNMPNTW
SQLShare=logs$
Table=LocationRoles
Parameters=DefaultGateway
[MMSettings]
SQLServer=srv-sql01.vansurksum.local
Database=MDT
Netlib=DBNMPNTW
SQLShare=logs$
Table=MakeModelSettings
Parameters=Make, Model
[MMPackages]
SQLServer=srv-sql01.vansurksum.local
Database=MDT
Netlib=DBNMPNTW
SQLShare=logs$
Table=MakeModelPackages
```

```
Parameters=Make, Model
Order=Sequence
[MMApps]
SQLServer=srv-sql01.vansurksum.local
Database=MDT
Netlib=DBNMPNTW
SQLShare=logs$
Table=MakeModelApplications
Parameters=Make, Model
Order=Sequence
[MMAdmins]
SQLServer=srv-sql01.vansurksum.local
Database=MDT
Netlib=DBNMPNTW
SQLShare=logs$
Table=MakeModelAdministrators
Parameters=Make, Model
[MMRoles]
SQLServer=srv-sql01.vansurksum.local
Database=MDT
Netlib=DBNMPNTW
SQLShare=logs$
Table=MakeModelRoles
Parameters=Make, Model
[RSettings]
SQLServer=srv-sql01.vansurksum.local
Database=MDT
Netlib=DBNMPNTW
SQLShare=logs$
Table=RoleSettings
Parameters=Role
[RPackages]
SQLServer=srv-sql01.vansurksum.local
Database=MDT
Netlib=DBNMPNTW
SQLShare=logs$
Table=RolePackages
Parameters=Role
Order=Sequence
[RApps]
SQLServer=srv-sql01.vansurksum.local
Database=MDT
Netlib=DBNMPNTW
SQLShare=logs$
Table=RoleApplications
Parameters=Role
```

```
Order=Sequence
[RAdmins]
SQLServer=srv-sql01.vansurksum.local
Database=MDT
Netlib=DBNMPNTW
SQLShare=logs$
Table=RoleAdministrators
Parameters=Role
```

Filling the MDT Database Using PowerShell

After you configure the MDT database and define access to it, you can add computers to the database and define their settings. If you need to perform this task for hundreds of computers, you don't want to do it one by one. You can instead use PowerShell to perform a bulk import of computer objects in the MDT database. In this example, we are going to use a CSV file that contains information about the computers we want to import.

SETTING UP THE MODULE

To begin, you'll use the MDT PowerShell module, provided by Michael Niehaus described in his blog posting:

http://blogs.technet.com/b/mniehaus/archive/2009/05/15/manipulating-the-microsoft-deployment-toolkit-database-using-powershell.aspx

Also keep in mind that you need PowerShell 2.0, which is included in Windows Server 2008 R2 by default. Follow these steps:

1. Download the MDTDB.zip file from the blog posting and unblock the file after you downloaded it. You can do this by opening the properties of the MDTDB.zip file and clicking Unblock on the General tab.

2. Unzip the contents of MDTDB.zip to a new folder and explore that folder. The zip file contains the MDTDB.psm1 file, which is the PowerShell module, and the MDTDB_Test.ps1 script, which contains samples on how to use the module in your own script. Notice that you should make a reference in your script to the module using the import-module cmdlet in PowerShell.

3. Be sure you set the PowerShell Execution policy to Unrestricted.

CREATING THE CSV FILE

You will use Microsoft Excel to create an input CSV file, which you can use to import a batch of machines into the database.

1. In Excel, open a new workbook and create three columns named Name, MAC, and Rules, respectively (Figure 11.5).

FIGURE 11.5
Create an Excel spreadsheet.

2. Fill the rows with the information you have on each computer you want to import: its name, its MAC address, and which role it should belong to.

3. Export the spreadsheet to a CSV file (Figure 11.6) and name it **bulkimport.csv**.

FIGURE 11.6
The CSV file opened in Notepad

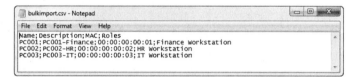

SETTING THE CORRECT SEPARATOR

Depending on your regional settings, sometimes when exporting an Excel sheet to a CSV file, you can end up having a semicolon (;) instead of a comma (,) as the separator. You can modify this by going to Control Panel ➤ Region And Language, selecting the Formats tab, and clicking Additional Settings. Here you have the option to set the list separator value, which should be set to comma. If you don't use the comma as a separator, PowerShell will not understand the CSV when using the import-csv cmdlet.

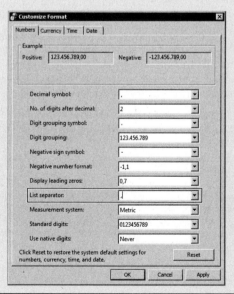

USING THE CSV FILE WITH THE POWERSHELL MODULE

You can use the following PowerShell script to import your CSV file into your MDT database. You should modify the `Connect-MDTDatabase` cmdlet line with your own SQL Server name and MDT database name. If you are using a named instance, you should also add the option `-instance instance name` after the provided SQL Server computer name. Make sure that the PowerShell script, the CSV file, and the `MDTDB.psm1` file are in the same folder.

```
Import-Module -name .\MDTDB.psm1
Connect-MDTDatabase -sqlServer SRV-SQL01 -database MDT
$computers = Import-Csv .\bulkimport.csv
$computers
For ($x=1; $x -le $computers.count; $x++)
{
    New-MDTComputer -macAddress $computers[$x-1].mac -description
$computers[$x-1].description -settings @{
        OSInstall='YES';
        OSDComputerName=$computers[$x-1].name;
    }
    Get-MDTComputer -macAddress $computers[$x-1].mac ? Set-MDTComputerRole -roles
$computers[$x-1].roles
}
```

If you want to see the output of the scripts directly, run a refresh on your database in order for the new computers to be reflected.

This is just one example of what you can do with the PowerShell module provided by Michael Niehaus.

Extending the MDT Database with Custom Settings

In addition to working with the default tables and views in the database, you can extend the schema of the MDT database so that you can add custom values. In this scenario, you are going to add the name of an application server that differs for each location, so that you can automatically use this name when you configure the custom application during the installation of the workstation.

Before extending your MDT database, make sure that you have created a backup of the database in case something goes wrong. To create the new `ApplicationServer` variable, you must add a new column to the settings table called ApplicationServer, which will contain the name of the application server you are going to use in a specific location:

1. Open SQL Server Management Studio, and in the Object Explorer browse to the MDT database ➤ Tables ➤ dbo.settings ➤ Columns (Figure 11.7).

2. Right-click Columns and select New Column.

3. Type the name of the new column you want to define (in this case, **ApplicationServer**), select nvarchar(50) as the data type, and make sure that Allow Nulls is selected.

4. Refresh all views that have a reference to the settings table by running the `sp_refreshview` stored procedure. You can do this by defining a new query in SQL Server Management Studio that contains the following lines:

```
Execute sp_refreshview ComputerSettings
Execute sp_refreshview LocationSettings
Execute sp_refreshview MakeModelSettings
Execute sp_refreshview RoleSettings
```

5. Execute this query against the MDT database by clicking "! Execute" on the main toolbar.

6. You should now have a new option available on the Details tab of your computer settings, in your location settings, in your make and model settings, and in your role settings. Figure 11.8 details this.

FIGURE 11.7
Microsoft SQL
Server Manage-
ment Studio

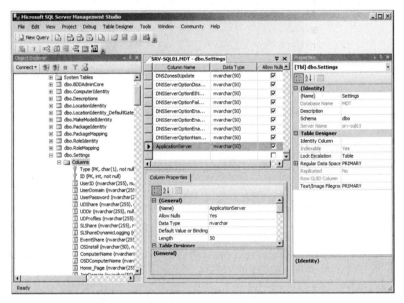

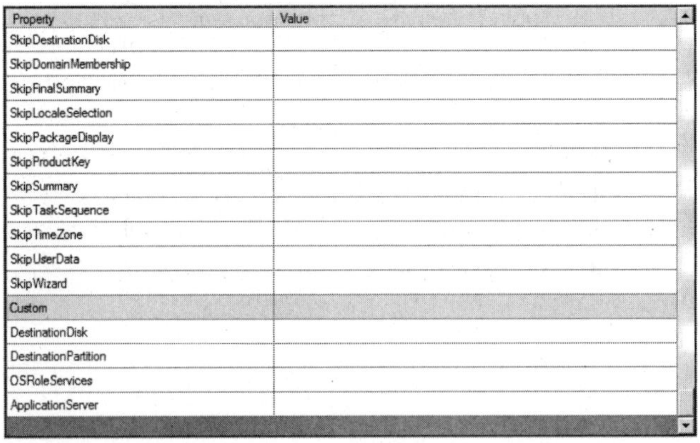

FIGURE 11.8
Newly added
option
ApplicationServer

Next you must provide the name of the application server in the location settings:

1. Open the location for which you want to set the ApplicationServer setting.

2. Select the Details tab and scroll all the way down to the ApplicationServer setting.

3. Modify its value with the name of the application server for that location.

Before you can use the new ApplicationServer value, you need to create a reference in your CustomSettings.ini file so that this value is queried:

1. Open the CustomSettings.ini file using a text editor and find the Settings section. Find the Properties setting and modify its value from MyCustomProperty to ApplicationServer, as follows:

```
[Settings]
Priority=CSettings, CPackages, CApps, CAdmins, CRoles, Locations, LSettings,
LPackages, LApps, LAdmins, LRoles, MMSettings, MMPackages, MMApps, MMAdmins,
MMRoles, RSettings, RPackages, RApps, RAdmins, Default
Properties=ApplicationServer
```

2. You can now use the %ApplicationServer% variable in your MDT task sequence step to install the application, providing %ApplicationServer% as an argument for the installation procedure.

The Bottom Line

Use selection profiles to create flexibility.   Selection profiles can help you create deployment shares with different content.

    Master It   How can you create deployment shares with different content—for example, one for workstation deployments and one for server deployments?

Use linked deployment shares.   By creating linked deployment shares, you can replicate the content of a master deployment share to one or more destination deployment shares.

    Master It   Because DFS-R replicates the exact contents of the source folder to the destination folders, how can you make sure that each deployment share stays unique?

Create stand-alone media from which you can deploy the operating system.   Stand-alone media can be used in specific offline scenarios; you can create stand-alone media using the New Media wizard.

    Master It   What will be the output of the New Media wizard?

Create and fill the MDT database.   MDT can leverage a database running on SQL Server, which can help you make your deployment solution even more flexible.

    Master It   What is the purpose of the MDT database?

Chapter 12

Zero Touch Installations

Microsoft provides excellent free tools in the form of Windows Deployment Services (WDS) and the Microsoft Deployment Toolkit (MDT). They offer light touch installation (LTI) methods, whereby an administrator or delegated user can install Windows in an unattended manner with a small amount of effort at the PC. Larger enterprises may want something more. What if you need to deploy Windows 7 to hundreds of PCs at once on a scheduled basis? Are you going to pay dozens of help desk staff the required overtime to run around to all of these PCs to initiate the installation and then verify that Windows and the required applications were installed?

The combination of MDT and System Center Configuration Manager 2007 enables you to perform ZTI operating system deployment (OSD). This huge systems management product allows administrators to create template images and deploy them from a central console to targeted PCs on both an ad hoc and a scheduled basis. This approach allows an entire department to be upgraded at night. An administrator can get reports on the success of the deployment and visits need only be done on an exceptional basis.

We strongly recommended that you read and understood the technologies used in Windows System Image Manager (WSIM — Chapter 4), WDS (Chapters 6–8), and MDT (Chapters 9–11) before proceeding with this chapter.

Also, MDT 2010 Update 1 offers a new user-driven installation (UDI) deployment method, which allows end users to initiate and customize an OS install on their PCs with an easy-to-use wizard. For more information on UDI, go to www.sybex.com/go/masteringwin7deployment for a free bonus chapter titled "User-Driven Installation."

In this chapter, you will learn to:

◆ Understand and set up Configuration Manager for OSD

◆ Capture customized images

◆ Deploy Windows 7 using task sequences

Understanding Configuration Manager

System Center Configuration Manager (also known as SCCM or ConfigMgr) is the successor to System Management Server (SMS). It is Microsoft's systems management solution for accomplishing the following:

◆ Auditing computer hardware and software

◆ Measuring software usage

◆ Deploying software

◆ Auditing machine and software settings

Two other features are of great interest to us:

◆ Operating system deployment (OSD)

◆ Software update deployment

LEARNING MORE ABOUT CONFIGMGR

The subject of Configuration Manager is pretty huge and there are a lot of architectural options. We're going to give you a quick run-through. Our focus will be entirely on OSD and you will see only a fraction of the possible ConfigMgr installation options. If you want to learn more, check out *Mastering System Center Configuration Manager 2007 R2* (Sybex, 2009).

We're going to take a few moments now to introduce ConfigMgr to those who have not done much with it before. After that we'll look at why it is important to OSD. Then we'll look at installing ConfigMgr and getting it to the point of being ready for the processes of OSD.

Introducing Configuration Manager

As of this writing, Microsoft System Center Configuration Manager 2007 R2 is the current release of the product and Configuration Manager 2007 R3 was in the process of completing its prerelease testing. Also known as SCCM or ConfigMgr, this product sometimes requires you to run many variations of a search when researching the product or trying to troubleshoot an issue. It is the successor to System Management Server (SMS) 2003 R2. Since SMS, it went through ConfigMgr 2007 (a major release) and was followed by the minor release of 2007 R2. Service Pack 2 has also been released and applied to the 2007 and 2007 R2 releases.

2007, 2007 R2, 2007 R3, AND LICENSES

Each of the releases of Configuration Manager is a differently licensed product. Each one requires server licensing for the site servers and for the agent computers. That means you cannot deploy ConfigMgr 2007 R3 if you have only purchased ConfigMgr 2007 licenses. You will either need to purchase Software Assurance with the original license acquisition or purchase new licenses once again. Consult with a large account reseller (LAR) for Microsoft licensing to learn more.

ConfigMgr is what it says on the tin: It allows an organization to manage the configuration of desktops, laptops, servers, and mobile devices. That may include distributing software, performing updates (including custom ones from third parties and those you create yourself), auditing hardware and software, checking how often software is being used, verifying and implementing security policies, and reporting on all of those activities. It is one of the biggest and most powerful products that Microsoft has. OSD was considered to be significantly important when ConfigMgr 2007 was originally developed. In fact, it is rumored that over 25 percent of the entire engineering effort was focused on OSD.

Configuration Manager has a number of basic components in the architecture:

Site Server A site server is used for managing computers in a site. All managed computers in the site communicate with the site server to receive instructions.

Database A SQL database is used for a primary site. You'll learn about primary sites when we talk about architecture next. The SQL database can be on a dedicated server or on a SQL cluster. Normally, however, this is a small database and it can be kept on the primary site server to keep backup and recovery operations more manageable. What is best practice? The unfortunate answer is: it depends. SQL licensing and the desire to cluster the database for fault tolerance are some factors that will lead you to not placing the SQL database on the site server.

Site A site is an administrator-defined boundary made up of networks. The administrator, engineer, or consultant who defines the site will take WAN and LAN traffic into consideration when planning the placement of site servers and roles.

Site System Role Each role enables a feature of ConfigMgr to be deployed. This allows certain things to be done. For example, a Service Locator Point allows clients that are not Active Directory members to find a Management point. The management point provides instructions to the client.

Client This is the piece of software that is deployed onto desktops, laptops, and servers that you wish to manage using ConfigMgr. It is capable of running a number of task-specific agents, such as hardware auditing or software distribution.

Collection A collection is a group that is used for targeting tasks at clients. The members are either statically defined by an administrator or are based on some query. For example, an administrator can have a collection for all computers in a specific site. Out of the box you will see sample collections such as the one that contains all Windows XP computers. Tactful use of collections can make a ConfigMgr administrator's work much easier; for example, you could have a specific job to audit all Windows XP computers that meet the criteria of Windows 7 and then automatically use that for something, as you might well figure out in a little while!

Management Point This is the site system role that provides instructions to clients in the site.

Distribution Point Any package that must be delivered to a client will be shared via a distribution point.

PXE Service Point Preboot Execution Environment (PXE) allows computers with no operating system to download a Windows PE client. This site system role enables those machines to connect to ConfigMgr with a ConfigMgr client for operating system deployment.

State Migration Point This site system role provides a location for the User State Migration Toolkit to temporarily store any captured user states during the installation of a new operating system in place of an old one.

Figure 12.1 includes a possible architecture with many sites in a WAN. This does get confusing; a physical site is one thing; then you have an Active Directory site and a ConfigMgr site. Often they are the same thing, but this architecture will show you that there are more options depending on interoffice bandwidth, server placement, and how you must deploy administrator delegation.

FIGURE 12.1
FIGURE 12.1
A Configuration
Manager site
architecture

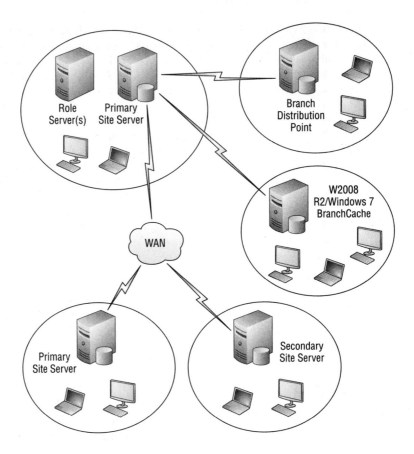

Every ConfigMgr architecture has at least one primary site with one site server. It's a primary site server because it has a SQL database. This allows administrators to perform administration that is unique to this site on this server. Any sites that are below it will inherit the configuration done by administrators in the root primary site. If the site is quite big, then site system roles might be deployed onto other servers.

Child sites may be either primary sites or secondary sites. You'll choose a primary site if you wish to allow administrators in that site to manage their own site server and how things work in their site. However, they do inherit configuration details or instructions from the primary site. Clients in the child primary site will report to their site server. The child primary site server will roll up this data to its parent site server. This allows root primary site administrators to view the status of all tasks. For example, they may control security updates in the root site and want to get a report on the update status of the entire enterprise.

Secondary site servers are there for WAN optimization reasons. They don't allow for custom deployments to be done on the secondary site server. For this sort of work, the parent primary site administrators would need to do some role creation and collection delegation on the parent primary site of the secondary site. Clients in a secondary site will communicate with local site system roles. The secondary site server will inherit tasks from the parent site and feed back the results. This optimizes cross-WAN traffic for larger offices that don't require much of a local ConfigMgr administration presence or customization and enables clients to work well.

It is possible to include remote locations into a site's boundaries. However, the responsible engineer should understand the architecture, how to employ the site role services, and the potential impact on the WAN. One optimization is the use of the branch distribution point. Normally a client downloads packages that it must install from a distribution point on a site server. It then feeds back the results of the installation to the site server.

Consider this scenario. Say your retail operation has hundreds of branch offices with just a few computers, adding up to thousands of computers. Would you want to deploy a site server into each one to optimize WAN traffic? There would be a significant cost in hardware, software, complexity, and administration effort. You certainly could not have them all connect to a central distribution point on the site server because it would clog the WAN. For example, a scheduled download and install of Office 2010 could shut down your entire retail outlet network. Instead, a branch distribution point can be deployed into each branch office. Then, packages can be replicated once to each office in a controlled manner. Clients in that office will use the local branch distribution point to download from. Results from the installation and management instructions still do communicate between the central site server and the remote clients across the WAN, but that issue might not be too bad.

Placement of a branch distribution point usually requires a server, and it is something that still must be managed in the ConfigMgr architecture. Hundreds of branch offices means there are hundreds of branch distribution points to replicate software to every time you create a new package. Windows Server 2008 R2 and Windows 7 (Ultimate and Enterprise editions) have a number of "better together" technologies. One of these is BranchCache. When used with Background Intelligent Transfer Service (BITS) to share packages from the site server distribution point, remote offices can optimize how they download the package on an on-demand basis:

◆ BranchCache is enabled on the distribution point and on the Windows 7 Enterprise/ Ultimate computers in the branch office.

◆ One of two architectures is used for BranchCache in the branch office. A distributed model is used when there are no servers. In this situation, the first computer to download the package from the distribution point will share it with the others. If a server is in the office, it can be used as the sharing point. This arrangement is preferred if Windows clients are powered off or are mobile on a frequent basis, thus making their local cache share unavailable and requiring a new cross-WAN download.

Why Use Configuration Manager for OSD?

When ConfigMgr deploys a client to a computer, the hardware auditing agent is usually enabled. The agent gathers hardware information about a managed computer. But it also gathers information such as the software installed and the operating system information. So the known information about any computer might include the following:

◆ The computer name

◆ The location

◆ The operating system edition, version, and service pack

◆ The software installed

◆ The amount of memory, the size of the hard disk, and the processor

This is the sort of information that could be used to tell if a computer could run Windows 7. Potentially, an administrator could create a ConfigMgr collection and use that as a target for a job to upgrade the operating system.

Speaking of which, ConfigMgr does have the ability to deploy operating systems. It uses the same basic building blocks that you have already learned about when reading about WSIM, WDS, or MDT. In fact, WDS is used by ConfigMgr behind the scenes for OSD.

ConfigMgr also has the concept of task sequences as found in MDT. This feature allows a scripted set of tasks to be executed in a specific order. For example, a user state could be captured on a Windows XP computer and saved to somewhere safe, a new operating system installed, and the user state restored.

ConfigMgr is primarily used as a software and update distribution system. The task sequence can include this functionality. If the computer is targeted with Office 2010, Visio 2010, Adobe Reader, or others, then all of those programs can be automatically installed and patched by ConfigMgr. The computer can be completely provisioned by the user by the time they log in. MDT can be installed and integrated with ConfigMgr to extend its task sequencing.

But why not just use the free-to-download MDT? It can do a lot of this work. MDT is what is referred to as a light touch installation (LTI). An administrator still has to walk to a computer and kick off that installation. ConfigMgr is a zero touch installation (ZTI). An IT department can deploy a ConfigMgr site server. Clients can be deployed automatically from the administrator desktops (using a locally installed ConfigMgr console) to all computers on the network. An OSD package can be created. Then the administrator can target all computers to run that package according to a task sequence and on a scheduled basis. For example, all XP computers meeting Windows 7 requirements can be rebuilt with Windows 7 at 5:00 p.m. on Friday night. At no point has the administrator or any help desk engineer visited those XP computers. Success or failure data is sent back to the site server as the jobs run on the targeted computers. This is more than you can get with MDT. Hopefully all will go well. However, a help desk engineer can visit those desktops that do fail to rebuild correctly. This by-exception visit is much more efficient than the LTI deployment.

An organization with hundreds or tens of thousands of computers will see the benefits of this. A little engineering up front, which is pretty similar to what is required for MDT, yields a ZTI deployment that will live with the organization forever. The Windows 7 project will be more efficient. Future rebuilds or new PC purchases will be easier. ZTI is a long-term investment too; the project to deploy the replacement for Windows 7 will also be easier.

Now that we've whetted your appetite, let's look at installing ConfigMgr.

Understanding the ZTI Flow

The processes that you will go through to set up ZTI are long and time consuming. There are a number of high-level steps that you will go through:

1. *Install Configuration Manager*: It is a lengthy and manual process to get a functional ConfigMgr server up and running. You can skip this step if the ConfigMgr server is already installed and healthy.

2. *Prepare and configure boot images*: This step is when the OSD work begins. Drivers are brought into the control of ConfigMgr and boot images are created for image capture and OSD operations.

3. *Create and capture a reference image*: A bare-metal machine with no operating system will be booted up on the network using PXE and configured with Windows 7. The machine is configured, Sysprep is run, and a reference image is created.

4. *Identify and target machines for rebuilding*: A collection or collections of Windows 7–capable machines is created so that Windows 7 deployments can be completed.

5. *Deploy Windows 7*: The Windows 7 reference image is deployed to preexisting computers that are a part of the Windows 7 deployment collection(s). New machines with no operating system are booted up using PXE to download the reference image over the network.

6. *Monitor deployment progress*: The progress of the deployment can be tracked using the reports that ConfigMgr provides.

It is a lot of work, but the effort will be worth it when you see how powerful and flexible the final solution can be. Most of the work is reusable.

Installing Configuration Manager 2007

Before we go any further, let's consider the versions of Configuration Manager you can use to deploy Windows 7:

Configuration Manager 2007/2007 R2 with Service Pack 2   This provides support for Windows Server 2008 R2 and Windows 7. You can install Configuration Manager 2007 and undergo the process of deploying Service Pack 2. Alternatively, you can install from slip-streamed media that deploys ConfigMgr 2007 and Service Pack 2 in one sweep.

Configuration Manager 2007 R3   This is the latest version of Configuration Manager and was undergoing early public beta testing during the development of this book.

In this book, we are going to install Configuration Manager 2007 with Service Pack 2 with Configuration Manager 2007 R2 in our lab onto the server DeploySrv. The lab network consists of an Active Directory domain controller called DC in the domain deploy.com, the deployment server called DeploySrv, some Windows XP virtual machines, and a blank virtual machine that we can deploy Windows 7 to. DHCP is enabled and configured for the lab network on the domain controller—which is required to provide a network configuration to any machine booting up with the Windows PE client.

CONFIGURATION MANAGER 2007 R3

Configuration Manager 2007 R3 was still an unfinished product as of this writing.

The newest release of ConfigMgr focuses mainly on power management. It allows the application of power-saving policies and reporting on the savings.

There is one new feature that will be beneficial in operating system deployment. Prestaged media support allows you to create an OSD when new PCs are going to be prepared by resellers or OEMs. When the new PC is delivered, it will boot up into the Windows PE client, connect to the network, and initiate the deployment.

The requirements for ConfigMgr are long and complex, and change depending on the architecture you decide on. It is best that you refer to the Microsoft site with all of the relevant information at `http://technet.microsoft.com/en-us/library/bb680717.aspx`. As you saw with WDS, you should have a second volume for storing data. Our DeploySrv has a D: drive. You will need Internet access for a fully functional ConfigMgr installation to download various updates, as you will see as you read on.

We'll now move on with an actual installation of the product. Your first steps will be to prepare the environment. There is a deep integration with Active Directory, and you should configure this before you install Configuration Manager.

Prepare for a ConfigMgr Installation

A significant amount of work is required before you even start to install ConfigMgr. Prerequisites in the Active Directory forest and domain must be configured, and the server must be prepared.

PREPARE ACTIVE DIRECTORY

A container will be created in Active Directory to contain information that will help ConfigMgr clients find the management point for their site. The contents of this container will be populated by ConfigMgr site servers. You'll want to ensure that write access is controlled, and this requires a security group. Take the following steps:

1. Create a security group in Active Directory to contain the computer accounts of all your planned ConfigMgr site servers. The name of this group in our lab will be `ConfigMgrSiteServers` but you should name your group according to your organization's naming standards.

2. Be sure to add the computer accounts for your site servers into the group.

3. Reboot the servers to pick up the new group membership (once the local domain controllers have replicated).

   The next few steps will require domain administrator rights for your domain.

4. You will use ADSI Edit (`ADSIedit.msc`) to create the container. Navigate into System and create a new container object called System Management.

   You now need to grant the site servers full control access rights to the new System Management container.

5. Right-click on System Management to access the properties of the container. Select the Security tab.

6. Click the Add button and add the `ConfigMgrSiteServers` group.

7. Grant that group Full Control rights to the container. You will end up with something similar to Figure 12.2.

8. Edit the entry for `ConfigMgrSiteServers` in the Advanced view to ensure the permissions apply to this object and all descendent objects.

   The final step in the Active Directory preparation is to extend the schema. This will allow you to create ConfigMgr-specific objects in the Active Directory forest. This task will require Schema Admins group membership in the root domain of the forest.

FIGURE 12.2

The System Management container

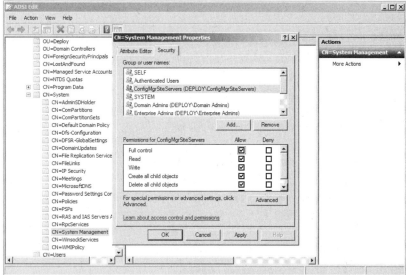

EXTENDING THE SCHEMA FOR CONFIGURATION MANAGER

The schema extension is highly tested and we've yet to hear of a problem with the process or results. But you might want to do a few things just in case. You could temporarily power down a domain controller before the schema extension. If there is a problem, then you at least have a copy of your domain before the new objects were added. However, the ConfigMgr schema extension is quite small and is unlikely to cause a problem.

You should also try to do this extension process from a computer that is located physically close to the Schema Master FSMO role holder in the Active Directory forest.

---

9. Extending the schema is pretty simple. All you have to do is run the `Extadsch.exe` utility in `\SMSSetup\Bin\i386\` from the ConfigMgr 2007 with SP2 installation media. You should end up with a result like the one shown in Figure 12.3.

FIGURE 12.3

Extending the Active Directory schema

```
Administrator: C:\Windows\system32\cmd.exe

D:\SMSSETUP\BIN\I386>EXTADSCH.EXE

Microsoft System Center Configuration Manager v4.00 (Build 6487)
Copyright (C) 2005 Microsoft Corp.

Successfully extended the Active Directory schema.

Please refer to the SMS documentation for instructions on the manual configurati
on of access rights in active directory which may still need to be performed.  (
Although the AD schema has now be extended, AD must be configured to allow each
SMS Site security rights to publish in each of their domains.)

D:\SMSSETUP\BIN\I386>
```

10. You will require some Active Directory user accounts. Create these on your domain controller:

    `ConfigMgrJoin` This is an account that will have rights to create computer accounts in the OU where you normally store those Active Directory objects. You can use it to automatically join new computers to the domain.

    `ConfigMgrSvc` You will require at least one user account that will have local administrator rights on the computers that you wish to manage using ConfigMgr. Initially, it will be used to deploy the ConfigMgr client from a central location. You can grant it local administrator rights using the Restricted Groups feature of Group Policy.

    `ConfigMgrNW` Some operations in ConfigMgr require that a client provide domain credentials to access network resources. This account can be used for those operations.

11. Create any OUs that you need to store any computer accounts. Ensure that the `ConfigMgrJoin` user account has the required rights. To start with, these two advanced permissions are required on the OU (This Object And All Descendent Objects):

    ◆ Create Computer Objects

    ◆ Delete Computer Objects

12. You also need to grant some advanced permissions to `ConfigMgrJoin` on the OU(s). Set the following to Allow For The Descendent Computer Objects:

    ◆ Read All Properties

    ◆ Write All Properties

    ◆ Read Permissions

    ◆ Modify Permissions

    ◆ Change Password

    ◆ Reset Password

    ◆ Validate Write To DNS Host Name

    ◆ Validate Write To Service Principal Name

You're now ready to start preparing your very first ConfigMgr site server. There are a number of things you need to do to it before you install ConfigMgr.

Prepare the ConfigMgr Site Server

You should install a server operating system on your site server. This OS can be either a 32-bit or a 64-bit operating system. We recommend a 64-bit operating system to future-proof the installation. Our example server, DeploySrv, is set up with Windows Server 2008 R2.

The next step is to install SQL Server. For this example, we are installing SQL Server 2008 and Service Pack 1 onto the site server. Once the installation of both the server and service pack is complete, you will need to make one change to the standard configuration: Named pipes must be enabled in SQL. You can do so using the SQL Server Configuration Manager.

From that point, take the following steps:

1. Launch the SQL Server Configuration Manager from Configuration Tools in the Microsoft SQL Server 2008 program group.

2. Navigate into SQL Server Network Configuration and expand Protocols for MSSQLSERVER.

3. Right-click on Named Pipes and select Enable. You are informed that the SQL services will need to be restarted in order to pick up this new configuration change. Make sure you coordinate with other administrators before doing the restart if this machine is monitored or if this SQL instance is used by other applications. You should end up with the setup shown in Figure 12.4.

FIGURE 12.4
SQL Server with Named Pipes enabled

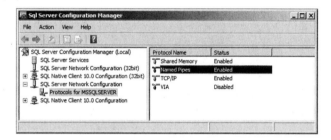

MANAGING WINDOWS SERVER 2008 OR 2008 R2

You should read *Mastering Microsoft Windows Server 2008 R2* (Sybex, 2010) if you wish to learn more about installing or configuring Windows Server 2008 or Windows Server 2008 R2.

Server Manager is used to add roles and features. For example, Windows Server Update Services (WSUS) 3.0 can be enabled and installed as a role on Windows Server 2008 R2 using Server Manager. IIS can be enabled and installed as a role on Windows Server 2008 or Windows Server 2008 R2.

4. Install IIS. This is a mandatory requirement. You will also use Server Manager to enable this role.

    A few additional pieces will be needed. A handy tip from Microsoft is to install IIS by enabling the BITS Server Extensions feature. BITS is a requirement and it subsequently requires IIS.

5. Choose to add the Remote Differential Compression features.

6. The Add Features Wizard will ask if you want to customize the IIS role installation. Add the following IIS role services and any dependencies:

    ◆ Common HTTP Features\WebDAV Publishing

    ◆ Application Development\ASP.NET

♦ Application Development\ASP

♦ Security\Windows Authentication

♦ Management Tools\IIS 6 Management Compatibility\IIS 6 Metabase Compatibility

♦ Management Tools\IIS 6 Management Compatibility\IIS 6 WMI Compatibility

The last role service, WebDAV, is not included with Windows Server 2008; you must download it from the official Microsoft IIS site at `www.iis.net/download/webdav`.

7. Next, WebDAV must be configured with an authoring rule to enable your ConfigMgr clients to use it. Open the IIS Manager from Administrative Tools. Navigate into the Default Web Site in the left navigation pane and enter the WebDav Authoring Rules in the center contents pane.

8. Click Enable WebDAV in the Actions pane. It will be disabled by default.

9. Click Add Authoring Rule in the Actions pane. Allow all users to have read access to all content, as shown in Figure 12.5.

FIGURE 12.5
Add Authoring Rule

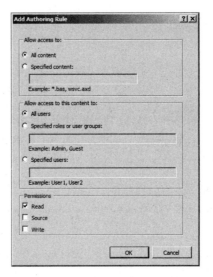

10. You also need to set up how WebDAV will behave. Do this by clicking on WebDAV Settings in the Actions pane. You should configure the following settings:

♦ Set Property Behavior\Allow Anonymous Property Queries to True

♦ Set Property Behavior\Allow Custom Properties to False

♦ Set Property Behavior\Allow Property Queries With Infinite Depth to True

11. If you plan on enabling BITS on this distribution point (which you probably will in order to optimize how clients connect and download content), set WebDAV Behavior\Allow Hidden Files To Be Listed to True. You can see the final configuration in Figure 12.6.

FIGURE 12.6
WebDAV settings
and behavior

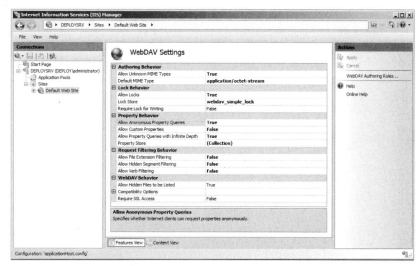

12. ConfigMgr will use components of WDS, so install this role.

13. When it is installed, launch the WDS console and configure the server to use D:\
    RemoteInstall as the Remote Installation Folder Location. Accept all the default settings
    in the Windows Deployment Services Configuration Wizard. At the end, do not add any
    images to the server.

14. It is likely that you will want to manage Windows updates using ConfigMgr if you are
    using it to deploy operating systems. If so, you will need to install WSUS 3.0 SP2. This is
    a simple task in Server Manager if you are using Windows Server 2008 R2. Install this
    role, but be sure not to configure WSUS in any way. The configuration will be handled by
    ConfigMgr if you decide to enable the Software Update Point site server role.

15. A number of file shares will be used for ConfigMgr OS deployment. You will need to
    create these file shares. Create the folders on the D: drive of the ConfigMgr site server
    (deploysrv.deploy.com) and share them with the appropriate permissions. You'll note
    that they are hidden shares, as detailed in Table 12.1.

TABLE 12.1: Shared folders that ConfigMgr will need

SHARE NAME	SHARE PERMISSIONS	NTFS PERMISSIONS	NOTES
Packages$	All Site Servers: Read ConfigMgr Administrators: Change		This is used to store Configuration Manager packages that you will create. They will be copied from here to the distribution points by ConfigMgr.

TABLE 12.1:   Shared folders that ConfigMgr will need   *(CONTINUED)*

SHARE NAME	SHARE PERMISSIONS	NTFS PERMISSIONS	NOTES
Images$	Everyone: Change	ConfigMgrNW: Modify	OSD images are kept here.
USMT$	Everyone: Change	Everyone: Modify	User state data can be captured and stored here temporarily while a computer is being rebuilt. You may need to use an alternative location with more available storage when performing large concurrent deployments. The User State Migration Toolkit might not be required in tightly controlled environments where all user data is stored on the network.
Drivers$	Everyone: Change		You can extract and store drivers here that will be required for OS distribution and for boot images.

You have now configured Active Directory and set up the server prerequisites for the Configuration Manager installation. It's time to install it.

Install the Site Server

You can install ConfigMgr once the prerequisites are installed and configured. These steps will install Configuration Manager 2007 with Service Pack 2, update the site server to Configuration Manager 2007 R2, and add additional components that assist OSD.

INSTALL CONFIGURATION MANAGER 2007 WITH SERVICE PACK 2

Take the following steps to install Configuration Manager 2007 with Service Pack 2:

1. Insert your Configuration Manager with Service Pack 2 media into the site server. If Autorun is disabled, you can run the Splash file on the root of the media. Click the Configuration Manager 2007 SP2 link under Install to launch the setup wizard.

2. Choose the default option of Install A Configuration Manager Site Server.

3. Choose the Custom setting when you get to the Installation Settings screen. The site type will be Primary. You should have a D: drive so you can install ConfigMgr onto it—for example, you can choose D:\ConfigMgr.

4. Every site in ConfigMgr has a three-letter code and a site name. Think these through without rushing the installation before you deploy a production system. For this exercise, you'll be using DPL as the site code and Deploy as the site name in the Site Settings screen. Enter the code and site name you've chosen.

5. For a production system, this would be a pure ConfigMgr 2007 system, so you will choose Configuration Manager Native Mode as the site mode. For a site with legacy SMS 2003 clients, you would choose the Mixed mode. Note that a Native mode site requires a PKI infrastructure. That requires a bit of work and a lot of explanation. To speed things along, we're going to take a shortcut for this exercise and choose to have a Mixed mode site. This won't affect OSD exercises.

6. A ConfigMgr client can have a number of agents enabled. For this exercise, accept the default settings for the SQL Server Computer settings as well as the installation location in the SMS Provider Settings screen.

7. You should accept the default setting for creating a management point on the Port Settings screen.

8. At the Update Prerequisite Component Path screen, create a folder for the installer. The wizard will then download updates to the installation packages so that the newest files can be installed on your site server.

9. After a summary screen, a prerequisite check is run. If you've followed all the steps correctly, you should have a single green check mark giving you the good news. Click Begin Install to install your site server.

At this point in the book, you'll be a progress bar veteran and know where to find a snack or a hot drink to occupy you for the next 10 minutes.

UPGRADE TO CONFIGURATION MANAGER 2007 R2

If you have the licensing, you can insert the media for ConfigMgr 2007 R2 and perform an upgrade of your site server. The installer is quite simple and will install the new components that are included in the R2 release. Three OSD features were added with the R2 release:

Unknown Computer Support   Prior to R2, you had to either already manage a computer or provision a computer account in advance for a new machine. R2 allows unknown computers to connect to the PXE service point.

Multicast Deployment   ConfigMgr 2007 R2 is capable of taking advantage of the multicast feature of WDS on Windows Server 2008 or later.

Alternative Command-Line Credentials   Command-line tasks that are used in OSD can use credentials other than Local System. This will be useful when accessing secure network resources.

INSTALL MDT 2010

Configuration Manager is capable of leveraging MDT 2010 to extend its ability to create and manage task sequences for OSD. To take advantage of this ability, you should install MDT 2010 after you have installed Configuration Manager with Service Pack 2.

1. MDT 2010 requires the free-to-download Word Viewer. You can get that from `www.microsoft.com/downloads/en/details.aspx?FamilyID=3657ce88-7cfa-457a-9aec-f4f827f20cac&displaylang=en` and install it on your ConfigMgr site server. Then install MDT 2010.

2. When MDT is installed, launch the MDT Deployment Workbench and create a new deployment share:

   ◆ Deployment share path: `D:\DeploymentShare`

   ◆ Share name: **DeploymentShare$**

   ◆ Deployment share name: **DeploymentShare**

3. Leave the remaining screens in the New Deployment Share Wizard with the default settings and close the Deployment Workbench.

4. The last step is to integrate MDT 2010 with your ConfigMgr site server. You can do this using the Configure ConfigMgr Integration utility, which is in the Microsoft Deployment Toolkit program group in the Start menu. The default settings for Site Server Name and Site Code should be okay, so leave them in place, as shown in Figure 12.7.

FIGURE 12.7
Integrate MDT 2010 with Configuration Manager

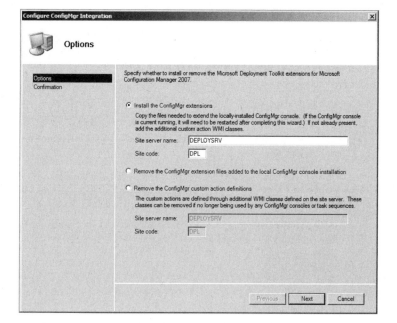

You've now installed the components that you'll be using to create operating system packages and deploy them. We're not quite done yet. Some other configurations must be done in ConfigMgr to prepare for our OSD exercises. We'll have a look at that next.

Your last step, as always with any new server, should be to run Windows Update to ensure all security updates are installed and to install any other patches that you require.

Configure the Site Server

You will now start working in the Configuration Manager Console, which you can find in Microsoft System Center ➤ Configuration Manager 2007 in the Start menu. You can see the console in Figure 12.8. The console is split into the usual navigation pane on the left, contents pane in the center, and context-sensitive Actions pane on the right.

FIGURE 12.8
The Configuration Manager Console

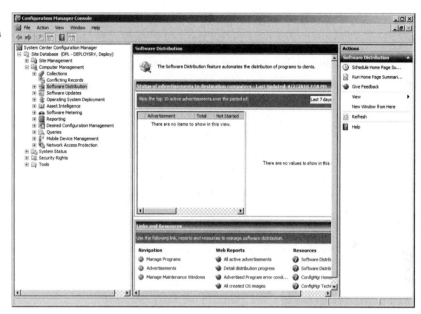

CONFIGURE THE SITE

The navigation pane reveals the site database for this primary site, DPL or Deploy on the server DeploySrv. The navigation pane breaks down into a number of areas:

Site Management   This area is where the site administrators will configure things like the role services, database operations, client deployment, discovery, and client agent configuration.

Computer Management   This area will be the most frequently used part of ConfigMgr. Here you will create and use collections, manage software distribution, run update deployment, run reports, and of course, do your OSD.

System Status   This area is where you can check on the health of your site systems and start your troubleshooting.

Security Rights By default, the administrator of the site server has complete rights over the entire site. You can delegate rights to specific parts of ConfigMgr, a class of objects, or selected objects. We recommend that you learn how to do this if you will be responsible for ConfigMgr.

Tools This area allows you to manage the many services that are used by ConfigMgr.

SYSTEM STATUS

You should make a habit of visiting Component Status and Site System Status for your site on a frequent basis. ConfigMgr does a very good job of keeping an eye on its own health. The errors and warnings also come with a lot of good information explaining any issues and some potential solutions.

You may be thinking how much work goes into installing a ConfigMgr site server. You've only seen the tip of a real-world deployment. Many things can go wrong, and a visit to System Status will usually shine a spotlight on any problems.

However, be aware that you will get some warnings no matter how well your installation goes. For example, some automated behind-the-scenes tasks won't run correctly directly after an installation. Typical of these are some of the warnings for the database.

You should start by preparing your ConfigMgr site. Some of the actions will take a while to run behind the scenes.

The first thing you should do is configure your site boundaries. Boundaries provide a way of specifying which computers should be a member of ConfigMgr site. You can use things like IP subnets, IPv6 prefixes, or Active Directory sites. The latter is handy because your ConfigMgr site can quickly take advantage of AD sites, which probably match up nicely. In this exercise, you can use the default Default-First-Site-Name site as your boundary. By this stage of the book, you are familiar with the use of Windows PE. You probably noticed that your boot image is not a domain member and therefore does not know about the Active Directory sites. Configuration Manager uses Windows PE as a boot image for OS deployment and image capturing. You should also add the IP subnet (192.168.1.0) as a boundary so that non-AD members (such as boot images) will be aware of what ConfigMgr site they are in (DPL - DeploySrv).

PATIENCE

You will learn very quickly that little happens immediately in ConfigMgr. It is a product designed to manage thousands of computers. You rarely expect immediate results in those circumstances. That means you can get frustrated when working in a lab. There are a few tricks to speed some things along, but you must learn to sit back and relax more than you might be used to.

When we work with bare-metal PCs, they are not members of the Active Directory. This means that they must access ConfigMgr resources, such as the distribution point(s), using the network access account (`deploy\configmgrnw`). You need to configure this access in ConfigMgr.

Navigate into Client Agents and edit the properties of Computer Client Agent. You should set the Network Access Account option as `deploy\configmgrnw` and enter the password for the account by clicking the Set button. Failing to do so will cause all boot images (CD, PXE, or USB) to not be able to access the distribution point and then cause OSD operations to fail.

You will want to deploy the ConfigMgr client to your lab network computers. You can do this manually (using `Ccmsetup.exe` in `\\DeploySrv\SMS_DPL\Client\`) or using a Client Push Installation method in Client Installation methods. You need to enable the process and provide credentials for it. You should already have a domain-based account that has local administrator rights on all required computers. That is the `ConfigMgrSvc` user account. Make sure your clients have had time to apply Group Policy if you are using the GPO Restricted Groups method to add that user to the local Administrators group of your computers. You can always run `gpupdate /force` on those machines to speed things along.

A client installation requires that you have Discovery Methods enabled. Active Directory System Discovery should be configured. You might want to enable the other Active Directory methods in a production environment. Associate the discovery method with an OU or the domain (the latter is perfect for this exercise), configure a polling schedule, and select the check box Run Discovery As Soon As Possible. You'll note the default schedule is every day, which is perfect in a real-world scenario but not always useful in a lab.

You can start seeing the results of your efforts by looking at the contents of your collections under Computer Management. Collections also have an update schedule. This means data must be discovered. Then this data is queried on another (per collection) schedule to populate a collection. You can alter that schedule, and you can also force a collection update by right-clicking on the collection and selecting Update Collection Membership.

After a while (you must be patient!), you will see that your lab computers will start to appear in the relevant collections. You will also start to see the client status change from No to Yes for each machine, assuming that the computer's domain account is okay and that the `ConfigMgrSvc` does have the required rights on the computer. Any computer with a client status of Yes will now be running a client with the configured client agents. A number of new objects will now appear in the Control Panel of those computers.

You'll notice collections for Windows XP and Windows Server 2003. You can create a Windows 7 collection using the following query criteria:

```
Operating System.Name is like "Microsoft Windows 7%"
```

Collections for other operating systems can be created similarly. You can pull in collected hardware information to get even more specific.

CONTROL WHERE CONFIGMGR STORES DATA

Configuration Manager will probably try to store data on the C: drive of your server. This could be quite annoying if you have gone to the expense of provisioning a D: drive with a lot of space. You can prevent this from happening by creating a file called `NO_SMS_ON_DRIVE.SMS` on your C: drive.

You can control where ConfigMgr will store Software Distribution files, or the distribution point, by navigating into `\Site Management\<Site Name>\Site Settings\Component Configuration` and editing the properties of Software Distribution. You can enter a drive where you want the distribution point to be located, for example `D:\`.

ADD SITE ROLES

The previously discussed client discovery process will take some time. As mentioned, ConfigMgr requires patience so you should move on by doing some other work to help pass the time.

A number of site roles must be deployed within a ConfigMgr site to allow the complete OSD process to work. Take the following steps:

1. Navigate into the Site Systems area under Site Settings.

2. Right-click on the site server and select New Roles. Add roles (if not already added to the site) in the following list. You can see the screen for enabling these roles in Figure 12.9.

   Server Locator Point   This will enable non-AD members to find the site server.

   State Migration Point   This will allow captured user states to be temporarily stored in the previously created shared folder. USMT can instead use hard-link migration which is a more efficient process.

   PXE Service Point   This will allow you to use network-located boot images to boot up computers with no operating system for OSD.

   Reporting Point   Using this, you can generate reports from the ConfigMgr database and track the process of running deployment jobs.

   Software Update Point   This allows ConfigMgr to deploy security updates to managed computers.

3. You are asked if you want ports to be opened to allow the PXE service point to work. Click Yes if you plan to capture a user state using USMT and store it on the network. You can use the site database for the Server Locator Point.

FIGURE 12.9
Enabling site roles

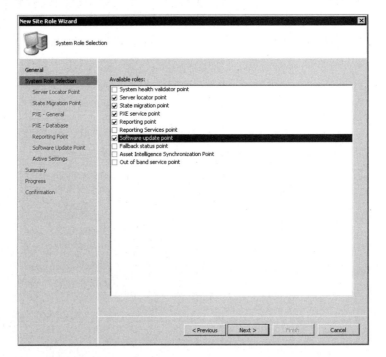

USMT 4.0 AND HARD-LINK MIGRATION

The User State Migration Toolkit has traditionally used a file share or the state migration point to temporarily store the user state in a safe location. You can choose to do so if you wish to keep data off the machine. USMT 4.0 introduces a feature called hard-link migration. It is much faster. Rather than copying a captured user state to a file share and then restoring it later, it remaps the locations of the files in the file system. These files are left untouched during the operating system rebuild and are moved back into the correct location afterward.

---

4. Configure the state migration point, if installed, as shown in Figure 12.10, with the location of the folder you created. In this example, it is D:\USMT.

NOTE Note that if you use MDT (which is discussed later in this chapter) you won't have to install the state migration point. You can configure multiple locations. You can specify the maximum number of clients that can be installed and how much free space should be left in the location.

You can also use the state migration point properties to specify how long data should be retained after being restored to a PC. You can delete the data immediately or accept the default of keeping it for one day. Keeping the data consumes disk space but does allow you to recover from glitches that might happen. Would you really want to lose a user's profile and data when you could have the option to keep it around for a few days before having it automatically deleted?

FIGURE 12.10
Setting up the state migration point

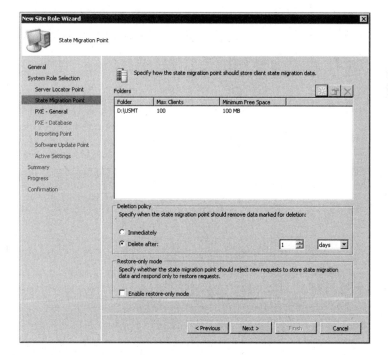

The PXE service point has a number of options, as you can see in Figure 12.11. By default, ConfigMgr will not allow unknown computers to boot up using a network-provided boot image. Any new computer would need to be pre-provisioned. This would be required in highly secure networks. However, most organizations might want something a little more administrator- and user-friendly.

FIGURE 12.11
Setting up the PXE service point

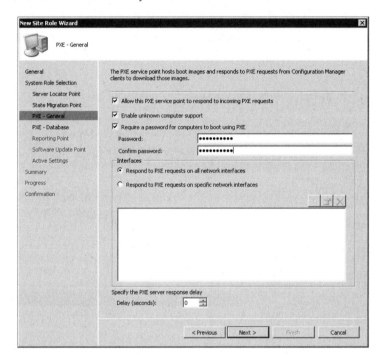

5. On the PXE - General screen, select the Enable Unknown Computer Support check box to allow ConfigMgr to facilitate PXE service for these new machines. You can optionally protect the PXE service with a password, enable it on only selected interfaces, and delay the response (which is useful in multi-VLAN networks with many PXE services).

FAILED PXE BOOTS

A PXE boot might fail for a number of reasons. If the DHCP part of the boot times out, then you should start by checking for an Active Directory–approved DHCP server with a valid scope for your network. There should be free IP addresses in the scope. Check that the PXE service point is listed as an approved DHCP server using the DHCP console. This is because PXE is based on the same network protocol. If you see an error related to architectures, ensure that you have both x86 and x64 boot images available on the PXE distribution point.

---

6. Continue to accept the defaults until you get to the Software Update point configuration. You might need to configure a proxy server if you have one.

7. In Active Settings, configure the Port Number and SSL Port Number to match the ports that your WSUS server installation uses. You can then set up the Microsoft Catalog synchronization. This includes the schedule, the classifications of updates, and the products that you wish to update.

   Note that Windows 7 won't appear in here as a product until the first synchronization has taken place. Don't select too much if you are just working on a lab because it will take time to process.

8. Finally there is the annoying Languages screen. Clear the unwanted languages here. A number of languages are selected by default and there is no quick way to clear them other than going through each one, one at a time. Not clearing the unwanted ones will increase the work you need to do later when working with update management in ConfigMgr. Production environments should download all the languages that are supported on the network.

9. Check on the System Status a little while after the role installation is completed. Any problems with dependencies will be highlighted and you should resolve them before progressing. Note that some errors or warnings will be created just because the roles are only being created or starting up for the first time. They could eventually work themselves out.

10. You could allow time for the initial Microsoft catalog software update synchronization to take place. Or you could force a synchronization to happen by navigating into \Computer Management\Software Updates, right-clicking on Update Repository, and selecting Run Synchronization. Wait a few minutes, and check the site status (Component Status\SMS_ WSUS_SYNC_MANAGER) to see the results. Then you can go into Site Settings\Component Configuration\Software Update Point Component and select whatever products you wish to manage updates for (such as Windows 7, which is now visible). The selected update types for the selected products can now be updated and managed using Software Updates.

    If you install the Software Update Point role, then also return to Client Installation Methods in Site Settings and enable Software Update Point Client Installation.

The setup of Configuration Manager is all done! It was a long process. It might make you wonder about the value of using ConfigMgr for OSD at all. Think of this work as an investment. You need to put in a big investment to get big returns. ConfigMgr is aimed at large organizations. You put in the work early on and are rewarded with completely automated OSD for the entire WAN. Next, we are going to look at creating and managing boot images in ConfigMgr 2007.

Preparing and Configuring Boot Images

In earlier chapters you read about how Windows Deployment Services and the Microsoft Deployment Toolkit use boot images. They are used to boot up bare-metal machines and to allow a setup routine to wipe an existing PC and replace its operating system. ConfigMgr has the same needs. Nothing new is used here. The same core technologies are reused. The only thing that is different is how the boot images are created and how they are shared.

A boot image is created in the Configuration Manager Console. Drivers are added to allow access to the network and to mass storage controllers. The boot image is shared to existing PCs via a distribution point, which is one of the Site Role Services that was deployed. The boot image is shared to bare-metal machines via the PXE service point (which makes use of the underlying Windows Deployment Services), which also has a distribution point that will be populated.

Creating Boot Images

Let's start by creating the 32-bit or x86 boot images. ConfigMgr gives you the tools to create 32- and 64-bit boot images from within the Configuration Manager Console.

1. Navigate into `Computer Management\Operating System Deployment`, as shown in Figure 12.12. You are going to be spending a lot of time here if you plan on doing ZTI using ConfigMgr.

FIGURE 12.12
Operating System
Deployment folder

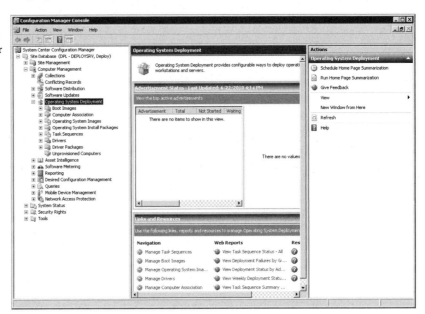

2. To create a new boot image, right-click on Boot Images and select Create Boot Image Using Microsoft Deployment. This launches a wizard, as you can see in Figure 12.13.

3. On the first screen, enter a path for where, in the distribution point shared folder that you created earlier, you want to store the new boot image. Try to use a naming standard.

4. As with previous package creations, enter descriptive content into Name and Version, which is shown in Figure 12.14.

FIGURE 12.13
Boot image package source

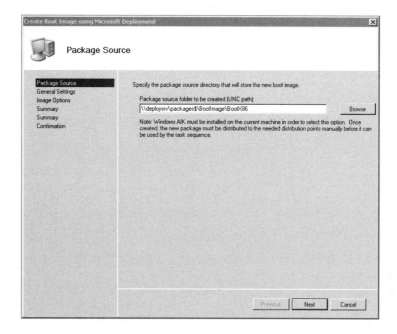

FIGURE 12.14
Boot image General Settings

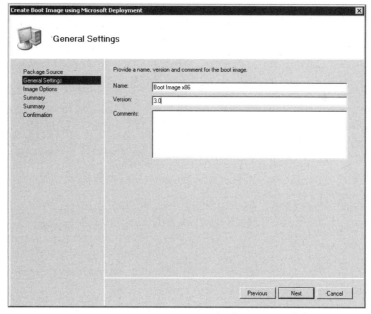

5. The Image Options screen allows you to configure the boot image. You can choose the architecture (x86 or x64). We will start by creating a 32-bit (x86) boot image, as shown in Figure 12.15. You can select optional fonts for Asian regional settings support. You can even add a custom image as the background when the boot image is running or additional files for troubleshooting. Make sure that ADO is selected as it will be required.

FIGURE 12.15

Boot Image
Options

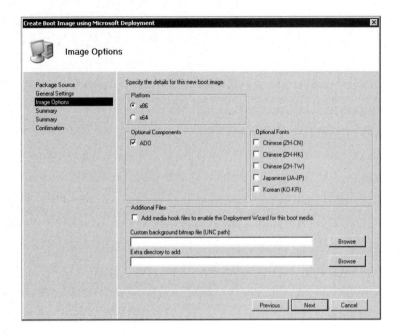

The boot image is created. All that remains is to make the boot image available to machines on the network. As you might remember, you need to add the boot image to a distribution point.

6. Navigate into the Boot Images folder, select the new boot image, right-click on it, and select Manage Distribution Points Wizard. Choose the option to copy the package to new distribution points.

7. Select both the normal distribution point and the PXE distribution point. The normal distribution point will be used to distribute the boot image when an existing installation of Windows will be replaced with a ConfigMgr-distributed installation image. The PXE distribution point will be used when a computer (for example, bare metal) is booted up onto the network to do a fresh installation.

8. Repeat this process to create and share an x64 or 64-bit boot image. It is required to handle some hardware that reports itself as x64 even if you are distributing an x86 installation image.

Once a boot image is created, you can open its properties to view or edit the settings. For example, you might develop your boot image and later add that background image to brand the deployment solution with the company logo. You could enable distribution points to be updated on a recurring schedule to accommodate changes to the boot image.

Adding Drivers to a Boot Image

A boot image is like any other operating system. If the hardware that it boots up on has hardware that has no native driver support, then the device won't work. For an OSD boot image, that can be a bit of a problem. What if there is no network card driver? You won't be able to download an installation image. What if there is no mass storage controller driver? You won't be able to see the hard disks and therefore won't be able to install the operating system. A boot image can be updated with drivers to allow access to those devices that would otherwise be unavailable.

ConfigMgr allows you to do something that will be familiar if you have worked with the Microsoft Deployment Toolkit. Drivers can be imported into ConfigMgr and then added to a boot image. The next sections will deal with the process of importing drivers into ConfigMgr and updating the boot images.

This is a simple enough task. The hardest part can be finding the right drivers and extracting them. You are looking to find a folder that contains an INF and a SYS file. Sometimes you have to extract a self-decompressing executable file or search through a cabinet file.

Real World Scenario

DRIVERS AND VIRTUAL LABS

This chapter was written using virtual machines that were running on a laptop. The operating system was Windows Server 2008 R2 Hyper-V. This provided a powerful and economic way to make the most of the hardware. You may want to consider something like Hyper-V, Xen, or one of VMware's desktop or server products to get a large lab network running on a minimum number of physical machines.

You may be familiar with the concept of integration components, virtual machine additions, or whatever the vendor has labeled them. Without them, your operating system has no drivers to access things like the virtual network card in the virtual machine. How do you get those drivers so you can import them into ConfigMgr?

The solution is to load the ISO image that contains the additions into your virtual machine. You can do this by telling the virtualization software to update the additions or install them. Do not actually complete this process if they are already installed. Instead, log into the virtual machine and navigate to where the drivers are kept. Hyper-V, for example, has a CAB file in the \support\amd64 and \support\x86 folders that contains the drivers for 64-bit and 32-bit virtual machines, respectively.

Extract the files and then you will have what you need to work with ConfigMgr, WDS, or MDT.

In this exercise we are keeping a copy of the extracted drivers in the D:\Drivers folder, which can be found on the network as \\deploysrv\drivers$. It is a good idea to have some sort of folder structure and naming standard. This approach makes it easy to find OEM drivers and specific versions, and enables you to keep track of, maintain, and/or replace driver versions as manufacturers release them. It will also allow you to maintain x86 and x64 drivers as well as drivers from different manufacturers for similar but slightly different chipsets.

To add drivers to ConfigMgr, take the following steps:

1. Select the Drivers folder, right-click, and select Import. This opens the Import New Driver Wizard, which is shown in Figure 12.16.

   You have two options here. If you are adding many drivers you can choose the "Import all drivers in the following network path (UNC)" option. You can see that \\deploysrv\

drivers$\X64 is selected. All folders within the specified UNC path will be searched for drivers. This makes the process nice and easy. In this example we have two folders in \\deploysrv\drivers$\. X64 contains all of the 64-bit drivers. We want to import them and categorize them as 64-bit drivers. That will make it easier to update 64-bit boot images with just the 64-bit drivers. There is also an X86 folder, allowing us to do the same with 32-bit drivers.

FIGURE 12.16
Import New
Driver Wizard

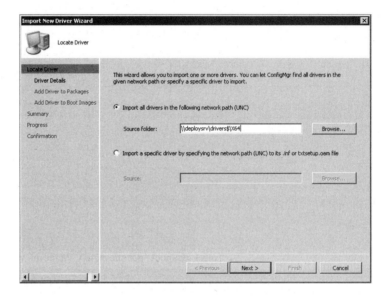

If you are adding just a single driver, then you can specify the exact folder where the driver's INF or txtsetup.oem file can be found. This will only import that driver instead of wasting time processing drivers that were already imported.

2. The Driver Details screen, in Figure 12.17, displays every driver that was found in the location that you specified. You can see that a check box beside each driver is selected by default, indicating that the driver is to be imported. Clear this check box if you do not want that driver. A check box at the bottom of the list also informs us that, by default, these drivers will be enabled and that computers will be able to install them. Clear this if you want. At the bottom, click the Categories button to add the selected drivers to a category. You can create new categories as well. You can see that we have added the imported drivers to the 64-bit category, making drivers easier to manage based on category.

3. On the next screen, shown in Figure 12.18, add your imported drivers to a driver package. You will want to do this to allow drivers be added to newly built computers. You can select an existing package or you can create a new package. A new package called All 64-bit Drivers was created in \\deploysrv\packages$\Drivers\X64. Check the "Update distribution points when finished" check box at the bottom to save a few clicks.

FIGURE 12.17
Driver Details

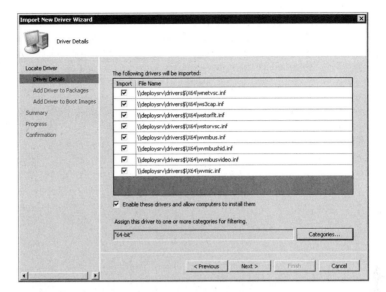

FIGURE 12.18
Adding drivers
to packages

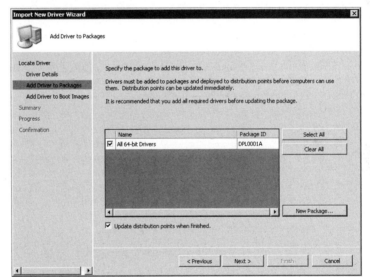

UPDATING DISTRIBUTION POINTS

Depending on your ConfigMgr architecture, some distribution points might be in remote locations at the other end of congested WAN links. You should work with ConfigMgr and network administrators to decide how and when distribution points will be updated. For example, would you want to replicate a large file across a 1 MB link while people are trying to work? This might be a scenario where schedules will be used to update the distribution points.

4. Figure 12.19 shows the Add Driver To Boot Images screen. Here, decide if you want to add your newly imported drivers to one or more existing boot images. We will update the 64-bit boot image that we created earlier and check the "Update distribution points when finished" check box. The newly updated boot image will be automatically installed on the distribution points when this wizard is complete.

FIGURE 12.19
Add Driver To Boot Images screen

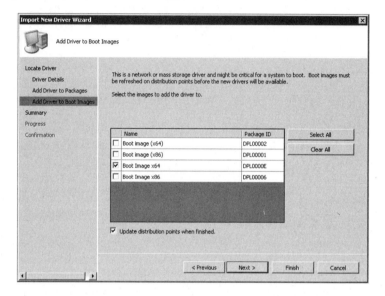

CHOOSING DRIVERS TO ADD TO BOOT IMAGES

Microsoft strongly recommends that only network and mass storage controller drivers be added to boot images. Adding every possible driver will unnecessarily increase the size of the boot image. To do this, you would not add the drivers to the boot image during a mass import. Instead, you would skip the Add Driver To Boot Images screen, finish the import, categorize the drivers by function, and add the network and mass storage controller drivers to your boot images.

5. When the import is complete, you will be able to see your drivers in the Drivers folder. You can select drivers and add them into other categories such as Networking or Mass Storage Controllers. Verify that the driver package was created in Driver Packages.

6. You should repeat this process with the x86 or 32-bit drivers if you think that there is a possibility that you will work with 32-bit machines in the future.

REMEMBER TO UPDATE DISTRIBUTION POINTS

Every time you modify a boot image, you need to remember to update the distribution points. Failing to do so will mean that you and users will continue to use the old boot image.

You can expand a package and view Package Status to see the replication status of a package. The Targeted value shows how many distribution targets are assigned with the package, and the Installed value shows how many distribution points have the package.

7. Take the time to view the properties of your boot images when they are created. The Windows PE tab is especially interesting. Normally, the ConfigMgr boot images disable the use of the command prompt. This can make troubleshooting driver and network access issues very difficult. You can enable this by checking the Enable Command Support (Testing Only) check box. The bottom of this tab also allows you to update the background for your boot image with a graphic of your choice, such as an organization or IT department logo.

Creating and Capturing a Reference Image

The reference image is a Sysprep-prepared build of a Windows installation that will be deployed to existing and new computers. There are a number of approaches to creating a reference image using the traditional Windows Sysprep and capture:

A Bare Operating System   A computer is prepared with just the operating system and nothing else. This is captured and deployed to all new computers. It requires patching and all software deployment, consuming more time during deployment. This will be done by Configuration Manager.

A Bare Operating System with Patches   An operating system is deployed to a reference computer. All available patches are deployed to the machine before a reference image is captured. All deployments of this image require all software to be deployed by Configuration Manager after the operating system image is installed.

Standard Computer Image   A common computer image is defined, typically consisting of the operating system, Microsoft Office, common utilities, management and security agents, and all patches. This definition is used to build a computer and this machine is captured as a reference image. The image is deployed and Configuration Manager deploys all other software that is assigned to the machine/user that is not contained within the image.

Specialized Computer Images   An image is built with all of the required software for serving a specific role. This image is not a generic one that can be deployed to everybody—it is appropriate where a large number of computers must be deployed with specialized software that might take a long time to deploy. The benefit of this solution is that the fully functional computer can be delivered in a short amount of time.

There are merits to the many approaches. The key to the decision-making process is finding a balance between the following:

◆ Building and testing the image

◆ Updating/replacing the image as updates to patches and software are released

◆ The time it takes for a fully functional PC to be deployed

We are going to focus on the simpler process of creating an image that contains the operating system and the security updates. The ConfigMgr site server that has been built contains everything that is needed. The good news is that we can automate the entire operating system installation, patch installation, Sysprep, and capture process using a task sequence.

There are a number of prerequisite packages (a collection of files shared from a distribution point) that are used during a Configuration Manager task sequence to deploy or capture an operating system. You can create them by hand, but we are going to do this the quick way by letting the Create Microsoft Deployment Task Sequence Wizard do the work for us.

1. Start this wizard (Figure 12.20) by navigating into Operating System Deployment and then into Task Sequences, and then clicking on the link in the Actions pane.

FIGURE 12.20
Choose a template
for the Reference
Task sequence.

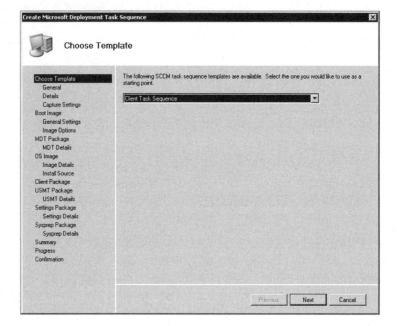

2. On the Choose Template screen, choose from a number of task sequence templates. We will use the Client Task Sequence. If you expand the drop-down list box you will see there are more options, including the ability to work with servers. Operating system deployment isn't limited to PCs and laptops!

3. On the General screen, shown in Figure 12.21, you assign a name to and describe the task sequence. Choose something that is as descriptive as possible. You might end up with a large number of task sequences after a while and you should make it easy to find the one you want when doing some work. You might append version numbers to the names as you start to customize your task sequences.

4. On the Details screen, shown in Figure 12.22, leave the machine in Workgroup. Reference machines should not be joined to a domain. You should enter the product key (the one shown is not a real one); otherwise the installation will stop and wait for someone to enter one. That would not be very zero touch.

5. On the Capture Settings screen (Figure 12.23), tell ConfigMgr where to store the captured installation image and what to call it. You must enter the UNC path to the folder and the

desired name of the WIM file that will be created. The path of `\\deploysrv\image$\`
`Windows 7 Pro x64.wim` is used in this example. You must define a capture account.
This example is using `deploy\configmgrnw`, but you can use any account that has modify rights on the `image$` share.

FIGURE 12.21
The Reference Task
sequence, General
screen

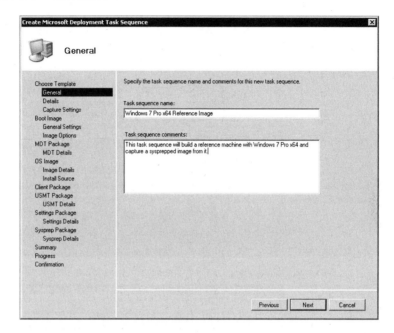

FIGURE 12.22
Details for the
Reference Task
sequence

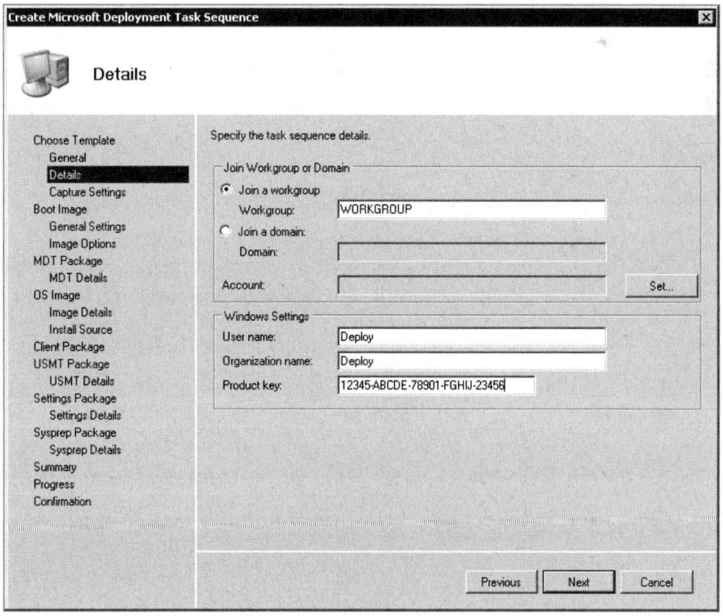

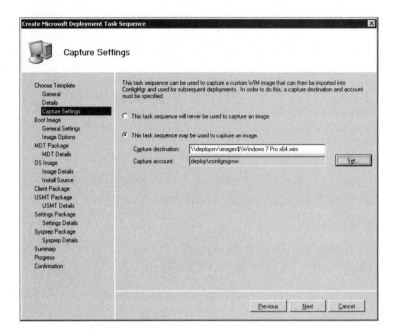

6. You created a boot image earlier, and you want to add drivers to it. On the Boot Image
   screen, shown in Figure 12.24, select one. We are working with 64-bit hardware and we
   want to deploy a 64-bit copy of Windows 7, so we will use the 64-bit boot image that we
   created earlier and add drivers to it.

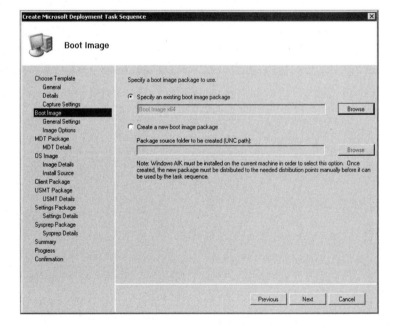

7. On the MDT Package screen (Figure 12.25), either use an existing or create an MDT package. The package will be used to temporarily download the content of MDT to a machine while the task sequence is running. This allows the task sequence to do many complicated tasks while it runs. We will choose to create an MDT package in the packages share at \\deploysrv\packages$\MDT\MDT 2010. The wizard will know where to find the MDT installation on this machine to create the package.

You should note how we are using a subfolder called MDT 2010. This will allow the single MDT folder to contain many future versions of MDT as they are released and will keep things easy to find.

FIGURE 12.25
Create an MDT
Package

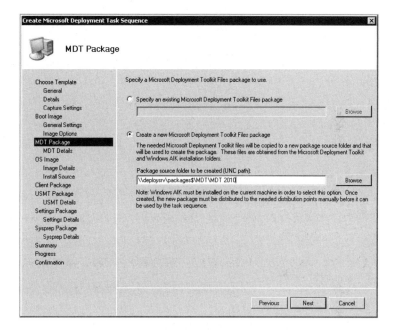

8. Name the package as Microsoft Deployment Toolkit 2010 in the following MDT Details screen.

9. The OS Image screen (Figure 12.26) allows you to do a number of things. You can choose an existing captured image (OS image) that is managed by ConfigMgr, create a new OS image from a captured WIM file, choose an OS install package (containing the Windows installation media files), or create a new OS install package. For the purposes of this exercise, do the latter. The Windows 7 installation media is loaded or mounted (E:\) and the destination for the new package is \\deploysrv\packages$\Windows\Windows 7.

10. Name the OS Image **Windows 7** in the Install Source screen.

11. On the next screen either select an existing package to install the Configuration Manager client or create a new package. We will select the Create A New ConfigMgr Client option.

12. The User State Migration Toolkit (USMT) will be used for capturing user states and restoring them. It won't be necessary to do this during the build of a reference image, but it won't hurt us to create the package now. Do that in the USMT Package screen (Figure 12.27). The default location of USMT is detected by ConfigMgr and entered for you. This is in the WAIK installation location in a subfolder called \tools\USMT. The package should be created in \\deploysrv\packages$\USMT\USMT 4.0.

FIGURE 12.26
Create an OS installation package

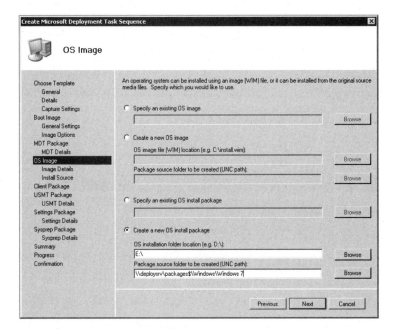

FIGURE 12.27
USMT Package screen

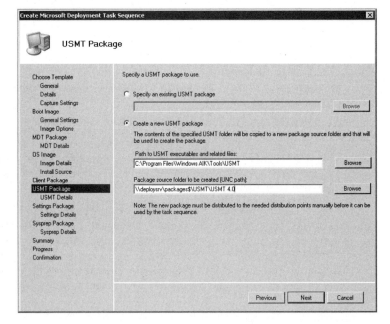

13. Name the package as User State Migration Toolkit 4.0 in the following USMT Details screen.

14. There are two files required for an MDT installation of Windows 7. Unattended installations require an answer file. It's the same XML file you might have created in WAIK, or used in WDS or MDT. MDT deployments also require some settings in the form of a file called `CustomSettings.ini`. We will supply these settings in a package. The package is created in the Settings Package screen (Figure 12.28). The files will be created in `\\deploysrv\packages$\Settings\Build and Capture Settings`. You will have to change the `CustomSettings.ini` file in a little while. You can optionally tweak the answer XML file to change the way that Windows 7 is installed.

FIGURE 12.28
Custom Settings

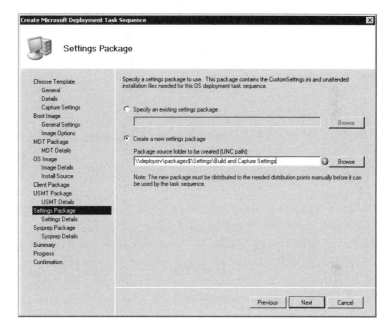

The package name can be called **Build and Capture MDT Settings** in the following Settings Details screen.

15. The Sysprep screen is similar to the previous ones. Legacy operating systems such as Windows XP didn't come with Sysprep, so you would have to create a package if you were working with them. Sysprep has been included with Windows since the Vista release. This means we can choose the "No Sysprep package is required" option on the Sysprep Package screen.

You accomplished a lot of work. The good news is that once these packages are created, you can just select them for reuse later. You might choose to use different settings packages, or maybe use a captured WIM file later on, but those involve minor amounts of work.

The wizard will then start to create packages and the task sequence. This might take a while, thanks to the creation of the OS installation package, so it will be another of the many opportunities to check your email or to take a watercooler break.

> **TASK SEQUENCE TEMPLATE**
>
> We are using a MDT 2010 task sequence template for the tasks in this exercise. The template will contain a number of ordered individual tasks. You can choose to create a native ConfigMgr template. Alternatively, you can choose to create a custom template and add each task or step in by hand.

16. A couple of minor edits must be completed in the task sequence. You can find the task sequence in `Computer Management\Software Distribution\Task Sequences`. Launch the Task Sequence Editor (Figure 12.29) by right-clicking a task sequence and selecting Edit.

FIGURE 12.29
The Task Sequence Editor

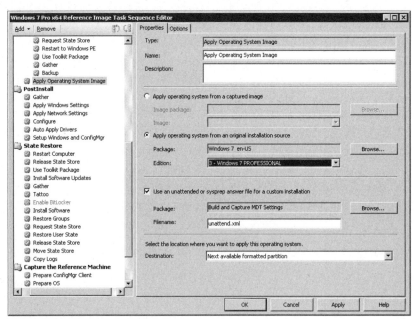

17. Navigate to the Apply Operating System Image task in the left navigation pane. Change the Edition in the right pane to the edition of Windows that you want to install, such as Windows 7 Professional. By default the Task Sequence Editor installs the Home Basic edition of Windows 7, which would be of no use in an enterprise network.

18. The Setup Windows and ConfigMgr task must also be edited. Click on this task in the left pane and change the entry in the Installation box to

`SMSSLP=DEPLOYSRV`

The operating system that this task sequence will build will be a workgroup member. Workgroup members cannot use Active Directory to figure out what their ConfigMgr site server should be. They must be told to use a Service Locator Point on a specific server. This ConfigMgr client installation parameter will tell them to use the site server role that was installed on DeploySrv.

INSTALL SOFTWARE USING A TASK SEQUENCE

You can use the Install Software action to install a software distribution package on the resulting machine. Doing so allows you to include ConfigMgr managed software in the reference image. You can add additional Install Software tasks to the task sequence.

Any desired software distribution package must have the "Allow this program to be installed from the Install Software task sequence without being advertised" option enabled in the required program. This setting is not enabled by default. You can find instructions for changing this setting in all of your packages at once at `http://blogs.technet.com/b/mniehaus/archive/2008/10/02/allow-this-program-to-be-installed-from-the-install-software-task-sequence-without-being-advertised.aspx`.

You need to return to the MDT settings package once the packages are created. This is your opportunity to change the unattended installation XML file. You should also change the `CustomSettings.ini` file.

19. Navigate to `D:\Packages\Settings\Build and Capture Settings` and open `CustomSettings.ini` using Notepad. You should change the contents to the following:

```
[Settings]
Priority=Default
[Default]
DoCapture=YES
_SMSTSORGNAME=Deploy Inc. IT Department
```

This will force MDT to capture the image and will change the default label of IT Organization on the task sequence progress bar to a label of your choosing, such as **Deploy Inc. IT Organization**.

20. Save the changes, and then it will be time to make the packages available to the network.

Install Packages on the Distribution Points

The packages, as they are, are residing in a shared folder called `\\deploysrv\packages$`. The packages have to be installed into a distribution point for them to be available to ConfigMgr clients. This process replicates the package files across the network to any remote distribution points that you may have, so you need to be careful about configuring schedules for this process. You can do so by opening the properties of a package, navigating to the Data Source tab, and checking the option Update Distribution Points On A Schedule.

So far we have created packages in the following:

Computer Management\Software Distribution\Packages   There are four packages here: the ConfigMgr client package, the MDT 2010 package, the MDT settings package, and the USMT package. Additional packages may be created to distribute software to PCs.

Computer Management\Operating System Deployment\Operating System Install Packages   The OS install package for Windows 7 resides here.

Computer Management\Operating System Deployment\Driver Packages   The driver packages for any imported drivers are here. They are used not only for the boot images, but as additional drivers for plug-and-play during operating system deployments.

Each of these packages must be selected in turn and be installed on the required distribution points. Take the following steps for each package:

1. Launch the Manage Distribution Points Wizard by right-clicking on each package and selecting Manage Distribution Points.

2. Choose the option to copy the package to new distribution points.

3. Choose the normal distribution point, such as DeploySrv. Do not select the PXE distribution point, for example `DeploySrv\Smspxeimages$`, because it is not intended for the use of package distribution.

4. Watch out for one unusual error that can occur. Sometimes, the package containing the MDT settings will not install correctly on the distribution point. This will cause your task sequence to fail when it runs. You can prevent this from happening by right-clicking on the package, choosing Manage Distribution Points, and clicking the "Update all distribution points with a new package source version" action. Doing so forces the version of the package to increment and forces it to be reinstalled on any selected distribution points.

5. There are a couple of really big packages in this process. The OS install package contains several gigabytes of files, and the boot image is not too small either. You need to be careful about scheduling their installation on remote distribution points in a production network. Use the scheduling options on the Data Source tab of the package properties to control the timing of the installations.

You will not be able to launch the task sequence until all the packages are installed on distribution points. You can track the process of this process by drilling down into the Package Status of each package in the Configuration Manager Console, as shown in Figure 12.30. The status of Install Pending means that the package is not ready on the distribution point. The status of Installed means it is ready.

FIGURE 12.30
Package installation status

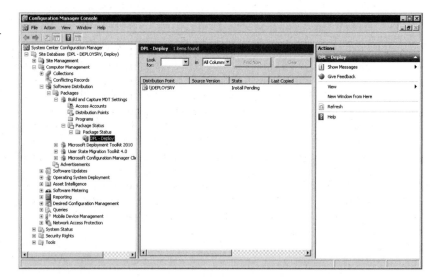

You can do other work while the packages are copied to the distribution point(s).

HAND-BUILT REFERENCE IMAGES

The process that we are using in this chapter will install Windows 7 Professional x64, install the ConfigMgr client, install any ConfigMgr-managed software distribution packages or software updates, run Sysprep, and then capture an image.

You might prefer to build, or have already built, a computer. If that is the case, you can create capture media in ConfigMgr to capture an image of this machine that ConfigMgr can later deploy.

The requirements for the machine are as follows:

◆ The machine must be a workgroup member.

◆ The administrator password must be blank.

◆ Password complexity should be turned off in the local policy settings.

Browse to Operating System Deployment in the Configuration Manager Console. You will launch a wizard by right-clicking on Task Sequences and selecting Create Task Sequence Media. From there you can create capture media. This allows you to create a USB or CD/DVD ISO image that can be used to boot up your reference machine and capture an image. A boot image will be used for the media. Make sure the drivers required for hard disk and network access are in the boot image.

When you boot up the machine with the capture media, the machine will be prepared with Sysprep, and an image will be captured and stored in a location of your choosing.

Create a Collection and a Computer Association

ConfigMgr uses collections as a way of targeting actions at computers. A collection can contain one or more computers. The membership is either statically defined or is generated based on a query. This query is done using data in the ConfigMgr database and can be done automatically on a scheduled basis.

OS deployment and collections is a complex topic. You may remember that we enabled unknown computers to access the PXE service point. By default, that check box is not selected and ConfigMgr will not respond to the machines that it was not previously aware of. Those machines fail to access a boot image and will not boot up from the network.

To prevent that, you can pre-create a computer object for the new-to-the-network machine, referred to as a computer association, in ConfigMgr. This is done in the Operating System Deployment folder in the Configuration Manager Console. When you do this, you need to provide something unique from the hardware such as the GUID or the MAC address. You name the computer and specify a collection that it should join.

Alternatively, if PXE access is not a huge issue, you can allow unknown computers to access the PXE service point (managed in Site Systems under Site Settings). An unknown computer will temporarily join the All Unknown Computers collection until its work is completed or it is joined to another collection via a discovery.

Think about this for a few moments. You are about to advertise a task sequence to build a reference computer and capture an image from it. All computers in that collection will receive this task. Later on, you will create an advertisement and link it to a collection to deploy the operating system. When new computers are purchased they will be a part of the All Unknown Computers collection. Do you want to advertise the reference image task sequence to a collection where new computers will join? New computers would end up building and capturing reference images.

Instead, you need to create a collection that will contain the computer that will be used for building and capturing reference images. This sort of specific targeting is strongly recommended for all development and test work in ConfigMgr. Now let's create that collection.

1. Browse to Collections under Computer Management in the Configuration Manager Console. Click on New Collection in the task pane on the right to start the New Collection Wizard, shown in Figure 12.31. Name the collection **Operating System Deployment**.

FIGURE 12.31
New Collection
Wizard

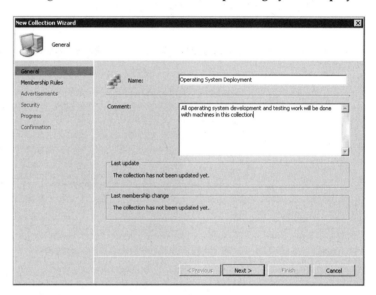

2. The next screen allows you to specify membership rules for the collection. This can be a query based on any stored details of discovered computers in the ConfigMgr database, or it can be something more specific. Skip this step for now. A collection has the ability to rebuild the membership on a scheduled basis. This is not required for this collection because the membership will be statically defined. Clear the "Update this collection on a schedule" check box at the bottom and complete the wizard.

The computer that we are going to work with does not yet have an operating system on it. We want it to be forced into the new Operating System Deployment collection. We can do this by using a Computer Association. If your desired computer was discovered already by ConfigMgr, then you can edit the membership rules of the collection to include it.

3. To create a computer association, navigate back into Operating System Deployment and then into Computer Association. Select the Import Computer Information task. This opens the Import Computer Information Wizard.

   If you have several machines, you can enter their details into a CSV file. You will need the GUID or the MAC address of each machine to import. You can get these from the BIOS or from the PXE boot screen (which requires the use of a digital camera because it is visible only for a short time). The format of this file is:

   ```
   <computer name>,<GUID-GUID-GUID-GUID-GUID>,
   <MAC:MAC:MAC:MAC:MAC:MAC:MAC:MAC>
   ```

4. You are going to import a single computer. Select it and skip to the next screen, shown in Figure 12.32. Enter the name of the computer and either the MAC address (of the network card that will boot onto the network with PXE support) or the machine's GUID.

FIGURE 12.32
Importing a single computer

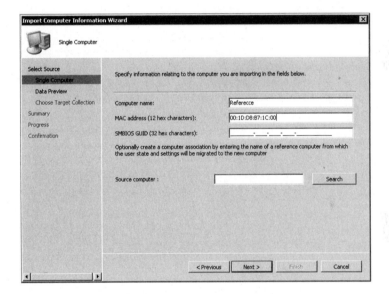

5. Choose whether to join the machine to the All Unknown Computers collection (by default) or to another collection. As you can see in Figure 12.33, we will join this machine to the Operating System Deployment collection.

6. Right-click on the collection and force the collection to update its collection membership. You can refresh the details pane to ensure that the object has been added correctly.

At this point you now have a task sequence (a workload) and a collection (a target). The next thing to do is create an advertisement to link them.

FIGURE 12.33
Choose Target Collection screen

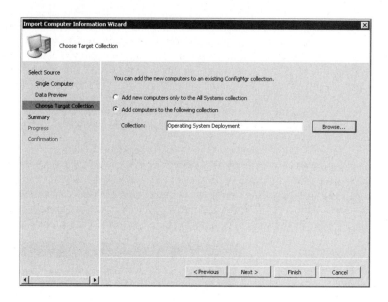

Advertise the Reference Image Task Sequence

ConfigMgr uses advertisements to tell computers what work they should do and when they should do it. An advertisement links the workload with a collection of computers. You have created a task sequence and now you are going to advertise it to the Operating System Deployment collection. The process to do so is quite easy:

1. Navigate to the task sequence in Configuration Manager Console, select it, and click on Advertise in the Actions pane.

2. The New Advertisement Wizard (shown in Figure 12.34) launches. The default name of the advertisement is inherited from the task sequence. Rename it if you wish. Pick a collection that this advertisement will target. In our case it will be the Operating System Deployment collection. This limits the task sequence to the machines that are members of the collection.

   A collection can have subcollections. For example, you could have subcollections called Reference, Test, and Pilot within the Operating System Deployment collection. That would allow for a complex test and development environment. By default, the advertisement will be inherited by subcollections, but to avoid this inheritance clear the "Include members of subcollections" check box.

3. Select the "Make this task sequence available to boot media and PXE" check box. (It must be selected, which it is not by default.)

4. The Schedule screen (Figure 12.35) allows you to define when an advertisement is available to clients and when it expires. The Mandatory Assignments box allows you to define when clients must run the advertisement. Click on the star-shaped button to create a new mandatory assignment with the As Soon As Possible value.

   There is another interesting check box which you don't need to use now but that will be of use later. The Enable Wake On LAN check box allows the advertisement to wake up a powered-down computer to run the advertisement. The requirements are that the hardware supports it and that the advertisement has been downloaded to the computer while it was powered up. Where could this capability be useful? You could advertise an OSD with a mandatory assignment of midnight on Saturday to existing computers with Wake On LAN enabled. Even if a PC is turned off, it will wake up and run the operating system installation task sequence. Nobody needs to be in and no users experience downtime. Users will come in after the weekend to find Windows 7 running instead of Windows XP or Windows Vista. That's zero touch installation at its best!

5. Skip through the rest of the wizard with the default values. Now the advertisement is ready to run.

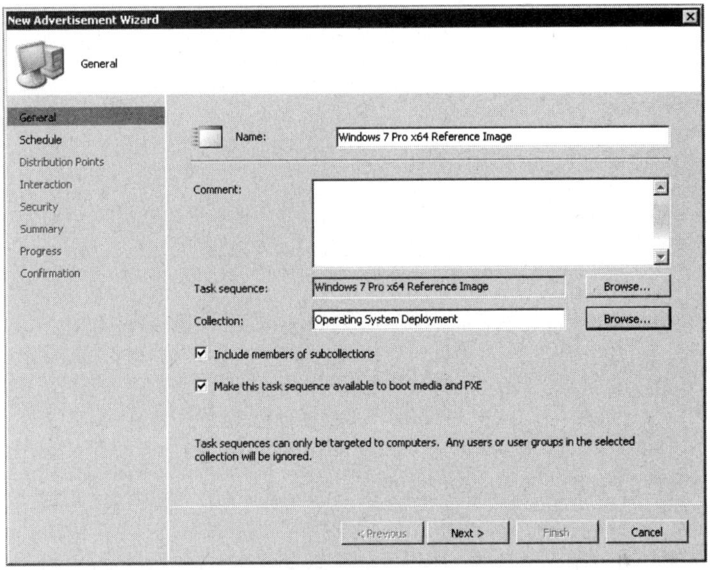

FIGURE 12.34
Advertising the Reference Task sequence

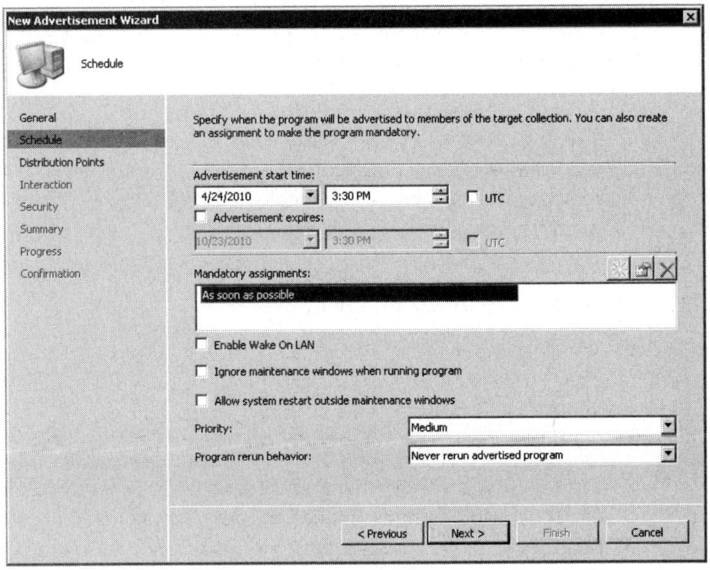

FIGURE 12.35
Advertisement schedule

Run the Reference Image Task Sequence

There are two ways to run the task sequence. The first way is to boot up the reference image computer using a PXE-based network boot. All the work to enable that capability has been completed. We'll come back to that in a few moments. The other way is to create some form of boot media. That approach will be useful if you cannot use PXE network boots.

You can create bootable media by selecting the task sequence and clicking on Create Task Sequence Media in the Actions pane. Select Bootable media in the Task Sequence Media Wizard and click Next. As you can see in Figure 12.36, you now have the choice of creating a USB stick that will run the task sequence or a CD/DVD ISO file.

FIGURE 12.36
Selecting the bootable media type

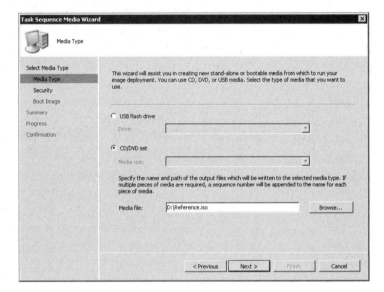

If you are using a virtual machine lab, then you might find using an ISO easier and quicker than setting up a PXE service point. But that would deprive you of the learning experience of doing all the required configurations. You can create the ISO file, copy it to the host machine, mount it with the blank reference virtual machine, and boot it up. You might not be able to create a USB flash drive if you are using some virtualization technologies. Such would be the case with Hyper-V without the use of third-party USB products.

You are going to use the already configured PXE boot option. The reference computer has the ability to boot up from the network. The PXE service point is configured. The task sequence is linked to a boot image. The task sequence is advertised to a collection. All we need to do is force the reference computer to boot up using PXE.

1. The reference machine needs to be configured to be able to boot from the network. Doing so requires a compatible network card and the feature enabled in the BIOS. A computer with no operating system will usually boot up from the network to find a boot image. If an operating system is installed, you can force a PXE boot during the power-on self-test (POST) just after the machine powers up. Quite often this is done by pressing the F12 key, but the method varies depending on the manufacturer. If you are using Hyper-V as your virtualization technology, you will need to use a Legacy Network Adapter (not the synthetic one) to have PXE functionality in the virtual machine.

2. Once the reference machine powers up, you should see the boot image download and start up. If your PXE service point is password protected, you have to enter the password. All of the work will be done by the task sequence so everything after this should be automated.

   If there are any problems with the PXE boot, you should inspect the smspxe.log file, which you can find in C:\Program Files\SMS_CCM\Logs on the site server that has the PXE service point. Your 64-bit computers will have that file in the C:\Program Files (x86)\SMS_CCM\Logs folder.

3. The task sequence begins. First, the availability of all the package dependencies on a distribution point is checked. A common problem is that the network access account has not been correctly configured for the Computer Client Agent. This will cause an error that says a particular package is not available. You need to keep an eye on things here. This is because the client will automatically reboot the machine after a few seconds if the task sequence fails.

4. This task sequence will install Windows 7, install the ConfigMgr client, install any available software updates or software distribution packages, run Sysprep, and create Windows 7 Pro x64.wim at \\deploysrv\image$\. The entire process will only require you to power up the machine (and maybe enter the PXE service point password if you enabled that). After that you can go for lunch, do some other work, or maybe go home for the day. The WIM file will be waiting there for you after a little while.

You now have a reference image with your customized Windows 7 build. You need to identify the Windows 7 capable machines that are on your network that you want to re-install with your Windows 7 reference image. And that is what we will do next.

Any errors during an OSD task sequence will appear the smsts.log file. The location of the file depends on the scenario:

♦ If task sequence completes when running in the full operating system with a ConfigMgr client installed on the computer, then it will be in %Windir%\System32\Ccm\Logs for 32-bit machines and %Windir%\SysWOW64\Ccm\Logs for 64-bit machines.

♦ If the task sequence completes when running in an installed operating system with no ConfigMgr client installed on the computer, then it will be in %Temp%\SMSTSLOG.

♦ If the task sequence completes while running in Windows PE, then it will be in <largest fixed partition>\SMSTSLOG.

Log files are the one thing that ConfigMgr is not short of. You can find a long list of log filenames, descriptions, and locations at http://technet.microsoft.com/library/bb892800.aspx.

Identifying and Targeting Machines for Rebuilding

We have seen that ConfigMgr uses collections to target actions such as an OSD. If you are performing a zero touch installation with ConfigMgr, you need a way to accurately identify which machines to upgrade, without even visiting them.

ConfigMgr will, by default, perform a hardware audit on all machines that the client is installed on. You can use this data to build a collection, or collections, and these collections can be used for targeting the deployment of the reference image.

A Deployment Strategy

One of the all-time classic quotes from comic book lore is "With great power comes great responsibility." ConfigMgr is the most powerful product that you can have on your entire Microsoft network. A forest or domain administrator can deploy the ConfigMgr client to every Windows machine in the Active Directory forest and do whatever they want via that client. It would be very easy to deploy an operating system image to every available machine, believing that all would go well.

When you've worked on complex projects for a while, you remember that Murphy's Law is never far away. Imagine you deploy an operating system image to a thousand PCs and something goes wrong. If a thousand people cannot work because of a mistake you made, you will be in the not-working category very quickly too. Not only will testing minimize the risk to a widespread, zero touch installation, but a documented and managed testing process will protect you to a certain extent from angry supervisors.

We have discussed how it is important to use a collection of machines for building and testing the operating system reference image. You should perform a series of tests with as many variations of the build as possible. Try to obtain access to various types of hardware. Thanks to the zero touch features of ConfigMgr, those machines could be on the other side of the planet, as long as they are in a ConfigMgr site with a nearby distribution point.

Eventually you will exit the testing phase. This is a good time to eat your own dog food. You should use ConfigMgr to deploy the reference image to a small set of PCs in IT and then increase the number gradually. You cannot expect someone to accept something that you will not do to your own machines.

DOG FOOD

You may wonder why we're talking about feeding a pet. Microsoft staff use the phrase "eating our own dog food" to describe how they test their products on themselves before releasing it to the public. This allows them to learn how to optimize the associated processes and to tweak the product.

You can apply this approach to your own production environment by applying an OSD solution to your own PCs. This method can be your first step outside of the test lab, where you can trial the solution in a real world environment. You can limit visibility and limit damage. If there are problems, you can return to the test lab to make the necessary changes. If all goes well, then you can publicize it to gain business confidence in your solution.

The PC ecosystem in a large enterprise is quite varied, no matter what controls you try to put in place. These variations can cause bugs that you do not expect. For example, BIOS issues could arise. If they do, that would be a perfect time to investigate whether the hardware manufacturer has an extension for ConfigMgr to upgrade the affected machines' firmware. The only way to detect these issues is to conduct a pilot. Try to involve a small set of IT-friendly power users from a variety of locations. You want them to be IT friendly because things might go wrong. Non- IT-friendly users will not react well to problems. If something does go wrong, then a power user will know to write down and communicate error messages, and they might even be able to help troubleshoot the issue.

If all goes well and you get approval from management, you will reach the point where you need to plan the deployment. ConfigMgr will be more than able to distribute a new operating system to every PC in the organization at once. But will your organization be able to handle that? You need to think of your colleagues in the help desk. You will communicate with users to let them know that a change is coming, but as you know few of these communication attempts receive much attention. Users who are confronted with a new and unexpected operating system when they walk in the following morning will be quick to call the help desk. Not everything will go as planned (some piece of software somewhere will slip through the cracks or some scanner with an odd driver will fail to load).

You should separate your deployment into manageable chunks. This strategy allows you to complete some basic training with users. The operating system can be deployed and the help desk will be able to handle the small increase in work. Once a team, site, department, or division is completed, you can move on to the next one.

Creating a Collection for Windows 7 Deployment

A collection or a set of collections must be created that will meet all of the following criteria:

◆ The collections must be suitable for your deployment strategy.

◆ All member machines do not run Windows 7.

◆ The hardware of the member machines meets the required specifications for running your applications and Windows 7.

The Microsoft Assessment and Planning Toolkit is one way of gathering this data. It could be used to generate a set of collections for an OSD.

Alternatively, you can use the data that is gathered by the ConfigMgr Hardware Inventory Client Agent to build a collection or collections. In this example you are going to create a collection where all machines that meet the following requirements will be targeted for deployment with the new reference image:

◆ The operating system is Windows XP.

◆ The CPU is faster than or equal to 1.8 GHz.

◆ The CPU is a 64-bit processor.

◆ The machine has 2 GB of RAM.

◆ The hard disk is at least 40 GB.

◆ The computer is a member of the HeadOffice Active Directory site.

You can accomplish this with a few minutes' work in the Configuration Manager Console.

1. Launch the New Collection Wizard by navigating into Collections and clicking on the New Collection action. Name the collection **Head Office Windows 7 Capable Systems** and click Next to progress to the Membership Rules screen.

2. Click the yellow database button on the right side to create a new query. This opens the Query Rules Properties dialog box shown in Figure 12.37. You can name the query (Head Office Windows 7 Capable Systems) and use the Limit To Collection option to limit this

query to members of the All Windows XP Systems collection. All members of this new collection must be running Windows XP. Click the Edit Query Statement button to generate the new query.

3. The Query Statement Properties dialog box opens. Select the Criteria tab to create a new part of the query statement. Clicking the button with a star icon will create a new criterion. This allows you to do a query from the database. Each criterion can be combined with other criteria using Boolean algebra. Clicking the Select button allows you to define the Where part of the statement. Clicking Operator allows you to say that something must be equal to a value, not equal to a value, greater than a value, and so on. You can either type in an explicit value or click the Value button to see values that have been collected by the installed ConfigMgr clients. Figure 12.38 shows a criterion where Processor - Max Clock Speed must be greater than or equal to 1800. That means only machines that meet this criterion can become a member of this collection. You can click OK and create more criteria that are combined with Boolean algebra.

FIGURE 12.37
Query Rule
Properties

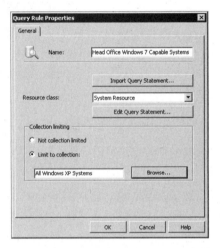

FIGURE 12.38
Defining a collection query statement criterion

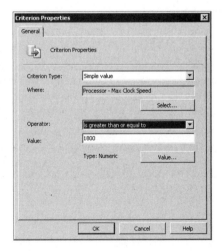

This tool allows you to build up quite a complex set of criteria for determining collection membership. An example that meets the criteria we just defined is shown in Figure 12.39.

You can see that there is an explicit statement in the criteria to exclude Windows 7 machines. A newly rebuilt Windows 7 machine may update its operating system status in a hardware audit when it boots up for the first time. But it will remain in the Windows XP collection until the Windows XP collection reruns its collection membership query (once a day by default). The Windows 7 exclusion will help to clean things up.

4. Click OK and continue through the New Collection Wizard. If you are doing lots of frequent deployments, then you might want to set the update the schedule for the collection to run more frequently than the default once per day. No results will appear in the collection until a membership update is done. You can select the collection, run the Update Collection Membership, and refresh the view to see the results.

FIGURE 12.39

The collection criteria for Windows 7 Deployment

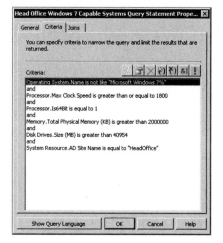

New Computers

How you deal with new bare-metal PCs depends on your network security policy:

Locked Down   If you only want to deploy the operating system image to known machines then you will need to create a computer association for every purchased machine and join it to a suitable collection. This will require some additional manual labor.

Password-Protected PXE Service Point   With this solution, a newly purchased computer will temporarily join the unknown the All Unknown Computers collection until the ConfigMgr client is installed and running and has fed enough details to ConfigMgr for other collections to update their membership according to their individual schedules. There is a single password on the PXE service point that will be controlled by IT staff and not shared with users. That way, all new builds of PCs must be initiated by IT or a trusted representative. The OSD advertisements must be linked to the All Unknown Computers collection.

Self-Service Provisioning The current trend in IT services is to empower users to help themselves as much as possible. Assuming that the PCs store no data and that there are no security issues, it should be possible for end users to boot a new PC using PXE and allow it to install the operating system. This means that a PC can be delivered straight to the desk and the end user can start work within a few minutes with no assistance from IT.

The lesson to take away is that the collections mechanism is very flexible. It allows you to create a Windows 7 deployment strategy that suits the needs and policies of your organization.

Deploying Windows 7

We have nearly reached the point where all the work you did to get ConfigMgr running and configured will reap a reward. It is time to see how to deploy Windows 7. Here are the required steps:

◆ Import the reference image WIM file to create a new operating system image. This package will be installed on distribution points.

◆ Create a new MDT settings package for an image deployment and install it on distribution points.

◆ Create a new task sequence to deploy the operating system image.

◆ Edit the task sequence.

◆ Advertise the task sequence to the required collection(s).

As before, we will be kind on the mouse and keyboard by allowing the task sequence wizard to create the new packages for us. Once the advertisement(s) are created, you can sit back and watch the status of your deployments in the reports that ConfigMgr creates.

Create a New Deployment Task Sequence

A new task sequence is required to deploy the reference image and use a new collection of MDT settings. As you will see, this task sequence will do a lot more work for us. In the real world, you might find that you will need a number of task sequences. This is because you can take a single reference image and perform a number of steps that might be unique to a team, department, site, or division in the organization.

1. As before, start the Create Microsoft Deployment Task Sequence Wizard from Task Sequences in the Configuration Manager Console. You will be using the Client Task Sequence template once again. Name the task sequence something like **Deploy Windows 7 Pro x64 Standard Image**.

2. On the Details screen (Figure 12.40) enter the name of the domain and the credentials for joining the new Windows 7 computer to the domain. This exercise will use the deploy\ configmgrjoin account that was given rights to join computer accounts to the domain.

3. Leave the Capture Settings screen with the default setting of "This task sequence will never be used to capture an image." This is because we do not want to run Sysprep on the resulting machine and create a reference image from it.

4. On the Boot Image screen, select the previously created boot image. You can select the Microsoft Deployment Toolkit 2010 package in the MDT package screen.

5. Figure 12.41 shows the OS Image screen. Here is where we will import the reference image WIM file to create a new OS image. Select Create A New OS Image. Enter the location and name of the file (`D:\Images\Windows 7 Pro x64.wim`) and the location where you wish to create a new package from it (`\\deploysrv\packages$\Images\Windows 7 Pro x64`).

FIGURE 12.40
Joining the
new computer to
the domain

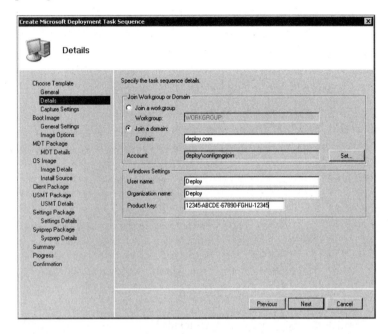

FIGURE 12.41
Creating a new
OS image

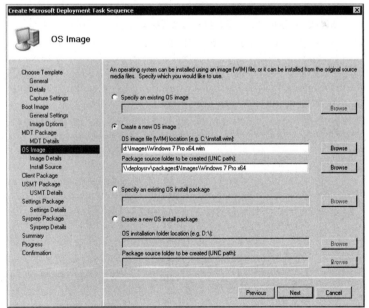

6. Name the image something descriptive in the following Image Details screen and give it a good description in the Comments box. Note that you can also perform this import action in the Configuration Manager Console in the OS Images folder in Operating System Deployment.

7. Select the existing ConfigMgr client package in the Client Package screen. You can also reuse the existing USMT package in the USMT Package screen.

    A new `CustomSettings.ini` file will be required to deploy your image, because the capture settings will be inappropriate. This gives you an opportunity to use a different unattended XML answer file for your deployment task sequence.

8. Create a new package (`\\deploysrv\packages$\Settings\Deploy Windows 7 Pro x64`) in the Settings Package screen, as shown in Figure 12.42.

FIGURE 12.42
Creating a deployment MDT settings package

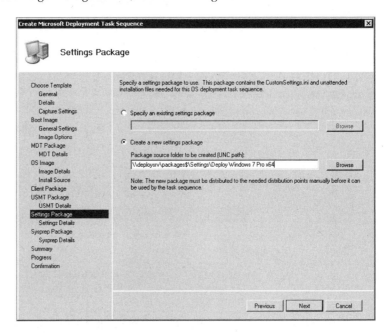

9. Name this package **Deploy Windows 7 Pro x64 Settings** in the Settings Details screen that follows.

    Once again, you will not require a Sysprep package. The task sequence will create the packages for you in the `\\deploysrv\packages$` share and the new task sequence will be created.

10. The `CustomSettings.ini` file in the MDT settings package (`D:\Packages\Settings\ Deploy Windows 7 Pro x64`) needs to be edited. Add the following settings to it:

```
[Settings]
Priority=Default
```

```
[Default]
DoCapture=NO
_SMSTSORGNAME=Deploy Inc. IT Department
```

Optionally, add the following line to the end of `CustomSettings.ini`:

```
MachineObjectOU=ou=computers,ou=deploy,dc=deploy,dc=com
```

This line will configure the domain join to create the computer account in the specified domain location. You should ensure that the join account (`deploy\configmgrjoin`) has the required permissions.

This is also your opportunity to edit the unattended installation XML file that is also contained within the package. You can alter how the Windows 7 image is installed.

11. Install these packages on the distribution point. You have to be careful:

   ◆ Do not install the packages on the PXE distribution point.

   ◆ The settings package will have to be updated on the distribution point after you install it. This is because of the previously mentioned potential of this package causing the task sequence to fail.

The task sequence is created and the packages are ready. Next you'll edit the task sequence to customize the installation of the image.

Edit the Deployment Task Sequence

The one-size-fits-all policy might apply to your reference image, but it most likely will not be the best approach when it comes to deployment task sequences. Your reference image is like a common denominator between all desktop and laptop computers in the organization. A task sequence that deploys that reference image can be varied depending on who or what it will be used to target. Some examples are as follows:

Kiosk-Like PCs   Some PCs, such as in a call center, might not have any user state or data on them. It is a waste of time to attempt to capture or restore a user state.

Executives   Rebuilding the PC of an executive or director using zero touch installation (or even manual) is a scary time. What happens if the build goes wrong? Have you anything you can quickly restore the machine to?

Specialization   You will find that some teams, departments, sites, or divisions have specific software that is licensed and used on all machines. It would be a requirement to quickly get that software onto the PC.

Having multiple task sequences allows you to do all of this and much more. You can then target each task sequence at the appropriate collection using an advertisement. You will edit the deployment task sequence (Deploy Windows 7 Pro x64 Standard Image) and make some changes.

By default, before an operating system is installed using the Client Task Sequence template, a backup is made of the existing installation. This backup would be very useful if you are performing an installation for users who are sensitive to downtime, such as executives. You can quickly recover the backup should something go wrong with the ZTI deployment. Would you really want to do this for every computer on the network? It would be time consuming and require a lot of storage space. Click the Options tab and check the Disable This Step check box (Figure 12.43) to prevent this task from running. The task will be grayed out when it is disabled.

FIGURE 12.43
Disabling a task sequence step

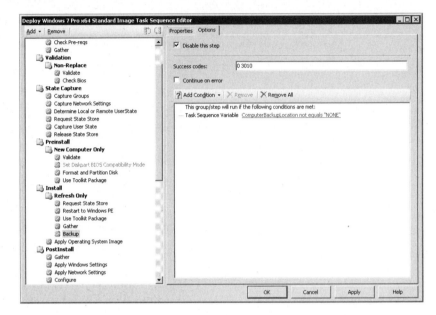

One of the most powerful security features of Windows 7 Ultimate and Enterprise editions is BitLocker. There is a task to enable and configure BitLocker (Figure 12.44) but it is disabled by default. Enable the Enable BitLocker step and configure it to match your organization's policies.

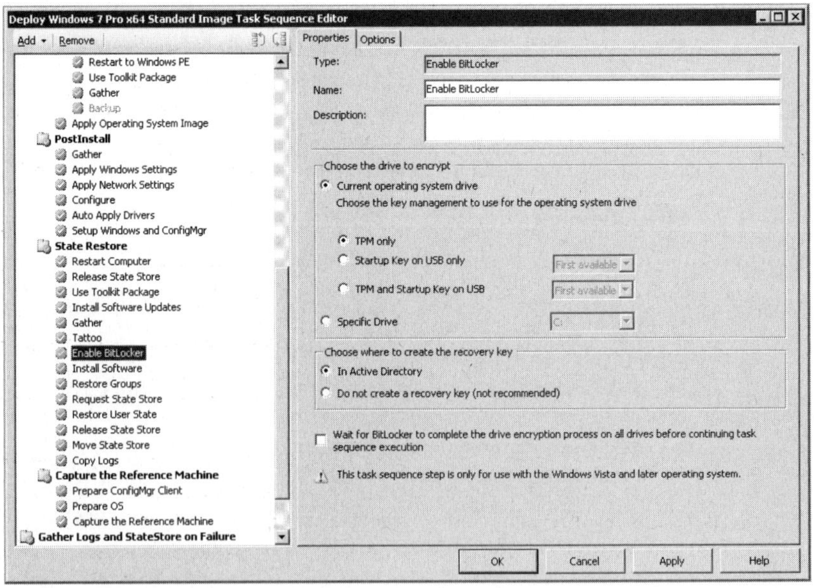

FIGURE 12.44
Enable and configure BitLocker

It is possible to force software to be installed onto the computer as a part of the task sequence. Normally, ConfigMgr will wait until the computer is built and the ConfigMgr client can evaluate policy to determine what software distribution advertisements apply to it.

The Install Software task, shown in Figure 12.45, allows you to pick a package and a program within that package to run. Doing so forces the software to install. Note that only programs with the "Allow this program to be installed from the Install Software task sequence without being advertised" setting will be able to run. Programs that do not allow execution without a user being logged in will not be visible in the Program selection box. This is because no one is logged into the PC when this task runs.

FIGURE 12.45
The Install
Software task

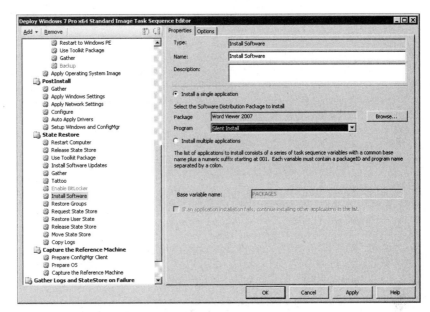

The easiest way to force more than one software distribution package to install is to add from Install Software tasks from the Add menu. Alternatively you can use the Base Variable Name in combination with Collection settings. You can learn more about this advanced technique at `http://blog.coretech.dk/confmgr07/software-distribution/installing-multiple-applications-using-variables/`.

COPY AN EXISTING TASK SEQUENCE

You can copy an existing task sequence to create a new one. Right-click on the source task sequence and select Duplicate. You can then customize the new copy.

You can add, configure, and disable tasks until you have a task sequence that meets the requirements for distributing the operating system reference image to the desired collection of PCs. You can then create more task sequences with different settings while still using the same reference image for other collections. When this is complete, it will be time to deploy the operating system.

Advertise for Bare-Metal Installation

As discussed previously, in a secure environment you can advertise the task sequence to a collection where the members are joined by computer association. This approach allows you to support many task sequences and many collections. This strategy requires more work to gather hardware information for new PCs, but it does allow a specialized PC to be quickly built.

Alternatively, if unknown computer support is enabled in the PXE service point, you can advertise a single task sequence to the All Unknown Computers collection. More traditional software distribution techniques can be used to install software once the computer is built. This approach requires no effort to gather information about new PCs but it does require more time to install software to specialize the PC beyond the single supported reference image.

SELF-SERVICE SOFTWARE PROVISIONING

Many organizations are turning to self-service software provisioning in the form of App-V, which is a part of the Microsoft Deployment Optimization Pack (MDOP). MDOP is an additional purchase that is available to Software Assurance customers. It allows applications to be sequenced into a virtualized package. Users can request an application, an optional approval process can be implemented to control license consumption, and the application is streamed to the user. App-V features integration with Configuration Manager.

A PC can now be built using PXE. This approach is suitable either for new machines or for machines where the operating system is broken beyond repair. A small amount of manual work is required to boot up the machine and enter the optional PXE service point password. Now it's time to move on to the fun part: zero touch installation.

Performing the Zero Touch Installation

This is the holy grail of OSD. If you have followed the exercises in this chapter, you are within grasping distance of it now. You will be able to deploy Windows 7 to hundreds or thousands of PCs without even leaving your desk. You can even do it at night when the PCs are turned off.

CONFIGURATION MANAGER WAKE ON LAN

Wake On LAN (WOL) is an Ethernet standard that allows a computer to be turned on or powered up over the network. This means you can schedule an advertisement for a time when some PCs might be powered down and ConfigMgr will wake them up to complete the work. You can learn more about WOL functionality in ConfigMgr at http://technet.microsoft.com/en-us/library/bb693668.aspx.

The process of deploying the Windows 7 reference image to an existing PC (whether it is XP, Vista, or Windows 7) is almost identical to the process of deploying it via PXE. An advertisement is created and associated with a collection. The only difference might be how the advertisement is scheduled. Normally, an advertisement that is used with existing computers will be scheduled to run at some point in the future.

You will advertise the deployment task sequence to the previously created Head Office Windows 7 Capable Systems collection. Start the New Advertisement Wizard for the task sequence (Figure 12.46). The collection that you wish to deploy Windows 7 to is selected. You will probably still want to select the option to allow the task sequence to be run from PXE and boot media. You never know what the future may hold. You might need to manually rebuild some computers at a later time if the operating system becomes unstable.

The Schedule screen (Figure 12.47) allows you to control exactly when an OSD will happen. Advertisement start time is when computers within the targeted collection will be able to start seeing the new task. A ConfigMgr client will become aware of the advertisement when it next refreshes its policy after this time.

FIGURE 12.46
The deployment
advertisement

FIGURE 12.47
The Schedule
screen

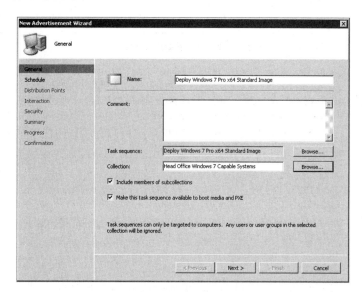

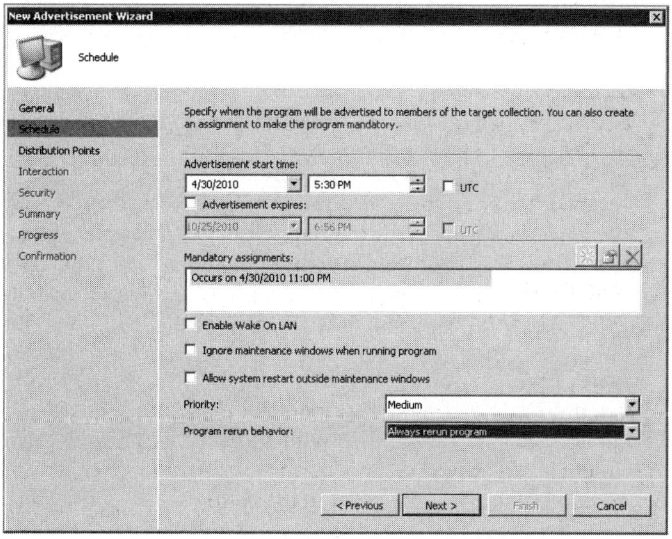

Advertisement Expires allows you to specify when computers will start to consider the advertisement to be not applicable anymore. You can think of it as like a use-by date on a carton of milk.

Mandatory assignments dictate when ConfigMgr clients will be forced to run the task sequence. They will have no option unless the date and time in the Advertisement Expires setting have been reached or passed.

You might want to use the As Soon As Possible option for your mandatory assignment if working in a lab.

The Program Rerun behavior is important to note. The default is Never Rerun Advertised Program. That means that once the program runs (even if it fails) on a computer, it will never run again. A new advertisement would be required to get the program to run on that computer again. You might want to consider the Always Rerun Program setting. This option allows help desk or possibly even end users to rebuild the PC via PXE using the advertisement if it breaks beyond repair.

You can move through the rest of the wizard and accept the default options unless otherwise directed by any deployment policies in your organization.

In the real world you will now sit back and relax. Nothing will usually happen for quite some time. In a lab, you will want to see things happen straight away.

You can force a ConfigMgr client to immediately look for new advertisements. To do this:

1. Open Control Panel.

2. Start the Configuration Manager item.

3. Click the Actions tab.

4. Select Machine Policy Retrieval & Evaluation Cycle.

The ConfigMgr client will now communicate with the ConfigMgr site server via the management point. Here it will learn of the new advertisement assuming that the advertisement start date and time has been reached. One of two things will now happen:

◆ *If the mandatory assignment date and time has been reached*: A warning will appear in the system notification area. It will let the user know that an advertised program will shortly start running. The user can force it to run straight away.

◆ *If the mandatory assignment date and time has not been reached*: A warning will appear in the system notification area. It will let the user know that an advertised program is available. The user can start Run Advertised Programs in the Control Panel to see if/when it will be forced to run. The user can also force the advertised program to run now if they choose.

The task sequence will run on the computer when the user starts the advertised program or when the mandatory date and time has been reached. If the PC is powered off at the time of the mandatory assignment, then it will run the advertised program when it powers up. But it will only do that if the assignment has not expired.

By default, a progress bar will appear to warn let the user know what is happening. After a while, the machine will complete its last reboot in the process and be waiting at the login prompt for the user to log in. Everything in the task sequence should be complete.

Monitoring Deployment Progress

It would be a very easy trap to think of zero touch installation as a fire-and-forget process. When you deploy an operating system to many critical business tools (end-user computers) at once, then you need to know exactly what is happening.

Configuration Manager has a rich set of reports (Reporting Point) that you can call upon to track the progress of any deployment. The Reporting Point can be accessed using your web browser at a URL that is based on the three-letter site code that you assigned when installing the ConfigMgr site server. For example, opening up `http://deploysrv.deploy.com/SMSReporting_DPL` (or `http://localhost/SMSReporting_DPL` when logged into the ConfigMgr server) will open up the window shown in Figure 12.48. The left pane contains report categories and individual reports that you can create. The Status summary of a specific task sequence advertisement report, found under Task Sequences - Advertisement Status, will allow you to monitor progress of a deployment. You can click the Values button on the right to select one of the advertisements and then click Display to open the report.

FIGURE 12.48
Configuration
Manager reports

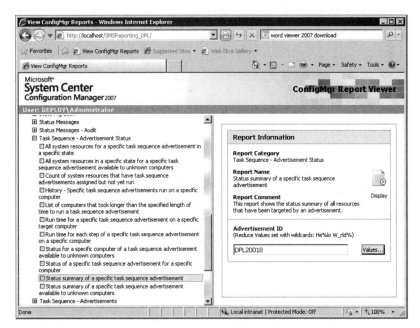

The report will open and give a summary of the status for the advertisement (Figure 12.49). Some clients might have no status, some might be running, some might be complete. The numbers of each status will be illustrated. The little arrow button on the left allows you to drill down. You can click on this to expand the report to see every computer with that status.

From there you can drill down into the detail of an individual computer (Figure 12.50). Normally you don't need to do this, but it will be useful for troubleshooting any deployments that fail or seem to be stuck at a specific point. An incredible amount of detail is available at this level to assist with identifying the cause of an issue.

FIGURE 12.49
Status summary of
the advertisement

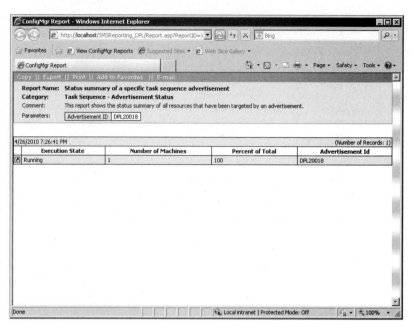

FIGURE 12.49
Status summary of
the advertisement

FIGURE 12.50
Detailed machine
progress

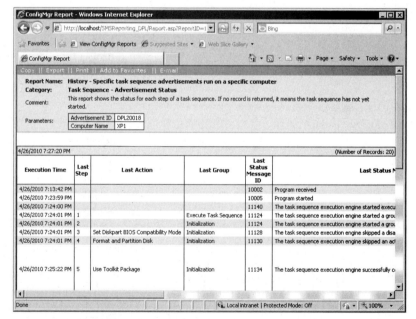

The status summary report will allow you to keep an eye on the deployment as time passes. You can then drill down into any computer that reports a problem, identify the cause, and remedy it. That will be a rare occasion if the process is well tested and planned.

ENABLING MULTICAST

ConfigMgr is capable of deploying a large operating system image to thousands of clients at once over the network. The bottleneck is the network. Enabling multicast allows many more clients to be targeted at once.

The distribution point must be installed on Windows Server 2008 or later. The WDS role must be enabled before multicast is enabled on the distribution point. IIS with ISAPI extensions and IIS 6 management compatibility must also be installed. The network and Windows firewalls must allow multicast UDP ports. ConfigMgr clients must be able to download content from the distribution point using BITS, HTTP, and HTTPS. Both Configuration Manager 2007 SP1 (or later) and Configuration Manager 2007 R2 (or later) must be installed.

Each of the following must be configured to use multicast:

◆ The distribution point

◆ The operating system image package

◆ The advertisement

You can learn more about enabling and using multicast in ConfigMgr at `http://technet.micro-soft.com/en-us/library/cc161973.aspx`.

Now you have the ultimate ability to deploy an operating system to many computers at once without leaving your desk and at a time that causes the least disruption to your end users. You can monitor the progress of the deployment using your reports. Imagine how impressed your boss will be when that Windows 7 deployment project ends early, with little disruption, and you hand over a ConfigMgr report to prove it.

The Bottom Line

Understand and set up Configuration Manager for OSD.   An understanding of how Configuration Manager works is required to plan even a small deployment.

> **Master It**   What are the functions of the management point, the distribution point, the software update point, and the PXE service point?

Capture customized images.   Configuration Manager allows you to create and capture a reference image that will be used for future deployment of Windows 7.

> **Master It**   A colleague reports to you that a prepared boot image fails to work. What are some of the possible causes?

Deploy Windows 7 using task sequences.   A reference image containing Windows 7 can be deployed with no human effort to many computers at once using a task sequence.

> **Master It**   A single generic Windows 7 OS install image has been created. It contains Microsoft Office, the usual utilities, and all of the latest security updates that are available. You are asked to prepare a deployment of Windows 7 for a department with 200 Windows XP computers. They will require two additional line-of-business applications and want the deployment to be as quick as possible.

Chapter 13

Taking Advantage of Volume Licensing

Volume licensing is often used in environments where multiple installations of the same product take place. When you employ volume licensing, you use a volume license key (VLK) to activate the product.

VLKs have been exploited by software pirates since their introduction. By using VLKs they found an easy way to distribute the software and have it activated as well. Each VLK is uniquely linked to the company which purchased it. Therefore, if that key is exploited, Microsoft could hold the company responsible and ultimately block the key from being used in the future.

With the launch of Windows Vista, Microsoft introduced technologies called the Software Protection Platform (SPP). These technologies help Microsoft identify counterfeit products and take appropriate actions against them. The SPP provides activation for new products and validates already activated products. Although the SPP has evolved since its introduction with Windows Vista, Microsoft and software pirates still play a cat and mouse game, where the software pirates crack an activation technology and Microsoft in turn introduces a new update for the SPP that neutralizes these workarounds.

With the release of Office 2010, Microsoft decided to also let activation of Office 2010 make use of the SPP technologies, and most likely other products will follow as well.

In this chapter, you will learn to:

◆ Decide which volume license key type to use

◆ Deploy, maintain, and troubleshoot a Key Management Service (KMS) infrastructure

◆ Centrally manage licenses throughout your organization

Choosing the Right Volume License Key for Windows

With the release of Windows Vista, Microsoft introduced two new license key types for Volume License customers: Key Management Service (KMS) and Multiple Activation Key (MAK). Because you can use both KMS and MAK in your environment, you need to understand how both keys work.

When you want to decide which license key to use for your Windows, you have to answer two main questions:

◆ Which products am I going to deploy?

◆ Which activation method am I going to use?

For Windows, license keys are organized in product groupings and generations. There are four product groupings that cover all the Windows client and Windows Server operating systems. One grouping is for the client editions; the other three cover the server editions. Currently there are two generations, the Vista/Windows Server 2008 generation and the Windows 7/Windows Server 2008 R2 generation. Table 13.1 gives an overview of the product groupings and generations for the Windows operating system.

TABLE 13.1: Volume License product groupings and generations

VOLUME LICENSE PRODUCT KEY GROUP	GENERATION: WINDOWS 7 AND WINDOWS SERVER 2008 R2	GENERATION: WINDOWS VISTA AND WINDOWS SERVER 2008
Windows Client VL	Windows 7 Professional	Windows Vista Business
	Windows 7 Enterprise	Windows Vista Enterprise
Server Group A	Windows Web Server 2008 R2	Windows Web Server 2008
	Windows Server 2008 R2 HPC Edition	Windows HPC Server 2008
	Windows HPC Server 2008 R2	Windows Client VL
	Windows Client VL	
Server Group B	Windows Server 2008 R2 Standard	Windows Server 2008 Standard
	Windows Server 2008 R2 Enterprise	Windows Server 2008 Enterprise
	Systems from Server Group A	Systems from Server Group A
	Windows Client VL	Windows Client VL
Server Group C	Windows Server 2008 R2 Datacenter	Windows Server 2008 Datacenter
	Windows Server 2008 R2 for Itanium-based systems	Windows Server 2008 for Itanium-based systems
	Systems from Server Group B	Systems from Server Group B
	Systems from Server Group A	Systems from Server Group A
	Windows Client VL	Windows Client VL

Volume License customers will receive a key for each product grouping, corresponding to the products that they are entitled to use based on their Volume License agreement. If a customer is entitled to use all Windows operating systems, the customer should see eight available Windows keys. The keys can be retrieved from the Microsoft Volume Licensing Service Center website at:

`www.microsoft.com/licensing/servicecenter/home.aspx`

DATACENTER LICENSES

If your environment has a Windows Server 2008 R2 datacenter license, you can use this key on your KMS host to activate all the Windows versions that are lower in version and generation—even Windows Vista and Windows Server 2008, because those operating systems belong to an earlier generation.

Deciding to use KMS, MAK, or a combination of these methods mainly depends on the type of environment and the number of systems for which you want to use product activation. As a best practice, always try to go for the KMS solution, because it's the solution that puts you in control of your volume licensing. However, in some scenarios the KMS solution isn't suitable and you must use MAK activation.

There are a few questions that need to be answered in order to determine the best activation method:

How many clients am I going to activate?   The KMS activation method only works when the activation threshold is reached. For the client OS the threshold is 25 and for the server OS it's 5. If the activation threshold cannot be reached, you must use the MAK activation method.

For example, if you have 3 servers and 3 clients, you will be able to activate the server OS because the activation count is greater than 5, but you will not be able to activate the client OS because the threshold is below 25.

Note that with the latest version of the KMS software there is no longer the requirement that the to-be-activated OS must be physical in order to count for the activation count limit.

How much risk to product key exposure do I want to take?   When you're using MAK activation, a unique product key for your organization is used to activate each product individually. This key could potentially be extracted by one of the many product extraction utilities circulating across the Internet and be used to activate other installations of the same product but not owned by the company. When using KMS, the product key that is used on the to-be-activated client is a generic one that is publicly known and indicates to the client that it should use a KMS infrastructure for its activation. The product key unique for your organization can only be found on the KMS server.

How often do my clients connect to the corporate network?   When using KMS for product activation, the clients using KMS try to contact the KMS host every 7 days; if after 180 days this attempt is still unsuccessful, the client will go into reduced functionality mode (RFM), which we will explore later in this chapter. When using MAK, clients connect to the Microsoft activation services over the Web directly or by using a Volume Activation Management Tool (VAMT) proxy scenario.

Does the environment that hosts my clients have Internet access?   When your environment doesn't have any Internet access and the number of clients is above the KMS activation threshold, you should use KMS in order to activate your clients. If the KMS activation threshold can't be reached, the MAK proxy scenario provided by the VAMT can help you activate your MAK clients. Or you could use MAK activation by phone. If your environment provides Internet access, you can use either method for activation.

As mentioned earlier, there's also a hybrid solution using both KMS and MAK. You could, for example, choose to use MAK activation for clients that aren't connected to the internal network within the required time frame, while using KMS for clients that are located within your internal network.

Microsoft developed the VAMT to help you activate clients centrally; while the first version could only help you activate KMS clients, version 2 can also help you configure KMS clients. The VAMT will be described in more detail in the section "Tracking Your Licenses: The Volume Activation Management Tool" later in this chapter.

OFFICE 2010 USES SPP

With the release of Microsoft Office 2010, Microsoft announced that Office 2010 will use the SPP as its activation method. This means that both MAK and KMS are available as activation methods for Microsoft Office 2010, Microsoft Project 2010, and Microsoft Visio 2010 as well. When using a KMS server, you have to extend that server with an update to support activation of Office 2010. The Office KMS server can run beside the KMS server you already have for your Windows Activation.

Tracking Your Licenses with the Key Management Service

The Key Management Service is a service that is installed on top of the Windows Server or Client. KMS is responsible for activating clients. In this section you will learn what the KMS host does and how to install it.

Learning the KMS Process

Each client that attempts to activate with a KMS host is given a client machine identification (CMID) designation. The CMID is stored on both the KMS host and the KMS client, and each CMID counts for the activation threshold. Activated clients attempt to contact the KMS host every seven days by default; if this attempt fails, the client will retry every 2 hours by default. If an activated client cannot contact the KMS host within 180 days, it will deactivate and go into reduced functionality mode.

The KMS host caches twice the amount of CMIDs that are required by the KMS clients in order to prevent the CMID count from dropping below the activation threshold unexpectedly. The KMS host will decrement its activation counter by 1 when a client doesn't contact the KMS host within 30 days.

MIND THE ACTIVATION THRESHOLD

Suppose you have activated six server OSes and 20 client OSes, which leads to an activation count of 26.

Now, if four of the clients OSes don't contact the KMS host within 30 days of their last contact, the activation count will drop below 25 (which is the threshold for client activation).

As long as activation count stays below 25, this will result in a potential situation where all registered and activated client OSes will revert to not activated after 180 days. Also, no more new clients will be activated until the threshold is above 25.

The server OSes will remain activated though, because the servers are still above their activation threshold.

Systems that use KMS as their activation method find the KMS host using Domain Name System (DNS) and its Service (SRV) Resource Records (RR) functionality.

For scalability, you have the option to install multiple KMS hosts in your environment. By using DNS priority and weight parameters, you can control how clients connect to the KMS hosts; this technique works for Windows 7 and Windows Server 2008 R2 clients only, though. Windows Vista and Windows Server 2008 clients just pick a KMS host returned from the DNS query. KMS hosts do not coordinate with each other; they are stand-alone systems. Therefore, it is important that you design your KMS infrastructure with caution.

Choosing Your KMS Host

Before you can install your KMS host, you must first decide on which platform you are going to install your KMS. Choosing the KMS host platform depends on the type of KMS product key group you have available. When choosing the KMS host system, you must consider the operating system editions that will be activated with KMS. A KMS that is hosted on Windows 7 can only activate client operating systems, but a KMS that is hosted on Windows Server 2008 R2 Enterprise can activate both client and server computers. You must have a corresponding KMS key to activate Windows Server 2008 R2 Enterprise in the first place.

Table 13.2 provides an overview of the KMS host OS that should be used depending on the type of clients you want to activate.

TABLE 13.2: KMS host OS by Windows Edition

WINDOWS PRODUCT EDITIONS ACTIVATED BY KMS	KMS SHOULD BE INSTALLED ON
Windows 7 Professional	Windows Vista
Windows 7 Enterprise	Windows 7
Windows Vista Business	KMS for Windows Server 2003 v1.2
Windows Vista Enterprise	
Products above and	KMS for Windows Server 2003 v1.2
Windows Web Server 2008 R2	Windows Web Server 2008
Windows Web Server 2008	Windows Web Server 2008 R2
Windows HPC Server 2008 R2	Windows HPC Server 2008
Windows HPC Server 2008	Windows HPC Server 2008 R2
Products above and	Windows Server 2008 R2 Standard
Windows Server 2008 R2 Standard	Windows Server 2008 R2 Enterprise
Windows Server 2008 R2 Enterprise	Windows Server 2008 Standard
Windows Server 2008 Standard	Windows Server 2008 Enterprise
Windows Server 2008 Enterprise	
Products above and	Windows Server 2008 R2 Datacenter
Windows Server 2008 R2 Datacenter	Windows Server 2008 Datacenter
Windows Server 2008 Datacenter	Windows Server 2008 for itanium-based systems
Windows Server 2008 for itanium-based systems	

ACTIVATING WINDOWS 7 CLIENTS ONLY

When you only want to activate Windows 7 clients using KMS, keep in mind that you cannot use Windows Server 2008 or Windows Server 2008 R2 as your KMS host.

Selecting the KMS Host Manually

When DNS is not available for KMS host assignment, you can assign a KMS host to KMS clients by using KMS host caching. When you assign a KMS host manually, you disable auto-discovery of KMS. A KMS host is manually assigned to a KMS client by running this command:

```
slmgr.vbs /skms <value>:<port>
```

where *value* is the KMS host's fully qualified domain name (FQDN), the KMS host's IPv4 address, or the KMS host's NetBIOS name. The *port* is the TCP port used by the KMS host.

Installing and Initializing KMS

Depending on which version of the OS you want to install the KMS functionality, you may have to download software from the Internet. The latest KMS version, 1.2, is already included with Windows 7 and Windows Server 2008 R2. For Windows Vista, Windows Server 2003, and Windows Server 2008, you should check for an update available that updates the KMS functionality to at least version 1.2.

To enable the KMS functionality, you should first install a KMS key on the KMS host using the Windows Software Licensing Management tool. In order to do this you should supply the VLK with the highest authority that you have available, so you know for sure that the KMS can service all the OS types it needs to activate.

1. Use an elevated command prompt to install the KMS key:

   ```
   slmgr.vbs /ipk <Kms Key>
   ```

   This will install the Software Protection Service on your KMS host.

2. After the KMS key is installed, activate the host over the Internet or by phone. To activate online, use:

   ```
   slmgr.vbs /ato
   ```

   To display the Installation ID to activate over the phone, use:

   ```
   slmgr.vbs /dti
   ```

   To determine the number you should call to activate your KMS, enter the following command:

   ```
   slui.exe 4
   ```

   The output of this command will provide you with a window which asks you in which country you reside and will provide you with the various options to activate using a phone.

3. After the host is activated, restart the Software Protection Service. Your KMS host is now ready to activate clients. ·

When you're installing a KMS host key on Windows 7 or Windows Server 2008 R2 using the UI, a warning message will appear. The warning is designed to prevent you from accidentally installing KMS keys on computers that you do not intend to be KMS. You can verify that the KMS host is working correctly by checking the KMS count and determining if it is increasing as you add more KMS clients.

In a Windows command prompt window on the KMS host, enter the following:

```
slmgr.vbs /dli
```

This command will display the current KMS count (Figure 13.1).

FIGURE 13.1
Detailed license information

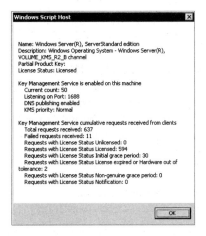

If you want even more information, you can use the /dlv option, which will give you verbose output. You can also check the Key Management Service event log for event ID 12290. This event displays the name of the computer and the timestamp of the activation request.

Configuring DNS to Let KMS Clients Find the KMS Server

If your network environment has Dynamic Domain Name System (DDNS) and allows computers to publish services automatically, deploying a KMS will automatically create the needed service resource records in DNS. If the organization has more than one KMS host or the network does not support DDNS, additional configuration tasks may be necessary.

You can verify whether the automatic creation succeeded by performing the following query targeting your DNS server:

```
NSLOOKUP -type=SRV _VLMCS._TCP
```

Your output should look similar to this:

```
Server:   dns01.domain.local
Address:  192.168.0.1
_vlmcs._tcp.domain.local    SRV service location:
          priority      = 0
```

```
            weight       = 0
            port         = 1688
            svr hostname = kms.domain.local
kms.domain.local  internet address = 192.168.0.2
```

If your environment does not support DDNS, you must either manually create your Service Resource Records (SRV RRs) in order to publish the KMS host, or you must point all your clients to the KMS server manually. To avoid failed DNS publishing events in your event log, you should also disable auto-publishing using the `slmgr.vbs /cdns` command-line option.

Manually created SRV RRs can coexist with SRV RRs that KMS hosts automatically publish in other domains for which DDNS is available. However, you must maintain all records to prevent conflicts and incidents.

Use the following settings on your DNS server if it doesn't support DDNS:

Service: _VLMCS

Protocol: _TCP

Port number: 1688

Service host: FQDN of KMS host

If your organization uses a non-Microsoft DNS server, the needed SRV RRs can be created as long as the DNS server is compliant with Berkeley Internet Name Domain (BIND) 8.2 or higher. Consider authorizing your KMS server so that it can perform RR updates. If this isn't possible, you should use the following parameters to register the service manually:

Name: _vlmcs._tcp

Type: SRV

Priority: 0 (or other priority value)

Weight: 0 (or other weight value)

Port: 1688

Hostname: FQDN of KMS host

Using Multiple Key Management Servers in Your Environment

By default, KMS clients query DNS for KMS service information. The first time a KMS client queries DNS for KMS service information, it chooses a KMS host from the list of SRV RRs that DNS returns. If the client is Vista or Server 2008, the KMS host is picked randomly, and if the client is Windows 7 or Windows Server 2008 R2, the priority and weight parameter provided in the DNS record are taken into account. Establishing KMS host priority groupings and weighting within each group allows you to specify which KMS host the clients should try first and balances traffic among multiple KMS hosts.

You can add priority and grouping under the `DnsDomainPublishList` Registry key, which you can find under:

```
HKEY_LOCAL_MACHINE\Software\Microsoft\Windows NT\CurrentVersion\
SoftwareProtectionPlatform
```

If the KMS host that a client selects does not respond, the KMS client removes that KMS host from its list of SRV RRs and randomly selects another KMS host from the list. When a KMS host responds, the KMS client caches the name of the KMS host and uses it for subsequent activation and renewal attempts. If the cached KMS host does not respond on a subsequent renewal, the KMS client discovers a new KMS host by querying DNS for KMS SRV RRs.

CONFIGURING DNS IN A MULTIPLE-DOMAIN SITUATION

By default, the KMS host registers itself in the DNS domain to which it belongs. If there are more than one DNS domain names in which the KMS host must be registered, a list of DNS domains can be created for a KMS host to use when publishing its SRV RR. To automatically let KMS publish its SRV RRs in multiple DNS domains, take the following steps:

1. Add each DNS domain suffix to the following multistring Registry value:

   `DnsDomainPublishList in HKEY_LOCAL_MACHINE\SOFTWARE\Microsoft\Windows NT\ CurrentVersion\SoftwareProtectionPlatform`

2. After changing the value, restart the Software Licensing Service, after which the KMS host will create the SRV RRs. Note that this key has changed from the original location in Windows Vista and Windows Server 2008, where the location was `HKEY_LOCAL_MACHINE\ SOFTWARE\Microsoft\Windows NT\CurrentVersion\SL`.

3. To verify that the procedure has been successful, check the Application event log on the corresponding KMS host. Event ID 12294 will be displayed when the KMS host has successfully created the SRV RRs; Event ID 12293 will be displayed when the process is unsuccessful.

Uninstalling KMS

When you want to decommission your KMS server or migrate the KMS functionality, you have to uninstall your KMS. To do so, take the following steps:

1. Uninstall the KMS host key by running the following command:

   `slmgr /upk`

2. Install the default KMS or your MAK by running the following command:

   `slmgr /ipk [KMS Client or MAK]`

3. Delete the necessary records from your DNS, or wait for DNS scavenging to delete the record for you.

Troubleshooting the KMS and the KMS Client

When troubleshooting KMS host and KMS client activation problems, you should start checking the Windows event log for KMS-related errors. The errors are displayed by error codes, but by using the Windows Activation Client tool, `slui.exe`, you can translate them back to understandable error messages. The following syntax shows how to use `slui.exe` to translate an error code back to an understandable error message:

```
slui.exe 0x2a <Error Code>
```

For example, using `SLUI.exe 0x2A 0xC004C008` launches the dialog box shown in Figure 13.2.

FIGURE 13.2
Windows Activation Client error code help

You can now use this error message to further troubleshoot your problem, by using it as a search term in your favorite search engine, for example. You can also use the VAMT to help you troubleshoot activation errors, because it provides you with detailed information about activation status.

Configuring KMS for Activation of Office 2010

Before you can extend your KMS server to also support activation of Office 2010 clients, you'll need to install the Microsoft Office 2010 KMS host license pack and your KMS server must already be the latest version—which is also a prerequisite in order to activate Windows 7 and Windows Server 2008 R2.

The Microsoft Office 2010 KMS Host License Pack consists of an executable called `KeyManagementServiceHost.exe`. When running the `KeyManagementServiceHost.exe` file, the KMS server functionality will be extended by installing the host license files so that activation of Microsoft Office 2010 will be possible. The KeyManagementServiceHost installer will also ask you to supply your Microsoft Office 2010 KMS host product key, so that the KMS server can start to activate Office 2010 products. The activation count threshold for Office 2010 is 5.

You can verify whether the Office 2010 KMS instance is working correctly by using the `slmgr .vbs` script. The only difference compared to using `slmgr.vbs` on a normal KMS instance is that you now have to provide the Activation ID (which is bfe7a195-4f8f-4f0b-a622-cf13c7d16864). The following command shows detailed license information for the Office 2010 KMS instance:

```
slmgr.vbs /dlv bfe7a195-4f8f-4f0b-a622-cf13c7d16864
```

Look for the License Status line in the output of this command and check that it states `Licensed`.

Microsoft Office 2010 Professional is by default equipped with a KMS key, so if the KMS server and DNS are set up correctly, any Microsoft Office 2010 professional installation will be able to find the KMS server and activate.

Monitoring the KMS Servers

So that you can monitor your KMS servers, Microsoft provides management packs for Microsoft Operations Manager (MOM) 2005 and System Center Operations Manager (SCOM) 2007. These management packs constantly monitor your KMS services and report problems to the centralized Operations Manager console; then you can take action.

The Key Management Service management pack monitors the status of the KMS service running on the KMS host. It can monitor DNS publishing and as well as Low Activation Count. Informational, warning, or critical alerts appear in SCOM.

Using Asset Intelligence Reports in SCCM 2007

System Center Configuration Manager provides the ability to report on client access licenses (CALs) using its Asset Intelligence feature. Before you can enable CAL data collection, you must make some changes in your environment:

◆ You must enable success logon event logging using Group Policy on all clients for which you want to receive CAL status.

◆ You must extend the `configuration.mof` file so that the corresponding WMI data classes will be inventoried.

At this point, the CAL reports can be run using the reporting functionality within System Center Configuration Manager.

KMS and the Client

In this section we will go into more detail on aspects of licensing from a client perspective. You can obtain licenses for Windows Vista, Windows 7, Server 2008, and Server 2008 R2 through three channels: retail, original equipment manufacturer (OEM), or volume licensing. Each channel has its own unique methods of activation. Organizations are free to choose how they obtain their operating systems, and based on that, they can choose among various activation methods.

Retail Windows Vista and Windows 7 products that are sold online, in a store from resellers or retailers, or from Microsoft are individually licensed. This means that each purchased copy comes with its own unique product key, which appears on the Certificate of Authenticity (COA) on the product packaging. When users start their computer for the first time, they can activate the product by entering the product key displayed on this COA, or by using the Active Windows option in the Control panel. This should be done within 30 days after the installation, the so-called grace period.

Original Equipment Manufacturers (OEMs) Most OEMs provide systems with an operating system installed. By associating the operating system with information in the BIOS of the computer, activation can take place. This is done before the computer is sent to the customer so that no additional activation actions are required by the user. This method of activation is known as OEM activation. OEM activation stays valid as long as the customer uses the OEM-provided image on that specific system.

OEM activation is a onetime activation that associates Windows with the firmware (BIOS) of a computer; this is called System Locked Preinstallation (SLP). The information is stored as a Windows marker in the ACPI_SLIC table of the BIOS, which will associate the computer with a specific installation type of the manufacturer. Reinstallation can only occur using the recovery media provided by the OEM.

Volume Activation   The Enterprise and Business versions of the Windows client and all the Windows server editions can be activated using Volume Activation. Volume Activation uses either KMS or MAK as an activation method, which we described earlier in this chapter.

Using a KMS Client Key and MAK During OS Installation

Clients using KMS employ a KMS client key. KMS client keys are publicly available and known. You can find those keys in the `pid.txt` file in the sources folder on your installation media and on TechNet. When you are automatically deploying clients in your environment and you want to use KMS for activation, you should use KMS client keys as the product key. Table 13.3 presents the operating systems and corresponding product keys.

TABLE 13.3:   KMS client keys

OPERATING SYSTEM EDITION	PRODUCT KEY
Windows 7 Professional	FJ82H-XT6CR-J8D7P-XQJJ2-GPDD4
Windows 7 Professional N	MRPKT-YTG23-K7D7T-X2JMM-QY7MG
Windows 7 Professional E	W82YF-2Q76Y-63HXB-FGJG9-GF7QX
Windows 7 Enterprise	33PXH-7Y6KF-2VJC9-XBBR8-HVTHH
Windows 7 Enterprise N	YDRBP-3D83W-TY26F-D46B2-XCKRJ
Windows 7 Enterprise E	C29WB-22CC8-VJ326-GHFJW-H9DH4
Windows Server 2008 R2 Web	6TPJF-RBVHG-WBW2R-86QPH-6RTM4
Windows Server 2008 R2 HPC edition	FKJQ8-TMCVP-FRMR7-4WR42-3JCD7
Windows Server 2008 R2 Standard	YC6KT-GKW9T-YTKYR-T4X34-R7VHC
Windows Server 2008 R2 Enterprise	489J6-VHDMP-X63PK-3K798-CPX3Y
Windows Server 2008 R2 Datacenter	74YFP-3QFB3-KQT8W-PMXWJ-7M648
Windows Server 2008 R2 for Itanium-based Systems	GT63C-RJFQ3-4GMB6-BRFB9-CB83V
Windows Vista Business	YFKBB-PQJJV-G996G-VWGXY-2V3X8
Windows Vista Business N	HMBQG-8H2RH-C77VX-27R82-VMQBT
Windows Vista Enterprise	VKK3X-68KWM-X2YGT-QR4M6-4BWMV

TABLE 13.3: KMS client keys *(CONTINUED)*

OPERATING SYSTEM EDITION	PRODUCT KEY
Windows Vista Enterprise N	VTC42-BM838-43QHV-84HX6-XJXKV
Windows Web Server 2008	WYR28-R7TFJ-3X2YQ-YCY4H-M249D
Windows Server 2008 Standard	TM24T-X9RMF-VWXK6-X8JC9-BFGM2
Windows Server 2008 Standard without Hyper-V	W7VD6-7JFBR-RX26B-YKQ3Y-6FFFJ
Windows Server 2008 Enterprise	YQGMW-MPWTJ-34KDK-48M3W-X4Q6V
Windows Server 2008 Enterprise without Hyper-V	39BXF-X8Q23-P2WWT-38T2F-G3FPG
Windows Server 2008 HPC	RCTX3-KWVHP-BR6TB-RB6DM-6X7HP
Windows Server 2008 Datacenter	7M67G-PC374-GR742-YH8V4-TCBY3
Windows Server 2008 Datacenter without Hyper-V	22XQ2-VRXRG-P8D42-K34TD-G3QQC

KMS KEYS VS. KMS CLIENT KEYS

Keep in mind that there is a difference between *KMS keys* and *KMS client keys*. The KMS key is the key you use to active your KMS and is unique for your Volume License agreement, whereas the KMS client key is publicly known and tells your client to use KMS for activation.

When you are using MAK during OS installation, the MAK key is added to the specialize pass in the unattended.xml file. The MAK key is stored in clear text, which is a requirement of the setup process. At the end of the installation, the MAK key is removed from the unattended.xml in order to avoid misuse.

Changing the Client License Type After Installation

You will have different usage rights depending on the channel you used to purchase your product. In general, converting an OEM-licensed product to volume licensing is prohibited, although exceptions exist.

CONVERTING RETAIL AND OEM EDITIONS TO VOLUME LICENSING

You are allowed to change an OEM installation to a Volume License installation if Software Assurance (SA) is purchased within 90 days after purchasing the OEM product. This exception applies only to Windows 7 or Windows Server 2008 R2, though.

Another exception is if the OEM product is the same product for which a Volume License agreement already is available. Volume License customers have reimaging rights and may be eligible to upgrade an OEM installation using Volume License media.

Retail and OEM editions of Windows 7 Professional and Server 2008 R2 can be changed to KMS or MAK clients. To change Windows 7 Professional and all editions of Windows Server 2008 R2 from retail to a KMS client, skip the Product Key page and when installation is complete, open an elevated command prompt window and type:

```
Slmgr.vbs /ipk <SetupKey>
```

where *<SetupKey>* is the KMS client key or MAK that corresponds to the edition of Windows 7 or Windows Server 2008 R2.

CONVERTING MAK CLIENTS TO KMS AND KMS CLIENTS TO MAK

By default, Windows 7 and Windows Server 2008 R2 operating systems use KMS for activation. To change existing KMS clients to MAK clients, you must install a MAK key. Similarly, to change MAK clients to KMS clients, run:

```
slmgr.vbs /ipk <KMS Client Key>
```

where *<KMS Client Key>* is one of the setup keys shown in Table 13.3. After installing the KMS setup key, you must activate the KMS client by running:

```
slmgr.vbs /ato
```

Postponing Activation

There are several scenarios in which you want to postpone activation, such as when you are testing functionality of the operating system or applications running on top of the operating system for a certain amount of time. Also, when building your corporate image you can run into a situation where you want to postpone activation.

POSTPONING ACTIVATION USING REARM

If you are not able to activate your Windows installation within 30 days on clients or 60 days on servers, you have the option to reset the initial grace period (a process known as *rearming*). For both client and server, you have the ability to do this three times, which means that you have 120 days on clients or 240 days on servers before you need to activate your systems. This extra time gives you some breathing space when you are setting up your environment.

When building reference images used for mass deployment, take these rearm restrictions into account as well, because running the `sysprep /generalize` option (discussed earlier chapters in this book) counts as one rearm. So when building your Windows image, keep in mind that you can use `sysprep /generalize` only three times in the life cycle of your Windows image. When you activate with KMS, though, your rearm count is increased by one each time you activate using KMS; this gives you some additional options to create your reference image.

REARMING OFFICE 2010

If you deploy Office 2010 within your image, the grace period for Office 2010 will probably begin right away. Therefore, it's possible to rearm the Office 2010 installation for 30 days so that you have some time to do activation. To rearm Office 2010, you should use the `Ospprearm.exe` file, which can be found in the `\<Program Files>\Common Files\Microsoft Shared\ OfficeSoftwareProtectionPlatform` folder. You can rearm Office 2010 five times.

WORKING WITH REDUCED FUNCTIONALITY MODE

If you fail to activate immediately after the operating system is installed, the OS still provides the full functionality of the operating system for a limited amount of time, or grace period. The length of the grace period is 30 days for a client OS and 60 days for a server OS and can be extended three times (except for Windows Vista Enterprise SP1, which can be rearmed up to five times). After the grace period expires, the OS reminds the user to activate by displaying notifications to activate the computer. This is called Notification mode.

During the initial grace period, periodic notifications that the computer requires activation are displayed. During the logon process, a notification appears to remind the user to activate the operating system and continues until there are three days left in the grace period. For the first two of the final three days, the notification appears every four hours. During the final day of the grace period, the notification appears every hour, on the hour.

After the initial grace period expires or activation fails, Windows continues to notify users that the operating system requires activation. Until the operating system is activated or rearmed, reminders that the computer must be activated appear in several places throughout the product.

After a user logs on, the user is presented with notification dialog boxes asking the user to activate. Notifications appear at the bottom of the screen above the notification area. A persistent desktop notification remains with a black desktop background (Figure 13.3). A reminder might appear when users open certain Windows applications.

FIGURE 13.3
Nongenuine desktop notification

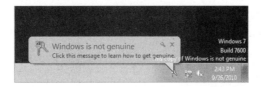

When significant hardware changes take place, a machine may fall Out-Of-Tolerance (OOT), which requires that it be reactivated. At that point, the machine reenters a grace period of 30 days.

Recovering from a Nongenuine State

When a KMS or MAK key is lost or exploited heavily, the key can be marked nongenuine by Microsoft and from that point on becomes invalid for activation.

When evidence of system tampering is detected, the system goes into a nongenuine state. If the computer has altered system files, the best way to recover is to initiate a system file check by using `sfc /scannow` or by reinstalling the operating system. If a KMS host is marked nongenuine because of a compromised product key, replace the KMS key on all KMS hosts configured with that specific key, using the VAMT for example. You should then force reactivation of the KMS clients by running `slmgr.vbs /ato`, or you could just allow the clients to reactivate according to their activation renewal schedule.

If the original key is compromised on a MAK-activated computer, install a new MAK key and reactivate. You can do this on each computer individually or by using the VAMT.

Before a computer can recover from a validation failure, you must first determine why the computer failed validation and then take appropriate recovery steps. When troubleshooting activation, examine the Application event log. The reason for the validation failure is listed in event ID 8209.

Understanding the Windows Software Licensing Management Tool

In Windows Vista and higher, `slmgr.vbs` is provided with the OS. The Windows Software Licensing Management (SLMGR) tool covers all aspects of client activation; it's used to install the KMS host but can also be used to configure clients.

By starting `slmgr.vbs` without any parameters, you are provided with five screens presenting all the options that the `slmgr.vbs` script has to offer. The options are detailed in Table 13.4.

TABLE 13.4:   `slmgr.vbs` options

GENERAL OPTIONS	DESCRIPTION
`/ipk<Product Key>`	Installs the product key (replaces the existing key).
`/ato [Activation ID]`	Activates Windows.
`/dli [Activation ID	All]`	Displays license information (default is the current license).
`/dlv [Activation ID	All]`	Displays detailed license information (default is the current license).
`/xpr [Activation ID]`	Expiration date for the current license state.

ADVANCED OPTIONS	DESCRIPTION
`/cpky`	Clears product key from the Registry (prevents disclosure attacks).
`/ilc <License file>`	Installs the license.
`/rilc`	Reinstalls system license files.
`/rearm`	Resets the licensing status of the machine.
`/upk [Activation ID]`	Uninstalls the product key.
`/dti [Activation ID]`	Displays the installation ID for offline activation.
`/atp <Confirmation ID> [Activation ID]`	Activates the product with the user-provided confirmation ID.

KMS CLIENT OPTIONS	DESCRIPTION
`/skms <Name[:Port]	: port>` `[Activation ID] [Activation ID]`	Sets the name and/or the port for the KMS computer this machine will use. The IPv6 address must be specified in the format `[hostname]:port`.
`/ckms [Activation ID]`	Clears the name of the KMS computer used (sets the port to the default).
`/skhc`	Enables KMS host caching.
`/ckhc`	Disables KMS host caching.

TABLE 13.4: slmgr.vbs options *(CONTINUED)*

TOKEN-BASED ACTIVATION OPTIONS	DESCRIPTION
/lil	Lists installed token-based Activation Issuance licenses.
/ril <ILID> <ILvID>	Removes installed token-based Activation Issuance license.
/ctao	Clears token-based Activation Only flag (default).
/stao	Sets token-based Activation Only flag.
/ltc	Lists token-based Activation Certificates.
/fta <Certificate Thumbprint> [<PIN>]	Forces token-based activation.

KMS OPTIONS	DESCRIPTION
/sprt <Port>	Sets TCP port KMS will use to communicate with clients.
/sai <Activation Interval>	Sets interval (minutes) for unactivated clients to attempt KMS connection. The activation interval must be between 15 minutes (min) and 30 days (max) although the default (2 hours) is recommended.
/sri <Renewal Interval>	Sets renewal interval (minutes) for activated clients to attempt KMS connection. The renewal interval must be between 15 minutes (min) and 30 days (max) although the default (7 days) is recommended.
/sdns	Enables DNS publishing by KMS (default).
/cdns	Disables DNS publishing by KMS.
/spri	Sets KMS priority to normal (default).
/cpri	Sets KMS priority to low.

Configuring Windows Firewall Settings When Using SLMGR Remotely

Client computers connect to the KMS host for activation by using anonymous Remote Procedure Calls utilizing TCP port 1688. After establishing a TCP session with the KMS host, the client sends a single request packet and the KMS host responds with the activation count. If the count is equal to or greater than the activation threshold for that operating system, the client will be activated and the session is closed.

The KMS client uses this same process for activation renewal requests. The communication each way is 250 bytes.

Because `slmgr.vbs` uses Windows Management Instrumentation (WMI), you must configure your firewall software to allow WMI traffic:

1. Open the Administrative Tools folder and click Windows Firewall With Advanced Security.

2. When you use KMS within a single subnet, allow the Windows Management Instrumentation (WMI) exception.

3. If you have multiple subnets, allow the connection for Windows Management Instrumentation (ASync-In), Windows Management Instrumentation (DCOM-In), and Windows Management Instrumentation (WMI-In). Additionally, allow remote access in the scope.

4. By default, Windows Firewall Exceptions in the Private and Public profiles only apply exceptions to traffic originating on the local subnet. To expand the exception so that it applies to multiple subnets, change the exception settings in Windows Firewall with Advanced Security or, if joined to an AD DS domain, choose the Domain Profile.

Allowing Standard Users to Perform Activation

If you want to allow standard users to activate their operating system, you must add a new Registry key. Create a DWORD Registry value named `UserOperations` with the value 1 in the following Registry subkey:

```
HKEY_LOCAL_MACHINE\SOFTWARE\Microsoft\Windows NT\CurrentVersion\
SoftwareProtectionPlatform
```

After you have created this Registry key, users will no longer need administrative rights for some operations, such as installing a product key, installing a license, or rearming. This means that a standard user can convert a KMS client to use MAK activation, activate a computer manually, and replace the current installed MAK with a new MAK.

No administrator permissions are needed to activate Office 2010 when using KMS. Normally activating Office 2010 using MAK requires administrator permissions. You can modify this behavior by adding a Registry key. Create a DWORD Registry value named `UserOperations` with the value 1 in the `HKEY_LOCAL_MACHINE\Software\Microsoft\OfficeSoftwareProtectionPlatform\registry` subkey.

Controlling Activation Notifications and Timing

You can turn off software licensing notifications by adding the following new Registry key. Create a DWORD Registry value named `NotificationDisabled` with the value 1 in the following Registry subkey:

```
HKEY_LOCAL_MACHINE\SOFTWARE\Microsoft\Windows NT\CurrentVersion\
SoftwareProtectionPlatform\Activation
```

This will disable all software licensing notifications. You should keep in mind, though, that this setting will be ignored if the grace period has expired.

You can modify the default values for activation timing by using `slmgr.vbs` or by using Registry settings.

When you want to modify the intervals using the SLMGR, you should use the following settings:

◆ By using `slmgr.vbs /sai <interval>`, you can modify the activation setting that specifies the retry interval after the client unsuccessfully accesses the KMS server; by default, this interval is set to 120 minutes, but you can change it to between 15 and 43,200 minutes (which is equal to 30 days).

◆ By using `slmgr.vbs /sri <interval>`, you can modify the renewal interval. The interval is set in minutes. The default value is 10,080 minutes (which is equal to 7 days), but you can change it to between 15 and 43,200 minutes.

Using Group Policy to Control Activation Behavior

You can control configuration and property data for Volume Activation using WMI and the Windows Registry, which can be controlled centrally by using Group Policy preferences. (Using Group Policy, you can also control the appearance of the black desktop during the notifications state; you can modify these settings in User Configuration, but its impact is much more than just suppressing the black desktop and therefore is not recommended.)

For both the KMS client and the KMS server, the following Registry settings can be modified. The settings can be found under this Registry key:

`HKLM\Software\Microsoft\Windows NT\CurrentVersion\SoftwareProtectionPlatform`

`Activation\AlternateURL` This is a REG_SZ value in which you can supply a URL to an alternate location where users are redirected after clicking the link "Learn more about activation online."

`Activation\NotificationDisabled` This is a DWORD value, which when set to 1 will hide all notifications about activation.

`UserOperations` This is a DWORD value that when set to 1 enables standard users to perform activation and rearm of machines, as well as install product keys.

`VLActivationInterval` This is a DWORD value that sets the activation interval, which by default is set to 120 minutes but can be set to 15 minutes minimal and 43,200 minutes maximal.

`VLRenewalInterval` This is a DWORD value that sets the renewal interval, which by default id set to 10,800 minutes but can be set to 15 minutes minimal and 43,200 minutes maximal.

For the KMS server, the following Registry settings apply:

`Activation\Manual` This is a DWORD value that when set to 1 disables automatic activation.

`DisableDNSPublishing` This is a DWORD value that when set to 1 disables the publishing to DNS.

`DnsDomainPublishList` This is a MULTI_SZ value that contains additional domain names in which you can register DNS SRV RRs.

`EnableKmsLowPriority` This is a DWORD value that can be set when contention from KMS in a co-hosted environment must be minimized.

KeyManagementServiceListeningPort This is a REG_SZ value that can be used to modify the default port, which is set to 1688.

KeyManagementServiceVersion This REG_SZ value is set so that the machine can be found by the KMS management pack for MOM.

For the KMS client, the following Registry settings can be set:

KeyManagementServiceName This is a REG_SZ value that is set in order to force the client to a specific KMS host.

KeyManagementServicePort This is a REG_SZ value that sets the TCP port that the KMS client uses on the KMS host.

Tracking Your Licenses: The Volume Activation Management Tool

The Volume Activation Management Tool (VAMT) can help you centrally manage both MAK and KMS volume activation for Windows Vista, Windows 7, Windows Server 2008, Windows Server 2008 R2, and Office 2010. VAMT cannot manage computers installed with Volume License editions of Windows XP or Windows Server 2003. This chapter will cover VAMT version 2.0, which comes with the Windows Automated Installation Kit (WAIK) for Windows 7.

Understanding the VAMT Requirements

VAMT is a Microsoft Management Console (MMC) 3.0 snap-in that can be installed on the following Windows operating systems:

- Windows XP SP2

- Windows Server 2003 SP1

- Windows Vista

- Windows Server 2008

- Windows 7

- Windows Server 2008 R2

The minimum system requirements for the VAMT host computer are a 1 GHz or higher processor and a minimum of 512 MB of RAM.

The VAMT MMC snap-in only ships in a 32-bit version, so on a 64-bit OS you have to load the 32-bit version of MMC to load the snap-in. You can do this by specifying the /32 option when starting MMC.exe.

Exploring What the VAMT Can Do for You

The VAMT is able to manage activations centrally, which starts with adding computers to the VAMT console. This can be done using several methods, including Active Directory querying or using an LDAP query or Workgroup querying, or by specifying a single computer or IP address.

After you have discovered client computers, you are able to scan those computers for installed software, and based on that, the VAMT can provide you with information about its installed software activation status. To retrieve license status, VAMT must have administrative permissions on all selected computers and WMI must be accessible through the Windows firewall. If you want to manage workgroup computers, network discovery must be enabled on each client and you must create a Registry key to enable remote administrative actions under User Account Control (UAC).

To enable remote administrative actions under UAC, create a DWORD Registry value named `LocalAccountTokenFilterPolicy` with the value 1 under the following Registry subkey:

```
HKLM\SOFTWARE\Microsoft\Windows\CurrentVersion\Policies\system
```

Based on the activation status information you receive, you can choose to manage the product keys installed on that host, such as changing the product key type to KMS.

The activation data can be stored in a Computer Information List (CIL) file, which is in XML format. You can export this data to other VAMT hosts or use it in other programs.

REPORTING

The information stored in a CIL file can be exported in two ways. One approach includes all the information available within the VAMT, and the other technique involves exporting the CIL file, excluding all sensitive information and thus making it suitable to publish publicly. You can export the information by selecting the Export Only Installation ID And Production ID option in the Save List As dialog box.

Because the CIL file is in XML, it can easily be imported in programs like Excel. The CIL file provides a way to report on the licensing status of the latest computer scan.

MAK PROXY ACTIVATION

When you're using MAK activation and you have clients that are not connected to the Internet, you can configure MAK proxy activation.

MAK proxy activation takes the information needed for activation from the clients that are not Internet connected and proxies that information to the Internet using the server or clients on which VAMT is installed. A prerequisite in this case is that the VAMT machine be connected to the Internet.

If having the VAMT machine connected to the Internet isn't an option either, you can export the information needed for licensing as CIL files, and then import this information on another VAMT machine that is connected. This machine can then perform the activation on behalf of the clients with the Microsoft Activation Service. After this activation is performed, the Confirmation ID (CID) data can be exported from the Internet-facing VAMT machine and then imported in the non-Internet-facing machine, which can update the status of the clients to activated by providing Activation IDs.

COMMAND-LINE INTERFACE

You can also use the VAMT tool from the command line so that you can use it in scripts. The executable is called `VAMT.exe`. The `VAMT.exe` command-line tool provides arguments that can help you perform the tasks you need. Call VAMT by providing a switch and, depending on the switch, typing a parameter:

```
Vamt <Switch [Parameter]>
```

Here are the available commands:

/?   Lists all available commands

/<cmd> /?   Shows help and usage information for a command

/a   Adds computers discovered by the query specified and refreshes the computers

/c   Applies the Confirmation IDs obtained from Microsoft to the respective products

/d   Activates the non–Generic Volume License Key (GVLK) and non-OEM product key products online

/e   Adds the specified product key to the product key list

/m   Merges two CIL files

/p   Installs the product key on the products listed in the input file

/r   Refreshes the status of products in the given CIL file

/s   KMS activates the products that were installed with GVLK

/t   Token activates the products installed with GVLK

/u   Acquires Confirmation IDs from Microsoft

/x   Exports the Installation IDs for the products eligible for proxy activation, such as products installed with non-GVLK and non-OEM product keys

The Bottom Line

Decide which volume license key type to use.   Before you install and configure your KMS infrastructure, you should determine which VLK type you are going to use.

Master It   You plan to install a KMS infrastructure used for activating your Windows clients and servers. The clients are Windows 7 based and the servers consist of Windows Server 2008 R2 Enterprise and Windows Server 2008 standard. From which product group should you use a key?

    A.   Server Group A

    B.   Server Group B

    C.   Server Group C

    D.   Windows Client

Deploy, maintain, and troubleshoot a Key Management Service (KMS) infrastructure. Depending on the type of KMS activation key, you have limited options available as to the type of operating system on which you are going to install your KMS server.

Master It   You are about to activate Windows 7 clients using a KMS server. For this you received a KMS activation key of the type Windows Client VL. On which OS can't the KMS server be installed?

    A.   Windows 7

    B.   Windows Vista

    C.   Windows Server 2003

    D.   Windows Server 2008

Centrally manage licenses throughout your organization.   When your company changes licensing terms, you could be assigned to change the license type of your clients. For example, you might have to change your VLK keys back to MAK keys.

Master It   You are assigned to change the product key of several Windows 7 clients from MAK to KMS. How will you proceed?

Appendix

The Bottom Line

Each of The Bottom Line sections in the chapters suggest exercises to deepen skills and understanding. Sometimes there is only one possible solution, but often you are encouraged to use your skills and creativity to create something that builds on what you know and lets you explore one of many possible solutions.

Chapter 1: Does Your Hardware Measure Up?

Identify the Windows 7 requirements.   You should know the minimum Windows 7 requirements and understand the difference between minimum and recommended requirements.

Master It   You are working as a consultant in a client site. The client is a publishing company. You are performing an assessment of the desktop and laptop computers with the intent of doing a Windows 7 deployment. You have been invited to a meeting to discuss the reports. A junior IT manager wants to reduce the amount of hardware upgrades to save money. She has stated that the minimum Windows 7 requirements should have been used in the assessment. What will your response be?

Solution   The minimum requirements of Windows 7 are the smallest amount of hardware that is required to install Windows 7. This hardware specification will not provide good performance. Additional applications will require additional hardware. For example, desktop publishing and graphics applications will have significant hardware requirements in addition to those of the operating system.

Plan for and use the Microsoft Assessment and Planning Toolkit.   MAP can be installed and used in a number of ways, depending on the organization and the project.

Master It   You are working as a senior engineer in a multinational organization. You have been tasked with performing an assessment of all desktop and laptop computers in the organization for a deployment of Windows 7. The project manager has told you that you must not impact the WAN connections in any way. How will you perform the assessment?

Solution   Identify each location that must be assessed and the local network ranges that will have computers on them. You can install MAP on a laptop computer and travel to each site. You can perform a local discovery using the Scan An IP Address Range discovery method and entering the IP range of the office that you are visiting. This will eliminate any cross-WAN discovery traffic.

Produce reports and proposals from the Microsoft Assessment and Planning Toolkit.
MAP can produce a report and a proposal from a MAP discovery and assessment database.

Master It You work for a software development company that is planning to deploy Windows 7. You have been asked to generate an assessment based on two hardware requirements: one for the support desk with low requirements and one for the developers with high requirements. Each group is contained within an Active Directory organizational unit. How will you perform the assessment and generate the necessary reports and proposals?

Solution You will generate two MAP databases using a single MAP installation. The first MAP database will be called Support and will be used to discover and assess the support desk. The assessment properties will be set according to the needs of the support desk hardware. A report and proposal will be generated for the support desk. This procedure will be repeated for the developers using a MAP database on the same MAP installation called Developers. The reports and proposals can be manually merged for a single set of documents.

Chapter 2: Evaluating Applications for Windows 7 Compatibility

Plan for and install the Application Compatibility Toolkit. The Application Compatibility Administrator allows for a flexible deployment based on the scale of the organization and the design of the network.

Master It You have been assigned the task of designing an ACT deployment for a large organization. There are many branch offices, some with lightly used high-speed links, some with moderately used high-speed links, and some with congested slow-speed links. You must design the solution so that enough data is gathered to plan any application compatibility operations while not affecting company operations.

Solution Each branch office will have at least one customized DCP. Branch offices with congested links will upload their data to a local file share. The file share will not be replicated. Instead, the data will be compressed and sent to you using secured removable storage when the life of the DCP has expired. You can then add this data to the ACT log share for processing. Branch offices with moderately used high-speed links will also upload their data to a local file share. This file share will be replicated to the ACT log share during off peak times for processing. Branch offices with high-speed links could upload their data directly from the DCP to the log share but on a very infrequent basis.

Use ACT to identify incompatible applications. The Application Compatibility Toolkit provides tools for identifying applications with compatibility issues.

Master It You have a large library of applications. Many of them are off-the-shelf purchases. You wish to avail yourself of as much community and vendor knowledge as possible to speed up the process of identifying compatibility issues. What is the best course of action?

Solution   The Application Compatibility Manager includes the ability to share data with the community via a Microsoft repository. By clicking the Send And Receive button, you can upload your discovered application data and download compatibility information, sometimes including solutions for certain issues. This information comes from Microsoft and original third-party vendors, and includes assessment results by the community.

Use ACT and XP Mode to solve compatibility issues.   When combined with Virtual PC for Windows 7, Windows XP Mode provides you with a way to run legacy applications that have no possible fixes on Windows 7 computers.

Master It   You are working as a consultant. A client site is replacing Windows XP with Windows 7. They have a small number of laptop users who need to run a critical application that does not work on Windows 7. All attempts to resolve this issue with ACT have failed. You have been asked to find a way to make the application work when the users are roaming and to make it as simple as possible to use. What can you do?

Solution   You can install Virtual PC for Windows 7 and XP Mode on the users' laptops. The required application can be installed in the Windows XP virtual machine. Ensure that the shortcut is made available in the Windows 7 Start menu. Then the users can start the application from their Windows 7 user interface. It will run in the Windows XP virtual machine but users will be unaware of that fact.

Chapter 3: Installing Windows 7: Meet the Panther

Choose the correct edition of Windows 7.   One of the primary tasks you'll have when considering Windows 7 is to determine what edition to purchase. Different editions have different capabilities, and if you purchase the wrong edition, you may not have the desired capabilities.

Master It   Your organization purchases licenses using Software Assurance contracts with Microsoft. Management wants to use the AppLocker capabilities of Windows 7. What edition should you select?

- **A.** Windows 7 Business
- **B.** Windows 7 Professional
- **C.** Windows 7 Enterprise
- **D.** Windows 7 Ultimate

Solution   The answer is C, the Enterprise edition. Only Enterprise and Ultimate editions include support for AppLocker. However, Enterprise is purchased through the Software Assurance program and the Ultimate edition is purchased through retail channels. Windows 7 doesn't include a Business edition. Windows 7 Professional won't enforce AppLocker settings.

Identify the correct method to install Windows 7. There are some specific upgrade requirements that restrict your upgrade paths. However, tools are available that will assist with migrating data as long as you follow the procedures when installing Windows 7.

Master It Your organization has Windows XP running on computers that will support Windows 7. You have purchased Windows 7 licenses and you want the computers to run Windows 7 when you're done. What should you do?

    A. Perform a bare-metal install of the computers.

    B. Perform an upgrade to Windows 7.

    C. Replace the computers and use USMT.

    D. Refresh the computers and use USMT

Solution The answer is D. You should refresh the computers and use the User State Migration Tool (USMT) to capture and restore the user state data. It's not necessary to perform a bare-metal install since the systems already have an operating system. You can't upgrade Windows XP to Windows 7. Since you are keeping the computers, you would not replace them.

Install Windows 7. One of the basic deployment tasks of Windows 7 is performing an installation. While you may ultimately choose to create images and deploy the images, you still have to start with a basic reference computer.

Master It Begin and complete an installation of Windows 7.

Solution Place the installation DVD into a system and boot the system. Follow the onscreen prompts or the procedure in this chapter to complete the installation.

View the current activation status. There may be times when you want to view the activation status of a system. You can use the slmgr command from the command prompt to view and manipulate the activation on any system.

Master It Execute the command needed to view detailed activation information for a system.

Solution Launch a command prompt and enter the following command: **slmgr /dlv**.

Chapter 4: Cloning the Panther: Automating Windows 7 Installation

Create a dual-boot system using a VHD. You want to create a dual-boot system so that you can boot into two different versions of Windows 7. You plan to use the second installation to test applications for compatibility. However, you have only one drive.

Master It You need to use a single system to install two versions of Windows 7. How can you accomplish this?

Solution Boot into the Windows 7 installation program, press Shift+F10 to access the command prompt, and use DiskPart to create a VHD file as a virtual disk. Install Windows 7 on the VHD file.

Prepare a system to be imaged. You want to capture an image that will be deployed to multiple systems. However, before you can capture the image, it must be prepared.

Master It What should you use to prepare the system to be imaged?

Solution You should use Sysprep. You can run it by browsing to the `C:\Windows \system32\sysprep` folder and running the Sysprep program. You can run Sysprep from the command line with the following command:

```
C:\windows\system32\sysprep\sysprep /oobe /generalize /shutdown
```

Capture an image. After you've prepared an image, you can capture it so that it can be deployed to other computers. This can be much more efficient than installing Windows 7 individually on each computer. There are tools available within the Windows Automated Installation Kit (WAIK) that can be used to capture an image.

Master It What tool can you use to capture an image?

    A. Sysprep

    B. ImageX

    C. LoadState

    D. ScanState

Solution The answer is B. The ImageX tool can capture an image after the image has been prepared with Sysprep. Sysprep prepares the system but it can't capture an image. ScanState and LoadState are used to capture and restore the user's state data.

Modify an image offline. There are some instances where you want to modify an offline image instead of deploying, modifying, and recapturing it. The WAIK provides tools that can be used for offline servicing of an image.

Master It You have captured an image but want to apply additional drivers to the image. What tool can you use?

Solution The Deployment Image Service and Management (DISM) tool can be used for offline servicing of images.

Apply an image. After capturing an image, you can then deploy it to other systems. While you can use tools such as Windows Deployment Services (WDS) to deploy the image to multiple systems through multicasting, you can also use tools within the WAIK to deploy images to a single system at a time.

Master It You have captured an image from a Windows 7 reference computer. You now want to apply the image to a system. What should you do?

Solution You can use the ImageX tool to apply the image. ImageX can be included in the WinPE, allowing you to boot into the WinPE and run the ImageX tool.

Create an unattended answer file. There are some times when you want to install Windows 7 without standing in front of the computer to answer all the questions. You can do this if you first create an unattended answer file that you can use to answer the questions automatically.

Master It You want to create an unattended answer file named `unattend.xml` to install Windows 7 without user intervention. What should you use to create the `unattend.xml` file?

Solution You can create `unattend.xml` files using the Windows System Image Manager (WSIM), which is available as part of the WAIK.

Chapter 5: Migrating the Existing User Data

Identify folders holding user state data. User state data can be migrated from a user's old system to the new system. This gives the user a lot of the same settings and data as they had before the OS change.

Master It You are preparing to upgrade several systems from Windows XP to Windows 7. You want to view some users' folders to determine where their documents are stored. Where are user profiles stored in Windows XP and Windows 7?

- **A.** In the `\Documents and Settings\`*username* folder in both operating systems
- **B.** In the `\Users\`*username* folder in both operating systems
- **C.** In the `\Documents and Settings\`*username* folder in Windows XP and in the `\Users\`*username* folder in Windows 7
- **D.** In the `\Documents and Settings\`*username* folder in Windows 7 and in the `\Users\`*username* folder in Windows XP

Solution The answer is C. Profiles are stored in the `\Documents and Settings` folder in Windows XP and in the `\Users\`*username* folder in Windows 7.

Identify the best tool to use to transfer user state data for a single user. You may occasionally need to transfer a single user's user state data from one computer to another. For example, you may want to ensure that an executive's user state data is transferred due to some special needs.

Master It What is the best tool to use to transfer user state data for a single user?

- **A.** Windows AIK
- **B.** ScanState
- **C.** LoadState
- **D.** Windows Easy Transfer

Solution The answer is D. The Windows Easy Transfer wizard can be used to transfer data for just a few users. It isn't the best tool for migration of many computers since it is very labor intensive.

Capture user state data. The first step in user state migration is to capture the user state data. The USMT includes tools used to capture this data.

Master It You have copied the USMT tolls to the `C:\`USMT folder on a source computer. You want to use these tools to capture user state data. What command should you use to capture user state data on a source system?

Solution ScanState is the USMT tool used to capture user state data. You can use the following command:

```
c:\usmt\scanstate /auto:c:\usmt\ c:\USMTStore /l:myscanstate.log
```

Apply user state data.   The last step in migrating user state data is to apply the user state data to the new system. The USMT includes tools used to apply the data.

Master It   You have captured user state data and stored it on a removable hard drive. You have installed Windows 7 on a new computer and copied the USMT tools into the C:\USMT folder. You now want to apply the captured user state data to the new computer. What command should you use to apply the captured state data onto a target computer?

Solution   LoadState is the USMT tool. Assuming the data is stored on an external drive assigned the letter E:, you can use the following command:

```
c:\usmt\loadstate /auto:c:\usmt\ e:\USMTStore /l:myloadstate.log /lac
```

Capture and apply user state data from the Windows.old folder.   User state data can be retrieved from the Windows.old folder after Windows 7 has been installed. You can even apply user state data after the Windows 7 installation if you didn't capture the data before the installation.

Master It   You performed a refresh of a PC that originally had Windows XP. You performed a clean installation of Windows 7 without modifying the partitions and a copy of the Windows.old folder was created. You also installed the USMT tools into the C:\USMT folder. You now want to apply the user state data from the Windows.old folder to the Windows 7 installation. What command(s) should you use?

Solution   You would first run ScanState, and then run LoadState. The following two commands could be used:

```
c:\usmt\scanstate c:\usmtstore /auto:c:\usmt\ ~lb
 /offlinewinold:c:\windows.old\windows  ~lb
 /hardlink c:\HardLinkStore  /l:myscanstate.log /nocompress
c:\usmt\loadstate c:\usmtstore /auto:c:\usmt\ /lac /hardlink /nocompress
```

Chapter 6: Windows Deployment Services: The Basics

Understand how WDS works.   WDS is an operating system image deployment solution that is based on the ability to boot up a computer using PXE.

Master It   What are the requirements for installing and using WDS to deploy Windows installation images?

Solution

- ◆ The WDS server must be running Windows Server 2003 with Service Pack 2 or later.

- ◆ The server must be a member of an Active Directory domain if it is a pre–Windows Server 2008 R2 WDS machine. DHCP must be configured to support the networks with potential WDS clients. DNS must be available for name resolution.

- ◆ The WDS image store will be on an NTFS volume on the WDS server.

◆ You must have local administrator rights on the WDS server to enable the role.

◆ You must have Enterprise Administrator rights to authorize the WDS server in the DHCP console.

◆ The WDS client user must have domain-based authorization to the installation images on the WDS server.

◆ The WDS clients will ideally have network cards with Net PC/PC98-compliance to allow them to boot up using PXE.

Install and configure WDS.   You will use the components of the server operating system to add the WDS component or role.

Master It   What two ways can you use to install the WDS role on a Windows Server 2008 R2 machine?

Solution   You can use the Server Manager console or you can use the Server Manager PowerShell module to add the WDS role to a Windows Server 2008 R2 machine.

Add boot and installation images.   You can add boot images and installation images to your WDS server to allow Windows 7 deployment operations.

Master It   You want to add a variety of Windows 7 Professional images to your WDS server. You need to keep the amount of storage space to a minimum. You have a standard desktop image but you have been forced to create several variations to allow for 32-bit and 64-bit architectures, as well as departmental customizations. How will you accomplish your goals?

Solution   You will create two image groups. Image groups provide single-instance storage for all contained installation images. The contents of the images are stored in a RWM file. The WIM file contains the metadata for the installation image. The first image group will be called Windows 7 Professional x86. All 32-bit images of Windows 7 Professional will be added to this image group. The second image group will be called Windows 7 Professional x64. All 64-bit images of Windows 7 Professional will be added to this image group.

Chapter 7: WDS from the Client's View

Use and customize the PXE client.   A user or administrator can start the PXE client of a capable machine once it is enabled in the BIOS and a special key or key sequence is entered during the POST of the machine when it starts up.

Master It   The WDS PXE client requires the person who is sitting at the client machine to observe and quickly respond to a prompt to press **F12**. Failure to do so causes the PXE client to time out and exit. You are receiving complaints about this and have been asked to disable this prompt. How will you accomplish this?

Solution   Open up the properties of the WDS server in the WDS console. Navigate to the Boot tab of the window. You will need to change the PXE Boot Policy option to either Always Continue The PXE Boot or Continue The PXE Boot Unless The User Presses The ESC Key.

Create a customized installation image. You can create customized installation images and deploy them using WDS.

> **Master It** A junior administrator is working in a lab to learn how WDS works. She has created a reference machine. A capture boot image was created with all the required drivers. The administrator has booted up the machine with the capture boot image but is unable to create a new image. What could be the cause?
>
> **Solution** It is likely that the junior administrator has forgotten to run Sysprep to generalize the machine. WDS will refuse to capture a nongeneralized reference machine.

Automate WDS. Although WDS is not a light-touch or a zero-touch operating system deployment solution, it is possible to automate much of what it does.

> **Master It** How can you automate image operations in WDS?
>
> **Solution** You can use WSIM (from WAIK) to create two types of unattended answer files. The first will configure the Windows PE boot environment and be associated with the boot images. The second will be associated with the installation image, allowing the image to be deployed without requiring human interaction.

Chapter 8: Tweaking Your WDS Server

Implement a machine naming policy using WDS. You can automate the naming of machines that are built using WDS.

> **Master It** Users will build their own computers using WDS. You have been asked to name computers using the first two letters of the user's forename and the first six characters of their surname. Some users may have up to 10 PCs. The computer name should be 10 characters long. What client naming policy will you use?
>
> **Solution** The client naming policy should be %2First%6Last%2#. This means that the user Rachel Handelman can have computers that are called RaHandel01 to RaHandel99.

Manage domain membership of WDS clients. It is possible to control where new computer objects are created when WDS prepared machines are joined to a domain.

> **Master It** You receive a call from a branch office help desk engineer. They are delighted to see that machines that are rebuilt will retain their original computer name. She asks you how this is accomplished. What will you tell her?
>
> **Solution** The computer object has an attribute called netbootGUID. This attribute stores the unique MAC or GUID of the machine. When the machine is rebuilt, this value is used to determine if the machine had a previous computer object and computer name. The name is reused if it did.

Understand how multicast WDS image deployments work. WDS can optimize the usage of network capacity for large-scale deployments by using a multicast transmission.

> **Master It** A colleague has set up a multicast transmission for 100 clients. He has gone home with an illness and you have taken over the deployment task. You notice that the deployment is taking longer than expected. What will you do?

Solution Open the WDS console and view the clients that are connected to the multicast transmission. Check the details there to see if anything stands out.

Check with the network administrators or network management tools to see if there is a fault on the network or any unusual loads. Verify that the cabling is of sufficient quality (minimum of CAT5 or CAT5e) and that there are no hubs being used.

Ensure that the multicast transmission allows different sessions for clients of different speeds.

Use the WDSUTIL command to identify the master client. This will be the slowest machine in the session and will cause all other WDS client downloads to run at its speed. Determine if it has a fault that is causing the issue. Disconnect the machine if it does.

Chapter 9: Microsoft Deployment Toolkit 2010

Set up a technician machine/deployment server (install MDT 2010 Update 1). The technician machine/deployment server is the computer on which you install MDT. If you install MDT on a desktop OS (Windows Vista SP1 or Windows 7), it is called a technician machine. If you install MDT on a Server OS (Windows Server 2003 R2, Windows Server 2008 or R2), it is referred to as a deployment server.

Master It You have chosen to create a deployment server; which operating system should you use? What is the required software that will need to be installed? Which architecture of WAIK and MDT should be installed?

    A. Server 2003 R2; .NET Framework 2.0, MSXML 6.0, WAIK, and MDT 32-bit

    B. Server 2008, WAIK, and MDT 64- bit

    C. Server 2008 R2, WAIK, and MDT 32-bit

    D. Server 2008 R2, WAIK, and MDT 64-bit

Solution The answer is D because you should always install the WAIK and MDT on the latest operating system available to ensure that you get the most up-to-date feature sets. Windows Server 2008 R2, WAIK, and MDT 64-bit make up the most current operating system and only come in 64-bit (there isn't a 32-bit version). The required software (.NET Framework 2.0 and MSXML 6.0) is built into Windows Server 2008 R2 so there is less to install.

Create an image containing an operating system, drivers, packages (patches), and applications. MDT's greatest strength is in how easy it is to create an image that you can deploy to a bare-metal machine that will install an operating system, applications, drivers, and patches.

Master It Create an image in MDT that will deploy Windows 7, Office 2010, and all necessary drivers and is fully patched.

Solution Create the image in MDT by importing Windows 7 as an OS, import the Office 2010 application complete with the command to install silently, and import drivers and patches. Create a task sequence that will deploy your Windows 7 OS, Office 2010 application, drivers, and patches. Update the deployment share.

Deploy an image using MDT client wizard.   MDT client wizard launches automatically when you boot using one of the custom WinPEs created by updating your deployment share. By default there will be two WinPEs created: LiteTouchPE_x86 and LiteTouchPE_x64. MDT's client wizard walks you through the deployment process.

Master It   Boot the LiteTouchPE_x64 custom MDT WinPE that is generated for you. The MDT client wizard launches and you choose to install an OS, but when the Task Sequence page is displayed there are no task sequences to choose from. What is the problem?

Solution   You created a 32-bit task sequence and then booted a 64-bit WinPE, which only displays 64-bit task sequences—but you have not created any 64-bit task sequences yet. To resolve this issue, you will need to boot the target machine with the 32-bit MDT WinPE (LiteTouchPE_x86); then your 32-bit task sequence will be available for you to select. Remember the 32-bit MDT WinPE (LiteTouchPE_x86) only displays 32-bit task sequences and the 64-bit MDT WinPE (LiteTouchPE_x64) only lists 64-bit task sequences.

Chapter 10: MDT's Client Wizard

Customize your deployment share, applications, operating systems, drivers, and packages. Updating your deployment share by default creates both 32-bit and 64-bit custom MDT WinPE image files (LiteTouchPE_x86.iso and LiteTouchPE_x64.iso). You can customize the platforms that are supported to reduce the amount of time it takes to update your deployment share.

Master It   You are planning on deploying 64-bit images only. How can you configure your deployment share to create the custom MDT WinPE image files needed for 64-bit deployment and not waste time creating the image files needed for 32-bit deployment?

Solution   In the Deployment Workbench, right-click your deployment share and choose Properties. The General tab shows the platforms that are supported. By default both 32-bit (x86) and 64-bit (x64) are supported. To support only 64-bit deployments, remove the check mark from the x86 box.

Create custom task sequences.   Task sequences drive the installation by controlling which tasks are performed and the order in which those tasks are performed. You can customize task sequences at any time by editing a previously created task sequence. To edit a task sequence from within the Deployment Workbench, right-click your task sequence and choose Properties. Or you could also double-click the task sequence to open its properties.

Master It   You have created a custom task sequence by first selecting the default Standard Client Task Sequence template and editing it. You now need to do two things: add an application to be installed via this task sequence and change the password for the local administrator account for any target machines that install Windows 7 using this task sequence. What are the steps for further customizing the task sequence to include these new requirements?

Solution   To add an application to be deployed via this task sequence, follow these steps:

In the Deployment Workbench, open the properties of the task sequence and select the Task Sequence tab. Expand the State Restore phase. Highlight Install Applications under the State Restore phase. Under the Install Applications Properties, choose Install A Single Application and click the Browse button. Select the application and click OK.

To change the password of the local administrator account on all target machines that receive this task sequence, you'll need to edit the task sequence properties. In the Deployment Workbench, open the properties of the task sequence by right-clicking the task sequence and choosing Properties. Go to the OS Info tab and click the Edit Unattend .xml button. Wait until Windows Image System Manager opens the unattended.xml file. Expand configuration pass 7 OOBE System - Microsoft-Windows-Shell-Setup_Neutral component – UserAccounts. Highlight AdministratorPassword. Change the value of the password to whatever you would like. Close and save.

Automate the MDT Deployment Wizard to show only the pages you want displayed during deployment.   The MDT Deployment Wizard utilizes two files to determine which pages are displayed during the deployment process and which pages are hidden. These files are the CustomSettings.ini and the Bootstrap.ini found in your F:\MDTLab\Control folder. You can view both files from within the Deployment Workbench by right-clicking your deployment share and opening the properties. The CustomSettings.ini file is displayed on the Rules tab. You can view the contents of Bootstrap.ini by clicking the Edit Bootstrap.ini button at the bottom-right corner.

Master It   You are a non-Enterprise client and all deployments require a product key that is mandated by management. You want the product key 11111-22222-33333-44444-55555 automatically supplied so no one has to type it in every time a deployment occurs. In addition, you want to hide the Welcome Windows Deployment page. Which file do you have to edit (CustomSettings.ini or Bootstrap.ini) and what entries do you need to provide?

Solution   From within the Deployment Workbench, right-click the deployment share and open Properties. On the Rules tab, add these two lines at the bottom of the [Default] section heading:

```
SkipProductKey=YES
OverrideProductKey=11111-22222-33333-44444-55555
```

To hide the Welcome Windows Deployment page, you'll need to click the Edit Bootstrap.ini button and add SkipBDDWelcome=YES in the [Default] section under the DeployRoot entry. The SkipBDDWelcome entry is the only entry that should be in Bootstrap.ini and not CustomSettings.ini. If placed in the CustomSettings.ini file, the entry will be ignored.

Chapter 11: Fine-Tuning MDT Deployments

Use selection profiles to create flexibility.   Selection profiles can help you create deployment shares with different content.

Master It   How can you create deployment shares with different content—for example, one for workstation deployments and one for server deployments?

Solution   Add all the folders that are used during workstation deployment to a selection profile, and add all the folders used during server deployment to another selection profile. Create two new linked deployment shares and provide each selection profile when configuring these linked deployment shares.

Use linked deployment shares. By creating linked deployment shares, you can replicate the content of a master deployment share to one or more destination deployment shares.

> **Master It** Because DFS-R replicates the exact contents of the source folder to the destination folders, how can you make sure that each deployment share stays unique?

> **Solution** When using DFS-R to replicate the content of your deployment share, you should modify your `Bootstrap.ini` so that the `DeployRoot` variable points to `%WDSServer%` instead of a server name. When a client boots a boot image from a specific WDS server, it automatically fills the `WDSServer` variable with the computer name of the server from which it booted the Windows PE image.

Create stand-alone media from which you can deploy the operating system. Stand-alone media can be used in specific offline scenarios; you can create stand-alone media using the New Media wizard.

> **Master It** What will be the output of the New Media wizard?

> **Solution** The New Media wizard will by default generate a folder structure, which can be copied to a USB drive or portable hard disk, and an ISO file, which can be burned to DVD directly. You have the option to disable the creation of the ISO file.

Create and fill the MDT database. MDT can leverage a database running on SQL Server, which can help you make your deployment solution even more flexible.

> **Master It** What is the purpose of the MDT database?

> **Solution** The MDT database provides a central repository that contains the settings which you would typically set in your `CustomSettings.ini`. Using the MDT database gives you the flexibility to define unique settings for different machines in a central location.

Chapter 12: Zero Touch Installations

Understand and set up Configuration Manager for OSD. An understanding of how Configuration Manager works is required to plan even a small deployment.

> **Master It** What are the functions of the management point, the distribution point, the software update point, and the PXE service point?

> **Solution** Configuration Manager clients communicate with the site server via the management point. They receive all deployment instructions from this site role. The distribution point is where clients download packages from. The software update point is used to interact with WSUS so that Configuration Manager can deploy software updates to clients. The PXE service point is used to allow clients to start up using a boot image over the network.

Capture customized images. Configuration Manager allows you to create and capture a reference image that will be used for future deployment of Windows 7.

> **Master It** A colleague reports to you that a prepared boot image fails to work. What are some of the possible causes?

> **Solution** The boot image must be installed on the PXE distribution point. Some 64-bit hardware will require an x64 boot image and will fail to start if there is only an x86 or

32-bit one available. The default boot image might not have the required network card or mass storage controller drivers to access the network from the computer or access the hard disk in the computer. The task sequence must be configured to use a boot image and then be advertised to a collection that contains the computer. The collection must be updated to have an up-to-date membership.

Deploy Windows 7 using task sequences. A reference image containing Windows 7 can be deployed with no human effort to many computers at once using a task sequence.

Master It A single generic Windows 7 OS install image has been created. It contains Microsoft Office, the usual utilities, and all of the latest security updates that are available. You are asked to prepare a deployment of Windows 7 for a department with 200 Windows XP computers. They will require two additional line-of-business applications and want the deployment to be as quick as possible.

Solution You will work with the owner of the line-of-business applications to prepare software distribution packages for installing those applications in an unattended manner. The silent install programs must be configured to allow an installation without a user being logged in. They must also allow execution from a task sequence. The software distribution packages will be installed on a distribution point that is close to the affected department. An additional task sequence can be created by duplicating the original default task sequence. Two new Install Software steps can be added by editing the new task sequence. Each of these steps will run the silent install program of each of the software distribution packages. The resulting task sequence can be advertised to a collection containing the 200 Windows XP computers. The default Windows 7 reference image will be deployed, and the task sequence will install each of the two line-of-business applications before the users can log in.

Chapter 13: Maintenance and Monitoring

Decide which volume license key type to use. Before you install and configure your KMS infrastructure, you should determine which VLK type you are going to use.

Master It You plan to install a KMS infrastructure used for activating your Windows clients and servers. The clients are Windows 7 based and the servers consist of Windows Server 2008 R2 Enterprise and Windows Server 2008 standard. From which product group should you use a key?

A. Server Group A

B. Server Group B

C. Server Group C

D. Windows Client

Solution In this case you can use the Server Group B KMS key, which is able to activate all the used operating systems.

Deploy, maintain, and troubleshoot a Key Management Service (KMS) infrastructure. Depending on the type of KMS activation key, you have limited options available as to the type of operating system on which you are going to install your KMS server.

Master It   You are about to activate Windows 7 clients using a KMS server. For this you received a KMS activation key of the type Windows Client VL. On which OS can't the KMS server be installed?

> **A.**   Windows 7
>
> **B.**   Windows Vista
>
> **C.**   Windows Server 2003
>
> **D.**   Windows Server 2008

Solution   In this scenario, you cannot install the KMS server on Windows Server 2008.

Centrally manage licenses throughout your organization.   When your company changes licensing terms, you could be assigned to change the license type of your clients. For example, you might have to change your VLK keys back to MAK keys.

Master It   You are assigned to change the product key of several Windows 7 clients from MAK to KMS. How will you proceed?

Solution   When you have to change the product key of several Windows installations, it's best to use the VAMT.

Index